Barbara Uttmann, who introduced the lace manufacture into the Erzgebirge.

From an ivory statuette by Koehler, Green Vault, Dresden.

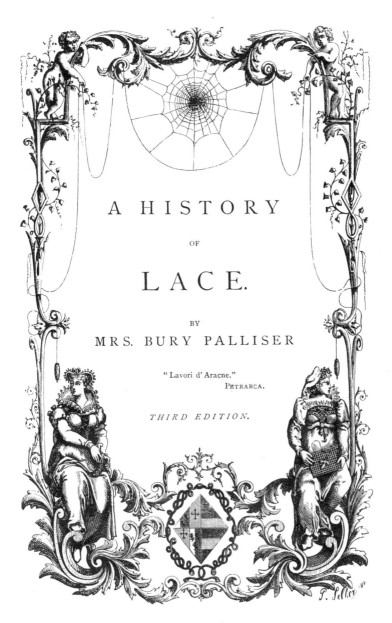

A HISTORY

OF

LACE.

BY

MRS. BURY PALLISER

"Lavori d' Aracne."
PETRARCA.

THIRD EDITION.

Tower Books
Book Tower - Detroit
1971

This is a facsimile reprint of the
1875 edition published in London
by Sampson Low, Marston, Low, &
Searle.

Library of Congress Catalog Card Number 75-78219

PREFACE TO THE THIRD EDITION.

IT is now eleven years since the HISTORY OF LACE was written. With the exception of the "Colbert Correspondence," which throws great light upon the establishment of the lace manufacture in France, little has been added to our general knowledge on the subject. On many important points we are still in the dark. We have no evidence where the pillow was first invented. Of the beautiful products of the Spanish Peninsula and of the once opulent towns of Nuremberg and Augsburg, we have no records. Modern writers question the fact of point d'Angleterre being made at Brussels, and reject the history of Barbara Uttmann's lace-teaching in the Erzgebirge. All that is left to us is to continue to collect scattered documents as they present themselves, and leave to posterity the task of writing the HISTORY OF LACE.

Kensington, July 1875.

PREFACE TO THE SECOND EDITION.

In sending forth a second edition of the HISTORY OF LACE, the Author has to acknowledge the flattering reception of her book.

It has now been carefully revised, with the addition of a copious index, a few new illustrations have been added, and the history of the different fabrics brought down to the International Exhibition of 1867.

The work has been translated into French by the elegant pen of the Comtesse de Clermont-Tonnerre, and is now in course of publication by Messrs. Firmin Didot.

13A *Upper Brook Street, January* 1869.

PREFACE.

"A HISTORY OF LACE." The title of this book may at first call forth surprise, and many folks wonder how so trivial a matter as lace can require a history.

This fabric, however, like those of porcelain, stained glass, and others essentially artistic, has, from its first origin, been an object of interest to all classes, from the potentate to the peasant, and, from the cradle to the coffin, has served as a favourite decoration to all those whose means permitted its acquirement.

Church, court, camp, and state, all alike valued the productions of the needle and the pillow, and by their patronage encouraged the prosperity of the manufacture.

Little, indeed scarce any, knowledge on this subject can be gained from books; one author copies his statistics from another, seldom troubling himself to verify the accuracy of his predecessor. Wardrobe accounts, household bills, and public acts are the most truthful guides; and from these documents alone we write, as a running commentary at the foot of each page will testify.

We cannot conclude this short notice without expressing our sincere thanks to T. DUFFUS HARDY, Esq., Deputy Keeper of the Records, and to the COUNT DE LABORDE, Keeper of the Imperial Archives, for the valuable assistance they have afforded the Author in granting free access to the public documents both of England and France; also to various librarians of Europe, for their kind and patient researches in our cause; and lastly, among many others from whom we have received much useful information, to the Miss LOCKES, from whose untiring exertions both in Italy and Germany, we derive much that is interesting in our volume.

And again, before taking leave of our readers, we beg to state that, in case this work should, at some distant period, reach a second edition, any contributions derived from well-authenticated sources—wills, inventories, family documents, or ancient publications, overlooked or as yet unsearched—will, if addressed to the Publishers, be gratefully welcomed by

The obliged Author,

FANNY BURY PALLISER.

Upper Brook Street, October 1864.

HISTORY OF LACE.

CHAPTER I.

NEEDLEWORK.

"As ladies wont
To finger the fine needle and nyse thread."—*Faerie Queen.*

"Needlework sublime."—*Cowper.*

THE art of lace-making has from the earliest times been so mixed
up with that of needlework, it would be impossible to enter on the
subject of the one without making some mention of the other.

From the first homely attempts of our mother Eve, we have,
throughout the Old Testament, constant mention of embroidery,
of curtains of "fine twined linen wrought with needlework, and
blue, and purple, and scarlet, with cherubims of cunning work." [1]

Again, the robe of the ephod was worked with "pomegranates
of blue, purple, and scarlet," [2] around the hem thereof. We have
mention in Isaiah of women's "cauls," [3] of "nets of checker-work" [4]
in Solomon's temple, with pomegranates and other matters too
numerous here to record.

Aholiab is specially recorded as the great embroiderer in blue; [5]
and the description of a virtuous woman in the Proverbs, who
"layeth her hands to the spindle," [6] and "clotheth herself in
tapestry," and that of the king's daughter, in the Psalms, who
"shall be brought unto the king in raiment of needlework," [7] all
plainly show how much the art was appreciated amongst the Jews. [8]

Both needlework and embroidery were highly esteemed by the

---

[1] Exodus xxvi. xxvii.
[2] Exodus xxviii. [3] Chap. iii. 18.
[4] 1 Kings vii. 17. [5] Exodus xxxv. 35.
[6] Chap. xxxi. [7] Psalm xlv.
[8] Again, in the song of Deborah, the

mother of Sisera says, "Have they not
divided the prey; . . . to Sisera a prey
of divers colours of needlework, of divers
colours of needlework on both sides?"—
Judges v. 30.

ancient Greeks. We read how Minerva, goddess of wisdom, though she scarcely can be said to have encouraged the art, took it under her especial patronage, and dire was the punishment inflicted upon Arachne, who dared to rival the goddess in this her favourite pursuit:—

> "Arachne once, as poets tell,
> A goddess at her art defied;
> But soon the daring mortal fell
> The hapless victim of her pride." [9]

In Homer, and other early authors, we have constant mention of veils,[10] cauls, and networks of gold, as well as of embroidered garments, while the outer tunics of the Egyptian robes of state, as depicted on the tombs, appear fashioned of a looped network or crochet, darned around the hem in patterns of gold, silver, and divers colours, realising the saying of Isaiah: "They that work in fine flax, and weave networks." [11] It was doubtless from the Egyptians that the Israelites learned the art.

Alexander the Great and Augustus Cæsar both showed their estimation of the needle; and the perfection of the Phrygian women caused all fine embroidery to be called by their name.[12] Gold threadwork was known to the Romans.

The author of "Letters from Italy," [13] speaking of the cabinet at Portici, mentions an elegant marble statue of Diana, dressed "after the purple gowns worn by the Roman ladies; the garment is edged with a lace exactly resembling point; it is of an inch and a half broad, and has been painted purple."

But nations far removed from civilisation were by no means ignorant of this handicraft, as the discovery of gold needles and other working implements in the Scandinavian tumuli can testify. Of these works little now exists even in the Northern museums.

---

[9] Goldsmith.

[10] So Pallas:

"Within her father's threshold dropped her veil
Of airy texture—work of her own hand."

Iliad, book viii., Lord Derby's trans.

And again, when Diomed wounds Venus, his spear pierces

"Th' ambrosial veil, the Graces' work."
Ibid.

[11] Chap. xix. 9. Also: "Fine linen with broidered work from Egypt was that which thou spreadest forth to be thy sail"—*Ezekiel* xxvii. 7; and again, ver. 16: "Syria was thy merchant . . . they occupied in thy fairs with emeralds, purple, and broidered work, and fine linen, and coral, and agate."

[12] "Opus phrygianum."

[13] In the years 1770 and 1771. By an Englishwoman (Mrs. Miller). London, 1777.

In the "London Chronicle" of 1767 will be found an account of the opening of a Scandinavian barrow, near Wareham, in Dorsetshire. Within the hollow trunk of an oak were found many bones, wrapped in a covering of deerskins neatly sewn together. There were the remains of a piece of lace of gold wire 4 inches long, and 2½ inches broad, Fig. 1 ; black and much decayed, of the old lozenge pattern, that oldest and most universal of all designs, again found depicted on the coats of the ancient Danes, where the borders are edged with an open or network of the same pattern.[14] Professor Worsaae ascribes this specimen to the Iron age.

Fig. 1.

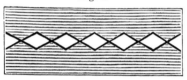

Gold lace found in a barrow.

Our Anglo-Saxon ladies excelled in this womanly accomplishment ; and gorgeous are the accounts of the gold-starred and scarlet-embroidered tunics and violet sarks worked by the nuns. The "opus anglicanum" was sought for by foreign prelates, and made the subject of papal correspondence.[15] Nor did our Anglo-Saxon kings ever fail, in their pilgrimages to Rome, to bestow on the sovereign Pontiff garments richly embroidered in gold and precious stones.

Royal and noble ladies plied their needles for the adornment of the church ; and great St. Dunstan himself designed patterns to be executed by their hands.[16]

The four daughters of Edward the Elder were famed for their ability. Their father, says William of Malmesbury, caused them in childhood "to give their whole attention to letters, and

[14] Strutt.

[15] The richly-embroidered orphreys of the English clergy excited the admiration of Pope Innocent IV. (1246), who inquired where they were made, and being answered in England, he exclaimed, " Truly England is our garden of delight, in sooth, it is a well inexhaustible, and where there is great abundance ; from thence much may be extracted." And immediately he despatched official letters to some of the Cistercian abbots in England, enjoining them to procure a certain quantity of such embroidered vestments, and send them to Rome for his own use. —Matthew of Paris.

[16] Ethelwynne, a noble lady, is recorded to have enlisted him in her service, to design the ornaments of a stole; and Dunstan sat daily in the lady's bower, superintending her work, together with the maidens.

afterwards employed them in the labours of the distaff and the needle."

Edgitha, Queen of Edward the Confessor, was, says the same historian, "perfect mistress of her needle." [17]

Though needlework was greatly cultivated in France, and "Berthe aux grands pieds," mother of Charlemagne, was a celebrated worker—

"à ouvrer si com je vous dirai
N'avoit meillor ouvriere de Tours jusqu'à Cambrai";

and of Charlemagne [18] it is chronicled that he

"Ses filles fist bien doctriner,
Et aprendre keudre et filer"—

still the palm may be accorded to our Anglo-Saxon ancestresses, for William the Conqueror, on his first appearance in public, after the battle of Hastings, clad himself in a richly wrought cloak of Anglo-Saxon embroidery,[19] an improvement, no doubt, upon the reputed handiwork of his queen, the far-famed tapestry of Bayeux.

Perhaps the finest specimens of "opus anglicanum" extant are the cope and maniple of St. Cuthbert, removed from his coffin some years since in the cathedral of Durham, and now preserved in the chapter library of that city. The embroidery, in beauty, baffles all description. One side of the maniple is of gold lace stitched on, worked, apparently, on a parchment pattern.

It was the custom in feudal times for knightly families to send their daughters to the castles of their suzerain lords, there to be trained to spin, weave, and embroider, under the eye of the lady châtelaine ; [20] a custom which, in the more primitive countries, continued even to the French Revolution.[21] In French romances

---

[17] The Anglo-Saxon Godric, sheriff of Buckingham, granted to Alcuid half a hide of land, as long as he should be sheriff, on condition she taught his daughter the art of embroidery.

[18] The skill of his wife, Fastrade, and that of Constance, queen of Robert, King of France, is also recorded.

[19] His secretary, William of Poictiers, states that "the English women are eminently skilful with the needle, and in weaving of gold."

[20] We read, for instance, that Gabrielle de Bourbon, wife of Louis de la Trémouille, "jamais n'estoit oyseuse, mais s'employoit, une partie de la journée en broderies et autres menus ouvrages appartenant à telles dames, et y occupoit ses damoyselles dont avoit bonne quantité, et de grosses, riches et illustres maisons."
—*Panegyric de Loys de la Trémoille, par Jean Bouchet.*

Again, Vecellio dedicates his "Corona" to Signora Nani, not only on account of the pleasure she takes in works of the needle, but for " il diletto che prende in farne essercitar le donne di casa sua, ricetto delle più virtuose giovani che hoggidì vivono in questa città."

[21] "It is usual here," writes a lady

these young ladies are termed "chambrières," in our English, simply, "the maidens." Great ladies prided themselves upon the number of their attendants, and passed their mornings at work, their labours beguiled by singing the "chansons à toile," as the ballads, written for these occasions, were termed.[22] In the wardrobe accounts of our kings appear constant entries of working materials purchased for the royal ladies.[23]

During the Wars of the Roses, when a duke of the blood royal is related to have begged alms in the streets of the rich Flemish towns, ladies of rank, more fortunate in their education, gained, like the French emigrants of modern days, their subsistence by the products of their needle.[24]

Without wishing to detract from the industry of mediæval ladies, it must be owned that the swampy state of the country, the absence of all roads, save those traversed by pack-horses during the fine season, and the deficiency of all suitable outdoor amusement but that of hawking, caused them to while away their time within doors the best way they could. Out of doors exercise for women is but of modern date. Not fifty years

from Madrid, in 1679, "for good families to put their daughters to ladies, by whom they are employed to embroider in gold and silver, or various colours, or in silk, about the shift, neck, and hands."

[22] "I jor fist es chambre son pere,
Une estole et i amict pere
De soie et d'or molt soutilment,
Si i fait ententevement
Mainte croisette et mainte estoile
Et dist ceste chanchon à toile."
Roman de la Violette.

"One day, seated in her father's room, she was skilfully working a stole and amict in silk and gold, and she was making in it, with great care, many a little cross and many a little star, singing all the while this chanson à toile."

[23] In one of Edward I. we find a charge of eight shillings for silk bought for the embroidery work of Margaret, the king's daughter, and another for 4 oz. of silk 200 oz. of gold thread, a spindle, &c.— *Liber de Garderoba*, 23 Edw. I., Public Record Office.

In one of Edward III., the sum of 2l. 7s. 2d. is expended in the purchase of

gold thread, silk, &c., for his second daughter, Joanna. — *Liber Garderobæ*, 12-16 Edw. III., Public Record Office.

Elizabeth of York worked much at her needle. In the account of her household, preserved in the Public Record Office, every page of which is signed by Queen Elizabeth herself, we find—

"To Evan Petreson, joiner, for the stuff and making of 4 working stools for the Queen, price of the stool 16 pence, 5s. 4d.

"To Thomas Fissch, for an elne of linen cloth for a samplar for the Queen, 8d."

In the Inventory, 4 Edward VI., 1552 (Harl. MSS. No. 1419), are entries of—

"Item, xii. samplars" (p. 419).

"Item, one samplar of Normandie canvas wrought with green and black silk" (p. 524).

"A book of parchment containing diverses patternes" (p. 474), probably purchases for his sisters.

[24] See, for instance, the interesting account of the Countess of Oxford, given by Miss Strickland, in her "Life of Queen Elizabeth of York."

since, in the remote provinces of France, a lady who quitted her house daily was remarked on. "Elle sort beaucoup," folks would say, as though she were guilty of dissipation.

So queens and great ladies sewed on. We hear much of works of adornment, more still of piety, when Katharine of Aragon appears on the scene. She had learned much in her youth from her mother, Queen Isabella, and had assisted at those "trials of needlework established by that virtuous monarch among the Spanish ladies: [25]

"Her days did pass
In working with the needle curiously." [26]

It is recorded how, when Wolsey, with the papal legate, Campeggio, going to Bridewell, begged an audience of Queen Katharine, on the subject of her divorce, they found her at work with her maids, like Penelope of old, and she came to them with a skein of red silk about her neck.[27]

Queen Mary Tudor is recorded to have followed the example of her illustrious mother, though all we find among the entries is a charge " to working materials for Jane the Fole, one shilling."

---

[25] These are alluded to in the dialogue between Industria and Ignavia, as given in Sibmacher's "Modelbuch," 1601 (French translation): "La vieille dame raconte l'histoire des concours de travail à l'aiguille chez les anciens Espagnols; comme Isabelle, femme de Ferdinand, a hautement estimé les travaux de l'aiguille."

Queen Isabella, says Prescott, "was careful to instruct her daughters in these more humble departments of domestic duty, for she thought nothing too humble to learn which is useful. If we are to believe Florez, the king wore no shirt but of the queen's making."

The "Spanish stitch," so often mentioned, was brought in by Katharine, on her marriage with Prince Arthur, in 1501. We have constantly in her wardrobe accounts, sheets, and pillow-beres, "wrought with Spanish work of black silk at the edge."

In the Inventory of Lord Monteagle, 1523 (Public Record Office), are "eight partlets, three garnished with gold, the rest with Spanish work."

In 1556, among the New Year's gifts presented to Queen Mary Tudor, most of the smocks are " wrought with black silk, Spanish fashion."

In the Great Wardrobe Accounts of Queen Elizabeth, 3 and 4, Public Record Office, we have "Sixteen yards of Spanish work for ruffs."

" Twelve tooth-cloths, with the Spanish stitch, edged with gold and silver bone lace."—Ibid. Eliz. 5 & 6.

The Spanish stitch appears in France with Henry II., 1557. " Pour la façon d'ung gaban avec ung grant collet chamarrez à l'Espaignolle de passement blanc," &c.—Comptes de l'Argentier du Roy, Archives Nat. K. K. 106.

[26] Taylor, the Water Poet, " Katharine of Aragon."

[27] The industry of Henry's last queen was as great as that of his first. Specimens still exist at Sizergh Castle, Westmoreland, of Katharine Parr's needlework, a counterpane and a toilet cover. An astrologer, who cast her nativity, foretold she would be a queen; so when a child, on her mother requiring her to work, she would exclaim, " My hands are ordained to touch crowns and sceptres, not needles and spindles."

No one would suspect the Virgin Queen of solacing herself with the charms of the needle. Every woman, however, had to make one shirt in her lifetime, and the "Lady Elizabeth's Grace," on the second anniversary of Prince Edward's birth, then only six years of age, presented her brother with a cambric smock wrought by her own royal hands.

The works of Scotland's Mary, who early studied all female accomplishments under her governess, Lady Fleming, are too well known to require notice. In the letters of the ill-fated queen are constant demands for silk and other sewing materials wherewith to solace her long captivity. She had also studied under Catherine de Medicis, herself an unrivalled needlewoman. Assembling her youthful daughters, Claude, Elizabeth, and Margaret, with Mary Stuart and her Guise cousins, "elle passoit," says Brantôme,[28] "fort son temps les apres-disnées à besogner apres ses ouvrages de soye, où elle estoit tant parfaicte qu'il estoit possible." The ability of Reine Margot [29] is celebrated by Ronsard, who exalts her as imitating Pallas in the art.[30]

Needlework was the daily employment of the convent. As early as the fourteenth century it was termed "nun's work;"[31] and even now, in secluded parts of the kingdom, ancient lace is styled by that name.[32]

Nor was the occupation solely confined to females. Monks were commended for their skill in embroidery;[33] and in the frontispieces of early pattern books published in the sixteenth century men are

---

[28] "Dames illustres."

[29] The "Reine des Marguerites," the learned sister of Francis I., was not less accomplished at her needle, and entries for working materials appear in her accounts up to the year of her death, 1549.
"Trois marcs d'or et d'argent fournis par Jehan Danes, pour servir aux ouvraiges de la dicte dame."—*Livre de dépenses de Marguerite d'Angoulême, par le Comte de la Ferrière-Percy;* Paris, 1862.

[30] "Elle addonnoit son courage
A faire maint bel ouvrage
Dessus la toile, et encor
A joindre la soye et l'or.
Vous d'un pareil exercise
Mariez par artifice
Dessus la toile en maint trait
L'or et la soie en pourtrait."
Ode à la Royne de Navarre, liv. ii. od. vii.

[31] 1380. "Œuvre de nonnain."—*Inventaire de Charles V.*

[32] "My grandmother, who had other lace, called this" (some needle-point) "nun's work."—*Extract from a Letter from the Isle of Man,* 1862.
"A butcher's wife showed Miss O—— a piece of Alençon point, which she called 'nun's work.'"—*Extract from a Letter from Scotland,* 1863.
A lace-maker of Totness, now in her 94th year, still uses what she calls a "nun's pillow."
1763. In the "Edinburgh Advertiser" appears, "Imported from the Grand Canaries, into Scotland, nun's work."

[33] As, for instance, "the imbrothering" of the monks of the monastery of Wolstrope, in Lincolnshire.

represented working at frames, and these books are stated to have been written "for the profit of men, as well as of women." [34]

Many were composed by ecclesiastics; [35] and in the library of St.-Geneviève at Paris are several works of this class,[36] inherited from the monastery of that name. As these books contain little or no letterpress, they could scarcely have been collected by the monks, unless with a view to using them.

At the dissolution of the monasteries, the great Roman Catholic ladies came to the rescue. Of the widow of the ill-fated Earl of Arundel, it is recorded : " Her gentlewomen and chambermaids she ever busied in works ordained for the service of the church. She permitted none to be idle at any time." [37]

Instructresses in the art of embroidery were now at a premium. The old nuns had died out, and there were none to replace them.

Mrs. Hutchinson, in her " Memoirs," enumerates, among the eight tutors she had at seven years of age, one for needlework; while Hannah Senior, about the same period, entered the service of the Earl of Thomond, to teach his daughters the use of their needle, with the salary of 200l. a year. The money, however, was never paid; so she petitions the Privy Council for leave to sue him.[38]

When, in 1614, the King of Siam applied to King James for an English wife, a gentleman of " honourable parentage " offers his daughter, whom he describes of excellent parts for " music, her needle, and good discourse." [39] And these are the sole accomplishments he mentions. The bishops, however, shocked at the proceeding, interfered, and put an end to the projected alliance.

No ecclesiastical objection, however, was made to the epitaph of Catherine Sloper. She sleeps in the cloisters of Westminster Abbey, 1620:

" Exquisite at her needle."

---

[34] " Livre de Lingerie," Dom. de Sera, 1581. " Donne, donzelle, con gli huomini."—*Taglienti*, 15:0. Patterns which " les Seigneurs, Dames et Damoiselles ont eu pour agréables."—*Vinciolo*, 1587.

[35] Jehan Mayol, carme de Lyon; Fra Hieronimo, dell' Ordine dei Servi ; Père Dominique, religieux carme, and others.

[36] One in the Bibliothèque Nationale is from the " Monasterio St. Germani à Pratis."

[37] He died 1595. " Lives of the Earl and Countess of Arundel," from the original MS. by the Duke of Norfolk. London, 1857.

[38] P. R. O. Calendar of State Papers, Domestic, Charles I. vol. clxix. 12.

[39] P. R. O. Calendar of State Papers, Colonial, No. 789.

Till a very late date we have ample record of the esteem in which this art was held.

In the days of the Commonwealth, Mrs. Walker is described to have been as well-skilled in needlework "as if she had been brought up in a convent." She kept, however, a gentlewoman for teaching her daughters.

Evelyn, again, praises the talent of his daughter, Mrs. Draper. "She had," writes he, "an extraordinary genius for whatever hand can do with a needle."

The gay queen of Charles I., followed by the consorts of the younger Stuarts, wrought a change in the simple habits of their royal predecessors, for when Queen Mary, in her Dutch simplicity, sat for hours knotting fringe, her favourite employment, Bishop Burnet, her biographer, adds: "It was a strange thing to see a queen work so many hours of the day;" and her homely habits formed a never ending subject of ridicule for the wit of Sir Charles Sedley.[40]

From the middle of the last century, or, rather, from the French Revolution, the more artistic style of needlework and embroidery fell into decadence. The simplicity of male costume rendered it a less necessary adjunct to female or, indeed, male education; for, strange to say, two of the greatest generals of the Republic, Hoche and Moreau, added to their pay by embroidering satin waistcoats long after they had entered the military service.

The needle now became replaced by trumpery fancy works, which the better taste of the last few years has happily exploded. We may look on the art as almost at an end. The sewing-machine has added to the exigences of the distressed needlewoman, and those who could once gain a fair livelihood now fear starvation. On the other hand, locomotion and cheap travelling have rendered the life of our countrywomen so much less stay-at-home; they have little time for the homely employment of their ancestors. We may verily say, with the prophet Daniel, of the present generation, "Many shall run to and fro, and knowledge shall be increased."

---

[40] See his epigram, "The Royal Knotter," about "the Queen:"—

"Who, when she rides in coach abroad,
Is always knotting threads."

Describing her daily drive with Louis XIV., a contemporary writer states of Madame de Maintenon that, "à peine installée dans la voiture, avant que le cocher eût fouetté les chevaux, la dame mit ses lunettes et tirá de l'ouvrage qu'elle avait dans son sac."

CHAPTER II.

CUTWORK.

"Et lors, sous vos lacis à mille fenestrages,
Raiseuls et poinct couppés et tous vos clairs ouvrages."
Jean Godard, 1588.

IT is from that open-work embroidery which in the sixteenth century came into such universal use that we must derive the origin of lace, and, in order to work out the subject, trace it through all its gradations.

This embroidery, though comprising a wide variety of decoration, went by the general name of cutwork.

The fashion of adorning linen has prevailed from the earliest times. Either the edges were worked in close embroidery—the threads drawn and fashioned with a needle in various forms—or the ends of the cloth unravelled and plaited with geometric precision.

To judge from the description of the linen grave-clothes of St. Cuthbert, as given by an eye-witness[1] to his disinterment in the twelfth century, they were ornamented in a manner similar to that we have described. "There had been," says the chronicler, "put over him a sheet . . . . this sheet had a fringe of linen thread of a finger's length; upon its sides and ends were woven a border of projecting workmanship fabricated of the thread itself, bearing the figures of birds and beasts, so arranged that between every two pairs there were interwoven among them the representation of a branching tree which divides the figures. This tree, so tastefully depicted, appears to be putting forth its leaves," &c. There can be no doubt that this sheet, for many centuries preserved in the cathedral church of Durham, was a specimen of drawn or cut work, which, though later it came into general use, was at an early period of our history alone used for ecclesiastical purposes, and an art which was, till the dissolution of monasteries, looked upon as a church secret.

---

[1] Translated from the "Libellus de Admirandis beati Cuthberti Miraculis," of Reginald, monk of Durham, by Rev. J. Rain. Durham, 1855.

Though cutwork is mentioned in Hardyng's Chronicle,[2] when, describing the luxury in King Richard II.'s reign, he says—

> " Cut werke was greate both in court and townes,
> Both in menes hoddis and also in their gownes,"

yet this oft quoted passage, no more than that of Chaucer, in which he accuses the priests of wearing gowns of scarlet and green colours ornamented with cutwork, cannot be received as evidence of this mode of decoration being in general use. It refers rather to the fashion of cutting out[3] pieces of velvet or other materials, and sewing them down to the garment with a braid, the applied or "appliqué" work of later times.

That linen was then adorned with the needle, we have evidence in the work of his consort, Queen Anne of Bohemia. In the cathedral at Prague is preserved a priest's robe, executed by her hand, a curious piece of mediæval embroidery and cutwork, yellow with age, but in perfect condition.

Coeval with these styles of decoration was drawn-work, in which the weft and woof threads of the tissue were drawn, retaining the design and forming the threads into a square network, rendered firm by a stitch at each intersection. The design was then embroidered, often in colours.[4]

The linen shirt or smock was the special object of adornment, and on the decoration of the collar and sleeves much time and ingenuity were expended.

In the ancient ballad of "Lord Thomas,"[5] the fair Annette cries :—

> " My maids, gae to my dressing-room,
> And dress me in my smock;
> The one half is o' the Holland fine,
> The other o' needlework."

Chaucer, too, does not disdain to describe the embroidery of a lady's smock :—

> " White was her smocke, embrouded all before
> And eke behynde, on her colar aboute,
> Of cole blacke sylke, within and eke without."

---

[2] "Chronicle of John Hardyng," circ. 1470.

[3] Temp. Rich. II. In their garments "so much pouncing of chesell to make holes, so much dragging (zigzagging) of sheers," &c.—*Good Parson, Chaucer.*

[4] Drawn-work continued to a late period in Russia, and is still to be found in the productions of Brazil, Chili, and the Philippine Islands. It was revived in Europe during the last century, and specimens were executed closely resembling lace, under the various appellations of drawn-work (Fig. 28), Indian work (see "Denmark"), Dresden point (see "Germany"), Hamburg point, &c.

[5] Percy, "Reliques of Ancient Poetry," vol. iii.

The sums expended on the decoration of this most necessary article of dress sadly excited the wrath of Mr. Stubbs, who thus vents his indignation: "These shirtes (sometymes it happeneth) are wrought throughout with needlework of silke, and such like, and curiously stitched with open seame, and many other knackes besides, more than I can describe; in so much, I have heard of shirtes that have cost some ten shillynges, some twenty, some forty, some five pounds, some twenty nobles, and (which is horrible to heare) some ten pound a pece." [6]

In the time of Henry VIII. the shirt was "pynched" or plaited:—

> "C.me nere with your shirtes bordered and displayed,
> In foarme of surplois." [7]

These,[8] with handkerchiefs,[9] sheet, and pillow-beres[10] (pillow-cases), were embroidered with silks of various colours, until the fashion gradually gave place to cutwork.

[6] "Anatomie of Abuses," by Philip Stubbs, 1583.

[7] "The Shyp of Folys of the Worlde," translated out of Latin by Alex. Barclay, 1508.

[8] The inventories of all nations abound in mention of these costly articles. The "smocks" of Katharine of Aragon, "for to lay in," were wrought about the collar with gold and silk. Lord Monteagle, 1523, had "two fine smocks of cambric wrought with gold." (Inv. P. R. O.) Among the New Year's gifts offered to Queen Mary Tudor (1556), we find a smock wrought over with silk, and collar and ruffles of damask, gold purl, and silver. Again, in the household expenses of Marguerite de France, 1545, we find a charge of "4 livres 12 sols, pour une garniture de chemise ouvré de soye cramoisie pour madicte dame" (Bib. Nat. MSS. Fonds Français, 10,394). About the same date (G. W. A. Eliz. 1 & 2, 1558–59) appear charges for "lengthening one smocke of drawne work, 20s. Six white smocks edged with white needlework lace, 10s. To overcasting and edging 4 smockes of drawne work with ruffs, wristbands, and collars, three of them with black work, and three of them with red," &c. At the funeral of Henry II. of France, 1559, the effigy was described as attired in "une chemise de

toile de Hollande, bordée au col et aux manches d'ouvraige fort excellent."— Godefroy, Le Cérémonial de France, 1610.

[9] See "France."

[10] The pillow-bere has always been an object of luxury, a custom not yet extinct in France, where the "taies d'oreiller, brodées aux armes," and trimmed with a rich point, form an important feature in a modern trousseau. In the inventory of Margaret of Austria, the gentle governess of the Low Countries, are noted—

"Quatre toyes d'oraillers ouvrées d'or et de soye cramoysie et de verde.

"Autres quatres toyes d'oraillers faites et ouvrées d'or et de soye bleu à losanges qui ont estées données à Madame par dom Diego de Cabrera."—Corr. de l'Empereur Maximilian Ier et de Marguerite d'Autriche, par M. Leglay; Paris, 1839.

Edward VI. has (Harl. MSS. 1419) "18 pillow-beres of hollande with brode seams of silk of sundry coloured needle-work." And again, "One pillow-bere of fine hollande wrought with a brode seam of Venice gold and silver, and silk nedlework."

And, Lady Zouche presents Queen Elizabeth, as a New Year's gift, with "One pair of pillow-beares of Holland work, wrought with black silk drawne work."—Nichols' Royal Progresses.

The description of the widow of John Whitcomb, a wealthy clothier of Newbury, in Henry VIII.'s reign, when she laid aside her weeds, is the first notice we have of cutwork being in general use. "She came," says the writer, "out of the kitchen in a fair train gown stuck full of silver pins, having a white cap upon her head, with cuts of curious needlework, the same an apron, white as the driven snow."

Fig. 2.

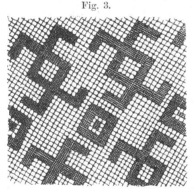

"Spiderwork," thirteenth century. Bock Coll. South Kensington Museum.

Fig. 3.

"Spiderwork," fourteenth century. Bock Coll. South Kensington Museum.

The embroidering on a net-work ground was a work of great antiquity. It is the "opus filatorium" of the fourteenth century,[11] the spiderwork or "opus araneum" of continental writers, revived, in modern times, under the names of "filet brodé" and "guipure d'art." We give two specimens of coloured silk network,

---

[11] Three pieces of this work are in the Exeter Inventory, dated 1327, quoted by Canon Rock.

the one (Fig. 2) ornamented with small embroidered shields and crosses, the other (Fig. 3) with the mediæval gammadion pattern.

We are now arrived at the Renaissance, a period when so close an union existed between the fine arts and manufactures ; when the most trifling objects of luxury, instead of being consigned to the vulgar taste of the mechanic, received from artists their most graceful inspirations. Embroidery profited by the general impulse, and books of designs were composed for that species which, under the general name of cutwork, formed the great employment for the women of the day. The volume most generally circulated especially among the ladies of the French court, for whose use it was designed, is that of the Venetian Vinciolo, to whom, some say,

Fig. 4.

Point coupé. Vinciolo.

we know not on what authority, Catherine de Medicis granted, in 1585, the exclusive privilege of making and selling the " collerettes gaudronnées "[12] she had herself introduced. This work, which passed through many editions, dating from 1587 to 1623, is entitled, " Les singuliers et nouveaux pourtraicts et ouvrages de Lingerie. Servans de patrons à faire toutes sortes de poincts,

---

[12] Goderonné—goudronné, incorrectly derived from pitch (goudron), has no relation to stiffness or starch, but is used to designate the fluted pattern so much in vogue in the sixteenth century—the " gadrooned " edge of silversmiths.

1588. " Il avait une fraise empesée et godronnée à gros godrons, au bout de laquelle il y avoit de belle et grande dentelle, les manchettes estoient goudronnées de mesme."

couppé, Lacis & autres.[13] Dedié à la Royne. Nouvellement inventez, au proffit et contentement, des nobles Dames et Damoiselles & autres gentils esprits, amateurs d'un tel art. Par le Seigneur Federic de Vinciolo Venitien. A Paris. Par Jean le Clerc le jeune, etc., 1587."

Two little figures, representing ladies in the costume of the period, with working-frames in their hands, decorate the title-page.[14]

Fig. 5.

(Ce Pelican contient en longueur 70 mailles et en hauteur 65.)

Lacis. Vinciolo, edition 1588.

The work is in two books. The first of point coupé, of rich geometric patterns, printed in white upon a black ground (Fig. 4).

The second of lacis, or subjects in squares, Fig. 5, with darned or counted stitches (point conté), like the patterns for worsted-work of the present day—the designs, the seven planets, Neptune, and various squares, borders, &c.

---

[13] " Reseau de poinct conté " is added to the subsequent editions.
[14] They are introduced into the frontispiece of this work.

Vinciolo dedicates his book to Louise de Vaudemont, the neglected queen of Henry III., whose portrait, with that of the king, is added to the later editions.

Various other pattern books for embroidery and other works of the needle had already been published. The earliest bearing a date is one printed at Cologne in 1527.[15]

These books are scarce; being designed for patterns, and traced with a metal style, or pricked through, many perished in the using. They are much sought after by the collector as among the early specimens of wood-block printing. We give therefore in the Appendix a list of those we find recorded, or of which we have seen copies, observing that the greater number, though generally composed for one particular art, may be applied indifferently to any kind of ornamental work.

Cutwork was made in several manners. The first consisted in arranging a network of threads upon a small frame, crossing and interlacing them into various complicated patterns. Beneath this network was gummed a piece of fine cloth, open like canvas, called quintain,[16] from the town in Brittany where it was made. Then, with a needle, the network was sewn to the quintain by edging round those parts of the pattern that were to remain thick. The last operation was to cut away the superfluous cloth; hence the name of cutwork.

The author of the "Consolation aux Dames," 1620, in addressing the ladies, thus specially alludes to the custom of working on quintain :—

> " Vous n'employrez les soirs et les matins
> A façonner vos grotesques quaintains,
> O folle erreur—O despence excessive."

Again, more simple was it to make the pattern detached without any linen at all; threads, radiating at equal distances from one common centre, served as a framework to others which were united to them in squares, triangles, rosettes, and other geometric forms, worked over with button-hole stitch (point noué), forming in some parts open-work, in others heavy, compact embroidery. This was the first needle-made lace, for the fineness and beauty of which Venice excelled, but it was produced in all

---

[15] See Appendix.
[16] Quintain—Quintin. French lawne. Randle Cotgrave, " Dictionarie of the

French and English Tongues," 1611. " 26 virges de Kanting pro sudariis pro ille 47/8."—*G. W. A.* Charles II. 1683-4.

other countries. In Italy it was called "reticella," and that derived from the Ionian Islands was styled "Greek lace."

Distinct from these geometric combinations was the lacis[17] of the sixteenth century, the old network revived. The ground consisted of a network of square meshes, on which was worked the pattern, sometimes cut out of linen and appliqué,[18] but more usually darned in or worked with counted stitches, "point conté," like tapestry. The ground, as we learn from a poem on lacis, affixed to the pattern book of "Milour Mignerak,"[19] was made by netting, beginning with a single stitch, and increasing a stitch on each side until the required size was obtained. If a strip or long border was to be made, the netting was continued to its prescribed length, and then finished off by reducing a stitch on each side till it was decreased to one; as garden nets are made in the present day.

This plain netted ground was called "réseau," "rézel," "rézeuil," and was much used for bed-curtains, vallances, &c.[20]

In the inventory of Mary Stuart, made at Fotheringay,[21] we find, "Le lict d'ouvrage de rezel;" and again, under the care of

---

[17] "Lacis, espèce d'ouvrage de fil ou de soie fait en forme de filet ou de réseuil dont les brins etaient entrelacez les uns dans les autres."—*Dict. d'Ant. Furetière*, 1684.

[18] "Béle Prerie contenant differentes sortes de lettres, etc., pour appliquer sur le reseuil ou lassis." Paris, 1601. Appendix.

[19] "Pratique de l'aiguille industrieuse du très excellent Milour Matthias Mignerak." Paris, 1605. Appendix.

[20] The inventories of Charles de Bourbon, ob. 1613, with that of his wife, the Countess of Soissons, made after her death, 1644 (Bib. Nat. MSS. F. Fr. 11,426), alone prove how much this rézeuil was in vogue for furniture during the seventeenth century.

"Item un pavillon de thoille de lin à bende de reseuil blang et noir faict par carel prisé, vi l. t. (livres tournois).

"Item quatre pentes de ciel de cotton blanc à carreaux.

"Item trois pentes de ciel de thoille de iln à carreaux et raiseuil recouvert avec le dossier, pareil estoffe, et petit carreau à point couppé garny de leur frange, le fonds du ciel de thoille de lin, trois custodes et une bonne grace et un drap pareille thoille de lin à bandes de reseuil recouvert . . . prisé xviii l. t."—*Inv. de Charles de Bourbon*.

"Item une autre tapisserie de rezeuil de toile blanche en huit pièces contenant ensemble vingt aulnes ou environ sur deux aulnes trois quarts de haute.

"Item une autre tenture de tapisserie de rézeau tout de leine (lin) appliquée sur de la toille blanche en sept pièces contenant dix-huit aulnes de cours sur trois aulnes de haute.

"Item trois pantes, fonds de dossier, les deux fourreaux de piliers, la couverture de parade, le tout en point couppé et toille.

"Item une garniture de lict blanc, faict par carré d'ouvrage de poinct couppé, le tout garny avec la couverte de parade, prisé la somme de soixante livres tournois."—*Inv. de la Comtesse de Soissons*.

[21] Dated 20 Feb. 1587. Now in the Record Office, Edinburgh.

Jane Kennethee, the "Furniture of a bedd of network and Holland intermixed, not yet finished."

When the réseau was decorated with a pattern, it was termed "lacis," or "darned netting," and, combined with point coupé, much used for bed-furniture and altar-cloths.[22]

In the inventory of Sir John Foskewe (modern Fortescue), Knight, time of Henry.VIII., we find in the hall, "A hanging of green saye, bordered with darning."

Queen Mary Stuart, previous to the birth of James I. (1560), made a will, which still exists, with annotations in her own handwriting.[23] After disposing of her jewels and objects of value, she concludes by bequeathing "tous mes ouvrages masches et collets aux 4 Maries, à Jean Stuart, et Marie Sunderland et toutes les filles." "Masches,"[24] with "punti a maglia," being among the numerous terms applied to this species of work.

Fig. 6.

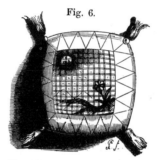

Impresa of Queen Margaret of Navarre, in lacis. Mignerak.

These "ouvrages masches" were doubtless the work of Queen Mary and her ladies. She had learned the art at the French court, where her sister-in-law, Reine Margot—herself also a prisoner for many long years—occupied herself in the same manner, for we find in her accounts,[25] "Pour des moulles est esguilles pour faire rezeuil la somme de iiii L. tourn." And again, "Pour avoir monté une fraize neufve de reseul la somme de x sols tourn."

Though the work of Milour Mignerak, already quoted, is dedi-

---

[22] 1781. "Dix-huit Pales de differentes grandeurs, tous de toile garnis tant de petite dentelle que de filet brodé."—*Inv. de l'Eglise de St.-Gervais.* Arch. Nat. L. L. 654.

[23] In the Record Office, Edinburgh.

[24] "Mache. The masches (meshes) or holes of a net between the thread and thread."—*Cotgrave.*

[25] *Comptes de la Reine de Navarre,* 1577. Arch. Nat. K. K. 162.

Plate I.

Sampler. Seventeenth century.

To face page 19.

cated to the "Trés-Chrestienne Reine de France et de Navarre, Marie de Médicis," and bears her cipher and arms, yet in the decorated frontispiece is a cushion, with a piece of lacis in progress, the pattern a daisy looking at the sun, the favourite impresa of her predecessor, the divorced Marguerite, now, by royal ordinance, "Marguerite Reine, Duchesse de Valois" (Fig. 6).

These pattern books being high in price and difficult to procure, teachers of the art caused the various patterns to be reproduced in "sam cloths," [26] as samplers were then termed, and young ladies worked diligently at their cutwork, lacis, and rézeuil,[27] much as a dame-school child did her A B C in the country villages of our own day. Proud mothers caused these chefs-d'œuvre to be framed and glazed; hence many have come down to us, chiefly of the seventeenth century, uninjured at the present time. (Coloured Plate I.)

A most important specimen of lacis was exhibited at the Art International Exhibition of 1874, by Mrs. Hailstone, of Walton Hall, an altar frontal 14 feet by 4 feet, executed in point conté, representing eight scenes of the Passion of our Saviour, in all fifty-six figures, surrounded by Latin inscriptions. It is assumed to be of English workmanship of an early period.

When used for altar-cloths, bed-curtains, or coverlets, to produce a greater effect, it was the custom to alternate lacis with squares of plain linen :—

> " An apron set with many a dice
> Of needlework sae rare,
> Wove by nae hand, as ye may guess,
> Save that of Fairly fair."—*Ballad of Hardyknute.*

These works formed the great delight of the ladies of the age. Jean Godard, in his poem on the Glove,[28] alluding to the occupation, says :—

> " Une femme gantée œuvre en tapisserie,
> En raizeaux deliez et toute lingerie
> Elle file—elle coud et fait passement
> De toutes les fassons. . . ."

---

[26] Randle Holme, in " The School Mistris Terms of Art for all her Ways of Sewing," has, " A Samcloth, vulgarly, a Samplar."

[27] In the S. K. M. (Bock collection) are specimens of rézeuil d'or, or network with patterns worked in with gold thread and coloured silks. Such were the richly wrought " serviettes sur filez d'or " of Margaret of Austria.

" Autre servyette de Cabes (Cadiz) ouvrée d'or, d'argent sur fillez et bordée d'or et de gris.

" Autre serviette à Cabes de soye grise et verde à ouvrage de fillez bordée d'une tresse de verd et gris."—*Inventory already quoted.*

[28] " Le Gan, de Jean Godard, Parisien." 1588.

The armorial shield of the family, coronets, monograms, the beasts of the Apocalypse, with fleurs-de-lys, hearts, &c., for the most part adorned those pieces destined for the use of the church. If, on the other hand, intended for a pall, death's-heads, cross-bones, and tears, with the sacramental cup, left no doubt of its destination.

As late as the year 1850, a splendid cutwork pall still covered the coffins of the fisher tribe when borne in procession through the streets of Dieppe, a votive offering, worked by the hands of some lady saved from shipwreck, and presented as a memorial of her gratitude.

In 1866, when present at a peasant's wedding in the church of St.-Lô (Département de la Manche), the author observed that the " toile d'honneur," which is always held extended over the heads of the married pair while the priest pronounces the blessing, was of the finest cutwork, trimmed with lace.

Both in the north and in the south of Europe the art still lingers on. Swedish housewives pierce and stitch the holiday collars of their husbands and sons; and careful ladies, drawing the threads of the fine linen sheets destined for the " guest-chamber," produce an ornament of geometric design.

Scarce twenty years since an expiring relic of this art might be sometimes seen on the white smock-frock of the English labourer, which, independent of elaborate stitching, was enriched with an insertion of cutwork, running from the collar to the shoulder crossways, like that we see decorating the surplices of the sixteenth century.

CHAPTER III.

LACE.

" Je demandai de la dentelle :
Voici le tulle de Bruxelles,
La blonde, le point d'Alençon,
Et la Maline, si légère ;
L'application d'Angleterre
(Qui se fait à Paris, dit-on) ;
Voici la guipure indigène,
Et voici la Valenciennes,
Le point d'esprit, et le point de Paris ;
Bref les dentelles
Les plus nouvelles
Que produisent tous les pays."
Le Palais des Dentelles, Rothomago.

LACE [1] is defined as a plain or ornamental network, wrought of fine threads of gold, silver, silk, flax, or cotton, interwoven ; to which may be added " poil de chèvre," and also the fibre of the aloe, employed by the peasants of Italy and Spain. The term " lacez," rendered in the English translation of the statutes [2] " lace," implies braids, such as were used for decorating the different parts of the dress, and appears long before lace, properly so called, came into use. " Passament " [3] also was a general term for gimps and braids, as well as for lace. Modern industry has separated these two classes of work, but the words being formerly used to express both renders it difficult in historic research to separate one from the other.

The same confusion occurs in France, where the first lace was called " passement," because it was applied to the same use, to braid or lay flat over the coats and other garments. The lace trade was entirely in the hands of the " Passementiers " of Paris, who were

---

[1] Lace. French, "dentelle ;" German, " Spitzen ; " Italian, " merletto," "trina ;" Genoa, " pizzo ; " Spanish, " encaje ; " Dutch, "kanten."

[2] Statute 3 Edw. IV. c. iii.

[3] " Passement, a lace or lacing."—*Cotgrave.*

allowed to make all sorts of " passements de dentelle sur l'oreiller aux fuseaux, aux épingles et à la main, d'or, d'argent, tant fin que faux, de soye, de fil blanc et de couleur," &c. They therefore applied the same terms to their different products, whatever the material.

The word " passement " continued to be used till the middle of

Fig. 7.

Grande dantelle au point devant l'aiguille. Montbéliard, 1598.

the seventeenth century, it being specified as " passements aux fuseaux," " passements à l'aiguille ; " only it was more specially applied to lace without an edge. When with indented edge, it was so qualified, " passement à dentelle."

Nor will the term " dentelle " be found in the earlier French dictionaries.[4] It was not till fashion caused the passement to be made with a toothed edge that the expression of "passement dentelé" first appears.

In the acounts of Henry II. of France, and his queen, we have frequent notices of "passement jaulne dantellé des deux costez,"[5] "passement de soye incarnat dentellé d'un costé,"[6] &c. &c., but no mention of the word "dentelle." It does, however, occur, in an inventory of an earlier date, that of Marguerite de France, sister of Francis I., who, in 1545, paid the sum of "VI livres pour soixante aulnes, fine dantelle de Florance pour mettre à des colletz."[7]

After a lapse of twenty years and more, among the articles furnished to Mary Stuart in 1567, is "Une pacque de petite dentelle;"[8] and this is the sole mention of the word in all her accounts.

Fig. 8. Fig. 9.

Petite dantelle. 1598. Petite dantelle. 1598.

We have like entries in the expenses of Henry IV.'s first queen.[9] Gradually the "passement dentelé" subsided into the modern "dentelle."

It is in a pattern book, published at Montbéliard, in 1598,[10] we first find designs for "dantelles." It contains twenty patterns, of all sizes, "bien petites, petites (Figs. 8, 9, 10, 11), moyennes, et grosses" (Fig. 7), the term always applied to toothed edges.

---

[4] Not in those of Rob. Estienne, 1549; Frère de l'Aval, 1549; or Nicot, 1606. Cotgrave has, "Dentelle, small edging (and indented), bone-lace, or needle-work." In "Dict. de l'Académie," 1694, we find, "Dentelle, sorte de passement à jour et à mailles tres fines ainsi nommé parceque les premières qu'on fit etoient dentelées."

[5] *Comptes de l'Argentier du Roi*, 1557. Arch. Nat. K. K. 106. "Passement de fine soie noire dentelle d'un costé." "Passement blanc," "grise," also occur.

[6] *Argenterie de la Reine*, 1556. Arch. Nat. K. K. 118.

[7] *Dépenses de la Maison de Madame Marguerite de France, Sœur du Roi.* Bib. Nat. MSS. F. Fr. 10,394, fol. 62.

[8] "Plus de delivré une pacque de petite dentelle qui est estez cousu ensemble pour mettre sur les coutures des rideaux des ditz litz contenant 80 aunes." Rec. Off. Edin. This custom of trimming the seams of bed-curtains with a lace indented on both sides was common throughout Europe.

[9] 1577. "Pour deux aulnes de passement d'argent a hautte dantelle pour mettre à ung renvers, au pris de soixante solz l'aulne.

"Pour une aulne de dentelle pour faire deux cornettes pour servir à la dicte dame, quatre livres."—*Cptes. de la Reine de Navarre.* Arch. Nat. K. K. 162.

[10] Appendix.

The word "dentelle" seems now in general use; but Vecellio, in his "Corona," 1592, has "opere a mazette," pillow lace, and Mignerak first gives the novelty of "passements au fuzeau," pillow lace (Fig. 12), for which Vinciolo, in his edition of 1623,

Fig. 10.

Fig. 11.

Petite dantelle. 1598.

Petite dantelle. 1598.

Fig. 12.

Fig. 13.

Passement au fuseau. Mignerak, 1605.

Passement au fuseau. Vinciolo, edition 1623.

also furnishes patterns (Figs. 13 and 14); and Parasole, 1616, gives designs for "merli a piombini" (Fig. 15).

In the inventory of Henrietta Maria, dated 1619,[11] appear a

---

[11] "Petits et grands passements; id. à l'esguille; id. facit an mestier; id. de Flandres à poinctes; id. orangé à jour; id. de Flandres satiné;" with "reseuil, dantelles, grandes et petites, or, argent,"

&c.—*Inv. de Madame Sœur du Roi.* Arch. Nat. K. K. 234.

So late as 1645, in the inventory of the church of St.-Médard at Paris (Arch. Nat. L. L. 858), the word is used. We

variety of laces, all qualified under the name of " passement ;" and in that of the Maréchal La Motte, 1627, we find the term applied to every description of lace.

" Item, quatre paires de manchettes garnyes de passement tant de Venise, Gennes, et de Malines." [12]

Another " terme de passementier " which has given rise to some confusion is the word " guipure." Strictly speaking, it was used to express a thick thread or cord over which was twisted a silk, gold, or silver thread.[13] Originally slips of parchment (cartisane) were used, but this was found to perish from damp, and was replaced by a cotton material called " canetille."

Fig. 14.

Fig. 15.

Passement au fuseau. Vinciolo, edition 1623.

Merletti a piombini. Parasole, 1616.

When in the seventeenth century passements were made of linen thread, to imitate the high reliefs of the needle-made points, then in so much estimation, a thick cord worked over with the thread (guipé) was introduced to mark the salient points of the pattern. Thus the term of guipure was applied to the thread laces with guipure reliefs, and the designation has since remained

find, " Quatre tours de chaire de thoille baptiste, ung beau surplis pour le predi- cateur, six autres, cinq corporaulx," all " à grand passement." Also, " deux pe- tits corporaulx à petit passement," and " trois tours de chaire garnyz de grand passement à dentelle."

[12] Inv. apres le decès de Mgr. le Maré- chal de La Motte. Bib. Nat. MSS. F. Fr. 11,426.

[13] " Guiper. Tordre les fils pendans d'une frange par le moyen de l'instrument qu'on nomme guipoir, fer crochu d'un côté, et chargé de l'autre d'un petit mor- ceau de plomb pour lui donner du poids." —Savary.

" Guipure. A grosse black thread covered or whipt about with silk."— Cotgrave.

to all laces without grounds of which the various patterns are united by brides ;[14] the term is also applied to the bold flowing patterns of Flanders and Italy, united by a coarse réseau ground, and indeed is almost indefinitely amplified.

Lace consists of two parts, the ground and the flower, pattern, or " gimp."

The older laces, points, and guipures, are not worked upon a network ground ; the flowers are connected by irregular threads overcast with button-hole stitch, and sometimes fringed with loops or knots, styled " thorns "; in Italian, " punti a spina." These uniting threads are called by our lace-makers " pearl ties "— Randle Holme [15] styles them " cockscombs "—the Italians " legs," the French " barrettes " or " brides ;" the latter term is that now universally adopted.

To express the honeycomb or network ground, we likewise use the French term " réseau." It is also called " fond," " champ," " treille," and sometimes " entoilage," on account of its containing the " toilé " flower or ornament so styled from its flat, close texture resembling linen, and also from its being often made of that material, or of muslin.[16]

The flower, or ornamental pattern, is either made together with the ground, as in Valenciennes or Mechlin, or separately, and then either worked in or sewn on (appliqué.)

The open-work stitches introduced into the pattern are called " modes," " jours ;" by our Devonshire workers, " fillings."

All lace is terminated by two edges, the " pearl," " picot," [17] or " couronne,"—a row of little points at equal distances, and the " footing " or " engrêlure,"—a narrow lace, which serves to keep the stitches of the ground firm, and to sew the lace to the garment upon which it is to be worn.

Lace is divided into two distinct classes, point and pillow. The first is made by the needle on a parchment pattern, and termed " needle point," " point à l'aiguille," " punto in aco."

---

[14] In an inventory of the church of the Oratoire, at Paris, of the seventeenth century, are veils for the host : one, " de taffetas blanc garny d'une guipure ;" the other, " de satin blanc à fleurs, avec une dentelle de guipure." Bib. Nat. MSS. F. Fr. 8621.

[15] "Store-house of Armory and Blason," 1688.

[16] " Grillé," " grillage," is another term applied to the flowers, but distinguished from toilé by having little square spaces between the thread ("grillé," grating), the work not being so compact as the toilé.

[17] " Une robe et tablier, garnis d'une dentelle d'Angleterre à picot."—Inv. de decès de la Duchesse de Bourbon. Arch. Nat. X. 10,064.

The word point is sometimes incorrectly applied to pillow-lace, as "point de Malines," "point de Valencienne," "point de Paris," [18] "point de neige," [19] "point à la reine." "Cette homme est bien en points" was a phrase used to denote a person who wore rich lace.[20] The manner of making pillow lace [21] need hardly be described. The "pillow" [22] is a round or oval board, stuffed so as to form a cushion, and placed upon the knees of the workwoman. On this pillow a stiff piece of parchment is fixed, with small holes pricked through to mark the pattern. Through these holes pins are stuck into the cushion. The threads with which the lace is formed are wound upon "bobbins," small round pieces of wood, about the size of a pencil, having round their upper ends a deep groove, so formed as to reduce the bobbin to a thin neck, on which the thread is wound, a separate bobbin being used for each thread. By the twisting and crossing of these threads the ground of the lace is formed. The pattern or figure, technically called "gimp," is made by interweaving a thread much thicker than that forming the groundwork, according to the design pricked out on the parchment.[23] Such has been the pillow, and the method of using it, with but slight variation, since its introduction.

To avoid repetition, we propose giving a separate history of the manufacture in each country; but in order to furnish some general notion of the relative ages of lace, it may be as well to enumerate the kinds most in use when Colbert, by his establishment of the Points de France, in 1665, caused a general develop-

---

[18] "Une chemisette de toile d'Hollande garnye de point de Paris."—*Inv. d'Anne d'Escoubleau, Baronne de Sourdis, veuve de François de Simiane.* 1681. Arch. Nat. M. M. 802.

[19] 1651. "Huit aulnes de toile commune garnies de neige."—*Inv. des meubles de la Sacristie de l'Oratoire de Jésus, à Paris.* Bib. Nat. MSS. F. Fr. 8621.

"Neuf autres petites nappes; les deux premières de toile unie; la troisième à dentelle quallifié de neige."—*Ibid.*

"Point de neige" recalls the quarrel of Gros René and Marinette:—

"Ton beau galant de neige, avec ta nonpareille,
Il n'aura plus l'honneur d'être sur mon oreille."

Molière, Dépit amoureux, 1656.

Point also means a particular stitch, as "point noué," "point d'esprit," "à chaînette."

[20] "Dict. d'Ant. Furetière. Augmenté par M. Basnage. La Haye, 1727."

[21] French, "dentelle à fuseaux;" Italian, "merli a piombini;" Dutch, "gespeldewerkte kant;" Old Flemish, "spelle werk."

[22] French, "carreau," "cousin," "oreiller;" Italian, "tombolo;" Venetian, "ballon;" Spanish, "mundillo."

[23] The number of bobbins is generally equal to 50 to each square inch. If the lace be one inch wide, it will have 625 meshes in each square inch, or 22,500 in a yard. The work, therefore, goes on very slowly, though generally performed with the greatest dexterity.

ment of the lace manufacture throughout Europe. Acccording to
M. Aubry, the laces known at that period were :—
1. Point or needle-made lace.—Principally made at Venice,
Brussels, and in Spain.
2. Bisette.—A narrow, coarse, indented thread pillow lace of
three qualities, made in the environs of Paris [24] by the peasant-
women, principally for their own use. Though proverbially of
little value : " Ce n'est que de la bisette," [25] it formed an article
of traffic with the mercers and lingères of the day.
3. Campane.[26]—A white, narrow, fine, indented thread pillow
edging,[27] used to sew upon other laces,[28] either to widen them or
to replace a worn-out picot or pearl.
4. Gueuse.—A thread lace, which owed to its simplicity the
name it bore. The ground was network (à réseau), the flowers a
loose, thick thread, worked in on a pillow, what is now called
" torchon." Gueuse was formerly an article of extensive con-

[24] At Gisors, Saint-Denis, Montmorency, and Villiers-le-Bel.— Savary,
Grand Dict. du Commerce, 1720.
Cotgrave gives, " Bisette. A plate (of
gold, silver, or copper) wherewith some
kinds of stuffes are stripped." Oudin,
" Feuille ou paillette d'or ou d'argent."
As " terme de passementier" it frequently
occurs in old inventories.
1545. " 55 sols pour une once bizette
d'argent pour mectre à des colletz."—Accounts of Madame Marguerite de France.
Bib. Nat.
1579. " Petite bizette d'or fin dentellez
des deux costez pour servir à des manches
de satin cramoisy" of Catherine de
Medicis.— Trésorerie de la royne mère du
roy. Arch. Nat. K. K. 115.
In the Chartley Inv. 1586, of Mary
Stuart, is mentioned, " Un plotton de
bisette noire."
[25] " Dict. de l'Académie."
[26] Campane, from " sonnette, clochette,
même grêlot." " Les festons qu'on met
aux etoffes et aux dentelles."—Oudin.
[27] Like bizette, a " terme de passementier." Campane lace was also made of
gold, and of coloured silks, for trimming
mantles, scarfs, &c. We find, in the
Great Wardrobe Accounts of George I.,
1714, an entry of " Gold Campagne
buttons."

Evelyn, in his " Fop's Dictionary,"
1690, gives, " Campane, a kind of
narrow, pricked lace ; " and in the
" Ladies' Dictionary," 1694, it is described as " a kind of narrow lace, picked
or scalloped."
In the Great Wardrobe Account of
William III., 1688–9, we have, " le poynt
campanie tæniæ."
[28] In the last century it was much the
fashion to trim the scalloped edges of
a broader lace with a narrower, which
was called " campaner."
1720. " Une garniture de teste à trois
pièces de dentelle d'Angleterre à raiseau,
garni autour d'une campane à dents."—
Inv. de la Duchesse de Bourbon.
1741. " Une paire de manches à trois
rangs de Malines à raizeau campanée."—
Inv. de decès de Mademoiselle Marie
Anne de Bourbon de Clermont. Arch.
Nat. X. 11,071. (Daughter of Mademoiselle de Nantes and Louis Duke de
Bourbon.)
" Une coëffure de Malines à raizeau à
deux pièces campanée."—Ibid.
In the lace-bills of Madame du Barry,
preserved in the Bib. Nat., are various
entries of " Angleterre et point à l'aiguille, campanée des deux côtés," for
ruffles, camisoles, &c.

sumption in France, but, from the beginning of the last century, little used, save by the lower classes. Many old persons may still remember the term, " beggars' lace."

5. Mignonette.[29]—A light, fine, pillow lace, called " blonde de fil," [30] also " point de tulle," from the ground resembling that fabric. It was made of Lille thread, bleached at Antwerp, of different widths, never exceeding 2 or 3 inches. This lace was manufactured at Lille and Arras, and also in the environs of Paris, in Lorraine, Auvergne, Normandy, and Switzerland. It was an article of considerable export, and at times in high favour, from

Fig. 16.

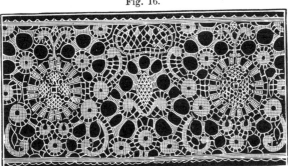

Old Mechlin.

its lightness and clear ground, for head-dresses [31] and other trimmings.[32]

6. Point de Paris, or point double.

---

[29] 1729. " Huit palatines tant points que mignonettes." — Inv. de decès de Louise Henriette de Bourbon-Conty, Princesse du Sang, Duchesse de Orléans. Arch. Nat. X. 10,077.

" Trente-vingt paires de manchettes, quatre coëffures, le tout tant de differents point qu'Angleterre, mignonettes que tulles."—Ibid.

1761. " Fichus garnis à trois rangs de blonde de fil sur entoilage."—Inv. de Charlotte Aglaë d'Orléans, Princesse du Sang, Duchesse de Modène (daughter of the Regent).

1789. Ruffles of blonde de fil appear also in the Inv. de decès de Monseigneur le Duc de Duras. Bib. Nat. MSS. F. Fr. 11,440.

[30] 1758. " Une paire de manchettes à

trois rangs de blonde de fil sur en-toilage."—Inv. de Mademoiselle Louise Anne de Bourbon Condé de Charollais (sister of Mademoiselle de Clermont). Arch. Nat. X. 10,076.

[31] " On employe aussi pour les coëffures de la mignonette, et on a tellement perfectionné cette dentelle, que estant peu de chose dans son commencement est devenue de consequence et même très chère, j'entends, la plus fine qu'on fait sur de beaux patrons."—Le Mercure Galant, 1699.

[32] It frequently appears in the advertisements of the last century. In the " Scottish Advertiser," 1769, we find enumerated among the stock in trade, " Mennuet and blonde lace."

7. Valenciennes.

8. Mechlin.—All the laces of Flanders, with the exception of those of Brussels, were known in commerce at this period under the general name of Mechlin (Fig. 16).

9. Guipures.

10. Gold lace.

Most of these laces are enumerated in a jeu d'esprit, entitled "La Révolte des Passemens," published at Paris in 1661.[33]

In consequence of a sumptuary edict against luxury in apparel, "Mesdames les Broderies—

> " Les Poinctes, Dentelles, Passemens,
> Qui, par une vaine despence,
> Ruinoient, aujourd'huy la France "—

meet, and concert measures for their common safety. Point de Gênes, with Point de Raguse, first address the company; next, Point de Venise, who seems to look on Raguse with a jealous eye, exclaims—

> " Encore pour vous, Poinct de Raguse,
> Il est bon, crainte d'attentat,
> D'en vouloir purger un estat.
> Les gens aussy fins que vous estes
> Ne sont bons que, comme vous faites,
> Pour ruiner tous les estats.
> Et vous, Aurillac on Venise,
> Si nous plions notre valise,"

what will be our fate?

The other laces speak, in their turn, most despondently, till a "vieille broderie d'or," consoling them, talks of the vanity of this world :—"Who knows it better than I, who have dwelt in kings' houses?" One "grande dentelle d'Angleterre" now proposes they should all retire to a convent. To this the "Dentelles de Flandres" object; they would sooner be sewn at once to the bottom of a petticoat.

Mesdames les Broderies resign themselves to become "ameublement;" the more devout of the party to appear as "devants d'autel;" those who feel too young to renounce the world and its vanities will seek refuge in the masquerade shops.

"Dentelle noire d'Angleterre" lets herself out cheap to a

---

[33] In the "Recueil de pièces les plus agréables de ce temps, composées par divers autheurs. Paris, chez Charles Sercy. MDCLXI."

The poem is dedicated to Mademoiselle de la Trousse, cousin of Madame de Sévigné, and was probably written by one of her coterie.

fowler, as a net to catch woodcocks, for which she felt "assez propre" in her present predicament.

The Points all resolve to retire to their own countries, save Aurillac, who fears she may be turned into a strainer "pour passer les fromages d'Auvergne," a smell insupportable to one who had revelled in civet and orange flower.

All were starting,—

> "Chacun, dissimulant sa rage,
> Doucement ploit son bagage,
> Resolu d'obéir au sort,"

when

> "Une pauvre malheureuse,
> Qu'on apelle, dit on, la Gueuse,"

arrives in a great rage, from a village in the environs of Paris. "She is not of high birth, but has her feelings all the same. She will never submit. She has no refuge—not even a place in the hospital. Let them follow her advice, and 'elle engageoit sa chaînette,' she will replace them all in their former position."

Next morn, the Points assemble. "Une grande Cravate [34] fanfaron" exclaims:—

> "Il nous faut venger cet affront,
> Revoltons-nous, noble assemblée."

A council of war ensues:—

> "La dessus, le Poinct d'Alençon
> Ayant bien appris sa leçon
> Fit une fort belle harangue."

Flanders now boasts how she had made two campaigns under Monsieur, as a cravat; another had learned the art of war under Turenne; a third was torn at the siege of Dunkirk.

> "Racontant des combats qu'ils ne virent jamais,"

one and all had figured at some siege or battle.

> "Qu'avons nous à redouter?"

cries Dentelle d'Angleterre. Not so, thinks Point de Gênes, "qui avoit le corps un peu gros."

---

[34] The Cravates or Croates soldiers had a band of stuff round their throats to support an amulet they wore as a charm to protect them from sabre-cuts. What began in superstition ended in fashion.

They all swear—

> " Foy de Passement,
> Foy de Poincts et de Broderie,
> De Guipure et d'Orfévrerie,
> De Gueuse de toute façon,"

to declare open war, and to banish the parliament.

The Laces assemble at the fair of St.-Germain, there to be reviewed by General Luxe.

The muster-roll is called over by Colonel Sotte Depense. Dentelles de Moresse, Escadrons de Neige, Dentelles de Hâvre, Escrues, Soies noires, and Points d'Espagne, &c., march forth in warlike array, to conquer or to die. At the first approach of the artillery they all take to their heels, and are condemned by a council of war. The Points to be made into tinder, for the sole use of the King's Mousquetaires; the Laces to be converted into paper; the Dentelles, Escrues, Gueuses, Passemens, and Silk Lace to be made into cordage and sent to the galleys; the Gold and Silver Laces, the original authors of the sedition, to be " burned alive."

Finally, through the intercession of Love,

> " Le petit dieu plein de finesse,"

they are again pardoned and restored to court favour.

The poem is curious, as giving an account of the various kinds of lace, and as a specimen of the taste of the time, but the " ton précieux " of the Hôtel Rambouillet pervades throughout.

The lace trade, up to this period, was entirely in the hands of pedlars, who carried their wares to the principal towns and large country-houses. It was through his relative, a lace colporteur of Lorraine, that the youthful Claude Gelée was taken to Rome to study.

"One Madame La Boord," says Evelyn, " a French peddling-woman, served Queen Katherine with petticoats, fans, and foreign laces." These hawkers attended the great fairs[35] of Europe, where all purchases were made.[36]

---

[35] These were, in France, Guibray, Beaucaire, and Bordeaux ; in Germany, Frankfort ; in Italy, Novi.

[36] All articles of luxury were to be met with at the provincial fairs. When, in 1671, Catherine of Braganza, the Duchess of Richmond, and the Duke of Buckingham, visited Saffron Walden fair, the queen asked for a pair of yellow stockings, and Sir Bernard Gascoyne, for a pair of gloves stitched with blue.

Even as early as King Henry III.[37] we have a notice " to purchase robes at the fair of St. Ives, for the use of Richard our brother;" and in the dramas of the sixteenth and seventeenth centuries, we find constant allusion to these provincial markets :—[38]

" Seven
Pedlars' shops, nay all Sturbridge fair,[39] will
Scarce furnish her." [40]

The custom of carrying lace from house to house still exists in Belgium, where, at Spa and other places, colporteurs,[41] with packs similar to those borne by our pedlars, bring round to the visitors laces of great value, which they sell at cheaper rates than those exposed in the shops.[42]

Many travellers, too, through the counties of Buckingham and Bedford, or the more southern regions of Devon, will still call to mind the inevitable lace box handed round for purchase by the waiter at the conclusion of the inn dinner ; as well as the girls who, awaiting the arrival of each travelling carriage or postchaise, climbed up to the windows of the vehicle, rarely allowing the occupants to go their way until they had purchased some article of the wares so pertinaciously offered to their inspection.

---

[37] 10 Hen. III., Devon's " Issues of the Exchequer."

[38] " No lace-woman," says Ben Jonson, "that brings French masks and cutworks." That lace was sold by pedlars in the time of Henry VIII., we find from a play, " The Four P's," written in 1544, by John Heywood. Among the contents of a pedlar's box are given " lasses knotted," "laces round and flat for women's heads," " sleve laces," &c.

On opening the box of the murdered pedlar (" Fool of Quality," 1766), " they found therein silk, linen, laces," &c.

[39] Defoe describes Sturbridge fair as the greatest of all Europe. " Nor," says he, " are the fairs of Leipsig in Saxony, the Mart at Frankfort-on-the Maine, or the fair of Nuremburg or Augsburg, any way comparable to this fair of Sturbridge."

In 1423, the citizens of London and the suburbs being accused of sending works of " embroidery of gold, or silver, of Cipre, or of gold of Luk, togedre with Spanish Laton of insuffisant stuff to the fayres of Sturesbrugg, Ely, Oxenford, and Salisbury "—in fact, of palming off inferior goods for country us —" all such are forfeited."—*Rot. Parl.* 2 Hen. VI. Nu. 49.

[40] " Lingua, or the Combat of the Tongue," a Comedy, 1607.

[41] This system of colporteurs dates from the early Greeks. They are termed both in Greek and Hebrew, "voyageurs."

[42] " She came to the house under the pretence of offering some lace, holland, and fine tea, remarkably cheap."—*Female Spectator,* 1757.

CHAPTER IV.

ITALY.

" It grazed on my shoulder, takes me away six parts of an Italian cutwork band
I wore, cost me three pounds in the Exchange but three days before."
Ben Jonson, Every Man Out of his Humour, 1599.

" Ruffles well wrought and fine falling bands of Italian cutwork."
Fair Maid of the Exchange, 1627.

THE Italians claim the invention of point or needle-made lace.
It has been suggested that they derived the art of fine needlework
from the Greeks who took refuge in Italy from the troubles of the
Lower Empire; and what further confirms its Byzantine origin
is, that those very places which kept up the closest intercourse
with the Greek Empire are the cities where point lace was
earliest made and flourished to the greatest extent.[1]

A modern Italian author,[2] on the other hand, asserts that
the Italians learned embroidery from the Saracens of Sicily,
as the Spaniards acquired the art from the Moors of Granada
or Seville, and brings forward, as proof of his theory, that the
word " to embroider," both in Italian and Spanish,[3] is derived
from the Arabic, and no similar word exists in any other European
language.

This theory may apply to embroidery, but certainly not to
lace, for how could the Easterns teach an art of which they were
ignorant themselves? With the exception of the Turkish crochet,
" oyah," and some darned netting and drawn-work which occur on
Persian and Chinese tissues, there is nothing approaching to lace
to be found in any article of Oriental manufacture.

Leaving to the learned these doubtful disputations, we proceed
to show that evidences of lace appear in Italy as early as the
fifteenth century.

---

[1] " Industrial Arts of the Nineteenth
Century," Sir Digby Wyatt.

[2] Francesco Nardi, "Sull' Origine

dell' Arte del Ricamo," Padova, 1839.

[3] Ricamare, Recamar.

The Cavaliere Antonio Merli, in his interesting pamphlet on Italian lace,[4] mentions an account preserved in the municipal archives of Ferrara, dated 1469, as probably referring to lace;[5] but he more especially brings forward a document of the Sforza family, dated 1493,[6] in which the word "trina"[7] (under its ancient form, "tarnete") constantly occurs, together with bone and bobbin lace.

Again, the Florentine poet, Firenzuola, who wrote from 1520 to 1530, composed an elegy upon a collar of raised point, made by the hand of his mistress. See "Florence."

Cavaliere Merli cites, as the earliest-known painting in which lace occurs, a maiolica disc, after the style of the Della Robbia family, in which, surrounded by a wreath of fruit, is represented the half-figure of a lady, dressed in a rich brocade, with a collar of white lace. The costume is of the fifteenth century; but as Luca della Robbia's descendants worked to a later period, the precise date of the work cannot be fixed.

Evidences of white lace, or passement, are said to appear in the pictures of Carpaccio, in the gallery at Venice, and in another by Gentile Bellini, where the dress of one of the ladies is trimmed round the neck with a white lace. The date of this last painting is 1500. We have not seen them.

Lace was made throughout Italy mostly by the nuns, and ex-

---

[4] "Origine ed Uso dell Trine a filo di refe" (thread). 1864. Privately printed.

[5] "1469. — Io, Battista de Nicollo, d'Andrea da Ferrara, debio avere per mia manifatura et reve per cuxere et candelle per inzirare . . . It. per desgramitare e refilare e inzirare e ripezare e reapicare le gramite a camixi quatordece per li signori calonexi, et per li, mansonarij le qual gramite staxea malissimamente, p. che alcune persone le a guaste. Lire 1 10. It. per reve et p. candelle. L. 0 5."

"1469.—I, Baptist de Nicollo, of Andrea da Ferrara, have owing to me for my making, and thread to sew, and candles to wax . . . Item, for untrimming and reweaving and waxing and repiecing and rejoining the trimmings of fourteen albs for the canons and attendants of the church, the which trimmings were in a very bad state because some persons had

spoiled them. L. 1 10. It. for thread and wax. L. 0 5."

These trimmings (gramite), Cav. Merli thinks, were probably "trine."

[6] See "Milan."

[7] "Trina," like our word lace, is used in a general sense for braid or passement. Floris, in his Dictionary ("A Worlde of Words," John Floris, London, 1598), gives:—

"Trine,—cuts, snips, pincke worke on garments; and Trinci,—gardings, fringings, lacings, &c., or other ornaments of garments."

"Merlo," "merletto," are the more modern terms for lace. We find the first as early as the poet Firenzuola. (See "Florence.") It does not occur in any pattern book of an older date than the "Fiori da Ricami," of Pasini, and the two works of Francesco de' Franceschi, all printed in 1591.

pressly for the service of the church.[8]   Venice was celebrated for
her point, and Genoa for her pillow lace.   The Italian laces best

Fig. 17.

Reticella.

known in the commercial world, in the earlier periods, were those
of Venice, Milan, and Genoa.

[8] At present, if you show an Italian a piece of old lace, he will exclaim : "Opera
di monache ; roba di chiesa."

It would be difficult to enumerate the various kinds of needle-made lace produced by Italy in her palmy days.

The Cavaliere Merli has endeavoured to classify them according to the names given in the pattern books, with which, as well as with her lace, Venice supplied the world. Out of more than a

Fig. 18.

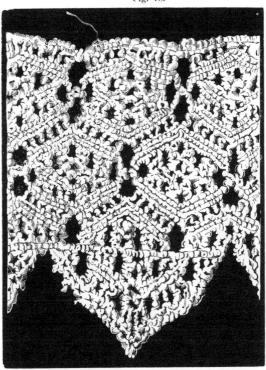

Punto a gropo. Knotted point.

hundred of these works, the names of which have been collected, above one-third were published in Venice.

1. Punto a reticella.[9]—Already described, p. 16 (Fig. 17).
2. Punto tagliato.[10]—Cutwork, already described, p. 16.
3. Punto in aria.[11]—See "Venice."

---

[9] First mentioned in the Sforza Inventory, 1493 (see "Milan"); not in the pattern books till Vecellio, 1592; but Taglienti (1530) gives "su la rete" and "Il Specchio di Pensieri" (1548) "punto in rede."

[10] First given in the "Honesto Esempio," 1550, and *passim*.

[11] Mentioned by Taglienti (1530), and afterwards in the "Trionfo" (1555), and *passim*.

4. Punto a fogliami.[12]—See " Venice."

5. Punto a gropo, or gropari.[13]—Groppo, or gruppo, signifies a knot, or tie, and in this lace the threads are knotted together, like the fringes of the Genoese macramè.[14]   After this manner is made the trimming to the linen scarfs or cloths which the Roman peasants wear folded square over the head, and hanging down the back (Fig. 18).

6. Punto a maglia quadra.—Lacis; square netting,[15] the " modano " of the Tuscans (Fig. 19).   This was much used for the

Fig. 19.

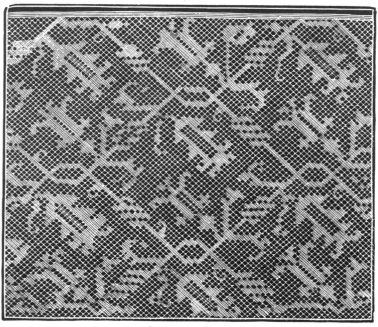

Punto a maglia. Lacis.

hangings of beds, and those curtains, placed across the windows, called " stores " by the French, by the Italians, " stuora." [16]

[12] Given in " Il Monte," circa 1550, but described earlier by Firenzuola. See " Florence."

[13] Taglienti (1530) has " groppi," " moreschi," and " arabeschi;" and " Il Specchio " (1548) " ponti gropposi." See also the Sforza Inventory, 1493.

[14] See " Genoa."

[15] Taglienti (1530) gives, "a ma-

gliata," Parasole (1600) " lavori di maglia."

[16] " Punti a stuora " occur in " Il Specchio " (1548), " I Frutti " (1564), and in the " Vera Perfettione " (1591). The word " stuora," modern " stuoja," means also a mat of plaited rushes, which some of these interlaced patterns may be intended to imitate.

7. Burato.—The word means a stiff cloth or canvas ("toille clere" of Taglienti, 1527), on which the pattern is embroidered, reducing it to a kind of rude lace. One of the pattern books[17] is devoted exclusively to its teaching.

8. Punto di Venezia.—The Venetian points, fine and wonderful works of the needle, that baffle all description, and are endless in variety.

The grounded laces fabricated at Burano will be noticed later.

9. Punto tirato.—Drawn-work.[18] Fig. 20 is a lace ground made by drawing the threads of muslin (fili tirati).[19] The present

Fig. 20.

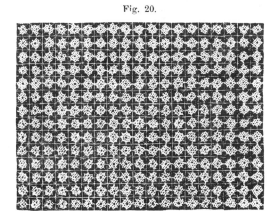

Punto tirato.   Drawn lace.

specimen is simple in design, but some are very complicated and beautiful.

Italy, we believe, furnished her own thread. "Fine white or nun's thread is made by the Augustine nuns of Crema, twisted after the manner as the silk of Bolonia," writes Skippin, 1631.

---

[17] Burato. See Appendix.

[18] There are many patterns for this work in "Le Pompe di Minerva," 1642. Taglienti (1530) has "desfilato" among his "punti."

[19] Many other points are enumerated in the pattern books, of which we know nothing, such as "gasii" (*I Frutti*, 1564), "trezola" (ibid.), "rimessi" (*Vera Perfettione*, 1591).

Fig. 21.

Venetian point in relief.

VENICE.

MRS. TERMAGANT. "I'll spoil your point de Venise for you.
                                    Shadwell, Squire of Alsatia.

              " Elle n'avoit point de mouchoir,
                Mais un riche et tres beau peignoir
                Des plus chers de point de Venise,
                En negligeance elle ivoit mise."
                                    Les Combats, &c. 1663.

To Venice belongs the invention of the two most perfect
productions of the needle, "point coupé," and the Venetian point
in relief (Fig. 21). In the sixteenth and seventeenth centuries,
the making of the first was almost universal in every household,

Fig. 22.

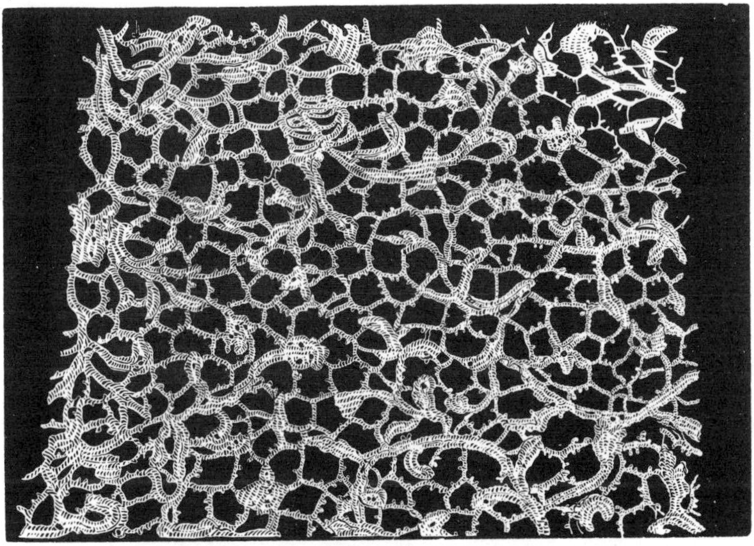

Venetian point.

but its use had become so general as to render it a commercial
speculation, and manufactories of it had been established in
different countries. The richness of its Gothic patterns and the
delicacy of its workmanship rendered it specially calculated for
the enrichment and adorning of linen.

The " punto in aria " of the pattern books, worked on a parchment pattern, and connected by brides, comprised an infinite

variety of patterns, answering to what is usually termed "flat Venetian." Various other wonderful products of the needle are

Fig. 23.

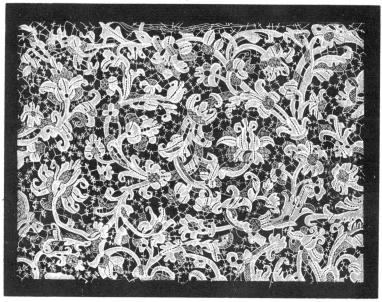

Venetian point.

included under the general name of Venetian points, all of exquisite workmanship, but which baffle description (Figs. 22, 23).

Fig. 24.

Mermaid's lace.

In the islands of the Lagune there still lingers a tale of the first origin of this most charming production.

A sailor youth, bound for the Southern Seas, brought home to his betrothed à bunch of that pretty coralline (Fig. 24) known to the unlearned as the " mermaid's lace." [20] The girl, a worker in points, struck by the graceful nature of the seaweed, with its small white knots united, as it were, by a " bride," imitated it with her needle, and after several unsuccessful trials produced that delicate guipure which before long became the taste of all Europe.[21]

The Venetian point in relief, the " punto a fogliami " (French,

Fig. 25.

Venetian point in relief.

" à ramages ") of the pattern books, is the richest and most complicated of all points. All the outlines in high relief are formed by means of cottons placed as thick as may be required to raise them. Sometimes the pattern is in double and triple relief; an infinity of beautiful stitches are introduced into the flowers, which are surrounded by a pearl of geometric regularity, the

---

[20] *Halimedia opuntia.*
[21] The fringed edging to a Venetian collar in the Dupont-Auberville col-lection in the International Exhibition has great resemblance to the mermaid's coralline.

pearls sometimes in scallops, "campanné," as the French term it. This is called "rose (from "raised") point," "gros point de Venise," &c. Coloured Plate II. is from the collerette of an Italian nobleman, worn only on state occasions. Coloured Plate III. is also a fine example; a " pale "[22] for covering the sacramental cup, made of silk of the natural cream colour, which with unbleached thread appears to have been greatly worn. Much lace of this colour has found its way to Paris for sale since the political changes in Italy.[23] Fig. 25 is an exquisite specimen of the fine raised point.

Though, to judge from the engravings of Vecellio,[24] lace was sparingly worn in general attire, yet at the reception of Henry III. of France, in 1574, by the Republic of Venice, he was astonished at the jewels and laced ruffs of the two hundred ladies who appeared in white, at the ball given by the Republic, and at the dresses trimmed with gold lace, "trina d' oro," and collars ("bavari,") made of wonderful design worked in needle-point at great expense.[25] The bed furniture of the monarch and his suite is described with hangings of cloth of gold, and as having a curtain made in network of precious works of the needle.[26]

If Venice exported largely her products, she seems also to have imported foreign lace, as appears by the sumptuary edicts of 1637 and 1653. In the first, the Provveditore alle Pompe prohibits the wearing, on the clothes of men and. women, silk lace, and pillow lace of Flanders, and others of excessive value, and in the other, prohibits " merli," or other ornament worked in " ponto in aria, ponti Fiamminghe, filo di pita," the thread of the aloe (*Agave*) worked in France, Flanders, and Lorraine, and at the end " merli " &c., worked in France, Flanders, England, and in every other place out of the state.

The secret of making the Venetian points in relief was probably long jealously preserved, and the monopoly of the trade was consequently confined to Venice, who exported annually to

---

[22] "Toile de la pale." A pasteboard about 8 inches square, enclosed in cambric or lace, used to cover the paten when laid over the cup.

[23] The whole furniture of a room was taken from a palace at Naples, comprising curtains, and vallance of a bed, window curtains, toilet, &c. of straw-coloured laces, reticella, embroidered netting, &c. ; the price asked was 18,000 francs = 720*l*.

[24] " Degli Habiti antichi et moderni," Venezia, 1590. Author of the " Corona " and "Gioiello."

[25] " Bavari fatti con maraviglioso disegno di lavori alle punta al aco di grand spesa."

[26] " Padiglioni fatti a rete di pretiosa opera di ago."—*Manlio della Croa,* 1574.

Plate II.

Rose or raised point, from the collar of a Venetian nobleman. Musée de Cluny.

To face page 44.

Plate III.

Venetian point in relief, bride picotée ground.

the amount of 400,000 crowns, all the convents and the greater part of the poor families subsisting upon this work.[27]

In 1626, foreign "dentelles et passemens au fuseau" were declared contraband in France, and Colbert determined to gain possession of the secret of the new point,[28] and establish a manufacture in the kingdom. His success will be related further on.

Venetian point is not mentioned by name until the ordinance of 1654. See "Greece."

Colbert's prohibitory edict and the introduction of the manufacture into France no doubt diminished the export of this artistic product, and inflicted a serious injury on the Venetian lace trade, which, says Daru, "occupait toute la population de la capitale," but Venetian point was not the less sought after.

A few weeks after the birth of Mary of Modena's first child, in 1675, there was sent to her from her native city a present of Venetian point and cloth of gold to the value of 3000l. Her consort, James II., paid 36l. 10s. for a cravat of the same point, to be worn on the day of his coronation.

There is a curious document in the library of St. Mark, a memorandum of instructions to an embassy extraordinary to the English court in 1695-6.[29] After various directions respecting their costume, the ambassadors are instructed to wear for their public entry collars of the finest Venetian point, adding that the laces of Venice are highly esteemed, and there is nothing more acceptable for presents than these laces. It is to be hoped, therefore, that in pursuance of his instructions the Venetian ambassador appeared at the lace-loving court of the Dutch William in a costume worthy the dignity and state of the Republic of St. Mark.

Our porte-bouquets and lace-trimmed nosegays are nothing new. On the occasion of the annual visit of the doge to the Convent delle Vergini, the lady abbess with the novices received him in the parlour and presented him with a nosegay of flowers placed in a handle of gold and trimmed round with the finest lace that Venice could produce.[31]

---

[27] Letter of De Banzy, Bishop of Beziers, and French ambassador at Venice, to Colbert, Nov. 1664.

[28] Again he writes, Dec. 1664: "Je vois que vous serez bien aise d'établir dans le royaume des manufactures de point de Venise, ce qui se pourrait faire en envoyant d'ici quelques filles des meilleures ouvrières qui puissent instruire celles de France."

[29] "Contarini Miscellany," communicated by Mr. Rawdon Brown.

[30] "Con profilo e senza."

[31] "Origine delle Feste veneziane, da Giustina R. Michiel." Milano, 1829.

Fynes Moryson [32] is the earliest known traveller who alludes to the lace products of Venice. "Venetian ladies in general," he says, "wear a standing collar and ruffs close up to the chin; the unmarried tie their hair with gold and silver lace." [33]

Evidently the collars styled "bavari," for which Vecellio [34] gives patterns "all' usanza veneziana," were not yet in general vogue. [35]

Fifty years later, Evelyn speaks of the veils of glittering taffetas, worn by the Venetian ladies, to the corners of which hang broad but curious tassels of point laces.

The Venetians, unlike the Spaniards, thought much of their fine linen, and the decorations pertaining to it. "La camicia preme assai più del giubbone," [36] ran the proverb. Young nobles were not allowed to wear lace on their garments until they put on the robe, which they usually did at the age of five-and-twenty, on being admitted to the council. [37]

Towards 1770 the Venice ladies, despising the sumptuary edicts of 1637 and 1653, began to forsake the fabrics of their native islands; for on the marriage of the doge's son, in that year, although the altar was decorated with the richest Venice point, the bride and her ladies wore their sleeves covered up to the shoulders with falls of the finest Brussels lace, and a tucker of the same material. [38]

During the carnival, however, the people, both male and female, wore a camail, or hood of black lace, covering the chin up to the mouth, called a "bauta." [39] It was one of these old black

---

[32] "An Itinerary, containing his Ten Yeeres Travel through Germany, Bohmerland, Switzerland, Netherland, Denmark, Poland, Italy, Turkey, France, England, Scotland, and Ireland." Lond. 1617.

[33] Venice noted "for needlework laces, called points."—*Travels thro' Italy and France, by J. Ray,* 1738.

F. M. Misson, "Nouveau Voyage d'Italie," 4me édition. La Haye, 1702.

[34] 1591.

[35] See, in Appendix, designs for bavari by Lucrezia.

[36] "La chemise avant le pourpoint."

[37] The entry of the Venetian ambassador, Mocenigo, is described in the "Mercure Galant," 1709 :

"Il avoit un rabat de point de Venise.

. . . Sa robe de damas noir avec des grandes manches qui pendoient par derrière. Cette robe etoit garnie de dentelle noir."

[38] "Letters from Italy." So, in a play of Goldoni, who wrote in the middle of the last century, the lady has a Brussels (Angleterre) head-dress.

"DON FLAMINIO. Mi par bellissima cotesto pizzo. BARBARA.—E un punto d'Inghilterra che ha qualche merito."— *Gli Amori di Zelinda e Lindoro.*

In Goldoni's plays all the ladies make lace on the pillow (merletti a mazzetta); so the art of making the needle Venetian point was probably at an end.

[39] "La plus belle dentelle noire fait l'espèce de camail qui, sous un chapeau noir emplumé, couvre leurs épaules et

lace hoods Walpole describes Lady Mary Wortley Montagu as wearing at Florence, 1762, in place of a cap. There is also another lace from Venice, "à réseau," or grounded. Its characteristic is its extraordinary delicacy and fineness; its most remarkable feature its flatness. Its meshes are very minute, the cordonnet which outlines the pattern worked flat; the ground has a horizontal appearance. It in some respects resembles the finest Brussels needle point.

M. Dupont d'Auberville had some exquisite specimens in the International Exhibition, which he assigns to the adjacent island of Burano, which evidently produced a lace of some celebrity, for Marini quotes from a document of the seventeenth century, in which, speaking of merletti, it is said that "these laces, styled 'punti in aria,' or 'di Burano,' because the greater part of them were made in the country so-called, are considered by Zannoni as more noble and of a greater whiteness, and for excellency of design and perfect workmanship equal to those of Flanders, and in solidity superior." [40]

From this it would appear as if punto in aria was made here and found occupation for a number of lace-workers. [41]

In the dictionary of Boerio, punto di Burano is described as fine needle point lace like that of Flanders, made by the women of that island. [42]

In 1845, when the late Mrs. Dennistoun, of Dennistoun, visited the island, a superannuated nun of ninety conversed with her on the subject, and said that she and her companions in her younger days employed their time in making punto di Burano, which was very costly and ordered for great marriages long beforehand. She showed specimens still tacked on paper, the ground à réseau, worked backwards and forwards, like the Alençon. Fig. 26 is taken from a specimen purchased at Burano by the Cavaliere Merli of the maker, an old woman known by the name of Ceccia la Scarpariola. It has no resemblance to the exquisite production we have described, but bears close analogy with point d'Alençon.

---

leur têt.."—*Madame du Boccage*, 1735, *Lettres sur l'Italie.*
"Quella specie di lungo cappuccio di finissimo merlo pur nero, chiamato baula."
—*Michiel.*
[40] Marini, "Com. di Venezia," t. viii.
[41] L'île de Burano où l'on fabrique les dentelles."—*Quadri, Huit Jours à Venise.*

[42] "Chiamasi il lavori di certe merletti finissimi e pregiatissimi fatti a punto d' ago—come quelle di Fiandra—che si fa dalle donne nelle Isole di Burano — singorlarmente, ed anche nelle vicino di Torcello a Mazzorbo del Veneto Estuario dov'è da molti anni introdotta questa arte."

In 1866, when the author's brother visited Burano, the art had entirely died out, and the "Contrada del Pizzo," once the head-quarters of the lace-makers, was a mystery to the natives, who could no longer account for its denomination. In the church is preserved a splendid series of altar cloths of so-called Burano

Fig. 26.

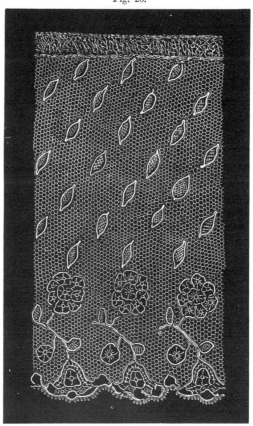

Burano point.

point, Venetian point in relief, and a fine "storiato" piece, representing the mysteries of the Passion.

But Venetian point is now no more. The sole relic of this far famed manufacture is the coarse torchon lace of the old lozenge pattern. The peasant-women of Palestrina sit working at their "ballon," and no sooner does a stranger appear than he is mobbed by the whole population, eager to sell their lace, the same as that mentioned by Lady Mary Wortley Montagu, when she speaks of "peddling-women that come on pretext of selling pennyworths of lace."

MILAN.

"Milano la Grande."

"MARGARET. I saw the Duchess of Milan's gown that they praise so.

"HERO. O that exceeds, they say.

"MARGARET. By my troth, it's but a nightgown in respect of yours: cloth o' gold and cuts, and laced with silver."

Much Ado about Nothing, iv. 1.

The earliest records of Italian lace belong to Milan, and occur in an instrument of partition between the sisters Angela and Ippolita Sforza Visconti, dated 1493.

This document is of the highest interest, as giving the inventory of an Italian wardrobe of the fifteenth century. In it, amidst a number of curious entries, are veils of gold network, with cambric pillow-cases, linen sheets, mosquito curtains, and various articles, worked "a reticella," and "a groppi," with the needle, bobbins, bones, and other different ways [43] mentioned in the pattern books of the following century.

Among other items, we find, "Half of a bundle containing patterns for ladies' work." [44]

Though the fabric of these fine points dates back for so many centuries, there is little notice of them elsewhere.

Henry VIII. is mentioned as wearing one short pair of hose of purple silk of Venice gold, woven like a caul, edged with a "passamaine" lace of purple silk and gold, worked at Milan. [45]

In a wardrobe account of Lord Hay, gentleman of his majesty's

---

[43] "Velleto (veil) uno d' oro filato.
Payro uno fodrete (pillow case) di cambria lavorate *a gugia* (à l'aiguille).
Lenzuolo (sheet) uno di revo di tele (linen thread), cinque lavorato *a punto*.
Peza una de tarnete (trina) d' argento facte a stelle.
Lenzolo uno de tele, quatro lavorato a *radexelo* (reticello).
Peze quatro de *radexela* per mettere ad uno moscheto (zanzariere, mosquito curtain).
Tarneta una d' oro et seda negra *facta da ossi* (bones).

Pecto uno d' oro facto *a grupi*.
Lavoro uno de rechamo facto *a grupi* dove era suso le perle de Madona Biancha.
Binda una lavorata *a poncto de doii fuxi* (two bobbins) per uno lenzolo."
Instrumento di divizione tre le sorelle Angela ed Ippolita Sforza Visconti, di Milano. 1493, *Giorno di Giovedì,* 12 *Settembre.*

[44] "La mità de uno fagotto quale aveva dentro certi dissegni da lavorare le donne."

[45] Harl. MS. No. 1419.

E

robes, 1606,[46] is noted down to James I., "One suit with cannons thereunto of silver lace, shadowed with silk Milan lace."

Again, among the articles furnished against the "Queen's lying down," 1606, in the bills of the Lady Audrye Walsingham,[47] is an entry of "Lace, Milan fashion, for child's waistcoat."

A French edict, dated March, 1613, against superfluity in

Fig. 27.

Reticella from Milan.

dress, prohibiting the wearing of gold and silver embroidery, specially forbids the use of all "passement de Milan, ou façon de Milan," under a penalty of 1000 livres.[48] The expression, "à point de Milan," occurs in the statutes of the passementiers of Paris.[49]

---

[46] Roll. P. R. O.   [47] P. R. O.

[48] De la Mare, "Traité de la Police."

[49] "Statuts, Ordonnances et Reglemens de la Communauté des Maistres Passe-

Milan was early celebrated for its gold thread and beautifully wrought laces of that material.

" Les galons, passements et broderies, en or et en argent de Milan," says Savary,[50] were once celebrated.

Lalande, who writes some years later, adds, the laces formerly were an object of commerce to the city, now they only fabricate those of an inferior quality.[51]

Much was consumed by the Lombard peasants, the better sorts serving for ruffles of moderate price.[52] So opulent are the citizens, says a writer of the same epoch, that the lowest mechanics, blacksmiths and shoemakers, appear in gold stuff coats with ruffles of the finest point.[53]

And when, in 1767, the Auvergne lace-makers petition for an exemption from the export duty on their fabrics, they state as a ground, that the duty prevents them from competing abroad, especially at Cadiz, with the lace-makers of Piedmont, the Milanais, and Imperial Flanders. Milan must therefore have made lace extensively to a late period.

Fig. 27 is a specimen of what is termed old Milan point (reticella) from the convent of Santa Maria delle Grazie, in that city.

In the district of Cantu, near Lake Como, the making of white and black pillow lace gives employment to many thousands of women. The " torchon " lace of the country is original, and in much request with the peasantry.

In the underground chapel of San Carlo Borromeo, in Milan cathedral, are preserved twenty six " camicie " trimmed with flounces of the richest point, all more or less splendid, and worked in the convents of the city, but many of the contents of this sumptuous wardrobe have rotted away from the effects of the damp atmosphere.

FLORENCE.

Of Florence and its products we know but little, though the Elegy of its poet Firenzuola proves that ladies made the raised

mentiers, etc., de Paris, confirmez sur les anciens Statuts du 23 mars 1558. Paris, 1719."

[50] " Grand Dictionnaire Universel du Commerce," 1723.

[51] " Voyage en Italie," 1765.

[52] Peuchet (J.), " Dictionnaire Universel de la Géographie Commerçante." Paris, An VII. = 1799.

[53] " Letters from Italy," by a Lady. 1770.

point at an early period.[54] His expression, " scolpito," carved,
sculptured in basso rilievo, leaves no doubt upon the matter.

Henry VIII. granted to two Florentines the privilege of importing for three years' time all " manner of fringys and passements
wrought with gold and silver or otherwise,"[55] an account of which
will be found in the notice of that monarch's reign.

Beyond this, and the statute passed at the " Sute of the
Browderers," on account of the " deceyptful waight of the gold of
Luk, Florence, Jeane, and Venice,"[56] there is no allusion to the
lace of Florence in our English records.

In France, as early as 1545, the sister of Francis I. purchases
" soixante aulnes fine dantelle de Florence"[57] for her own use ;
and some years afterwards, 1582, the Queen of Navarre pays " 17
écus 30 sols " for " 10 aulnes et demye " of the same passement
" faict à l'esguille à haulte dantelle pour mettre à des fraizes."[58]

On the marriage of Elisabeth de France with Philip II. in
1559, purchases were made of " passements et de bisette, en fil
blanc de Florence."

Seeing the early date of these French accounts, it may be
inferred that Catherine de Medicis first introduced, on her arrival
as a bride, the products of her native city.[59]

Ray mentions that people of quality sent their daughters at
eight years old to the Florentine nunneries, to be instructed in all
manner of women's work.

Lace was also fabricated at Sienna, but it appears to have been
the " lavoro di maglia," or lacis, called by the Tuscans " modano
ricamato," embroidered network.

Early in the last century, two Genoese nuns of the convent of
Sta. Maria degli Angeli in Sienna executed pillow laces and gold

---

[54] " Questo collar scolpì la donna mia
Di basso rilevar, ch' Aracne mai,
E chi la vinse nol faria più bello.
Mira quel bel fogliame, ch' un acanto
Sembra, che sopra un mur vada carponi.
Mira quei fior, ch' un candido ne cade
Vicino al seme, apr' or la bocia l' altro.
Quei cordiglin, che 'l legan d' ognitorno,
Come rilevan ben ! mostrando ch' ella
E la vera maestra di quest' arte,
Come ben compartiti son quei punti !
Ve' come son ugual quei bottoncelli,
Come s' alzano in guisa d' un bel colle
L' un come l' altro !
· ·   · · · · · · · · ·

Questi merli da man, questi trafori
Fece pur ella, et questo punto a spina.
Che mette in mezzo questo cordoncello,
Ella il fe pure, ella lo fece."
Elegia supra un Collaretto, Firenzuola.
[55] Rymer's " Fœdera." 38 Hen. VIII. =
1546.
[56] 4 Hen. VII. = 1488-9.
[57] *Compte des dépenses de la maison de
Madame Marguerite de France, Sœur du
Roi.* Bib. Nat. MSS. F. Fr. 10,394.
[58] *Comptes de la Reine de Navarre.*
Arch. Nat. K. K. 170.
[59] In 1535.

and silver embroidery of such surpassing beauty that they are
still carefully preserved and publicly exhibited on fête days.
One Francesca Bulgarini also instructed the schools in the making
of lace of every kind, especially the Venetian reticella.[60]

STATES OF THE POPE.

Lace was made in many parts of Romagna. Besides the
knotted lace already alluded to,[61] the peasant-women wore on

Fig. 28.

Unfinished drawn work.

their collerettes much lace of that large-flowered pattern and
fancy ground found alike in Flanders and on the head-dresses of
the Neapolitan and Calabrian peasants.

Specimens of pillow lace of the province of Urbino, lately sent
to us from Italy, resemble in pattern and texture the fine close

---

[60] She died in 1862.   [61] See p. 38.

Brabant lace on the collar of Christian IV., figured in our notice of Denmark. The workmanship is of great beauty.

Fig. 28 represents a fragment of a piece of lace of great interest, communicated by the Countess Gigliucci. It is worked with the needle upon muslin, and only a few inches of the lace are finished. This incompleteness makes it the more valuable as it enables us to trace the manner of its execution, all the threads being left hanging to its several parts. The countess states that she found the work at a villa belonging to Count Gigliucci, near Fermo, on the Adriatic, and it is supposed to have been executed by the count's great-grandmother above 160 years ago—an exquisite specimen of " the needle's excellency."

Though the riches of our Lady of Loreto fill a volume in themselves,[62] and her image was fresh clad every day of the year, the account of her jewels and plate so overpower any mention of her lace, which were doubtless in accordance with the rest of the wardrobe, there is nothing to tell on the subject.

The laces of the Vatican and the holy Conclave, mostly presents from crowned heads, are magnificent beyond all description. They are, however, constantly in the market, sold at the death of a cardinal by his heirs, and often repurchased by some newly elected prelate, each of whom on attaining a high ecclesiastical dignity is compelled to furnish himself with several sets.

A lady,[63] describing the ceremony of washing the feet by the Pope, writes, in 1771, " One of his cardinals brought him an apron [64] of old point with a broad border of Mechlin lace, and tied it with a white ribbon round his holiness's waist." In this guise protected, he performed the ceremony.

Clement IX. was in the habit of making presents of Italian lace, at that period still prized in France, to Monsieur de Sorbière, with whom he had lived on terms of intimacy previous to his elevation. " He sends ruffles," cries the irritated Gaul, who looked for something more tangible, " to a man who never has a shirt." [65]

---

[62] *Inventaire du Trésor de N. D. de Lorette.* Bib. Nat. MSS.

[63] " Letters from Italy."

[64] " The gremial or apron placed on the lap of the Roman Catholic bishops when performing sacred functions in a sitting posture."—*Pugin's Glossary of Ecclesiastical Ornament.*

[65] This reminds one of the lines of Goldsmith, in his poem, " The Haunch of Venison," the giving of venison to hungry poets who were in want of mutton ; he says :—

" Such dainties to send them their health
   it would hurt ;
It's like sending them ruffles when wanting a shirt."

NAPLES.

When Davies, barber surgeon of London,[66] visited Naples in 1597, he writes, " Among the traffic of this city is lace of all sorts and garters."

Fynes Moryson, his contemporary, declares " the Italians care not for foreign apparel, they have ruffles of Flanders linen wrought with Italian cutwork so much in use with us. They wear no lace in gold and silver, but black ; " while Lassels says, all they care for is to keep a coach ; their point de Venise and gold lace are all turned into horses and liveries.[67]

Of this lace we find but scanty mention. In the tailor's bill of Sir Timothy Hutton, 1615, when a scholar at Cambridge, a charge is made for " four oz. and a half quarter and dram of Naples lace." And in the accounts of laces furnished for the marriage of the Princess Elizabeth to the Elector Palatine, 1612, is noted " narrow black Naples lace, purled on both sides."

The principal fabric of lace was in the Island of Ischia. Vecellio, in 1590, mentions the ladies' sleeves being trimmed with very fine thread lace.[68] Ischia lace may still be met with, and serves for trimming toilets, table-covers, curtains, &c., consisting generally of a square netting ground, with the pattern embroidered.

Much torchon lace, of well-designed patterns, was also made, similar in style to that given in Fig. 34.

Though no longer fabricated in the island, the women at Naples still make a coarse lace, which they sell about the streets.[69]

Towards the middle of the last century, many of the Italian sculptors adopted an atrocious system, only to be rivalled in bad taste by those of the Lower Empire, that of dressing the individuals they modelled in the costume of the period, the colours of the

---

[66] " A true Relation of the Travailes, and most miserable Captivitie of W. Davies." Lond. 1614.

[67] " An Italian Voyage, or a complete Journey through Italy, by Rich. Lassels, Gent." 2nd edit. Lond. 1698. A reprint, with additions by another hand, of the original edition. Paris, 1670. Lowndes' " Bibliographer's Manual." Bohn's new edit.

[68] " Portano alcune vesti di tela di lino sottile, lunghe fino in terra, con maniche larghe assai, attorno alle quali sono attaccati alcuni merletti lavorati di refe sottilissimo.—Habiti di donna dell' Isola d' Ischia."—Degli Habiti Antichi e Moderni di Diverse Parti del Mondo, di Cesare Vecellio. Venezia, 1590.

[69] We have among the points given by Taglienti (1530) " pugliese." Lace is still made in Puglia and the other southern provinces of Naples and in Sicily.

dress represented in varied marbles. In the villa of Prince Valguarnera, near Palermo, were some years since many of these strange productions with rich laces of coffee-coloured point, admirably chiselled, it must be owned, in giallo antico, the long flowing ruffles and head-tires of the ladies being reproduced in white alabaster.[70]

GENOA.

"Genova la Superba."

"Lost,—A rich needle work called Poynt Jean, a yard and a half long and half quarter broad."—*The Intelligencer*, Feb. 29, 1663.

"Genoa, for points."—*Grand Tour*, 1756.

The art of making gold thread, already known to the Etruscans, took a singular development in Italy during the fourteenth century.

Genoa[71] first imitated the gold threads of Cyprus. Lucca followed in her wake, while Venice and Milan appear much later in the field. Gold of Jeane formed, as already mentioned, an item in our early statutes. The merchants mingled the pure gold with Spanish "laton," producing a sort of "faux galon," such as is used for theatrical purposes in the present day. They made also silver and gold lace out of drawn wire, after the fashion of those discovered, not long since, at Herculaneum.

When Skippin visited Turin, in 1651, he describes the manner of preparing the metal wire. The art maintained itself latest at Milan, but died out towards the end of the seventeenth century.

In the wardrobe of Mary de Medicis is enumerated, among other articles, a "mouchoir de point de Gennes frisé."[72]

Moryson, who visited the Republic in 1589, declares "the Genoese wear no lace or gardes."

Genoa was as celebrated for its pillow lace as Venice for its needle-made. The characteristic of this lace was its design, a kind of barleycorn-shaped pattern, radiating into rosettes from a

---

[70] Brydone, "Tour through Sicily," 1773.

[71] "From the tax-books preserved in the Archives of S. George, it appears that a tax upon gold thread of four danari upon every lira in value of the worked material was levied, which between 1411 and 1420 amounted to L. 73,387. From which period this industry rapidly declined, and the workers emigrated."—*Merli*.

[72] *Garderobe de feue Madame*, 1646. Bib. Nat. MSS. F. Fr. 11,426.

centre. It was particularly adapted for the large turn-over collar of Louis XIII., and was produced by plaiting, and made entirely on the pillow (Fig. 29). We find little mention of Genoa point [73] before the seventeenth century,[74] when it formed an article of great commerce. The first allusion to these points is in the prohibitory edict of 1639, a period when Genoa point was in universal use for collars,[75] cuffs, and other articles of dress.[76]

No better customer was found for these luxurious articles of adornment than Madame de Puissieux.[77] " Elle étoit magnifique et ruina elle et ses enfans. On portoit en ce temps-là," writes St.-Simon, " force points de Gênes qui étoient extrêmement chers; c'étoit la grande parure—et la parure de tout age : elle en mangea pour 100,000 écus (20,000l.) en une année, à ronger entre ses dents celle qu'elle avoit autour de sa tête et de ses bras." [78]

"The Genoese utter a world of points of needlework," writes Lassels, at the end of the century, and throughout the eighteenth we hear constantly of the gold, silver, and thread lace, as well as of the points of Genoa, being held in high estimation.

Gold and silver lace was prohibited to be worn within the walls of the city, but they wear, writes Lady Mary Wortley Montagu, exceeding fine lace and linen.[79] Indeed, by the sumptuary laws of the Republic, the richest costume allowed to the ladies was black velvet trimmed with their home-made lace.

The "femmes bourgeoises" still edge their aprons with lace, and

[73] Signore Tessada, the great lace fabricant of Genoa, carries back the manufacture of Italian lace as early as the year 1400, and forwarded to the author specimens which he declares to be of that date.

[74] As late as 1597, writes Vulson de la Colombière, " ni les points de Gennes, ni de Flandre n'étoient en usage."—*Vray Théâtre d'Honneur et de Chevalerie.* Paris, 1648.

[75] Queen Christina is described by the Grande Mademoiselle, on the occasion of her visit, as wearing, "au cou, un mouchoir de point de Gênes, noué avec un ruban couleur de feu."—*Mém. de Mademoiselle de Montpensier.*

" Item, ung peignoir, tablier et cornette de toile baptiste garnie de point de Gênes."—*Inv. de la Comtesse de Soissons,* 1634.

" Une petit manteau brodé et son collet de point de Gênes."—*The Chevalier d'Albret.*

" Linge, bijoux et points de Gênes."—*Loret, Muse Historique,* 1650.

" Item, ung autre mouchoir de point de Gênes."—*Inv. du Maréchal de La Motte,* 1657.

[76] The " Lois de la Galanterie Françoise," 1644, speaking of the lace-trimmed "canons," says, " il sera toujours mieux s'il y peut avoir deux ou trois rangs de Point de Gênes, ce qui accompagnera le jabot qui sera de même parure."

[77] Madame de Puissieux died in 1677, at the age of 80.

[78] " Mém." t. xiv. p. 286.

[79] Signore Tessada has in his possession a pair of gold lappets of very beautiful design, made at Genoa about the year 1700.

Fig. 29.

Genoa point.   Pillow-made.   From a collar in the possession of the Author.

some of the elder women wear square linen veils trimmed with coarse lace.[80]

" That decayed city, Genoa, makes much lace, but inferior to that of Flanders," states Anderson, in his " Origin of Commerce," 1764.

Savary, speaking of the Genoa manufacture, says : " As regards France, these points have had the same lot as those of Venice— ruined by the act of prohibition."

In 1840, there were only six lace-sellers in the city of Genoa. The women work in their own houses, receiving materials and patterns from the merchant, who pays for their labour.[81]

Lace, in Genoa, is called " pizzo." " Punti in aco " were not made in this city. The points of Genoa were all the work of the pillow, " a piombini," [82] or " a mazzetta," as the Italians term it, of fine handspun thread brought from Lombardy. Silk was procured from Naples. Of this Lombardy thread is the magnificent collerette of which we give an example (Fig. 29). This was the Genoa point par excellence, and is still known by this appellation. The old Genoa point still finds favour in the eyes of the clergy, and on fête days, either at Genoa or Savona, may be seen splendid lace decorating the " camicie " of the ecclesiastics.

The barristers of Genoa retain as a part of their costume falling bands of rich lace.

The lace manufacture extends along the coast from Albissola, on the western Riviera, to Santa Margherita, on the eastern. Santa Margherita and Rapallo are called by Luxada [83] the emporium of the lace industry of Genoa. The workers are mostly the wives and daughters of the coral-fishers, who support themselves by this occupation during the long and perilous voyages of their husbands. In the archives of the parochial church of Santa Margherita is preserved a book of accounts, in which mention is made, in the year 1592, of gifts to the church, old nets from the coral fishery, together with pissetti (pizzi) ; the one a votive offering of some successful fishermen, the other the work of their wives or daughters, given in

---

[80] " Letters from Italy," 1770.

[81] Cavasco, " Statistique de Gênes," 1840.

[82] The bobbins appear to have been made in Italy of various materials. We have " merletti a fusi," in which case they are of wood. The Sforza inventory gives, " a doii fuxi," two bobbins ; then,

" a ossi," of bone ; and, lastly, " a piombini ;" and it is very certain that lead was used for bobbins in Italy, probably for weaving some kind of coarse guipure. See Parasole (1600).

[83] " Memorie Storiche di Santa Margherita."

gratitude for the safe return of their relatives. There was also found an old worn parchment pattern for a kind of tape guipure (Fig. 30). The manufacture, therefore, has existed in the province

Fig. 30.

Lace pattern found in the church at Santa Margherita.   Circa 1592.

of Chiavari for many centures.   Much of this description of lace is assigned to Genoa.   In these tape guipures, the tape or braid was first made, and the ground worked in on the parchment either by the needle or on the pillow (Fig. 31).   The laces consist of white thread of various qualities, either for wear, church decoration, or for exportation to America.

Later, this art gave place to the making of black blonde, in imitation of Chantilly. In the year 1850, the lace-workers began to make silk guipures for France, and these now form their chief

Fig. 31.

Tape guipure. Pillow-made. Genoa.

produce. The exportation is very great, and lace-making is the daily occupation not only of the women,[84] but the ladies of the commune.[85] The "maestri," or overseers, receive all orders from the trade, and find hands to execute them. The silk and thread required for the lace is weighed out and given to the lace-makers,

[84] In 1862, Santa Margherita had 2210 lace-workers; Rapallo, 1494.
[85] Communicated by Sig. Gio. Tessada, Junr., of Genoa.

and the work, when completed, is re-weighed, to see that it corresponds with that of the material given. The maestri contrive to realise large fortunes, and become in time signori; not so the poor lace-makers, whose hardest day's gain seldom exceeds a franc and a half.[86]

The laces of Albissola,[87] near Savona, of black and white thread, or silk of different colours, were once an article of considerable exportation to the principal cities of Spain—Cadiz, Madrid, and Seville. This industry was of early date. In many of the parochial churches of Albissola are specimens of the native fabric dating from 1600, the work of devout ladies; and parchment patterns, drawn and pricked for pillow lace, bearing the earlier

Fig. 32.

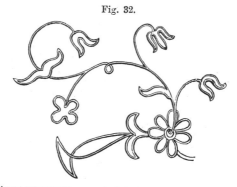

Parchment pattern used to cover a book, bearing the date of 1577.   (Reduced.)

date of 1577, have been lately found covering old law books, the property of a notary of Albissola. The designs (Fig. 32) are flowing, but poor, and have probably served for some shawl or apron, for it was a custom long handed down for the daughters of great nobles, previous to their marriage, to select veils and shawls of this fabric, and, in the memory of an aged workwoman, the last of these bridal veils was made for a lady of the Gentili family. Princes and lords of different provinces in Italy sent commissions to Albissola for these articles in the palmy days of the manufacture, and four women would be employed at one pillow, with sixty dozen bobbins at a time.[88] The making of this lace formed an occupation by which women in moderate circumstances were willing to increase their incomes. Each of these ladies, called a maestra, had

[86] Gandolfi, "Considerazioni agrario."   from Savona, on the road leading to Genoa:
[87] A small borgo, about an hour's drive   [88] Cav. Merli.

a number of workers under her either at home or out. She supplied the patterns, pricked them herself, and paid her workwomen at the end of the week; each day's work being notched on a tally.[89] The women would earn from ten soldi to two lire a day. The last fine laces made at Albissola were bought up by the lace merchants of Milan on the occasion of the coronation of Napoleon I. in that city.

Fig. 33.

Fringed macramè. Genoa.

A considerable quantity of lace was formerly made from the fibre of the aloe (filo d' erba spada),[90] by the peasants of Albissola, either of its natural cream colour or dyed black. This lace, however, like that fabricated in the neighbourhood of Barcelona, would not stand washing.[91]

There exists a beautiful and ingenious work, taught in the

---

[89] In the Albert Museum of Exeter are several of these tallies marked with the names of their owners—Bianca, Maria Crocera, and others.

[90] Called by the people of the Riviera, "filo del baccalà di Castellaro." Aloe fibre was formerly used for thread.— *Letter of Sig. C. G. Schiappapietra.* It is also styled "filo di pita" in the Venetian sumptuary ordinances (p. 44).

[91] The author has to express her grateful thanks to Signore Don Tommaso Torteroli, librarian to the city of Savona, and author of an interesting pamphlet ("Storia dei Merletti di Genova lavorati in Albissola," Sinigaglia, 1863), for specimens of the ancient laces of Albissola, and many other valuable communications.

schools and convents along the Riviera, derived from the "punto a groppo," and carried to great perfection at the Albergo de' l'overi at Genoa. It is almost the first employment of the fingers which the poor children of either sex learn. This art is principally applied to the ornamenting of towels, termed "macramè,"[92] a long fringe of thread being left at each end, for the purpose of being knotted together in geometrical designs (Fig. 33). Macramè at the Albergo de' Poveri were formerly made with a plain plaited fringe, till, in 1843, the Baroness A. d'Asti brought one from Rome, richly ornamented, which she left as a pattern. Marie Picchetti, a young girl, had the patience to unpick the fringe and discover the way it was made. A variety of designs are now executed, the more experienced inventing fresh patterns as they work. Some are applied to church purposes. Costly specimens of elaborate workmanship were in the Paris Exhibition of 1867. These richly trimmed macramè form an item in the wedding trousseau of a Genoese lady, while the commoner sorts find a ready sale in the country, and are also exported to South America and California.[93] The making of macramè has of late years become a favourite employment.

---

[92] A word of Arabic derivation, used for denoting fringe for trimming, whether of cotton, thread, or silk.

[93] This custom of ornamenting the ends of the threads of linen for household as well as for ecclesiastical purposes was from the earliest times common, and is still occasionally met with both in the North and South of Europe. "At Bayonne, they make the finest of linen, some of which is made open like network, and the thread is finer than hair."—

Ingenious and diverting Letters of a Lady's Travels into Spain, London, 1679.

There is a painting of the Last Supper at Hampton Court Palace, by Sebastian Ricci, in which the tablecloth is edged with cutwork; and in the great picture in the Louvre, by Paul Veronese, of the supper at the house of Simon the Canaanite, the ends of the tablecloth are likewise fringed and braided like the macramè.

CHAPTER V.

GREECE.

WE have already spoken of Greece as the cradle of embroidery; and in those islands which escaped the domination of the Turks the art still lingered on. Cyprus, to whom in after times proud Venice gave a queen, was renowned for its gold, its stuffs, and its needlework. As early as 1393, in an inventory of the Dukes of Burgundy, we find noted " un petit pourpoint de satin noir et est la gorgerette de maille d'argent de Chippre "—a collar of silver network.[1]

In our own country, thirty years later, we have a statute touching the deceitful works of the embroiderers of gold or of silver of Cipre, which shall be forfeited to the king.[2] But the secret of these cunning works became, after a time, known throughout Europe. Of cutworks or laces from Cyprus [3] and the islands of the Grecian seas, there is no mention; but we hear much of a certain point known to the commerce of the seventeenth century as that of Ragusa, which again, after an ephemeral existence, disappears from the scene. Of Ragusa, says Anderson, " her citizens, though a Popish state, are manufacturers to a man."

Certain it is that this little republic, closely allied with the Italian branches of the house of Austria, served them with its navy, and in return received from them protection. The commerce of Ragusa consisted in bearing the products of the Greek islands and Turkey to Venice, Ancona, and the kingdom of Naples;[4] hence it might be inferred that those fine productions of·the Greek convents which, of late years, have been so much brought before the public notice were first introduced into Italy by the merchants of Dalmatia, and received on that account the denomination of " points

---

[1] Laborde, " Glossaire," Paris, 1853.
[2] Statute 2 Hen. VI. c. x.=1423.
[3] Taglienti, 1530, among his punti,
gives " Ciprioto."
[4] " Description de Raguse." Bib. Nat. MSS. F. Fr. 10,772.

de Raguse." When Venice manufactured enough for herself, these cutworks and laces were no longer in demand; but the fabric still continued, and found favour in its native isles, chiefly for ecclesiastical purposes, the dress of the islanders, and for graveclothes.

In our English statutes we have no allusion to point de Raguse; in those of France,[5] it appears twice. Tallemant des Réaux[6] mentions it incidentally, and the "Révolte des Passemens"[7] give it honourable notice. Judging from the lines addressed to it in the last-named jeu d'esprit, point de Raguse was of a more costly character, "faite pour ruiner les estats," than any of those other points present. If, however, from this period it did still form an article of commerce, we may infer that it appeared under the general appellation of point de Venise. Ragusa had affronted Louis Quatorze by her attachment to the Austro-Italian princes; he kicked out her ambassadors,[8] and if the name of the point was unpleasant, we may feel assured it was no longer permitted to offend the royal ears. Though no manufacture of thread lace is known at Ragusa, yet much gold and silver lace is made for ornamenting the bodices of the peasants. They also still fabricate a kind of lace or gimp of coloured silks in the style of Fig. 34. Its resemblance, with its looped edges, to the pattern given from "Le Pompe,"[9] published at Venice in 1557, is very remarkable.

The conventionally termed Greek lace is the Italian reticella; the designs of geometric fashion. The Ionian Islands for many years belonged to Venice. Fig. 35 is from a specimen purchased in the island of Zante. This lace was much in vogue in Naples for curtains, bed-hangings, and coverlets. A room hung with bands of Greek lace, alternated with crimson or amber silk, has a most effective appearance.

The church lace of the Ionian Isles was not appreciated by the natives, who were only too glad to dispose of it to the English officers in garrison at Corfu. Much is still found in Cephalonia:

---

[5] Points de Raguse; first mentioned in edict of January 1651, by which the king raises for his own profit one quarter of the value of the "passemens, dentelles, points coupez de Flandres, pointinars, points de Venise, de Raguse, de Gênes," &c.—Recueil des Lois Françaises. Again, the ordinance of August 1665 establishes the points de France "en la manière des points qui se font à Venise, Cênes, Raguse et autres pays etrangers," recited in the Arrêt of Oct. 12, 1666.—De Lamare, Traité de la Police.

[6] "Alors les points de Gênes, de Raguse, ni d'Aurillac n'étaient point connus."

[7] In 1661.

[8] In 1667.

[9] See Appendix.

the natives bring it on board the steamers for sale, black with age, and unpleasant to the senses. This is not to be wondered at when we consider that it is taken from the tombs, where for centuries it has adorned the grave-clothes of some defunct Ionian. This hunt-

Fig. 34.

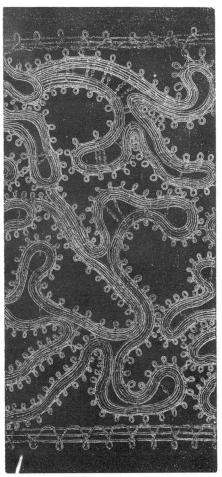

Coloured silk pillow guipure, or passementerie. Italy. South Kensington Museum.

ing the catacombs has now become a regular trade. It is said that much coarse lace of the same kind is still made in the islands, steeped either in coffee or some drug, and, when thus discoloured, sold as from the tombs.

The Greek islands now fabricate lace from the fibre of the
aloe, and a black plaited lace similar to the Maltese. In Athens,

Fig. 35.

Reticella, or Greek lace. From Zante.

and other parts of Greece proper, a white silk lace is made, mostly
consumed by the Jewish Church.

TURKEY.

"The Turks wear no lace or cut stuff," writes Moryson; [10]
winding up with, "neither do the women wear lace or cutwork on
their shirts;" but a hundred and fifty years later, fashions are
changed in the East. The Grand Turk now issues sumptuary laws
against the wearing of gold lace "on clothes and elsewhere." [11]

A fine white silk guipure is now made in modern Turkey at
Smyrna and Rhodes, Oriental in its style: this lace is formed
with the needle or tambour hook. Lace or passementerie of similar
workmanship, called "oyah," is also executed in colours representing flowers, fruits, and foliage superposed, standing out in
high relief from the ground. Numerous specimens were in the
French International Exhibition of 1867.

[10] 1589.   [11] " Edinburgh Advertiser," 1764.

The point lace manufactured in the harems is little known and costly in price. It is said to be the only silk guipure made with the needle. Specimens were in the International Exhibition of 1874.

MALTA.

The lace once made in Malta, indigenous to the island, was a coarse kind of Mechlin or Valenciennes of one arabesque pattern. In 1833, Lady Hamilton Chichester induced a woman, named Ciglia, to copy in white the lace of an old Greek coverlet, which she still has in her possession. The Ciglia family, from that time,

Fig. 36.

Loubeux de Verdale. From the cast of his tomb. Musée Nationale, Versailles.

commenced the manufacture of the black and white silk plaited guipures, so generally known under the name of Maltese lace. Much Maltese lace is now made at the orphanage in the little adjacent island of Gozo. Malta has certainly the first claim to the invention of these fine guipures, which have since made the fortune of Auvergne, where they have been extensively manufactured at Le Puy, as well as by our own lace-makers of Bedfordshire and in the Irish schools. The black is made of Barcelona silk, the same as that used in Catalonia for the fabrication of the black blonde mantillas of the Spanish ladies. Fig. 36 represents the trimming round the ecclesiastical robe of Hugues Loubeux de Verdale, cardinal and grand master of the Knights of Malta, who died 1595, and is buried in the church of St. John, where a magnificent tomb is erected to his memory.

Lace-making is the sole manual employment of the women of Ceylon. We mention it in this place because the specimens of thread pillow lace from Point de Galle and Candy bear a striking resemblance to the Maltese. (Fig. 37.) A lace of similar character has also been successfully made in the missionary schools at Madras.

Fig. 37.

Pillow lace. Ceylon.

CHAPTER VI.

SPAIN.

" Of Point d'Espagne a rich cornet,
  Two night rails and a scarf beset,
  With a large lace and collaret."
  Evelyn, Voyage to Marry-land.

" Hat laced with gold Point d'Espagne." [1]
  Wardrobe of a Pretty Fellow, Roderick Random.

THE COUNT. " Voglio una punta di Spagna, larga, massiccia, ben lavorata. Del disegno, della ricchezza, ma niente di luccicante."—*Goldoni, L'Avaro fastoso.*

SPANISH point, in its day, has been as celebrated as that of Italy. Tradition declares Spain to have learned the art from Italy, whence she communicated it to Flanders, who, in return, taught Spain how to make pillow lace. Be that as it may, Spanish point was highly prized, extensively made, and Spain had no occasion to import the products of Italy. Many reasons exist why Spanish point was less known to Europe in general than that of other nations. The dress of the court, guided not by the impulse of fashion, but by sumptuary laws, gave little encouragement to the manufacture ; while, on the other hand, the numberless images of our Lady and other patron saints, dressed and re-dressed daily in the richest vestments, together with the albs of the priests and the decorations of the altars, caused an immense consumption for ecclesiastical purposes. " Of so great value," says Beckford, " were the laces of these favoured Madonnas that in 1787 the Marchioness of Cogalhudo, wife of the eldest son of the semi-royal race of Medina Cœli, was appointed mistress of the robes to our Lady of La Solidad, at Madrid, a much coveted office." It may be surmised then that the supply scarcely exceeded the demand, and that the rich points of which we have lately heard so much were entirely employed for home consumption. At that early period, too, Spain, on whose empire the sun never set, had

---

[1] 1756. " Point d'Espagne hats."—*Connoisseur.*

an abundant outlet for her industry in those gold colonies of
South America which have since escaped from her grasp.

Point d'Espagne, in the usual sense of the word, signifies that
gold or silver lace, sometimes embroidered in colours, so largely
consumed in France during the reign of Louis XIV.

Dominique de Sera, in his " Livre de Lingerie," published in
1584, especially mentions that many of the patterns of point

Fig. 38.

The Work-room.
From an engraving of the sixteenth century, after Stradan.

coupé and passement given were collected by him during his
travels in Spain; and in this he is probably correct, for as early
as 1562, in the Great Wardrobe Account of Queen Elizabeth, we
have noted down sixteen yards of black Spanish laquei (lace) for
ruffs, price 5s.

The early pattern books contain designs to be worked in gold and silver,[2] a manufacture said to have been chiefly carried on by the Jews,[3] as indeed it is in many parts of Europe at the present time; an idea which strengthens on finding that two years after the expulsion of that persecuted tribe from the country, in 1492, the most Catholic kings found it necessary to pass a law prohibiting the importation of gold lace from Lucca and Florence, except such as was necessary for ecclesiastical purposes.

We find no mention of lace in the ordinances of Toledo and Sevilla of the fifteenth and sixteenth centuries, nor in those of Granada of the sixteenth and seventeenth, nor in the laws of Ferdinand and Isabella;[4] although there is preserved in the cathedral of Granada a lace alb said to have been presented to the church by these sovereigns. The late Cardinal Wiseman stated to the author that he had himself officiated in this vestment, which was valued at 10,000 crowns.

Our English translation of Don Quixote has led some authors into adducing a passage as an evidence that the art of making bone lace was already known in Spain in Cervantes' day. "Sanchica," writes Theresa Pança to her husband, the newly appointed Governor of Barataria, "makes bone lace, and gets eight maravedis a day, which she drops into a tin box to help towards household stuff. But now that she is a governor's daughter, you will give her a fortune, and she will not have to work for it."

In referring to the original Spanish, we find the words rendered "bone lace" are "puntas de randas," signifying works of lacis or réseuil.[5]

We may safely say that the fine church lace of Spain was but little known to the commercial world of Europe until the dissolution of the Spanish monasteries[6] in 1830, when the most splendid

---

[2] "Livre Nouveau de Patrons," and "Fleurs des Patrons," give various stitches to be executed "en fil d'or, d'argent, de soie, et d'autres." Both printed at Lyons. The first has no date, the second, 1549. "Le Pompe," Venezia, 1559, has "diversi sorti di mostre per poter far, d' oro, di sete, di filo," &c.

[3] Not many years since, a family at Cadiz, of Jewish extraction, still enjoyed the monopoly of manufacturing gold and silver lace.—*Letter from Spain,* 1863.

[4] "Ancient Needle Point and Pillow Lace," published under the sanction of the Science and Art Department of the Committee of Council on Education, edited by Mr. Alan Cole.

[5] "Ouvrage de lacis ou réseuil."— *Oudin, Trésor des Deux Langues Fr. et Esp.* 1660.

[6] Spain has 8932 convents, containing 94,000 nuns and monks.—*J. Townsend, Journey through Spain in the Years* 1786 *and* 1787.

specimens of nun's work came suddenly into the market; not only the heavy lace generally designated as "Spanish point," but pieces of the very finest description, so exquisite as to have

Fig. 39.

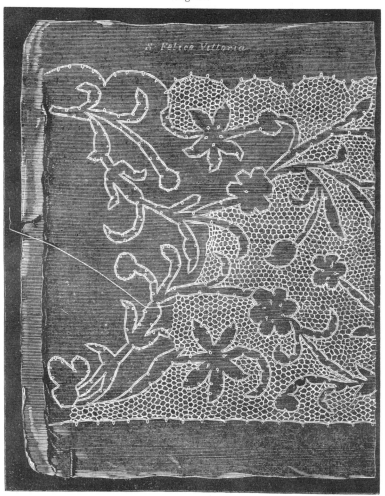

Unfinished work of a Spanish nun.

been the work only of those whose "time was not money." and whose devotion to the church and to their favourite saints rendered this work a labour of love, when in plying their needles they called to mind its destination. We have lately received from Rome photographs of some curious relics of old Spanish conventual work—parchment patterns with the lace in progress. They were found in the convent of Jesù Bambino, and belonged to some Spanish nuns who, in bygone ages, taught the art to the novices. None of the present inmates can give further information respecting them. The work, like all point, was executed in separate pieces given out to the different nuns, and then joined together by a more skilful hand. In Fig. 39 we see the pattern traced out by two threads fixed in their places by small stitches made at intervals by a needle and aloe[7] thread

Fig. 40.

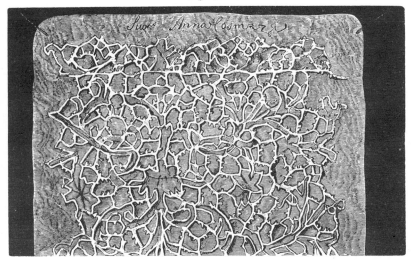

Unfinished work of a Spanish nun.

working from underneath. The réseau ground is alone worked in. We see the thread as left by Sister Felice Vittoria when last she plied her task.

Fig. 40 has the pearled ground, the pattern traced as in the other. Loops of a coarser thread are placed at the corners, either to fasten the parchment to a tight frame, like a schoolboy's slate, or to attach it to a cushion, as in Fig. 6, page 18. In Fig. 41 the pattern is first worked.

The ordinance of Philip III. against the wearing of lace, dated 1623, enjoining " simples rabats, sans aucune invention de point

[7] The aloe thread is now used in Florence for sewing the straw-plait.

couppé ou passement," for the men, with fraises and manchettes in like trim for the ladies, both, too, without starch,[8] was not cal-

Fig. 41.

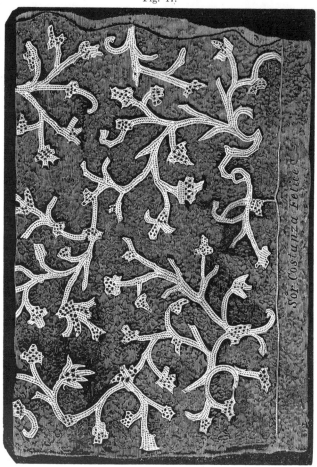

Unfinished work of a Spanish nun.

culated for the development of a national industry already ruined by the expulsion of the Moors, some years previously.[9]   This same

---

[8] This ordinance even extended to foreign courts. We read in the "Mercure Galant," 1679, of the Spanish ambassadress, "Elle etoit vestue de drap noir avec de la dentelle de soye ; elle n'avait ni dentelle ni linge autour de sa gorge."

[9] From the expulsion of the Moors, 1614, manufactures declined throughout Spain. The silk looms of Seville were reduced from 60,000 to 60.

ordinance, which extended to gold and silver lace, was suspended during the matrimonial visit of Prince Charles of England;[10] indeed, the Queen of Spain herself sent him, on his arrival at Madrid, ten trunks of richly laced linen. The prince had travelled incognito, and was supposed to be ill-provided. Whether the surmises of her majesty were correct, we cannot presume to affirm; we only know that, on the occasion of the Spanish voyage, a charge of two dozen and a half laced shirts, at twelve shillings each, for the prince's eight footmen, appears in the wardrobe accounts.[11]

The best account of Spanish manners of the seventeenth century will be found in the already mentioned "Letters of a Lady's Travels in Spain" (1679). "Under the vertingale of black taffety," she writes, "they wear a dozen or more petticoats, one finer than the other, of rich stuffs trimmed with lace of gold and silver, to the girdle. They wear at all times a white garment called sabenqua; it is made of the finest English lace, and four ells in compass. I have seen some worth five or six hundred crowns; . . . so great is their vanity, they would rather have one of these lace sabenquas than a dozen coarse ones;[12] and either lie in bed till it is washed or else dress themselves without any, which they frequently enough do." Describing her visit to the Princess of Monteleon, she says, "Her bed is of gold and green damask, lined with silver brocade and trimmed with point de Spain.[13] Her sheets were laced round with an English lace, half an ell deep. The young princess bade her maids bring in her wedding clothes. They brought in thirty silver baskets, so heavy, four women could only carry one basket; the linen and lace were not inferior to the rest." The writer continues to enumerate the garters, mantles, and even the curtains of the princess's carriage, as trimmed with "fine English thread, black, and bone lace."

Spain was early celebrated for its silk,[14] which with its

---

[10] "Mercure François."

[11] They have also provided—
14 ruffs and 14 pairs of cuffs laced, at 20s. . . . £14
For lacing 8 hats for the footmen with silver parchment lace, at 3s. . . . . . 1 4s.
Extraordinary Expenses of His Highness to Spain, 1623. P. R. O.

[12] Doctor Monçada, in 1660, and Osorio, in 1686, reckoned more than three millions of Spaniards who, though well dressed, wore no shirts.—*Townsend's Spain.*

[13] Speaking of the apartment of Madame d'Aranda, Beckford writes, "Her bed was of the richest blue velvet, trimmed with point lace."

[14] As early as the Great Wardrobe Account of Queen Elizabeth, 1587,

coloured embroidered laces, and its gold and silver points, have always enjoyed a certain reputation. Of the latter, during the seventeenth century, we have constant mention in the wardrobe accounts and books of fashion of the French court. The description of the celebrated gold bed at Versailles, the interior lacings of the carriages, the velvet and brocade coats and dresses, "chamarrés de Point d'Espagne," the laces of gold and coloured silk, would alone fill a volume of themselves.[15] Narciso Felin, a writer of the seventeenth century, says there were at that time many women occupied in the making of lace of gold, silver,[16] and thread (Fig. 42), with a perfection equal to that of Spanish Flanders. Campany, another old author, carries the number of lace-makers to 12,000. The Spaniards, nevertheless, are said, in

P. R. O., we have a charge for bobbin lace of Spanish silk, " cum uñ tag," for the mantle, 10s. 8d.

In a letter from Prestwich Eaton to Geo. Willingham, 1631, the writer sends 1000 reals (25l.), and in return desires him to send, together with a mastiff dog, some black satin lace for a Spanish suit.—State Papers, Domestic, Car. I. P. R. O.

[15] 1697. Marriage of Mademoiselle and the King of Spain. The queen, says the "Mercure," wore "une mante de Point d'Espagne d'or, neuf aunes de long."

1698. Fête at Versailles on the marriage of the Duc de Bourgogne. "La Duchesse de Bourgogne portoit un petit tablier de Point d'Espagne de mille pistoles."—Galérie de l'ancienne Cour, ou Mém. des Règnes de Louis XIV. et Louis XV. 1788.

1722. Ball at the Tuileries. "Tous les seigneurs étaient en habits de drap d'or ou d'argent garnis de Points d'Espagne, avec des nœuds d'épaule, et tout l'ajustement à proportion. Les moindres étaient de velours, avec des Points d'Espagne d'or et d'argent."—Journal de Barbier, 1718-62.

1722. "J'ai vu en même temps le carosse que le roi fait faire pour entrer dans Reims, il sera aussi d'une grande magnificence. Le dedans est tout garni d'un velours à ramage de Points d'Espagne d'or."—Ibid.

1731. Speaking of her wedding-dress, Wilhelmina of Bayreuth, the witty sister of Frederick the Great, writes, "Ma robe étoit d'une étoffe d'or fort riche, avec un Point d'Espagne d'or, et ma queue étoit de douze aunes de long"—Mémoires.

1751. Fête at Versailles on the birth of the Duke of Bourgogne. The coats of the "gens de cour, en étoffes d'or de grand prix ou en velours de toute couleurs, brodés or, ou garnis de Point d'Espage d'or."—Journal de Barbier.

[16] In the reign of William and Mary, we find, in a laceman's bill of the queen, a charge for forty-seven yards of rich, broad, scalloped, embossed point de Spain ; and her shoes are trimmed with gold and silver lace. B. M. Add. MSS. No. 5751.

At the entry of Lord Stair into Paris, 1718, his servants' hats are described as laced with Spanish point, their sleeves laced with picked silver lace, and dented at the edge with lace. "Edinburgh Courant."

In 1740, the Countess of Pomfret, speaking of the Princess Mary's wedding clothes, writes, "That for the wedding night is silver tissue, faced at the bottom before with pink-coloured satin, trimmed with silver Point d Espagne."—Letters of the Countess of Hartford to the Countess of Pomfret, 1740.

1634, to have derived a great part of their laces from the Isle de France, while the French, on their part, preferred those of Flanders.[17] That the lace trade was considered worth protecting is evident by the tariff of 1667; the import duty of twenty-five reals per pound on lace was augmented to two hundred and fifty. Much point was introduced into Spain at this time, by way of Antwerp to Cadiz, under the name of " puntos de mosquito e de transillas."

Madame des Ursins, 1707, in a letter to Madame de Maintenon, ordering the layette of the Queen of Spain from Paris, writes, " If I were not afraid of offending those concerned in the purchase, in

Fig. 42.

Old Spanish pillow lace.

my avarice for the King of Spain's money, I would beg them to send a low-priced lace for the linen."

This gold point d'Espagne was much fabricated for home consumption. The oldest banner of the Inquisition—that of Valladolid—is described as bordered with real point d'Espagne, of a curious Gothic (geometric) design. At the autos-da-fé, the grandees of Spain and officers of the holy office marched attired in cloaks, with black and white crosses, edged with this gold lace. Silver point d'Espagne was also worn on the uniform of the Maestranza, a body of nobility formed into an order of chivalry at Seville, Ronda, Valencia, and Granada. Even the saints were rigged out, especially St. Anthony, at Valencia, whose laced costume, periwig, and ruffles are described as " glorious."

---

[17] Marquis de la Gomberdière, 1634, " Nouveau Réglement général des Finances," &c.

Point d'Espagne was likewise made in France, introduced by one Simon Châtelain, a Huguenot, about 1596; in return for which good services he received more protection than his advanced opinions warranted. Colbert, becoming minister in 1662, guaranteed to Simon his safety—a boon already refused to many by the intolerant spirit of the times. He died in 1675, having amassed a large fortune.[18] Colbert, in 1669, writes, " En dentelles de toutes façons, la France fait grandissime commerce en Espagne et aux Indes occidentales." "France," says Anderson, "exports much lace into Spain."

Towards the middle of the eighteenth century, the Spanish manufactures seem to have been on the decline, judging from the constant seizures of vessels bound from St. Malo to Cadiz, freighted with gold and silver lace. The Eagle, French vessel, taken by Captain Carr, in 1745, bore cases to the value of 150,000*l*.[19] In 1789 we also read that the exports of lace from the port of Marseilles alone to Cadiz exceeded 500,000*l*.[20]

Gold and silver lace are made at Barcelona, Talavera de la Reyna, Valencia, and Seville. In 1808, that of Seville was flourishing. The gold is badly prepared, having a red cast.

The manufacture of blonde is almost entirely confined to Catalonia, where it is made in many of the villages along the sea-coast, and especially in the city of Barcelona. In 1809, it gave employment to 12,000 persons, a number now augmented to 34,000. There are no large manufactories, the trade is in the hands of women and children, who make it on their own account, and as they please.[21] Swinburne, who visited Spain in 1775, writes:— " The women of the hamlets were busy with their bobbins making black lace, some of which, of the coarser kind, is spun out of the leaf of the aloe. It is curious, but of little use, for it grows mucilaginous with washing." He adds, "at Barcelona, there is a great trade in thread lace."[22] The manufacture of silk lace or blonde in Almagro (La Mancha) occupies from 12,000 to 13,000

---

[18] "Eighty children and grandchildren attended his funeral, in defiance of the edict of 12 Sept. 1664, and were heavily fined."—*La France Protestante, par M. M. Haag.* Paris, 1846–59.

[19] " Gent'eman's Magazine," 1745.

[20] Peyron, 1789.

[21] "Itinéraire de l'Espagne," Comte Alph. de Laborde, t. v.

[22] Peuchet, " Dictionnaire Universel de la Géographie Commerçante" (An. VII. = 1799), speaking of Barcelona, says their laces are " façon de France," but inferior in beauty and quality. The fabrication is considerable, employing 2000 women in the towns and villages east of Barcelona. They are sold in Castile, Andalusia, and principally in the Indies.

people. The laces of New Castile were exported to America, to which colonies, in 1723, the sumptuary laws were extended, as more necessary than in Spain, "many families having been ruined," says Ustariz, "by the great quantities of fine lace and gold stuffs they purchased of foreign manufacture, by which means Spanish America is drained of many millions of dollars." [23] A Spanish lace-maker does not earn on an average two reals (5d.) a day.[24]

The national mantilla is, of course, the principal piece manufactured. Of the three kinds which, de rigueur, form the toilette of the Spanish lady, the first is composed of white blonde, a most unbecoming contrast to their sallow, olive complexion : this is only used on state occasions—birthdays, bull-fights, and Easter Mondays. The second is black blonde, trimmed with a deep lace. The third, "mantilla de tiro," for ordinary wear, is made of black silk, trimmed with velvet. A Spanish woman's mantilla is held sacred by law, and cannot be seized for debt.[25] The silk employed for the lace is of a superior quality. Near Barcelona is a silk-spinning manufactory, whose products are specially used for the blondes of the country. Spanish silk laces do not equal in workmanship those of Bayeux and Chantilly, either in the firmness of the ground or regularity of the pattern. The annual produce of this industry scarcely amounts to 80,000l.

Specimens of Barcelona white-thread lace have been forwarded to us from Spain, bearing the dates of 1810, 1820, 1830, and 1840. Some have much resemblance to the products of Lille—a clear ground, with the pattern worked in one coarse thread; others, of a double ground, bear evidence of a Flemish origin.

Spain sent to the international exhibitions, together with her black and white mantillas, fanciful laces gaily embroidered in coloured silks and gold thread—an ancient manufacture lately revived, but constantly mentioned in the inventories of the French court of the seventeenth century, and also by the lady whose letters we have already quoted. When describing a visit to Donna Teresa de Toledo, who received her in bed, she writes, "She had several little pillows tied with ribbons and trimmed

---

[23] "Theory of Commerce," from the Spanish of Don Ger. de Ustariz. Lond. 1751.

[24] When the holidays of the Roman Catholic Church are deducted, the workdays of the people amount only to 260 in the course of the year—fifty less than in a Protestant country.

[25] Ford, "Handbook of Spain."

with broad fine lace. She had 'lasses' all of flowers of point de
Spain in silk and gold, which looked very pretty." [26]

The finest specimen of Spanish work exhibited in 1862 was a
mantilla of white blonde, the ground a light guipure, the pattern
wreaths of flowers supported by Cupids.

Before concluding our account of Spanish lace, we must allude
to the " dentelles de Moresse," supposed by M. Francisque Michel [27]
to be of Iberian origin, fabricated by the descendants of the
Moors who remained in Spain and embraced Christianity. These
points are named in the before-mentioned " Révolte des Passemens," where the author thus announces their arrival at the fair
of Saint-Germain :—

> " Il en vint que, le plus souvent,
> On disoit venir du Levant;
> Il en vint des bords de l'Ibère,
> Il en vint d'arriver n'agueres
> Des pays septentrionaux."

What these points were, it would be difficult to state: in the
inventory of Henry VIII. is marked down, " a purle of morisco
work."

One of the pattern books gives on its title-page—

> " Dantique et Roboesque
> En comprenant aussi Moresque."

A second speaks of " Moreschi et arabesche." [28] A third is
entitled, " Un livre de moresque;" [29] a fourth, " Un livre de
feuillages entrelatz et ouvrages moresques." [30] All we can say on
the subject is—that the making cloths of chequered lace formed
for a time the favourite employment of Moorish maidens, and
they are still to be purchased, yellow with age, in the African
cities of Tangier and Tetuan. They may be distinguished from
those worked by Christian fingers by the absence of all animals
in the pattern, the representation of living creatures, either in
painting, sculpture, or embroidery, being strictly forbidden by
the Mahommedan law.

---

[26] 1678. " On met de la dentelle brodée
de couleur de points d'Espagne aux
jupes."—*Mercure Galant.*

[27] " Recherches sur le Commerce, la
Fabrication et l'Usage des Étoffes de
Soie etc. pendant le Moyen Age."
Paris, 1839.

[28] Taglienti, Venice, 1530.

[29] Paris, 1546.

[30] Pelegrin de Florence, Paris, 1530.

PORTUGAL.

"Her hands it was whose patient skill should trace
The finest broidery, weave the costliest lace;
But most of all—her first and dearest care—
The office she would never miss or share,
Was every day to weave fresh garlands sweet,
To place before the shrine at Mary's feet."

The Convent Child, Miss Procter.

Point lace was made in Portugal as well as in Spain, and held in high estimation. There was no regular manufacture; it formed the amusement of the nuns, and of a few women who worked at their own houses. The sumptuary law of 1749 put an end to all luxury among the laity. Even those who exposed such wares as laces in the streets were ordered to quit the town.[31]

In 1729,[32] when Barbara, sister of Joseph, King of Portugal, at seventeen years of age, married Ferdinand, Prince of Spain, before quitting Lisbon, she repaired to the church of the Madre de Dios, on the Tagus, and there solemnly offered to the Virgin the jewels and a dress of the richest Portuguese point she had worn on the day of her espousals. This lace is described as most magnificent, and was for near a century exhibited under a glass case to admiring eyes, till at the French occupation of the Peninsula the Duchesse d'Abrantès, or one of the imperial generals, is supposed to have made off with it. When Lisbon arose from her ashes after the terrible earthquake of 1755, the Marquis de Pombal founded large manufactures of lace, which were carried on under his auspices. Wraxall, in his "Memoirs," mentions having visited them.

The modern laces of Portugal and Madeira closely resemble those of Spain; the wider for flounces are of silk; much narrow is made after the fashion of Mechlin. Forty years ago a considerable quantity of white coarse lace, very effective in pattern, was made in Lisbon and the environs: this was chiefly exported, viâ Cadiz, to South America. Both black and white are extensively made in the peninsula of Peniche, north of Lisbon (Estremadura Province), and employ the whole female population.

---

[31] "Magazin de Londres," 1749.

[32] Mademoiselle Dumont, foundress of the Point de France Manufactory, in the Rue St.-Denis, quitted Paris after some years, and retired to Portugal: whether she there introduced her art is more than the author can affirm.

Children at four years of age are sent to the lace school, and
are seated at "almofadas" (pillows), proportioned to their height,
on which they soon learn to manage the bobbins, sometimes
sixty dozen or more, with great dexterity.[33]

Of the point lace made in the Spanish Peninsula, we have
evidently but scanty information. The Spanish raised point
would appear to be identical with that of Venice, but there are
others with different characteristics which are assigned to Spain,
such as the class in low relief, wanting the freedom and richness

Fig. 43.

Madeira lace, pillow-made.

of design of the Venetian, and passing in commerce as "flat
Spanish point."

The fine points in relief of Italy and Spain were the result of
such time and labour as to render them too costly for moderate
means. Hence they were extensively counterfeited. The principal scroll of the pattern was formed by means of tape on linen cut
out and sewn on, and the reliefs were produced by cords fixed
and overcast after the work was finished, thus substituting linen
and cords for parts of the needlework. These counterfeit points
were, in France, the occasion, in 1669, of an ordinance.

---

[33] "Queen," August 1872.

The nuns of Odivales were, till the dissolution of the monasteries, famed for their lace fabricated of the fibre of the aloe.

Pillow lace was made at Madeira some fifty years ago. The coarse kind, a species of dentelle torchon, served for trimming pillow-cases and sheets—" seaming lace," as it was called (Fig. 43). Sometimes the threads of the linen were drawn after the manner of cutwork; but the manufacture had entirely ceased till within these last fifteen years, when it was re-established by Mrs. Bayman. There are now seven families employed in the fabrication of Maltese lace, which is made almost entirely by men; the women occupy themselves in the open-work embroidery of muslin.

Brazil makes a coarse narrow pillow lace for home consumption (Fig. 44).

Fig. 44.

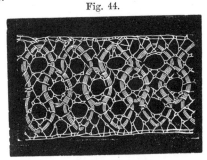

Brazilian lace, pillow-made.

The republics of Central and South America show indications of lace-making, consisting chiefly of darned netting and drawn work, the general characteristics of the lace of those countries. The lace-bordered handkerchiefs of Brazil, and the productions of Venezuela, with the borders of the linen trousers of the Guachos, and the Creva lace of the blacks of the province of Minas Geraes, are the finest specimens of drawn work. The lace of Chili is of the old lozenge pattern, and men also appear to be employed there in the work. That from Paraguay is likewise made on the pillow; all traditions of the European missionaries and traders who first colonised the country.

CHAPTER VII.

FLANDERS.

" For lace, let Flanders bear away the belle."
Sir C. Hanbury Williams.
" In French embroidery and in Flanders lace
I'll spend the income of a treasurer's place."
The Man of Taste, Rev. W. Bramstone.

FLANDERS and Italy together dispute the invention of lace. In many towns of the Low Countries are pictures of the fifteenth century, in which are portrayed personages adorned with lace,[1] and Baron Reiffenberg, a Belgian writer,[2] asserts that lace cornettes, or caps, were worn in that country as early as the fourteenth century. He also brings the evidence of contemporary paintings, to show how early it was made. In a side chapel of the choir of St. Peter's, at Louvain, is an altar-piece by Quentin Matsys, date 1495, in which a girl is represented making lace with bobbins on a pillow with a drawer, similar to that now in use. We have not seen the painting. There exists a series of engravings after Martin de Vos, 1581, giving the occupation of the seven ages of life: in the third,[3] assigned to "age mur," is seen a girl sitting with a pillow on her knees, making lace (Fig. 45): the occupation must have been then common, or the artist would scarcely have chosen it to characterise the habits of his country.

The historian of the Duke of Burgundy[4] declares Charles the Bold to have lost his "dentelles" at the battle of Granson, 1476; he does not state his authority: probably they were gold or silver.

In 1651, Jacob van Eyck, a Flemish poet, sang the praises of lace-making in Latin verse. "Of many arts, one surpasses all

---

[1] Those in the collegiate church of St. Peter's, at Louvain, and in the church of St. Gomar, at Lierre (Antwerp Province).—*Aubry.*

[2] "Mémoires de l'Académie de Bruxelles," 1820.

[3] Engraved by Collaert. Bib. Nat. Grav

[4] M. de Barante.

the threads woven by the strange power of the hand, threads which the dropping spider would in vain attempt to imitate, and

Fig. 45.

Lace-making. After Martin de Vos.

which Pallas would confess she had never known;" and a deal more in the same style.[5]

---

[5] It goes on : " For the maiden, seated at her work, plies her fingers rapidly, and flashes the smooth balls and thousand threads into the circle. Often she fastens with her hand the innumerable needles, to bring out the various figures of the pattern ; often, again, she unfastens them ; and in this her amusement makes as much profit as the man earns by the sweat of his brow ; and no maiden ever complains even at the length of the day. The issue is a fine web, open to the air

The lace manufacture of the Netherlands, as Baron Reiffenberg writes, has a glorious past. After exciting the jealousy of other European nations, in the sixteenth century, when every industrial art fled from the horrors of religious persecution, the lace fabric alone upheld itself, and by its prosperity saved Flanders from utter ruin. Every country of Northern Europe, France,[6] Germany, and England, has learned the art of lace-making from Flanders. After the establishment of the Points de France by Colbert, Flanders was alarmed at the number of lace-makers who emigrated, and passed an Act, dated Brussels, 26th December 1698, threatening with punishment any who should suborn her workpeople.

Lace-making forms an abundant source of national wealth to Belgium, and enables the people of its superannuated cities to support themselves, as it were, on female industry.[7] One-fortieth of the whole population (150,000 women) are said to be thus engaged. But a small number assemble in the ateliers; the majority work at home. The trade now flourishes as in the most palmy days of the Netherlands.

Lace-making forms a part of female education in Belgium. Charles V. commanded it to be taught in the schools and convents. Examples of the products of his period may be seen in the cap worn by him under his crown (Fig. 46), and in the contemporary portrait of his sister, Mary, Queen of Hungary. This cap, long preserved in the treasury of the bishop princes of Basle, has now passed into the Musée de Cluny. It is fine linen; the imperial arms are embroidered in relief, alternate with designs in lacis of exquisite workmanship.[8]

---

with many an aperture, which feeds the pride of the whole globe; which encircles with its fine border cloaks and tuckers, and shows grandly round the throats and hands of kings; and, what is more surprising, this web is of the lightness of a feather, which in its price is too heavy for our purses. Go, ye men, inflamed with the desire of the Golden Fleece, endure so many dangers by land, so many at sea, whilst the woman, remaining in her Brabantine home, prepares Phrygian fleeces by peaceful assiduity."—*Jacobi Eyckii Antwerpiensis Urbium Belgicarum Centuria.* Antw. 1651. 1 vol. 4to. Bib. Royale, Brussels.

[6] Alençon excepted.

[7] It destroys, however, the eyesight. "I was told by a gentleman well acquainted with Flanders," says McPherson, "that they are generally almost blind before thirty years of age."—*History of Commerce*, 1785.

[8] Together with the cap is preserved a parchment with this inscription: "Gorro que perteneccio à Carlos Quinto, emperad. Guarda lo, hijo mio, es memoria de Juhan de Garnica." ("Cap which belonged to the Emperor Charles V. Keep it, my son, in remembrance of John de Garnica.") J. de Garnica was treasurer to Philip II.

Queen Mary's cuffs (Fig. 47) are of the geometric pattern of
the age, and, we may presume, of Flanders make, as she was

Fig. 46.

Cap of the Emperor Charles V. Musée de Cluny.

Fig. 47.

Mary, Queen of Hungary, Governess of the Low Countries. +1558. From her portrait,
Musée Nationale, Versailles.

governess of the Low Countries from 1530 till her death. The
granddaughter of Charles V., the Infanta Isabella, who brought

the Low Countries as her dower,[9] appears in her portraits (Fig. 48) most resplendent in lace, and her ruff rivals in size those of our Queen Elizabeth, or Reine Margot.

But to return to our subject. Of the lace schools, there are now nearly 900, either in the convents or founded by private charity. At the age of five, small girls commence their apprenticeship; by ten, they earn their maintenance; and it is a pretty sight, an "école dentellière," the children seated before their pillows, twisting their bobbins with wonderful dexterity (Fig. 49).

In a tract of the seventeenth century, entitled "England's

Fig. 49.

A Belgian lace school.

Improvement by Sea and Land, to outdo the Dutch without Fighting,"[10] we have an amusing account of one of these establishments. "Joining to this spinning school is one for maids weaving bone lace; and in all towns there are schools according to the bigness and multitude of the children. I will show you how they are governed. First, there is a large room, and in the middle thereof a little box like a pulpit. Second, there are benches built about the room as they are in our playhouses. And in the box in the middle of the room, the grand mistress, with a long white wand

[9] Married, 1599, Albert, Archduke of Austria.

[10] By Andrew Yarranton, Gent. London, 1677. A proposal to erect schools for teaching and improving the linen manufacture as they do "in Flanders and Holland, where littte girls from six years old upwards learn to employ their fingers." Hadrianus Junius, a most learned writer, in his description of the Netherlands, highly extols the fine needlework and linen called cambric of the Belgian nuns, which in whiteness rivals the snow, in texture satin, and in price the sea-silk—Byssus, or beard of the Pinna.

Fig. 48.

Isabella Clara Eugenia, daughter of Philip II., Archduchess of Austria, Governess of the Netherlands.
Died 1633.

To face page 90.

in her hand. If she observes any of them idle, she reaches them
a tap, and if that will not do, she rings a bell, which, by a little
cord, is attached to the box. She points out the offender, and she
is taken into another room and chastised. And I believe this way
of ordering the young women in Germany (Flanders) is one great

Fig. 50.

Old Flemish (Trolle Kant).

(The piece of lace from which this woodcut is taken has five or six different
designs all joined together; probably patterns sent round for orders.)

cause that the German women have so little twit twat,[11] and I am
sure it will be as well were it so in England. There the children
emulate the father—here they beggar him. Child," he winds up,

---

[11] An old term, still used in Scotland, for gossip, chatter.

" I charge you tell this to thy wyfe in bed, and it may be that she, understanding the benefit it will be to her and her children, will turn Dutchwoman, and endeavour to save moneys." Notwithstanding this good advice, in 1768, England received from Flanders lace-work, 250,000*l.*, to her disadvantage, as compared to her exports.

The old Flemish laces are of great beauty. Fig. 50 represents a description of lace, called in the country Trolle Kant, a term which has been transferred to our own lace counties, in which lace of a peculiar make is styled Trolly.

The guipures of Flanders were always held in high estimation. The thread of which they were made was finer than that of France, and the fine flowing pattern, extending to some length like an architectural border, had a magnificent appearance when laid flat upon the vestment, as was the fashion in the seventeenth century.

At one period much lace was smuggled into France from Belgium by means of dogs trained for the purpose. A dog was caressed and petted at home, fed on the fat of the land, then, after a season, sent across the frontier, where he was tied up, half starved, and ill-treated. The skin of a bigger dog was then fitted to his body, and the intervening space filled with lace. The dog was then allowed to escape, and make his way home, where he was kindly welcomed with his contraband charge. These journeys were repeated till the French custom house, getting scent, by degrees put an end to the traffic. Between 1820 and 1836, 40,278 dogs were destroyed, a reward of three francs being given for each.[12]

BRUSSELS (BRABANT).

" More subtile web Arachne cannot spin."
Spenser.

" From Lisle I came to Brussels, where most of the fine laces are made you see worn in England."—*Lord Chesterfield,* 1741.

At what period the manufacture of Brussels lace commenced, we are ignorant. The ancient churches of Brabant possess, it is said, many precious specimens, the gifts of munificent princes,

---

[12] These dogs were of large size, and able to carry from 22 to 26 lbs. They also conveyed tobacco. The Swiss dogs smuggle watches.

who have at all periods shown a predilection for Brussels lace, and in every way promoted its manufacture. In usage, it is termed "point d'Angleterre," an error explained to us by history. In 1662, the English parliament, alarmed at the sums of money expended on foreign point, and desirous to protect the English bone lace manufacture, passed an act prohibiting the importation of all foreign lace. The English lace merchants, at a loss how to supply the Brussels point required at the court of Charles II., invited Flemish lace-makers to settle in England, and there establish the manufacture. The scheme, however, was unsuccessful. England did not produce the necessary flax, and the lace made was of an inferior quality. The merchants therefore adopted a more simple expedient. Possessed of large capital, they bought up the choicest laces of the Brussels market, and then, smuggling them over to England, sold them under the name of point d'Angleterre,[13] or "English point."[14]

The account of the seizure made by the Marquis de Nesmond, of a vessel laden with Flanders lace, bound for England, in 1678,[15] will afford some idea of the extent to which this smuggling was carried on. The cargo comprised 744,953 ells of lace, without enumerating handkerchiefs, collars, fichus, aprons, petticoats, fans, gloves, &c., all of the same material. From this period, "point de Bruxelles" became more and more unknown, and was at last effaced by "point d'Angleterre,"[16] a name it still retains.[17]

On consulting, however, the English royal inventories of the time, we find no mention of "English point." In France, on the other hand, the fashion books of the day[18] commend to the notice of the reader, "Corsets chamarrés de point d'Angleterre," with vests, gloves, and cravats trimmed with the same material. Among

---

[13] This fact is curiously enough corroborated in a second memorandum given by the Venetian ambassador to the English court in 1695, already mentioned (p. 45), by an informant in London, who states that Venetian point is no longer in fashion, but "that called English point, which you know is not made here, but in Flanders, and only bears this name of English to distinguish it from the others."

"Questo chiamato punto d'Inghilterra, si sappia che non si fa qui, ma in Fiandra, et porta solamente questo nome d'Inghilterra per distintione dagli altri."

[14] Black lace was also imported at this period from the Low Countries. Among the articles advertised as lost, in the "Newsman" of the 26th of May 1664, is: "A black lute-string gown with a black Flanders lace."

[15] "Mercure Galant," 1678.

[16] "Le corsage et les manches étaient bordés d'une blanche et légère dentelle, sortie à coup sûr des meilleures manufactures d'Angleterre."

[17] We have, however, one entry, in the wardrobe accounts of the Duc de Penthièvre: "1738. Onze aunes d'Angleterre de Flandre."

[18] "Mercure Galant," 1678.

the effects of Madame de Simiane, dated 1681, were many articles of English point;[19] and Monseigneur the Archbishop of Bourges, who died some few years later, had two cambric toilettes trimmed with the same.[20]

The finest Brussels lace can only be made in the city itself. Antwerp, Ghent, and other localities, have in vain tried to compete with the capital. The little town of Binche, long of lace-making celebrity, has been the most successful. Binche, however, now only makes pillow flowers (point plat), and those of an inferior quality.

When, in 1756, Mrs. Calderwood visited the Béguinage, at Brussels, she writes to a friend, describing the lace-making : " A part of their work is grounding lace; the manufacture is very curious. One person works the flowers. They are all sold separate, and you will see a very pretty sprig, for which the worker only gets twelve sous. The masters who have all these people employed give them the thread to make them; this they do according to a pattern, and give them out to be grounded; after this they give them to a third hand, who ' hearts ' all the flowers with the open work. That is what makes this lace so much dearer than the Mechlin, which is wrought all at once."[21]

The thread used in Brussels lace is of extraordinary fineness. It is made of flax grown in Brabant, at Hal and Rebecq-Rognon.[22] The finest quality is spun in dark underground rooms, for contact with the dry air causes the thread to break; so fine is it as almost to escape the sight. The feel of the thread as it passes through the fingers is the surest guide. The thread-spinner closely examines every inch drawn from her distaff, and when any inequality occurs, stops her wheel to repair the mischief. Every artificial help is given to the eye. A background of dark paper

---

[19] " Deux paires de manchettes et une cravatte de point d'Angleterre." —*Inventaire d'Anne d'Escoubleau, Baronne de Sourdis, veuve de François de Simiane.* Arch. Nat. M. M. 802.

[20] " Inv. après le decès de Mgr. Mich. Philippine de la Vrillière, Patriarche, Archevêque de Bourges," 1694. Bib. Nat. MSS. F. Fr. 11,426.

" Une toilette et sa touaille avec un peignoir de point d'Angleterre."—*Inv. de decès de Mademoiselle de Charollais,* 1758. Arch. Nat.

[21] " Mrs. Calderwood's Journey through Holland and Belgium, 1756." Printed by the Maitland Club.

[22] Flax is also cultivated solely for lace and cambric thread at St. Nicholas, Tournay, and Courtrai. The process of steeping (rouissage) principally takes place at Courtrai, the clearness of the waters of the Lys rendering them peculiarly fitted for the purpose. Savary states that fine thread was first spun at Mechlin.

is placed to throw out the thread, and the room so arranged as to admit one single ray of light upon the work. The life of a Flemish thread-spinner is unhealthy, and her work requires the greatest skill; her wages are therefore proportionably high.

It is the fineness of the thread which renders the real Brussels ground (vrai réseau) so costly.[23] The difficulty of procuring this fine thread, at any cost, prevented the art being established in other countries. We all know how, during the last fifty years of the bygone century, a mania existed in the United Kingdom for improving all sorts of manufactures. The Anti-Gallican Society gave prizes in London; Dublin and Edinburgh vied with their sister capital in patriotism. Every man would establish something to keep our native gold from crossing the water. Foreign travellers had their eyes open, and Lord Garden, a Scotch lord of session, who visited Brussels in 1787, thus writes to a countryman on the subject:— "This day I bought you ruffles and some beautiful Brussels lace, the most light and costly of all manufactures. I had entertained, as I now suspect, a vain ambition to attempt the introduction of it into my humble parish in Scotland, but on inquiry I was discouraged. The thread is of so exquisite a fineness they cannot make it in this country. It is brought from Cambray and Valenciennes in French Flanders, and five or six different artists are employed to form the nice part of this fabric, so that it is a complicated art which cannot be transplanted without a passion as strong as mine for manufactures, and a purse much stronger. At Brussels, from one pound of flax alone, they can manufacture to the value of 700l. sterling."

Of the two kinds of ground used in Brussels lace, the bride had, a century back,[24] been replaced by the réseau, and was only made to order. Nine ells of "Angleterre à bride" appear in the bills of Madame du Barry.[25] Sometimes

---

[23] It is often sold at 240l. per lb., and in the report of the French Exhibition of 1859 it is mentioned as high as 500l. (25,000 fr. the kilogramme). No wonder that so much thread is made by machinery, and that Scotch cotton thread is so generally used, except for the choicest laces. But machine-made thread has never attained the fineness of that made by hand. Of those in the Exhibition of 1862, the finest Lille was 800 leas (a technical term for a reel of 300 yarns),

the Brussels 600, the Manchester 700; whereas in Westphalia and Belgium hand-spun threads as fine as 800 to 1000 are spun for costly laces. The writer has seen specimens, in the Museum at Lille, equal to 1200 of machinery; but this industry is so poorly remunerated that the number of skilful hand-spinners is fast diminishing.

[24] "Dictionnaire du Citoyen," 1761.

[25] "Comptes de Madame du Barry." Bib. Nat. MSS. F. Fr. 8157 and 8.

bride [26] and réseau were mixed.[27] In the inventories the description of ground is always minutely specified.[28]

The réseau was made in two ways,[29] by hand (à l'aiguille), and on the pillow (au fuseau). The needle ground is worked from one flower to another, as in Coloured Plate IV. The pillow is made in small strips of 1 inch in width, and from 7 to 45 inches long, joined together by a stitch long known to the lace-makers of Brussels and Bayeux only,[30] called "point de raccroc;" in English, "fine joining," and consisting of a fresh stitch formed with a needle between the two pieces to be united. It requires the greatest nicety to join the segments of shawls and other large pieces. Since machine-made net has come into use, the "vrai réseau" is rarely made, save for royal trousseaux.

There are two kinds of flowers: those made with the needle are called "point à l'aiguille;" those on the pillow, "point plat."[31] The best flowers are made in Brussels itself, where they have attained a perfection in the relief (point brodé) unequalled by those made in the surrounding villages and at Binche, in Hainault.

---

[26] Albs of Brussels lace were much worn by the Church.

"Trois aubes de batiste garnies de grande dentelle de gros point d'Angleterre."—*Inv. des Meubles etc. de Louis, Duc d'Orléans, décédé* 4 *fév.* 1752 (son of the regent). Arch. Nat. X. 10,075.

"Deux aubes de point d'Angleterre servant à Messieurs les curez.

"Une autre aube à dentelle de gros point servant aussy à M. le curé."— *Inventaire et Description de l'Argenterie, Vermeil Doré, Ornemens, Linge etc. appartenant à l'Œuvre et Fabrique de l'église Saint-Merry à Paris,* 1714. Arch. Nat. L. L. 859.

[27] "Une coëffure à une pièce d'Angle terre bride et réseau."—*Comptes de Madame du Barry.*

"1 aune et quart d'Angleterre mêlé." —*Ibid.*

[28] Mrs. Delany writes ("Corr." vol. 2): "The laces I have pitched on for you are charming, it is grounded Brussels."

"Deux tours de gorge à raiseau, un tour de camisolle à bride."— *Inv. de la Duchesse de Bourbon,* 1720. Arch. Nat. X. 10,062-4.

"Six peignoirs de toile fine garnis par en haut d'une vieille dentelle d'Angleterre à raiseau."—*Inv. de decès de Monsieur Philippe, petit-fils de France, Duc d'Orléans, Régent du Royaume, décédé* 2 décembre 1723. Arch. Nat. X. 10,067.

The "fond écaillé" often occurs.

"Une coëffure à une pièce de point à l'écaille;

"Une paire de manchettes de cour de point à raizeau, et deux devants de corps de point à brides à écailles."—*Inv. de la Duchesse de Modène,* 1761. Arch. Nat. X. 10,082.

"Deux barbes, rayon et fond d'Angleterre superfin fond écaillé."—*Comptes de Madame du Barry.* See her Angleterre, Chap. XI. note [27].

[29] To which machinery has added a third, the tulle or Brussels net.

[30] The needleground is three times as expensive as the pillow, because the needle is passed four times into each mesh, whereas in the pillow it is not passed at all.

[31] "Trois oreillers, l'un de toile blanche picqueé garnis autour de chacun d'un point plat."—*Inv. de la Duchesse de Modène.*

Plate IV.

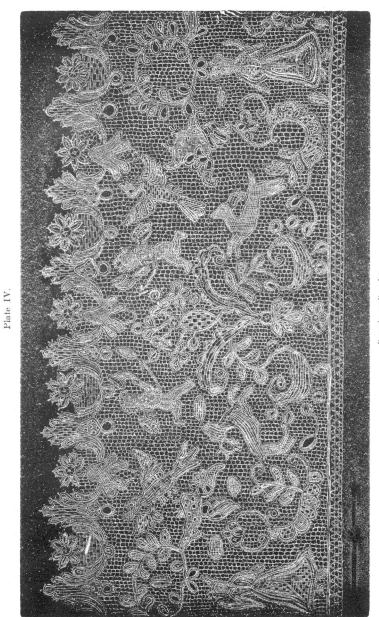

The last have one great fault. Coming soiled from the hands of the lace-makers, they have a reddish-yellow cast. In order to obviate this evil, the workwoman, previous to sewing the flowers on the ground, places them in a packet of white lead and beats them with the hand, an operation injurious to the health of the lace-cleaner. It also causes the lace to turn black when laid in trunks or wardrobes in contact with flannel or other woollen tissues bleached with sulphur, which discolours the white lead. Bottles containing scent, the sea air, or a heated room, will produce the same disagreeable change, and the colour is with difficulty restored. This custom of powdering yellow lace is of old date. We read in 1782:[32] "On tolère en même temps les dentelles jaunes et fort sales, poudrez-les à blanc pour cacher leur vetusté, dut la fraude paroître, n'importe, vous avez des dentelles vous êtes bien dispensé de la propreté mais non du luxe." Mrs. Delany writes in 1734: "Your head and ruffles are being made up, but Brussels always looks yellow;" and she was right, for flax thread soon returns to its natural hue. Yet,

"How curled her hair, how clean her Brussels lace!"

exclaims the poet.[33] Later, the taste for discoloured lace became general. The "Isabelle" or cream-coloured tint was found to be more becoming than a dazzling white, and our coquettish grand-mothers, who prided themselves upon the colour of their point, when not satisfied with the richness of its hue, had their lace dipped in coffee.

In the older laces the plat flowers were worked in together with the ground (Figs. 51 and 52). Application lace was unknown to our ancestors.[34] The making of Brussels lace is so complicated that each process is, as before mentioned, assigned to a different hand, who works only at her special department. The first, termed—

Drocheleuse (Flemish, drocheles), makes the vrai réseau.

2. Dentelière (kantwerkes), the footing.

3. Pointeuse (needlewerkes), the point à l'aiguille flowers.

4. Platteuse (platwerkes) makes the plat flowers.

---

[32] "Tableau de Paris, par S. Mercier," Amsterdam, 1782.

[33] "Fashion," J. Warton.

[34] Brussels lace-makers divide the plat into three parts, the "mat," the close part answering to the French "toilé" (see p. 26); "gaze au fuseau," in which small interstices appear, French "grillé;" and the "jours," or open work.

Fig. 51.

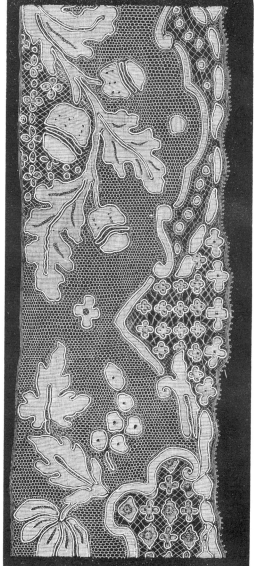

Old Brussels (point d'Angleterre), pillow-made.   Middle of eighteenth century.

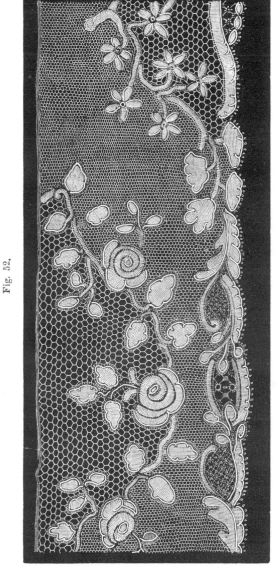

Fig. 52.

Old Brussels. (Point d'Angleterre.) Formerly belonging to H. M. Queen Charlotte.

H 2

5. Fonneuse (grondwerkes) is charged with the open work (jours) in the plat.

6. Jointeuse, or attacheuse (lashwerkes), unites the different sections of the ground together.

7. Striqueuse, or appliqueuse (strikes), is charged with the sewing (application) of the flowers upon the ground.

The pattern is designed by the head of the manufactory, who, having cut the parchment into pieces, hands it out ready pricked. The worker has no reflections to make, no combinations to study. The whole responsibility rests with the master, who selects the ground, chooses the thread, and alone knows the effect to be produced by the whole. (Coloured Plate V.)

The lace industry of Brussels is now divided into two branches, the making of detached sprigs, either point or pillow, for application upon the net ground, and the modern "point gazé." The first is the Brussels lace "par excellence," and more of it is produced than of any other kind. Of late years, it has been greatly improved, by mixing point and pillow-made flowers. Point gazé is so called from its gauze-like needle ground, "fond gaze," comprised of very fine, round meshes, with needle-made flowers, made simultaneously with the ground, by means of the same thread, as in the old Brussels. It is made in small pieces, the joining concealed by small sprigs or leaves, after the manner of the old point, the same lace-worker executing the whole strip from beginning to end. Point gazé is now brought to the highest perfection, and is remarkable for the precision of the work, the variety and richness of the "jours," and the clearness of the ground. In appearance, it somewhat resembles point d'Alençon, but the work is less elaborate and less solid. When flowers both of needle point and pillow lace are introduced upon the "fond gaze," it is erroneously termed "point de Venise."

Brussels was a favoured lace at the court of the First Empire.[35] When Napoleon and the Empress Marie Louise made their first public entry into the Belgian capital, they gave large orders for albs of the richest point, destined as a present for the Pope. The

---

[35] The veil presented by the city of Brussels to the Empress Josephine was sold in 1816, by Eugène Beauharnais, to Lady Jane Hamilton. It is described to have been of such ample dimensions that, when placed on Lady Jane's head, who was upwards of 6 feet high, it trained upon the ground. The texture of the réseau was exquisitely fine. In each corner was the imperial crown and cypher, encircled with wreaths of flowers. This chef-d'œuvre of art passed into the possession of Lady Jane's daughter, the Duchesse de Coigny.

Plate V.

Brussels. 1750—1800.

To face page 100

Plate VI.

Brussels needle point. Circa 1750.

To face page 101.

city, on its part, offered to the empress a collection of its finest lace, on vrai réseau; also a curtain of Brussels point, emblematic of the birth of the King of Rome, with Cupids supporting the drapery of the cradle. After the battle of Waterloo, Monsieur Troyaux, a manufacturer at Brussels, stopped his lace manufactory, and turned it into an hospital for English soldiers. His humane conduct did not go unrewarded: he received a decoration from his sovereign, while his shop was daily crowded with English ladies, who then, and for years after, made a point of purchasing their laces at his establishment. (Coloured Plate VI.) Monsieur Troyaux made a large fortune, and retired from business.[36]

MECHLIN.

" And if disputes of empire rise between
    Mechlin, the queen of lace, and Colberteen,
    'Tis doubt! 'tis darkness! till suspended Fate
    Assumes her nod to close the grand debate."
                        Young, Love of Fame.

" Now to another scene give place:
    Enter the Folks with silk and lace,
    Fresh matter for a world of chat,
    Right Indian this, right Macklin that."
                        Swift, Journal of a Modern Lady.

" Mechlin, the finest lace of all!"
                        Anderson, Origin of Commerce.

" ROSE. Pray what may this lace be worth a yard?
 " BALANCE. Right Mechlin, by this light!"
                        Farquhar, The Recruiting Officer.

Mechlin is the prettiest of laces, fine, transparent, and effective. It is made in one piece, on the pillow, with various fancy stitches introduced. Its distinguishing feature is the flat thread which forms the flower, and gives to this lace the character of embroidery

---

[36] To afford an idea of the intrinsic value of Brussels lace, we give an estimate of the expense of a fine flounce (volant) of " vrai réseau mélangé" (point and plat), 12 metres long by 35 centimetres wide (13¼ yards by 14 inches):—

		Francs.
Cost of the plat		1885·75
Needle point		5000
Open work, "jours" (fonnage)		390
Appliqué (stricage)		800
Ground (réseau)		2782
Footing (engrélure)		1·27
	Total	10859·02 = 434l. 7s. 6d.

Equals 36l. 3s. 9d. the metre, and the selling price would be about 50l. 16s., which would make the flounces amount to 609l. 12s.

—hence it is sometimes called " broderie de Malines." [37]   It was
made at Mechlin, Antwerp, Lierre, and Turnhout, but the manufacture has long been on the decline.   Lately, however, it appears
to have partially revived.   Previous to 1665, as elsewhere stated,
the name was given to all pillow laces of which the pattern was
relieved by a flat thread.   It was only this that distinguished it
from Valenciennes.   When in the eighteenth century the réseau
ground was adopted, Malines still continued the bride also, which
was generally preferred, especially in France.[38]   According to
Savary, the laces of Ypres, Bruges, Dunkirk, and Courtrai, passed
at Paris under that name.[39]

The statute of Charles II. having placed a bar to the introduction of Flanders lace into England, Mechlin neither appears
in the advertisements nor inventories of the time.

We find mention of this lace in France as early as Anne of
Austria, who is described in the memoirs of Marion de l'Orme as
wearing a veil " en frizette de Malines." [40]   Again, the Maréchal
de la Motte, who died in 1627, has, noted in his inventory,[41] a
pair of Mechlin ruffles.

Regnard, who visited Flanders in 1681, writes from Mechlin :
" The common people here, as throughout all Flanders, occupy
themselves in making the white lace known as Malines, and the
Béguinage, the most considerable in the country, is supported by
the work of the Béguines, in which they excel greatly." [42]

When, in 1699, the English prohibition was removed, Mechlin
lace became the grand fashion, and continued so during the succeeding century.   Queen Mary anticipated the repeal by some
years, for, in 1694, she purchased two yards of knotted fringe for
her Mechlin ruffles,[43] which leads us to hope she had brought the
lace with her from Holland ; though, as early as 1699, we have

---

[37] " Une paire de manchettes de dentelle de Malines brodée.

" Quatre bonnets de nuit garnis de
Malines brodée."—*Inv. de decès de Mademoiselle de Charollais*, 1758.

[38] *Inv. de la Duchesse de Bourbon*,
1720.

" 1704. Deux fichus garnis de dentelle
de Malines à bride ou rézeau.

" Une cravatte avec les manchettes de
point de Malines à bride.

" Deux autres cravattes de dentelle de
Malines à rézeau et trois paires de man-

chettes de pareille dentelle."—*Inv. de
Franç. Phelypeaux Loisel.*   Bib. Nat.
MSS. F. Fr. 11,459.

[39] *Inv. de decès de Madame Anne,
Palatine de Bavière, Princesse de Condé,*
1723.   Arch. Nat. X. 10,065.

[40] In the accounts of Madame du
Barry, we have " Malines bâtarde à
bordure."

[41] See p. 25.

[42] " Voyage en Flandre," 1681.

[43] B. M. Add. MSS. No. 5751.

advertised in the "London Gazette," August 17th to 21st:—"Lost from Barker's coach, a deal box containing," among other articles, "a waistcoat and Holland shirt, both laced with Mecklin lace." Queen Anne purchased it largely; at least she paid in 1713[44] 247*l*. 6*s*. 9*d*. for eighty-three yards, either to one Margaret Jolly or one Francis Dobson, "Millenario Regali"—the Royal Milliner, as he styles himself. George I. indulges in a "Macklin" cravat.[45]

"It is impossible," says Savary, about this time, "to imagine how much Mechlin lace is annually purchased by France and Holland, and in England it has always held the highest favour."

Fig. 53.

Mechlin. End of eighteenth century.

Of the beau of 1727, it is said—

"Right Macklin must twist round his bosom and wrists;"

while Captain Figgins, of the 67th, a dandy of the first water, is described, like the naval puppy of Smollett in "Roderick Random," "his hair powdered with maréchal, a cambric shirt, his Malines lace dyed with coffee-grounds." Towards 1755 the fashion seems to have been on the decline in England. "All the town," writes Mr. Calderwood, "is full of convents; Mechlin lace is all made there; I saw a great deal, and very pretty and cheap. They talk of giving up the trade, as the English, upon whom they depended, have taken to the wearing of French blondes. The lace merchants

[44] Gr. Ward. Acc. P. R. O.   [45] Ibid.

employ the workers and all the town with lace.   Though they gain
but two-pence halfpenny daily, it is a good worker who will finish
a Flemish yard (28 inches) in a fortnight."

Mechlin is essentially a summer lace, not becoming in itself,
but charming when worn over colour (Fig. 53).   It found great
favour at the court of the Regent, as the inventories of the period
attest. Much of this lace, judging from these accounts, was made
in the style of the modern insertion, with an edging on both sides,

Fig. 54.

Mechlin.   Formerly belonging to Queen Charlotte.   End of eighteenth century.

" campané," and, being light in texture, was well adapted for the
gathered trimmings, later termed " quilles," [46] now better known
as " plissés à la vieille." [47]   Mechlin can never have been used as a
" dentelle de grande toilette ;" it served for coiffures de nuit,
garnitures de corset, ruffles, and cravats. [48]

---

[46] " On chamarre les jupes en quilles
de dentelles plissées."—*Mercure Galant,*
1678.

" Un volant dentelle d'Angleterre
plissée."—*Extraordinaire du Mercure,
Quartier d'Esté,* 1678.

[47] " 1741. Une coiffure de nuit de Malines à raizeau campanée de deux pieces.

" Une paire de manches de Malines

brodée à raizeau campanée, un tour de
gorge, et une garniture de corset."—*Inv.
de Mademoiselle de Clermont.*

" 1761. Une paire de manches de
Malines bridés non campanée, tour de
gorge, et garniture de corset."—*Inv. de
la Duchesse de Modène.*

[48] " 1720. Une garniture de teste à
trois pièces de dentelle de Malines à bride.

Lady Mary Wortley Montagu, describing an admirer, writes—

> "With eager beat his Mechlin cravat moves—
> He loves, I whisper to myself, he loves!"

It was the favourite lace of her late Majesty Queen Charlotte (Fig. 54) and of the Princess Amelia. Napoleon I. was also a great admirer of this fabric, and when he first saw the light Gothic tracery of the cathedral spire of Antwerp, he exclaimed, "C'est comme de la dentelle de Malines."

ANTWERP.

"At Antwerp, bought some ruffles of our agreeable landlady, and set out at 2 o'clock for Brussels."—*Tour*, by G. L. 1767.

Before finishing our account of the laces of Brabant, we must touch upon the produce of Antwerp, which, though little differing from that of the adjoining towns, seems at one time to have been known in the commercial world.[49] In the year 1560 we have no mention of lace among the fabrics of Antwerp, at that period already flourishing, unless it be classed under the head of "mercery, fine and rare."[50] The cap, however, of an Antwerp lady[51] of that period is decorated with fine lace of geometric pattern (Fig. 55). As early as 1698, the "Flying Postman" advertises as follows: "Yesterday, was dropped between the Mitre Tavern and the corner

"Deux peignoirs de toile d'Hollande garnis de dentelle, l'une d'Angleterre à bride et l'autre de Maline à raiseau."—*Inv. de la Duchesse de Bourbon.*

"1750. Une dormeuse de Malines."—*Inv. de Mademoiselle de Charollais.*

"1770. 5½ grande hauteur de Malines pour une paire de manchettes, 264 francs.

"1 au. jabot pour le tour de gorge, 16.

"5 au. ½ Malines pour garnir 3 chemises au nègre à 12 fr." (the wretch Zamor who denounced her).—*Comptes de Madame du Barry.*

"1788. 6 tayes d'oreiller garnies de Malines."—*Etat de ce qui a été fourni pour le renouvellement de Mgr. le Dauphin.* Arch. Nat. K. 505, No. 20.

"1792. 2 tayes d'oreillier garnis de maline."—*Notes du linge du ci-devant Roi.* Ibid. No. 8.

"1792. 24 fichus de batiste garnis de Maline.

"2 taye d'orilier garnis de Maline."—*Renouvellement de M. le Duc de Normandie.* Ibid.

[49] An arrêt, dated 14 Aug. 1688, requires that "toutes les dentelles de fil d'Anvers, Bruxelles, Malines et autres lieux de la Flandre Espagnolle," shall enter only by Rousselars and Condé, and pay a duty of 40 livres per lb. Arch. Nat. Coll. Rondoneau.

[50] In the list of foreign Protestants resident in England, 1618 to 1688, we find in London, Aldersgate Ward, Jacob Johnson, born at Antwerp, lace-maker, and Antony du Veal, lace-weaver, born in Turny (Tournay).

[51] This portrait has been engraved by Verbruggen, who gives it as that of Catherine of Aragon.

of Princes-street, five yards and better of Antwerp lace, pinner breadth. One guinea reward."

According to Savary, much lace without ground, "dentelle sans fond," a guipure of large flowers touching each other, was made in all the towns of Brabant for especial exportation to the Spanish Indies, where the "Gothic" taste continued in favour up to a very late period. These envoys were expedited first to Cadiz, and there disposed of. In 1696, we find in a seizure made by Monsieur de la Bellière, on the high seas, "2181 pieces de dentelles grossières à l'Espagnole assorties." [52]

Fig. 55.

A lady of Antwerp, ob. 1598. After Crispin de Passe.

Since the cessation of this Spanish market, Antwerp lace would have disappeared from the scene had it not been for the attachment evinced by the old people for one pattern, which has been worn on their caps from generation to generation, generally known by the name of "pot lace" (potten kant). It is made in the Béguinages of three qualities, mostly "fond double." The pattern has always a vase (Fig. 56), varied according to fancy.[53] Antwerp now makes Brussels lace.

---

[52] "Mercure Galant," 1696.

[53] The flower-pot was a symbol of the Annunciation. In the early representations of the appearance of the Angel Gabriel to the Virgin Mary, lilies are placed either in his hand or set as an accessory in a vase. As Romanism de-clined, the angel disappeared, and the lily pot became a vase of flowers; sub-sequently, the Virgin was omitted, and there remained only the vase of flowers. The "Potten" design is not peculiar to Antwerp lace.

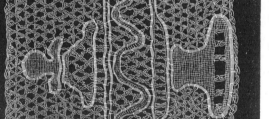

Fig. 56.

Antwerp pot lace. (Potten Kant.)

One of the earliest pattern books, that printed by Vorsterman [54]—the title in English—was published at Antwerp. There
is no date affixed to the title-page, but it only contains patterns
for Spanish stitch and other embroidery—no lace.

Turnhout, Antwerp, and Mechlin seem to have largely
manufactured lace up to the present century; as we find in 1803,
out of forty lace manufactories in the province, there were thirteen
at Antwerp, twelve at Turnhout, and nine at Malines.[55] Turnhout
now produces Mechlin.

FLANDERS (WEST).

The most important branch of the pillow lace trade in Belgium
is the manufacture of Valenciennes, which, having expired in its
native city, has now spread over East and West Flanders. The
art was originally imported into Flanders from French Hainault in
the seventeenth century. As early as 1656, Ypres began to make
Valenciennes lace. When, in 1684, a census was made by order
of Louis XIV., there were only three forewomen and sixty-three
lace-makers. In 1850, there were from 20,000 to 22,000 in Ypres
and its environs alone.

The productions of Ypres are of the finest quality and most
elaborate in their workmanship. On a piece not 2 inches wide,
from 200 to 300 bobbins are employed, and for the larger widths
as many as 800 or more are used on the same pillow.[56] The
ground is in large clear squares, which admirably throws up
the even tissue of the patterns.[57] In these there was little
variety until 1833, when a manufacturer [58] adopted a clear
wire ground with bold flowing designs (Fig. 57), instead of the
thick "treille"[59] and scanty flowers of the old laces. The change
was accepted by fashion, and the Valenciennes lace of Ypres

---

[54] See Appendix.

[55] " Tableau statistique du Dép. des
Deux-Nèthes, par le Citoyen Herbou-
ville. An X."=1802.

[56] In the International Exhibition of
1874, there were no less than 8000
bobbins on a Courtrai pillow used for
making a parasol cover.

[57] Ypres Valenciennes was exhibited, in
1867, at 80*l.* (the metre). The lace-maker,
working twelve hours a day, could scarcely
produce one-third of an inch a week. It

would take her twelve years to complete
a length of six or seven metres; her
daily earnings averaging two to three
francs. Ypres makes the widest Valenciennes of any manufacture except Courtrai, whence was exhibited a half-shawl
(pointe) of Valenciennes.

[58] M. Duhayon Brunfaut, of Ypres.

[59] " Treille" is the general term for the
ground (réseau) throughout Belgium and
the Dép. du Nord.

has now attained a high decree of perfection. Courtrai has made great advances towards rivalling Ypres in cheapness and quality.

Not a hundred years since, when the laces of Valenciennes prospered, those of Belgium were designated as "fausses Valenciennes." Belgium has now the monopoly to a commercial value of more than 800,000*l.*[60] The other principal centres of the manufacture are Bruges, Courtrai, and Menin, in West, Ghent and Alost, in East, Flanders. When Peuchet wrote in the last century, he cites "les dentelles à l'instar de Valenciennes" of Courtrai as being in favour, and generally sought after both in England and

Fig. 57.

Valenciennes lace of Ypres.

France, while those of Bruges are merely alluded to as "passing for Mechlin." From this it may be inferred the tide had not then flowed so far north. The Valenciennes of Bruges, from its round ground, has never enjoyed a high reputation. In forming the ground, the bobbins are only twisted twice, while in those of Ypres and Alost the operation is performed four and five times.[61] The oftener the bobbins are twisted the clearer and more esteemed is the Valenciennes.

The "guipure de Bruges," or "point duchesse," made at Bruges,

---

[60] France alone buys of Belgium more Valenciennes than all the other countries united; upwards of 12 millions of francs (480,000*l.*). Aubry.

[61] At Ghent two turns and a half, and at Courtrai three and a half. Each town has its own peculiar stitch.

is one of the prettiest laces imaginable. It is of a brilliant white, composed of pillow-made flowers united by " barrettes," or " brides à picot." It may be termed the Belgian Honiton, which lace it exactly resembles in workmanship. The patterns are larger, less delicate, and less firm, than those of the Devonshire product, but it is less costly. West Flanders has now a hundred and eighty manufactories and four hundred lace schools. Of these, 157 are the property of religious communities, and number upwards of 30,000 apprentices.[62]

FLANDERS (EAST).

No traveller has passed through the city of Ghent, for the last hundred years, without describing the Béguinage and its lace school. " The women," writes the author of the " Grand Tour," 1756, " number nigh 5000, go where they please, and employ their time in weaving lace."

Savary cites the " fausses Valenciennes," which he declares to equal the real in beauty. They are, continues he, " moins serrées, un peu moins solides, et un peu moins chères."

The best account, however, we have of the Ghent manufactures is contained in a letter addressed to Sir John Sinclair by Mr. Hey Schoulthem, in 1815. " The making of lace," he writes, " at the time the French entered the Low Countries, employed a considerable number of people of both sexes, and great activity prevailed in Ghent. The lace was chiefly for daily use; it was sold in Holland, France, and England. A large quantity of ' sorted ' laces of a peculiar quality were exported to Spain and the colonies. It is to be feared that, after an interruption of twenty years, this lucrative branch of commerce will be at an end: the changes of fashion have even reached the West Indian colonists, whose favourite ornaments once consisted of Flemish laces and fringes.[63] These laces were mostly manufactured in the charitable institutions for poor girls, and by old women whose eyes did not permit them to execute a finer work. As for the young girls, the quality of these Spanish laces, and the facility of their

---

[62] " L'Industrie dentellière belge, par B. v. d. Dussen. Bruxelles, 1860."

[63] Robinson Crusoe, when at Lisbon, sends " some Flanders lace of a good value," as a present to the wife and daughter of his partner in the Brazils.

execution, permitted the least skilful to work them with success, and proved a means of rendering them afterwards excellent work-women. At present, the best market for our laces is in France; a few also are sent to England." He continues to state that, since the interruption of the commerce with Spain, to which Ghent formerly belonged, the art has been replaced by a trade in cotton; but that cotton-weaving spoils the hand of the lace-makers, and, if continued, would end by annihilating the lace manufacture.[64]

Grammont and Enghien, ten years back, only manufactured cheap white thread lace, now entirely replaced by laces of black silk. The lace of Grammont of late years has greatly developed, but the lace has not the beauty of the French, the bobbins are more often twisted in making the ground, which deprives it of its elasticity, and the silk is weakened by the quantity of dye, which gives it a dull appearance. The quality of the silk is good, and the price much less than that of the Normandy manufacture. Grammont makes no small pieces, but shawls, dresses, &c., principally for the American market.

The lace industry of East Flanders is now most flourishing; it boasts 200 manufactories directed by the laity, and 450 schools under the superintendence of the nuns.

HAINAULT.

The laces of Mons and those once known as "les figures de Chimay," both in the early part of the eighteenth century, enjoyed a considerable reputation. The author, on visiting Chimay last year, could find no traces of the manufacture, beyond an aged lace-maker, an inmate of the hospice, who made black lace, "point de Paris;" and she said that, until within these last few years, Brussels lace has been also made at Chimay.

Binche was, as early as 1686, the subject of a royal edict, leading one to infer that the laces it produced were of some importance. In the said edict, the roads of Verviers, Gueuse, and Le Catelet, to those persons coming from Binche, are pro-nounced "faux passages." [65] Savary esteems the products of this

---

[64] "Answer to Sir John Sinclair," by Mr. H. Schoulthem, concerning the manu-factures of Ghent. 1815.   [65] Arch. Nat. Coll. Rondoneau.

little village. The same laces, he adds, are made in all the
" monastères " of the province, who are partly maintained by the
gains. The lace is good, equal to, if not surpassing, those
of Brabant and Flanders. It appears to have been " point
d'Angleterre," of which they had the reputation of making
finer pieces than Brussels or Bruges. Dentelle de Binche
was much in vogue in the last century. It is mentioned in the
inventory of the Duchesse de Modène,[66] daughter of the regent,
1761; and in that of Mademoiselle de Charollais, 1758, who has
a " couvrepied, mantelet, garniture de robe, jupon," &c., all of
the same lace. In the " Misérables " of Victor Hugo, the old
grandfather routs out from a cupboard " une ancienne garniture
de guipure de Binche," for Collette's wedding dress. M. Victor
Hugo told the author he had, in his younger days, seen Binche
guipure of great beauty. The Binche application flowers have
been already noticed.[67]

We have now named the great localities for lace-making
throughout the Low Countries. Some few yet remain unmen-
tioned.

Liége, in her days of ecclesiastical grandeur, carried on the
trade like the rest. We read, in 1620, of " English Jesuitesses at
Liège, who seem to care as much for politics as for lace-making."[68]

An early pattern book, that of Jean de Glen, a transcript of
Vinciolo, was published in that city in 1597. It bears the
mark of his printing press—three acorns with the motto, " Cuique
sua præmia," and is dedicated to Madame Loyse de Perez. He
concludes a complimentary dedication to the lady with the
lines :—

> " Madame, dont l'esprit modestement subtil,
> Vigoureux, se délecte en toutes choses belles,
> Prenez de bonne part ces nouvelles modelles
> Que vous offre la main de ce maistre gentil."

He states that he has travelled, and brought back from Italy some
patterns, without alluding to Vinciolo.

---

[66] " Une paire de manchettes de cour de dentelle de Binche ;
Trois paires de manchettes à trois rangs de dentelle de Binche ;
Deux fichus de mousseline bordées de dentelle de Binche ;
Deux devants de corps de dentelle de Binche."—Arch. Nat. X. 10,082.

[67] See page 94.

[68] Letter of Sir Henry Wotton to Lord Zouch. " State Papers, Domestic," Jas. I.
P. R. O.

"Dentelles de Liège, fines et grosses de toutes sortes," are mentioned with those of Lorraine and Du Comté (Franche-Comté) in the tariff fixed by a French edict of 18th September 1664.[69] Mrs. Calderwood, who visited Liége in 1756, admires the point edging to the surplices of the canons, which, she remarks, "have a very genteel appearance." The manufacture had declined at Liége, in 1802, when it is classed by the French Commissioners among the "fabriques moins considérables."

Some years since an establishment of "dentelle torchon" was established at Stavelot, near Spa. Upwards of a hundred children were then employed, and the manufacture flourished sufficiently to cause much irritation to the Belgian custom-house officers.

The lace products of St. Trond, in the province of Limburg, appear, by the report of the French commission of 1803, to have been of some importance. Lace, they say, is made at St. Trond, where from 800 to 900 are so employed, either at their own homes or in the workshops of the lace manufacturers. The laces resemble those of Brussels and Mechlin, and although they have a less reputation in commerce, several descriptions are made, and about 8000 metres are produced of laces of first quality, fetching from 12 to 14 francs the metre. These laces are chiefly made for exportation, and are sold mostly in Holland and at the Frankfort fairs.[70]

Within the last few years the immense development of the Belgian lace trade has overthrown the characteristic lace of each respective city. Lace, white and black, point and pillow, may at the present time be met with in every province of the now flourishing kingdom of Belgium.

---

[69] Arch. Nat. Coll. Rondoneau.
[70] "Statistique du Dép. de la Meuse-Inf., par le Citoyen Cavenne. An X."

CHAPTER VIII.

FRANCE TO LOUIS XIV.

" Il est une déesse inconstante, incommode,
　Bizarre dans ses goûts, folle en ses ornements,
　Qui paraît, fuit, revient, et renaît, en tout temps :
　Protée était son père, et son nom est la Mode."

Voltaire.

" To day the French
All clinquant, all in gold."

Shakespeare.

To the Italian influence of the sixteenth century France owes the fashion for points coupés and lace.[1] It was under the Valois and the Medicis that the luxury of embroidery, laces of gold, silver, and thread, attained its greatest height, and point coupé was as much worn at that epoch as were subsequently the laces of Italy and Flanders.

The ruff, or fraise, as it was termed, from its fancied resemblance to the caul[2] or frill of the calf, first adopted by Henry II.[3] to conceal a scar, continued in favour with his sons. The queen mother herself wore mourning from the day of the king's death ; no decoration, therefore, appears upon her wire-mounted ruff ;[4] but the fraises of her family and the " escadron volante " are profusely

---

[1] Italian fashions appeared early in France. Isabeau de Bavière, wearer of the Oriental " hennin," and Valentine de Milan, first introduced the rich tissues of Italy. Louis XI. sent for workmen from Milan, Venice, and Pistoia, to whom he granted various privileges, which Charles VIII. confirmed.

[2] In Ulpian Fulwell's " Interlude," 1568, Nichol Newfangle says—
" I learn to make gowns with long
　　sleeves and wings,
　I learn to make ruffs like calves'
　　chitterlings."

[3] " Collerettes et manchettes fraisés

firent leur première entrée dans le costume des hommes vers 1540."—*Quicherat, Histoire du Costume en France.*

[4] The queen was accused by her enemies of having, by the aid of Maître René, " empoisonneur en titre," terminated the life of Queen Jeanne de Navarre, in 1571, by a perfumed ruff (not gloves) (" Description de la Vie de Catherine de Medicis") ; and her favourite son, the Duke d'Alençon, was said, circa 1575, to have tried to suborn a valet to take away the life of his brother Henry, by scratching him in the back of his neck with a poisoned pin, when fastening his fraise.

trimmed with the geometric work of the period, and the making of lacis and point coupé, as before mentioned, was the favourite employment of her court. Catherine encouraged dress and extravagance, and sought by brilliant fêtes to turn people's minds from politics. In this she was little seconded either by her husband or gloomy son King Charles; but Henry III. and his "mignons frisés et fraisés" were tricked out in garments of the brightest colours, toques and toquets, pearls, earrings, and jewels. The ruff was the especial object of royal interest. With his own hand he used the poking-sticks and adjusted the plaits. "Gaudronneur des collets de sa femme" was the soubriquet bestowed on him by the satirists of the day.[5]

By 1579 the ruffs of the French court had attained such an outrageous size, "un tiers d'aulne"[6] in depth, that the wearers could scarcely turn their heads.[7] So absurd was the effect, the journalist of Henry III.[8] declares, "they looked like the head of John the Baptist in a charger."

Nor could they eat so encumbered. It is told how Reine Margot one day, when seated at dinner, was compelled to send for a spoon with a handle 2 feet in length wherewith to eat her soup.[9] These monstrosities, "so stiffened they cracked like paper,"[10] found little favour beyond the precincts of the Louvre. They were caricatured by the writers of the day; and in 1579 a band of students decked themselves out in large paper ruffs after the royal cut, and paraded the fair of St.-Germain, shouting, "A la fraise on connoit le veau." The king arrived unexpectedly, and sent them to prison for their impertinence.[11] Suddenly, in 1575, the fraise gave way to the "rabat," or turn-down collar, but both were worn alternately for some time. In vain

---

[5] "Satyre Menippée," Paris, 1593.

[6] "Chronologie novenaire," Vict. P. Cayet.

[7] "S'ils se tournoient, chacun se reculoit crainte de gater leurs fraizes."— *Satyre Menippée.*

" Le col ne se tourne à leur aise
Dans le long reply de leur fraise."
Vertus et Propriétés des Mignons, 1576.

[8] "Ces beaux mignons portoient . . . leurs fraizes de chemise de toute d'atour empesez et longues d'un demi-pied, de façon qu'à voir leurs testes dessus leurs fraizes, il sembloit que ce fut le chef de Saint-Jean dans un plat."—*Journal de Henri III., Pierre de l'Estoille.*

[9] "Perroniana," Cologne, 1691.

[10] "Goudronnées en tuyaux d'orgue, fraisées en choux crépus, et grandes comme des meules de moulin."—*Blaise de Viginière.*

"La fraize veaudelisée à six étages."
La Mode qui Court, Paris, N. D.

[11] "Appelez par les Espagnols 'lechuguillas,' ou petites laitues, à cause du rapport de ces gaudrons repliées avec les fraisures de la laitue."—*Histoire de la Ville de Paris, D. Mich. Félibien.*

I 2

were sumptuary edicts issued against luxury.[12]　The court set a
bad example; and in 1577, at the meeting of the states of Blois,
Henry wore on his own dress four thousand yards of pure gold
lace.　His successor, Henry IV., issued several fresh ordinances [13]
against " clinquants [14] et dorures."　Touching the last, Regnier,
the satirist, writers :—

> " A propos, on m'a dit
> Que contre les clinquants le roy faict un edict." [15]

Better still, the king tried the effect of example : he wore a
coat of grey cloth with a doublet of taffety, without either trimming
or lace—a piece of economy little appreciated by the public.　His
dress, says an author, " sentait des misères de la Ligue."　Sully,
anxious to emulate the simplicity of Louis XI., laughed at those
" qui portoient leurs moulins et leurs bois de haute futaie sur
leurs dos." [16]　" It is necessary," said he, " to rid ourselves of our
neighbours' goods, which deluge the country."　So he prohibited,
under pain of corporal punishment, any more dealings with the
Flemish merchants.

But edicts failed to put down point coupé; Reine Margot,
Madame Gabrielle, and Bassompierre were too strong for the
minister.

The wardrobe accounts of Henry's first queen are filled with
entries of point coupé and " passements à l'aiguille ; " [17] and though

---

[12] No less than ten were sent forth by
the Valois kings, from 1549 to 1583.

[13] These were dated 1594, 1600, 1601,
and 1606.

[14] Copper used instead of gold thread
for embroidery or lace.　The term was
equally applied to false silver thread.

"1582.　Dix escus pour dix aulnes de
gaze blanche rayée d'argent clinquant
pour faire ung voille à la Boullonnoise."—
Comptes de la Reine de Navarre.　Arch.
Nat. K. K. 170.

[15] Regnier, Math., "Ses Satyres," 1642.

[16] The observation was not new.　A
Remonstrance to Catherine de Medicis,
1586, complains that " leurs moulins,
leurs terres, leurs prez, leurs bois et leurs
revenuz, se coulent en broderies, pour-
filures, passemens, franges, tortis, cane-
tilles, recameurs, chenettes, picqueurs,
arrièrepoins etc. qu'on invente de jour à
autre."—*Discours sur l'extrême cherté etc.,*
presenté à la Mère du Roi, par un sien

fidelle Serviteur (Du Haillan), Bordeaux,
1586.

[17] " 1579.　Pour avoir remonsté trois
fraises à poinct couppé, 15 sols.

" Pour avoir monté cinq fraizes à poinct
couppé sur linomple, les avoir ourllés et
couzeus à la petite cordellière et au poinct
noué à raison de 30 sols pour chacune.

" Pour la façon de sept rabatz ourllés à
double arrièrepoinct et couzu le passement
au dessus.

" 1580.　Pour avoir faict d'ung mouchoir
ouvré deux rabats, 20 sols.

" Pour deux pieces de poinct couppé
pour servir à ladicte dame, vi livres.

" Pour dix huict aulnes de passement
blanc pour mestre à des fraizes a trois
escus l'aulne."

1582. The account for this year contains entries for " passement faict à les-
guille,"—" grand passement,"—" passement faict au mestier," &c.—*Comptes de*
la Reine de Navarre.　Arch. Nat.

Henry usually wore the silk-wrought shirts of the day,[18] we find in the inventory of his wife one entered as trimmed with cutwork.[19] Wraxall declares to have seen exhibited, at a booth on the Boulevart de Bondy, the shirt worn by Henry when assassinated. "It is ornamented," he writes, "with a broad lace round the collar and breast. The two wounds inflicted by the assassin's knife are plainly visible."[20]

In the inventory[21] made at the death of Madame Gabrielle, the fair Duchesse de Beaufort, we find entered sleeves and towels of point coupé, with fine handkerchiefs, gifts of the king to be worn at court, of such an extraordinary value that Henry requires them to be straightway restored to him. In the same list appears the duchess's bed of ivory,[22] with hangings for the room of réseuil.[23]

---

[18] "Vingt trois chemizes de toile fine à ouvrage de fil d'or et soye de plusieurs coulleurs, aux manchettes coulet et coutures.

"Ung chemize à ouvrage de soye noire.

"Quatre chemizes les trois à ouvrage d'or et d'argent et soye bleu."—*Inv. des meubles qui ont estés portés à Paris*, 1602. Arch. Nat.

[19] "1577. A Jehan Dupré, linger, demeurant à Paris, la somme de soixante douze livres tournois à luy ordonnée pour son payement de quatre layz d'ouvraige à poinct couppé pour faire une garniture de chemise pour servir à mon dict segneur, à raison de 18 liv. chacune."—*Comptes de la Reine de Navarre*. Arch. Nat. K. K. 162, fol. 655.

[20] "This shirt," he adds, "is well attested. It became the perquisite of the king's first valet de chambre. At the extinction of his descendants, it was exposed to sale."—*Memoirs*.

A rival shirt has lately turned up at Madame Tussaud's, with "the real blood" still visible. Monsieur Curtius, uncle of Madame Tussaud, purchased it at an auction of effects once the property of Cardinal Mazarin. Charles X. offered 200 guineas for it.

[21] "Item, cinq mouchoirs d'ouvrages d'or, d'argent et soye, prisez ensemble cent escuz.

"Item, deux tauayelles aussi ouvrage d'or, d'argent et soye, prisées cent escuz.

"Item, trois tauayelles blanches de rezeuil, prisées ensemble trente escuz.

"Item, une paire de manches de point coupé et enrichies d'argent, prisez vingt escuz.

"Item, deux mouchoirs blancz de point coupé, prisez ensemble vingt escuz.

"Toutes lesquelles tauayelles et mouchoirs cy dessus trouvez dans un coffre de bahu que la dicte defunte dame faisoit ordinairement porter avec elle à la court sont demeurez entre les mains du Sr de Beringhen, suivant le commandement qu'il en avoit de sa majesté pour les representer à icelle, ce qu'il a promis de faire."—*Inventaire apres le decès de Gabrielle d'Estrées*, 1509. Arch. Nat. K. K. 157, fol. 17.

[22] "Item, un lit d'yvoire à filletz noirs de Padoue, garny de son estuy de cuir rouge."—*Ibid.*

[23] "Item, une autre tenture de cabinet de carré de rezeau brodurée et montans recouvert de feuillages de fil avec des carrez de thoile plaine, prisé et estimé la somme de cent escus Soleil.

"Item, dix sept carrez de thoile de Hollande en broderie d'or et d'argent fait a deux endroictz, prisez et estimez à 85 escus.

"Item, un autre pavillon tout de rezeil avec le chapiteau de fleurs et feuillages. . . . .

"Item, un autre en neuf fait par carrez de point coupé."—*Ibid.* fols. 46 and 47.

The Chancellor Herault,[24] who died at the same period, was equally extravagant in his habits, while the shirts of the combatants in the duel between M. de Crequy and Don Philippe de Savoie (1598) are specially vaunted as " toutes garnies du plus fin et du plus riche point coupé qu'on eust pu trouver dans ce temps là, auquel le point de Gennes et de Flandres n'estoient pas en usage." [25]

The enormous wire-mounted collerette, rising behind her head like a fan, of Mary de Medicis, with its edgings of fine lace, are well known to the admirers of Rubens :—

> " Cinq colets de dentelle haute de demy-piè
> L'un sur l'autre montez, qni ne vont qu'à moitié
> De celuy de dessus, car elle n'est pas leste,
> Si le premier ne passe une paulme la teste." [26]

On the accession of Louis XIII. (1610) luxury knew no bounds. The queen regent was magnificent by nature, while Richelieu, anxious to hasten the ruin of the nobles, artfully encouraged their prodigality. But Mary was compelled to repress this taste for dress. The courtiers importuned her to increase their pensions, no longer sufficient for the exigencies of the day. The queen, at her wits' end, published in 1613 a "Réglement pour les superfluités des habits," prohibiting all lace and embroidery.[27]

France had early sent out books of patterns for cutwork and embroidery. That of Francisque Pelegrin was published at Paris in the reign of Francis I.

Six were printed at Lyons alone. The four earlier have no date,[28] the two others bear those of 1549 [29] and 1585.[30] It was to these first that Vinciolo so contemptuously alludes in his dedication " Aux Benevolles Lecteurs," saying, " Si les premiers ouvrages que vous avez vus ont engendré quelque fruit et utilité je m'assure que les miens en produiront davantage." Various editions of

---

[24] " Manchettes et collets enrichys de point couppé."—*Inventaire apres le decès de Messire Philippe Herault, Comte de Cheverny, Chancelier de France,* 1599. Bib. Nat. MSS. F. Fr. 11,424.

[25] Vulson de la Colombière, " Vray Théâtre d'Honneur et de Chevalerie," 1647.

[26] " Satyrique de la Cour," 1613.

[27] " Histoire de la Mère et du Fils," from 1616–19. Amsterdam, 1729.

[28] "Livre nouveau dict Patrons de Lingerie," &c.
" Patrons de diverses Manières," &c. (Title in rhyme.)
" S'ensuyvent les Patrons de Mesire Antoine Belin."
" Ce Livre est plaisant et utile." (Title in rhyme.)

[29] " La Fleur des Patrons de Lingerie."

[30] " Tresor des Patrons," J. Ostons.

Vinciolo were printed at Paris from 1587 to 1623; the earlier dedicated to Queen Louise de Lorraine; a second to Catherine de Bourbon, sister of Henry IV.; the last to Anne of Austria.

The "Pratique de Leguille de Milour M. Mignerak" was published by the same printer, 1605; and we have another work, termed "Bèle Prerie," also printed at Paris, bearing date 1601.[31]

Fig. 58.

Cinq-Mars.   After his portrait by Lenain.   Musée Nationale, Versailles.

The points of Italy and Flanders now first appear at court, and the church soon adopted the prevailing taste for the decoration of her altars and her prelates.[32]

The ruff, now discarded, is replaced by the "col rabattu," or "rabat," with its deep-scalloped border of point.   The "manchettes

---

[31] "Le Livre de Moresques" (1546), "Livre de Lingerie," Dom. de Sera (1584), and "Patrons pour Brodeurs," (no date), were also printed at Paris.

The last book on this kind of work printed at Paris is styled, "Méthode pour faire des Desseins avec des Carreaux," &c., by Père Dominique Donat, religieux carme. 1722.

[32] A point de Venice alb, said to be of this period, point rose, is preserved in the Musée de Cluny.

à revers" are trimmed in the same manner, and the fashion even extends to the tops of the boots.

Of these lace-trimmed boots, the favourite, Cinq-Mars, left three hundred pairs at his death (1642). From his portrait, after Lenain, which hangs in the National Gallery of Versailles, we give one of these boots (Fig. 58), and his rich collerette or falling collar of Italian point (Fig. 59).

The garters, now worn like a scarf round the knee, have the ends adorned with point.

Fig. 59.

Cinq-Mars. After his portrait by Lenain. Musée Nationale, Versailles.

A large rosette of lace completes the costume of the epoch (Fig. 60).

Gold lace shared the favour of the thread fabric on gloves,[33] garters, and shoes.[34]

---

[33]   "Quelques autres de frangez
        Bordent leur riche cuir, qui vient des lieux estranges."
                    Le Gan, de Jean Godard, Parisien, 1588.

[34] "1619. Deux paires de rozes à soulliers garnies de dentelle d'or."—*Inv. de Madame Sœur du Roi* (Henrietta Maria). Arch. Nat.

" De large taftas la jartière parée
Aux bouts de demy-pied de dentelle dorée." [35]

The cuffs, collars of the ladies either falling back or rising
behind their shoulders in double tier, caps, aprons descending to
their feet (Fig. 61), are also richly decorated with lace.

Fig. 60.

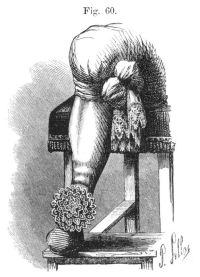

Lace rose and garter. After Abraham Bosse.

Fig. 61.

Young lady's apron, time of Henry III. After Gaignières. Bib. Nat. Grav.

The contemporary engravings of Abraham Bosse and Callot
faithfully portray the fashions of this reign.

---

[35] " Satyrique de la Court."

In the "Prodigal Son," of Abraham Bosse, the mother, waiting his return, holds out to her repentant boy a collar trimmed with the richest point. The "Foolish Virgins" weep in lace-trimmed handkerchiefs, and the table-cloth of the rich man, as well as his dinner napkins, are similarly adorned. Again, the "Accouchée" recovers in a cap of Italian point under a coverlet of the same. At the "Retour de Baptême," point adorns the christening dress of the child and the surplice of the priest.

When, in 1615, Louis XIII. married, Anne of Austria discarded the collerettes of the mother queen—the reign of Italy was at an end—all was now à l'espagnole and the court of Castile.

The prodigality of the nobles [36] having called down royal ordinances on their heads, [37] these new edicts bring forth fresh satires, in which the author deplores the prohibitian of cutwork and lace :—

> "Ces points couppez, passemens et dentelles,
> Las! qui venaient de l'Isle et de Bruxelles,
> Sont maintenant descriez, avilis,
> Et sans faveur gisent ensevelis ;" [38]

but

> "Pour vivre heureux et à la mode
> Il faut que chacun accommode
> Ses habits aux editz du roi."

Edict now follows on edict.[39]   One known as the Code

---

[36] The inventory of the unfortunate Maréchal de Marillac, beheaded 1632, has "broderye et poinctz d'Espagnes d'or, argent et soye; rabats et collets de point couppé ; taffetas nacarat garnye de dantelle d'argent; pourpoinct passementé de dantelle de canetille de Flandre," &c. Bib. Nat. MSS. F. Fr. 11,426.

[37] 1620. Feb. 8. "Déclaration portant deffenses de porter des clinquants, passements, broderies," &c. Arch. Nat. G. G. G.

1623. March 20. "Déclaration qui defend l'usage des étoffes d'or," &c.— Recueil des anciennes Lois Françaises, tome xvi. 107.

1625. Sept. 30. "Déclaration" prohibits the wearing "tant en collets, fraizes, manchettes, et autres linges des passements, Point coupez et Dantelles, comme aussi des Broderies et Decoupures surquintin ou autre toille." Bib. Nat. L. i. 8.

[38] "Consolation des Dames sur la Reformation des passemens," 1620.

[39] Again, 1633, Nov. 18, "Déclaration" restricts the prohibition ; permits "passements manufacturés dans le royaume qui n'excederont 9 ll. l'aune." Arch. Nat. G. G. G.

1634. May 30. "Lettres patentes pour la reformation du luxe des habits " prohibits "dentelles, passements et broderies " on boots, carriages, &c. British Museum.

1636. April 3. "Déclaration contre le Luxe." Again prohibits both foreign and home-made points coupés, &c., under pain of banishment for five years, confiscation, and a fine of 6000 francs. De la Mare, " Traité de la Police."

1639. Nov. 24. Fresh prohibition, points de Gênes specially mentioned. Not to wear on the collar, cuffs, or boots, " autres choses que de la toile simple sans aucune façon." Arch. Nat. G. G. G.

Michaud, entering into the most minute regulations for the toilet, especially excited the risibility of the people. It was never carried out. The caricatures of this period are admirable: one represents a young cavalier fresh rigged in his plain-bordered linen, according to the ordinance, eyeing with a look of despair a box of discarded laces:—[40]

> " Il me semble pourtant à mes yeux
> Qu'avec de l'or et la dantelle
> Je m'ajuste encore bien mieux."

Alluding to the plain-bordered collars, now ordered by the prohibition of 1639, the " Satyrique de la Court " sings:—

> " Naguères l'on n'osoit hanter les damoiselles
> Que l'on n'eust le colet bien garni de dentelles ;
> Maintenant on se rit et se moque de ceux là
> Qui desirent encore paroistre avec cela.
> Les fraises et colets à bord sont en usage,
> Sans faire mention de tous en dentellage."

France at this time paying large sums to Italy and Flanders for lace, the wearing of it is altogether prohibited, under pain of confiscation and a fine of 6000 livres.[41] The queen mother, regardless of edicts, has over passements d'or and all sorts of forbidden articles, "pour servir à la layette que sa majesté a envoyé en Angleterre."[42] Within scarce one year of each other passed away Marie de Medicis, Richelieu, and Louis XIII. The king's effigy was exposed on its "lit de parade vêtue d'une chemise de toile de Hollande avec de tres belles dantelles de point de Gennes au collet et aux manches."[43] So say the chroniclers.

---

[40] " Le Courtisan Reformé, suivant l'Edit de l'année 1633 ;" and again, " Le Jardin de la Noblesse Françoise dans lequel ce peut cueillir leur manière de Vettement," 1629.

[41] April 1636.

[42] 1631. " Trésorerie de la Reine Marie de Médicis." Arch. Nat. K. K. 191.

[43] Vulson de la Colombière, " Pompes qu'on pratique aux obsèques des Rois de France."

CHAPTER IX.

LOUIS XIV.

THE courtiers of the regency under Anne of Austria vied with the Frondeurs in extravagance. The latter, however, had the best of it.

"La Fronde," writes Joly, "devint tellement à la mode qu'il n'y avoit rien de bien fait qu'on ne dist être de la Fronde. Les étoffes, les dentelles etc., jusqu'au pain,—rien n'estoit ni bon, ni bien si n'estoit à la Fronde." [1]

Nor was the queen regent herself less profuse in her indulgence in lace. She is represented in her portraits with a berthe of rich point, her beautiful hand encircled by a double-scalloped cuff (Fig. 62).

The boot-tops had now reached an extravagant size. One writer compares them to the farthingales of the ladies, another to an inverted torch. The lords of the regent's court filled up the apertures with two or three rows of Genoa point (Fig. 63).

In 1653, we find Mazarin, while engaged in the siege of a city, holding a grave correspondence with his secretary Colbert concerning the purchase of some points from Flanders, Venice, and Genoa. He considers it advisable to advance thirty or forty thousand livres "à ces achapts," adding that by making the purchases in time he will derive great advantage in the price, but as he hopes the siege will soon be at an end, they may wait his arrival at Paris for his final decision. [2] Colbert again writes, November 25, pressing his eminence on account of the "quantité de mariages qui se feront l'hyver."

A passage in Tallemant des Réaux would lead one to suppose these laces were destined as patterns for the improvement of

---

[1] "Mémoirs de Guy Joly," from 1648–65.

[2] Dated 19 Nov. 1653. The letter is

given in full by Comte de Laborde "Le Palais Mazarin," Paris, 1845.

French manufactures, " per mostra di farne in Francia," as the
cardinal expressed himself.

Fig. 62.

Anne of Austria. Musée Nationale, Versailles.

Fig. 63.

A courtier of the regency. After Abraham Bosse.

Certainly in the inventory of Mazarin [3] there is no mention

---

[3] "Inv. fait apres la mort du Cardinal Mazarin," 1661. Bibl. Nat. MSS. Suite
de Mortmart, 37.

of Italian points, no lace coverlets to his "Lict d'ange moire tabizée, couleur de rose, chamarrée de dentelles d'or et d'argent."

We may almost imagine that the minister and his secretary combined were already meditating the establishment of Points de France.

In this reign, fresh sumptuary ordinances are issued. That of 27th November 1660 is the most important of all,[4] and is highly commended by Sganarelle in the "École des Maris" of Molière, which appeared the following year :—

> " Oh ! trois et quatre fois soit béni cet édit,
> Par qui des vêtemens le luxe est interdit ;
> Les peines des maris ne seront pas si grandes,
> Et les femmes auront un frein à leurs demandes.
> Oh ! que je sais au roi bon gré de ses décrets ;
> Et que, pour le repos de ces mêmes maris,
> Je voudrais bien qu'on fît de la coquetterie
> Comme de la guipure et de la broderie."

This ordinance, after prohibiting all foreign "passemens, dentelles, points de Gênes, points coupés," &c., or any French laces or passements exceeding an inch in width, allows the use of the "collerettes" and "manchettes" persons already possess for the space of one year, after which period they are only to be trimmed with a lace made in the kingdom, not exceeding an inch in width.

The ordinance then goes on to attack the "canons,"[5] which, it states, have been introduced into the kingdom with "un excès de dépense insupportable, par la quantité de passemens, points de Venise et Gênes," with which they are loaded. The use of them is now entirely prohibited, unless made of plain linen or of the same stuff as the coat, without lace or any ornament.

The lace-trimmed canons of Louis XIV., as represented in the picture of his interview with Philip IV., in the Island of

---

[4] It is to be found at the Archives Nat. or in the Library of the Cour de Cassation. In the Archives Nat. is a small collection of ordinances relative to lace collected by M. Rondoneau, extending from 1666 to 1773. It is very difficult to get at all the ordinances. Many are printed in De la Mare (" Traité de la Police"); but the most complete work is the "Recueil général des anciennes Lois françaises, depuis l'an 420 jusqu'à la Révolution de 1789," par MM. Isambert, Ducrusy et Taillandier. Paris, 1829. The ordinances bear two dates, that of their issue and of their registry.

[5] The " bas à bottes," afterwards called "canon," was a circle of linen or other stuff fastened below the knee, widening at the bottom so as to fill the enlargement of the boot, and, when trimmed with lace, having the appearance of a ruffle.

Fig. 64.

Louis XIV. Musée Nationale, Versailles.

To face page 127.

Pheasants, previous to his marriage, 1660 (Fig. 64), give a good idea of these extravagant appendages. These

> "Canons à trois étages
> A leurs jambes faisoient d'ombrages;"[6]

and, what was worse, they would cost 7000 livres a pair.

"At the court of France," writes Savinière, "people think nothing of buying rabats, manchettes, or canons, to the value of 13,000 crowns."[7]

These canons with their accompanying rheingraves,[8] which after the prohibition of Venice point were adorned with the new productions of France, suddenly disappeared. In 1682, the "Mercure" announces, "Les canons and les rheingraves deviennent tout à fait hors de mode."

At the marriage of the young king with the infanta, 1660, black lace,[9] probably in compliment to the Spanish court,[10] came into favour, the nobles of the king's suite wearing doublets of gold and silver brocade, "ornés," says the "Chronique,"[11] "de dentelles noires d'un point recherché."[12] The same writer, describing the noviciate of La Vallière at the Carmelites, writes, "Les dames portoient des robes de brocard d'or, d'argent ou d'azur, par dessus

---

[6] "Dictionnaire des Précieuses," 1660. Molière likewise ridicules them:
"Et de ces grands canons, où, comme des entraves,
On met tous les matins les deux jambes esclaves."
  L'École des Maris.
And again, in *L'École des Femmes:*
"Ils ont de grands canons, force rubans et plumes."

[7] "Les Délices de la France, par M. Savinière d'Alquie," 1670.

[8] The petticoat-shaped garment, fastened round the knee with a drawing string, as worn in the time of Charles II.

[9] The fashion of wearing black lace was introduced into England in the reign of Charles II. "Anon the house grew full, and the candles lit, and it was a glorious sight to see our Mistress Stewart in black and white lace, and her head and shoulders dressed with diamonds."—*Pepys' Diary.*
"The French have increased among us

many considerable trades, such as black and white lace."—*England's Great Happiness, &c.* Dialogue between Content and Complaint. 1677.
"Item, un autre habit de grosse moire garny de dantelle d'Angleterre noire."—*Inv. de Madame de Simiane,* 1691. Arch. Nat. M. M. 802.

[10] Of this custom a relic may still be found at the court of Turin, where ladies wear lappets of black lace. Not many years since, the wife of a Russian minister, persisting to appear in a suit of Brussels point, was courteously requested by the grand chamberlain to retire.

[11] "Chroniques de l'Œil-de-Bœuf."

[12] Madame de Motteville is not complimentary to the ladies of the Spanish court: "Elles avoient peu de linge," she writes, "et leurs dentelles nous parurent laides."—*Mémoires pour servir à l'histoire d'Anne d'Autriche.*

lesquelles elles avoient jetées d'autre robes et dentelles noires transparentes."[13] Under Louis XIV., the gold and silver points of Spain and Aurillac rivalled in fashion the thread manufactures of Flanders and Italy, but towards the close of the century,[14] we are informed, they have fallen into the "domaine du vulgaire."

The ordinance of 1660 had but little effect, for various others are issued in the following years, with the oft repeated prohibitions of the points of Genoa and Venice.[15] But edicts were of little avail. No royal command could compel people to substitute the laces of France[16] for the artistic productions of her sister countries. Colbert, therefore, wisely adopted another expedient. He determined to develop the lace manufacture in France, and to produce fabrics which should rival the coveted points of Italy and Flanders, so that if fortunes were lavished upon these luxuries, the money, at all events, should not be sent out of the kingdom to procure them.

By his order were suborned from Venice and the Low Countries a number of the most skilful workwomen, whom he distributed among the manufactories already existing, and in towns where he established new ones.

A declaration of the 5th August 1665 orders the establishment in the towns of Du Quesnoy, Arras, Rheims, Sedan, Château-Thierry, Loudun, Alençon, Aurillac, and others in the kingdom, of the manufacture of all sorts of works of thread, as well of the needle as on the pillow, in the manner of the points which are made at Venice, Genoa, Ragusa, and in other foreign countries, which shall be called "points de France."[17] An exclusive privilege is given for ten years, and a grant of 36,000 francs. A company was

---

[13] Madame de Sévigné mentions these dresses : " Avez-vous ouï parler des transparens ? . . . de robes noires transparentes ou des belles dentelles d'Angleterre?"—*Lettres.* Transparents were light tissues upon which were applied flowers and foliage painted by hand.

[14] 1690. " Chron. de l'Œil-de-Bœuf."

[15] 1661, May 27 ; 1662, Jan. 1 ; 1664, May 31, Sept. 18, and Dec. 12.

[16] "On fabriquait précédement ces espèces de dentelles guipures, dont nous voyont encore quelques restes, et dont on ornait les aubes des prêtres, les rochets des évêques et les jupons des femmes de qualité."—*Roland de la Platière.* The

articles on lace by Roland and Savary have been copied by all succeeding writers on the subject.

[17] We have in vain sought for this ordinance in the Library of the Cour de Cassation, where it is stated to be by the authors of the " Recueil des Lois françaises," but fortunately it is recited in a subsequent arrêt, dated 12 October 1666 (Arch. Nat. Coll. Rondoneau), by which it appears that the declaration ordered the establishment, in "les villes du Quesnoy, Arras, Reims, Sedan, Château-Thierry, Loudun, Alençon, Aurillac, et autres du royaume, de la manufacture de toutes sortes d'ouvrages de fil,

formed,[18] its members rapidly increased, and in 1668 the capital amounted to 22,000 livres. Eight directors were appointed, at salaries of 12,000 livres a year, to conduct the manufacture, and the company held its sittings in the Hôtel de Beaufort at Paris. The first distribution of profits took place in October 1669, amounting to 50 per cent. upon each share. In 1670, a fresh distribution took place, and 120,000 livres were divided among the shareholders. That of 1673 was still more considerable. In 1675, the ten years' privilege ceased, the money was returned, and the rest of the profits divided. Colbert likewise set up a manufactory at the Château de Madrid, built by Francis I., in the Bois de Boulogne. Such was the origin of point lace in France.

The difficulties met by Colbert in establishing his manufactories can only be estimated by reading his correspondence; in which there are not less than fifty letters[19] on the subject. The apathy of the town authorities and the constant rebellions of the lace-workers, who preferred their old stitch, were incessant sources of trouble to him, but eventually Colbert's plan was crowned with success. He established a lucrative manufacture, which brought large sums of money into the kingdom,[20] instead

---

tant à l'éguille qu'au coussin, en la manière des points qui se font à Venise, Gennes, Raguse et autres pays estrangers, qui seroient appellés points de France." In a subsequent arrêt (15 Oct. 1666) it is set forth that the entrepreneurs have caused to be brought in great numbers the best workers from Venice and other foreign cities, and have distributed them over the above-mentioned towns, and "qu'au moyen de l'application que l'on y a portée, il se fasse en France des ouvrages de fil si exquis, qu'ils esgellent, mesme surpassent en beauté les estrangers." Bibl. de la Cour de Cassation.

[18] Talon, "secrétaire du cabinet," was one of the first members.

We find by an arrêt, 15 Feb. 1667, that this patent had already been infringed. On the petition of Jean Pluymers, Paul, and Catherine de Marcq, "entrepreneurs de la Manufacture Royalle de toutes sortes de points de fil," that notwithstanding the prohibition of previous arrêts, the merchants continue to sell and

many to wear, "par une license qui ne peut étre permise," other points, old or new, than those made in the royal manufactory, the king renews the prohibition. Arch. Nat. Coll. Rondoneau.—Nov. 17 of the same year appears a fresh prohibition of wearing or selling the passements, lace, and other works in thread of Venice, Genoa, and other foreign countries (British Museum), and, 17 March 1668, "Itératives" prohibitions to wear these, either new or "commencé d'user," as injurious to a manufacture of point which gives subsistence to a number of persons in the kingdom. Ibid.—Again, 19 Aug. 1669, a fresh arrêt in consequence of complaints that the workers are suborned and work concealed in Paris, &c. Arch. Nat. Coll. Rondoneau.

[19] See "Correspondance administrative de Colbert," published by Depping.

[20] Colbert said to Louis XIV.: "There will always be found fools enough to purchase the manufactures of France, though France should be prohibited

of sending it out.   Well might he say that "Fashion was to
France what the mines of Peru were to Spain."[21]

Boileau alludes to the success of the minister in his "Epistle
to Louis XIV.":—

> "Et nos voisins frustrés de ces tributs serviles
> Que payait à leur art le luxe de nos villes."

The point de France supplanted those of Venice and Flanders;
but its price confined its use to the rich, and when the wearing of
lace became general, those who could not afford so costly a
production replaced it by the more moderate pillow lace.   This
explains the great extension of the pillow-lace manufacture at
this period—the production did not suffice for the demand.
Encouraged by the success of the royal manufactures, lace manufactories started up in various towns of the kingdom.   The number
of lace-workers increased rapidly: those of the towns being in-
sufficient, they were sought for in the surrounding country, and
each town became the centre of a trade extending round it in a
radius of several miles; the work being given out from the
manufactory to be executed by the cottagers in their own homes.[22]

---

from purchasing those of other countries.'   The king agreed with the minister, whom he made chief director of
the trade and manufactures of the
kingdom.

[21] A favourite saying of Colbert.

[22] "Rapport sur les Dentelles fait à la
Commission française de l'Exposition
Universelle de Londres, 1851."   Felix
Aubry.   One of the best histories of lace
published.

Fig. 65.

Le Grand Bébé. Musée Nationale, Versailles.

To face page 131.

CHAPTER X.

LOUIS XIV. (*continued*).

"Tout change : la raison change aussi de méthode ;
Écrits, habillemens, systèmes : tout est mode."
Racine fils, Épître à Rousseau.

THE point de France continued to be worn in the greatest
profusion during the reign of Louis XIV. The king affected his
new-born fabric much as monarchs of the present day do their
tapestries and their porcelains. It decorated the church and her
ministers. Ladies offered "tours de chaire à l'église de la
paroisse."[1] Albs, "garnies d'un grand point de France brodé
antique;"[2] altar-cloths, trimmed with Argentan,[3] appear in the
church registers.[4] In a painting at Versailles, by old Watteau,
representing the presentation of the grand dauphin to his royal
father, 1668, the infant is enveloped in a mantle of the richest
point (Fig. 65); and point de France was selected by royal
command to trim the sheets of holland used at the ceremony of
his "nomination."[5] At the marriages both of the Prince de
Conti and of Mademoiselle de Blois the toilette[6] presented by
the king was " garnie de point de France si haut qu'on ne voyait

---

[1] "Deux tours de chaire de point de France donnez depuis quelques années par deux dames de la paroisse."—*Inv. de l'église de Saint-Merry, à Paris.* Arch. Nat. L. L. 859.

[2] "Inv. de Madame Anne Palatine de Bavière, Princesse de Condé." Ibid. X. 10,065.

[3] "Inv. de l'église de Saint-Gervais, à Paris." Ibid. L. L. 854.

[4] The saints, too, came in for their share of the booty.

"There was St. Winifred," writes a traveller of the day, " in a point commode with a large scarf on and a loup in hand, as tho' she were going to mass. St.

Denis, with a laced hat and embroidered coat and sash, like a captain of the guards."—*Six Weeks of France,* 1691.

[5] "Toille de Hollande, avec des grands points de France."—*Le Cérémonial de la Nomination de Monseigneur le Dauphin,* 1668. Arch. Nat. K. K. 1431.

[6] "Le Mercure Galant," Juillet 1688. This periodical, which we shall have occasion so frequently to quote, was begun in 1672, and continued to July 1716. It comprises, with the "Extraordinaires," 571 vols. in 12mo.

"Le Mercure de France," from 1717 to 1792, consists of 777 vols. Brunet, "Manuel du Libraire."

K 2

point de toile." [7] The valance, too, and coverlet of the bed were
of the same material—wedding presents to his daughter and her
cousins from their royal father. [8]

In this luxury, however, England followed her sister kingdom ;
for we read in the " Royal Magazine " of 1763 that on the baptism
of the young prince, afterwards Duke of York, the company
went to the council chamber at St. James's, where a splendid bed
was set up for the queen to sit on, the counterpane of which is
described as of inimitable workmanship, the lace alone costing
3783*l*. sterling. [9] " What princes do themselves, they engage
others to do," says Quintilian, and the words of the critic were,
in this case, fully verified : jupes, [10] corsets, mantles, aprons with
their bibs, [11] shoes, [12] gloves, [13] even the fans were now trimmed
with point de France. [14]

At the audience given by the dauphine to the Siamese ambassadors, " à ses relevailles," she received them in a bed " presque
tout couvert d'un tres beau Point de France, sur lesquels on avoit
mis des riches carreaux." [15] On the occasion of their visit to
Versailles, Louis, proud of his fabric, presented the ambassadors

---

[7] " Le Mercure Galant."

[8] It was the custom, at the birth of a
dauphin, for the papal nuncio to go to
the palace and present to the new-born
child " les langes benites, ' or consecrated
layette, on behalf of his holiness the
Pope. The shirts, handkerchiefs, and
other linen, were by half-dozens, and
trimmed with the richest point. This
custom dates as early as the birth of
Louis XIII. Mercier describes the ceremony of carrying the layette to Versailles
in the time of Louis XV. " Vie du Dauphin, père de Louis XVI." Paris, 1858.

[9] In the Lancaster state bedroom, at
Fonthill, was sold in 1823: " A state
bed quilt of Brussels point, for 100
guineas, and a Brussels toilet cover, for
30 guineas."—*Fonthill Sale Catalogue.*

" 1694. Une toilette de satin violet
picquée garny d'un point d'Espagne d'or
à deux carreaux de mesme satin et aussi
piqué.'—*Inv. de Mgr. de la Vrillière,
Patriarche, Archevêque de Bourges.* Bib.
Nat.

" 1743. Une toilette et son bonhomme
garnie d'une vieille dentelle d'Angle-

terre."—*Inv. de la Duchesse de Bourbon.*

" 2758. Une toilette avec sa touaille
de point fort vieux d'Alençon."—*Inv. de
Mademoiselle de Charollais.*

" 1770. Une tres belle toilette de
point d'Argentan, et son surtout de 9000
livres.

" Une tres belle toilette d'Angleterre,
et son surtout de 9000."—*Cptes. de Madame du Barry.*

[10] " On voit toujours des jupes de point
de France."—*Mercure Galant,* 1686.

" Corsettes chamarrés de point de
France."—*Ibid.*

[11] Madame de Sévigné describes Mademoiselle de Blois as " belle comme un
ange," with " un tablier et une bavette
de point de France."—*Lettres.* Paris
27 Jan. 1674.

[12] " Garnis de point de France formant
une manière de rose antique."—*Mercure
Galant,* 1677.

[13] In the " Extraordinaire du Mercure"
for 1678, we have, in " habit d'este,"
gloves of " point d'Angleterre.

[14] " Mercure Galant," 1672.

[15] Ibid. 1686.

with cravats and ruffles of the finest point.[16] These cravats were either worn of point, in one piece, or partly of muslin tied, with falling lace ends [17] (Fig. 66).

In 1679, the king gave a fête at Marly to the élite of his brilliant court: when, at sunset, the ladies retired to repair their toilettes, previous to the ball, each found in her dressing-room a robe fresh and elegant, trimmed with point of the most exquisite texture, a present from that gallant monarch not yet termed " l'inamusable."

Nor was the Veuve Scarron behind the rest. When, in 1674, she purchased the estate from which she afterwards derived her

Fig. 66.

Louvois. 1691. From his statue by Girardon. Musée Nationale, Versailles.

title of Maintenon, anxious to render it productive, she enticed Flemish workers from the frontier to establish a lace manufacture upon her newly acquired marquisate. How the fabric succeeded, history does not relate, but the costly laces depicted in her portraits (Fig. 67) have not the appearance of home manufacture.

Point lace-making became a favourite employment among ladies. We have many engravings of this reign: one, 1691, of a "fille de qualité" thus occupied, with the motto, "Apres dîner vous travaillez au point." Another,[18] from an engraving of Le

---

[16] "Mercure Galant," Fév. 1685.

[17] Ibid. 1678.

[18] At the Mazarin Library there are four folio volumes of engravings, after Bonnard and others, of the costumes of the time of Louis XIV.; and at the Archives Nat. is a large series preserved in cartons numbered M. 815 to 823, &c., labelled "Gravures de Modes."

Paultre, dated 1676, is entitled "Dame en déshabille de chambre" (Fig. 68).

"La France est la tête du monde" (as regards fashion), says Victor Hugo, "cyclope dont Paris est l'œil;" and writers of all ages, whether prose or poet, seem to have been of the same opinion. It was about the year 1680 that the

> "Mode féconde en mille inventions,
> Monstre, prodige étrange et difforme,"

was suddenly exemplified in France.

Fig. 67.

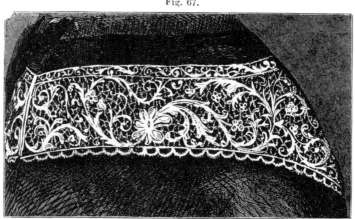

Madame de Maintenon. From her portrait. Musée Nationale, Versailles.

All readers of this great reign will recall to mind the story of the "Fontanges." How in the hurry of the chase the locks of the royal favourite becoming dishevelled by the wind, the fair huntress hurriedly tying the lace kerchief, with a ribbon that bound them, round her head, produced, in one moment, a coiffure so light, so artistic, that Louis XIV., enchanted, prayed her to retain it for that night at court. The lady obeyed the royal command. The ribbon mixed with lace, now worn for the first time, caused a sensation, and the next day all the ladies of the court appeared "coiffées à la Fontange." (See Madame de Lude, Fig. 70.)

But this head-dress, with its tiers of point mounted on wires,[19]

---

[19] "La Fontange altière."—*Boileau.*

soon ceased to be artistic; for thirty years it grew higher and higher. Poets and satirists attacked the fashion, much as they did the high head-dresses of the Roman matrons more than a

Fig. 68.

A lady in morning déshabille.   From an engraving by Le Paultre.   1676.

thousand years ago.[20] Of the extinction of this mode we have various accounts; some asserting it to have been preached down

[20] The wife of Trajan wore this coiffure, and her sister Marcina Faustina, wife of Antoninus, much regretted the fashion when it went out. Speaking of this head-dress, says a writer in the "Bibliothèque Universelle" of 1693, "On regarde quelque fois des certaines choses comme tout à fait nouvelles, qui ne sont que des vieilles modes renouvellées. L'auteur en appelle un exemple dans les coiffures élevées que portent les femmes aujourd'hui, croyant ajouter par là quelque chose à leur taille. Les dames Romaines avaient la même ambition et mettaient des ajustemens de tête tout semblables aux Commodes et aux Fontages de ce temps. Juvenal en parle expressément dans sa Satire VI."

by the clergy, as were the " hennins," in the time of Charles VI.;
but the most probable story is that which relates how in October
1699 Louis XIV. simply observed, " Cette coiffure lui paroissoit
désagréable." The ladies worked all night, and next evening, at
the Duchess of Burgundy's reception,[21] appeared for the first time
in a low head-dress. Fashion,[22] which the author of the before
quoted " Consolation" would call " pompeux," was " aujourd'hui
en reforme." Louis XIV. never appreciated the sacrifice ; to the
day of his death he persisted in saying, " J'ai eu beau crier contre
les coiffures trop hautes." No one showed the slightest desire to
lower them till one day there arrived " une inconnue, une guenille
d'Angleterre" (Lady Sandwich, the English ambassadress!!),
" avec une petite coiffure basse—tout d'un coup, toutes les
princesses vont d'une extrémité à l'autre."[23] Be the accusation
true or not, the " Mercure" of November 1699 announces that
" la hauteur des anciennes coiffures commence à paroître ridicule."

In these days lace was not confined to Versailles and the
court.[24]

" Le gentilhomme," writes Capefigue, " allait au feu en manchettes poudré à la maréchale, les eaux de senteur sur son mouchoir
en point d'Angleterre, l'élégance n'a jamais fait tort au courage,
et la politesse s'allie noblement à la bravoure." And Capefigue is
right; for who rallied more nobly round the throne than did the
French gallants of that luxurious century?

But war brings destruction to laces as well as finances, and, in
1690, the loyal and noble army was found, alas! in rags. Then
writes Dangeau: " M. de Castanaga, à qui M. de Maine et M. de
Luxembourg avoient demandé un passeport pour faire venir des
dentelles à l'armée, a refusé le passeport, mais il a envoyé des
marchands qui ont porté pour dix mille écus de dentelles, et apres
qu'on les eut achetées, les marchands s'en retournèrent sans
vouloir prendre d'argent, disant qu'ils avoient cet ordre de M. de
Castanaga."

" J'avois une Steinekerque de Malines," writes the Abbé de
Choisy, who always dressed in female attire. We hear a great

---

[21] " Galerie de l'ancienne Cour."

[22] " 1699. Oct. Le Vendredi 25, il y
eut grande toilette chez Madame la
Duchesse de Bourgogne où les dames
parurent, pour la première fois, en
coiffures d'une forme nouvelle, c'est à dire
beaucoup plus basses."—Mercure Galant.

[23] " Corr. de la Duchesse d'Orléans,
Princesse Palatine, mère du Régent."

[24] Speaking of the Iron Mask, Voltaire
writes :—" His greatest passion was for
linen of great fineness and for lace."—
Siècle de Louis XIV.

deal about these Steinkirks at the end of the seventeenth century. It was a twisted lace necktie, and owed its origin to the battle of that name in 1692,[25] when the young French princes of the blood were suddenly ordered into action. Hastily tying their lace cravats—in peaceful times a most elaborate proceeding—they rushed to the charge, and gained the day. In honour of this event, both ladies and cavaliers wore their handkerchiefs knotted or twisted in this careless fashion.

> " Je trouve qu'en été le Steinkerque est commode,
> J'aime le falbala,[26] quoiqu'il soit critiqué,"

says somebody. Steinkirks became the rage, and held good for many years, worn alike in England [27] and France by the women and the men. Fig. 69 represents the grand dauphin in his " longue Steinkerque à replis tortueux ; "[28] Fig. 70, the Duchesse du Lude [29] in similar costume and high fontange, both copied from prints of the time.

We must now allude to the prettiest fashion of the reign, a lace ruffle to the ladies' sleeves, concerning the wearing of which "à deux rangs," or "à trois rangs," there was much etiquette. We find constant mention of these in the fashion-books and inventories of the time.

" Les manches plates se font de deux tiers de tour, avec une dentelle de fil de point fort fin et fort haut. On nomme ces manches Engageantes." [30]

---

[25] Fought by Marshal Luxembourg— vieux tapissier de Notre-Dame—against William of Orange.

[26] Falbala,—a deep single flounce of point .or gold lace. The "Mercure Galant," 1698, describing the Duchess of Burgundy "à la promenade," states : " Elle avoit un habit gris de lin en falbala, tout garny de dentelles d'argent." " Femme de qualité en Steinkerke et Falbala."—*Engraving of* 1693.

[27] See " England.—William III."

[28] Regnard.

[29] Dame du palais to Queen Marie Thérèse, and afterwards first lady of

honour to the Duchess of Burgundy. She died 1726.

[30] " Mercure Galant," 1683.

Again, in 1688, he says: " Les points de Malines sont fort en règne pour les manches qu'on nomme engageantes. On y met des points très-hauts, fort plissés, avec des pieds."

They appear to have been soon intro- duced into England, for Evelyn, in his " Mundus Muliebris," 1690, says : " About her sleeves are engageants ;" and the " Ladies' Dictionary " of nearly the same date gives : " Ængageants, double ruffles that fall over the wrist."

In the lace bills of Queen Mary II., we find—

	£.	s.	d.
" 1694. 1¾ yd. Point for a broad pair of Engageants, at £5 10s.	9	12	6
3½ for a double pair of ditto, at £5 10s.	19	5	0
1 pair of Point Engageants	30	0	0

(B. M. Add. MSS. No. 5751.)

[" 1720

Fig. 70.

Madame du Lude en Steinkerque.

Fig. 69.

Le Grand Dauphin en Steinkerque.

This fashion, though introduced in 1688, continued in vogue till the French Revolution. We see them in the portrait of Madame Palatine, mother of the regent (Fig. 71), and in that of Madame Sophie de France, daughter of Louis XV., taken in 1782 by Drouais.

Before finishing with point de France, we must allude to the "équipage de bain," in which this favoured fabric formed a great item. As early as 1688, Madame de Maintenon presents Madame

Fig. 71.

Madame Palatine (Elis. Charlotte de Baviere), Duchesse d'Orleans. By Rigaud. Mus. Nat. Versailles.

de Chevreuse with an "équipage de bain de point de France" of great magnificence. It consisted not only of a peignoir, but a broad flounce, which formed a valance round the bath itself. You see them in old engravings of the day. Then there were the towels and the "descente," all equally costly.[31] To English

---

"1720. Six paires d'engageantes, dont quatre à un rang de dentelle, et les autres paires à double rang, l'une de dentelle d'Angleterre à raiseau et l'autre de dentelle à bride."—*Inv. de la Duchesse de Bourbon.* Arch. Nat.

"1723. Une paire d'engageantes à deux rangs de point plat à raiseau."—

Inv. d'Anne de Bavière, Princesse de Condé.

1770. "Six rangs d'engageantes de point à l'aiguille," with the same of point d'Argentan and Angleterre, appear in the lace-bills of Madame du Barry.

[31] "1725. Deux manteaux de bain et deux chemises, aussi de bain, garnis aux

notions this luxury may seem out of place; but French ladies of the seventeenth and eighteenth centuries admitted their habitués, not only to the honour of the ruelle,[32] but also to the bath-room.[33] In the latter case the bath was "au lait," i. e. clouded by the mixture of some essence. "Aux autres temps, autres mœurs."

The "fameuse poupée" of the reign of Louis XIV. must not be forgotten. The custom of dressing up these great dolls originated in the salons of the Hôtel Rambouillet, where one termed "la grande Pandore," at each change of fashion, was exhibited "en grande tenue;" a second, the little Pandore, in morning déshabille. These dolls were sent to Vienna and Italy, charged with the finest laces France could produce. As late as 1764, we read in the "Espion Chinois," "Il a débarqué à Douvres un grand nombre de poupées de hauteur naturelle habillées à la mode de Paris, afin que les dames de qualité puissent régler leurs goûts sur ces modèles."[34] Even when English ports were closed in war time, a special permission was given for the entry of a large alabaster doll, 4 feet high, the "Grand Courrier de la Mode."[35]

---

manches de dentelle, l'une à bride, et l'autre à raiseau."—*Inv. d'Anne de Bavière, Princesse de Condé.*

"1743. Ung Tour de baignoir de bazin garny de vieille dentelle.

"Trois lings de baignoire garnis de dentelle." — *Inv. de la Duchesse de Bourbon.*

[32] Describing the duties of the "critic of each bright ruelle," Tickell says :—

"Oft with varied art, his thoughts digress
  On deeper themes—the documents of dress;
  With nice discernment, to each style of face
  Adapt a ribbon, or suggest a lace ;
  O'er Granby's cap bid loftier feathers float,
  And add new bows to Devon's petticoat."   *Wreath of Fashion.*

[33] In the spring of 1802, Mr. Holcroft, when in Paris, received a polite note from a lady at whose house he visited, requesting to see him. He went, and was informed by her maid the lady was in her warm bath, but she would announce his

arrival. She returned, and led him to a kind of closet, where her mistress was up to her chin in water. He knew the manners of the place, and was not surprised. "Travels."

[34] Mercier also mentions, in his "Tableau de Paris," la poupée de la rue Saint-Honoré : "C'est de Paris que les profondes inventions en modes donnent des loix à l'univers. La fameuse poupée, le mannequin precieux, affublé des modes les plus nouvelles. . . . passe de Paris à Londres tous les mois, et va de là répandre ses graces dans toute l'Europe. Il va au Nord et au Midi, il pénètre à Constantinople et à Petersbourg, et le pli qu'a donné une main françoise se répète chez toutes les nations, humbles observatrices du goût de la rue Saint-Honoré."

[35] The practice was much more ancient. M. Ladomie asserts that in the royal expenses for 1361, figure so many livres for a doll sent to the Queen of England ; in 1496, another, sent to the Queen of Spain ; and in 1571, a third, to the Duchess of Bavaria.

Henry IV. writes in 1600, before his marriage to Marie de Medicis : "Fron-

In the war of the First Empire, this privilege was refused to our countrywomen; and from that time Englishwomen, deprived of all French aid for a whole generation, began to dress badly. Pitt has much to answer for. With this notice finishes our account of the reign of Louis XIV.

tenac tells me that you desire patterns of our fashion in dress. I send you, therefore, some model dolls." — *Miss Freer's Henry IV.*

It was also the custom of Venice, at the annual fair held in the Piazza of St. Mark, on the day of the Ascension (a fair which dates from 1180), to expose in the most conspicuous place of the fair a rag doll, which served as a model for the fashions of the year.—*Michiel, Origine delle Feste Veneziani.*

Fig. 72.

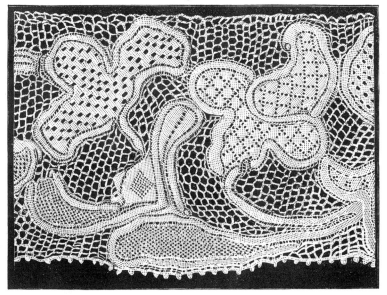

Guipure.   Seventeenth century.

CHAPTER XI.

LOUIS XV.

"Le luxe corrompt tout, et le riche qui en jouit, et le pauvre qui le convoite."
J.-J. Rousseau.

LOUIS XIV. is now dead and gone, to the delight of a wearied nation: we enter on the regency and times of Louis XV.—that age of "fourchettes," manchettes, and jabots—in which the butterfly abbés, "les porte-dentelles par excellence," played so conspicuous a part.

The origin of the weeping ruffles, if Mercier[1] is to be credited, may be assigned to other causes than royal decree or the edicts of fashion. "Les grandes manchettes furent introduites par des fripons qui voulaient filouter au jeu et escamoter des cartes." It never answers to investigate too deeply the origin of a new invented mode,—sufficient to say, ruffles became a necessary adjunct to the toilet of every gentleman. So indispensable were they the Parisians are accused of adopting the custom of wearing ruffles and no shirts.

"Les Parisiens," writes Mercier, "achètent quatre ajustemens contre une chemise. Un beau Monsieur se met une chemise blanche tous les quinze jours. Il coud ses manchettes de dentelle sur une chemise sale," and powders over his point collar till it looks white.[2] This habit passed into a proverb. The Maréchal de Richelieu, who, though versed in astronomy, could not spell, said of himself, "Qu'on ne lui avoit pas fourni des chemises, mais qu'il avoit acheté des manchettes."[3] This account tallies

---

[1] "Tableau de Paris," 1782.

[2] "The French nation are eminent for making a fine outside, when perhaps they want necessaries, and indeed a gay shop and a mean stock is like the Frenchman with his laced ruffles without a shirt."— *The Complete English Tradesman.* Dan

Defoe. Lond. 1726. Foote, in his Prologue to the "Trip to Paris," says, "They sold me some ruffles, and I found the shirts."

[3] "Souvenirs de la Marquise de Créquy, 1710-1802."

in well with former accounts,[4] and with a letter of Madame de Maintenon to the Princess des Ursins, 1710.[5]

At this period it was the custom for grisettes to besiege the Paris hotels, bearing on their arms baskets decked out with ruffles and jabots of Malines, Angleterre, and point. What reader of Sterne will not recollect the lace-seller in his "Sentimental Journey"?

The jabot[6] and manchettes of point were the customary "cadeau de noces" of the bride to her intended for his wedding dress— a relic of which practice may be found in the embroidered wedding shirt furnished by the lady, in the North of Europe.[7] The sums expended in these articles would now appear fabulous. The Archbishop of Cambray[8] alone possessed four dozen pairs of ruffles, Malines, point, and Valenciennes. The wardrobe bills of the Duke de Penthièvre, of 1738, make mention of little else. An ell and a quarter of lace was required for one pair of ruffles. A yard, minus $\frac{1}{16}$, sufficed for the jabot.[9] There were "manchettes de jour," "manchettes tournantes,"[10] and "manchettes de nuit": these last named were mostly of Valenciennes.[11] The point d'Alençon ruffles of Buffon, which he always wore, even when writing, were

---

[4] See p. 54, and note [65].

[5] "M. de Vendôme, at his marriage, was quite astonished at putting on his clean shirt a-day, and fearfully embarrassed at having some point lace on the one given him to put on at night. Indeed," continues she, "you would hardly recognise the taste of the French. The men are worse than the women. They wish their wives to take snuff, play, and pay no more attention to their dress." The exquisite cleanliness of Anne of Austria's court was at an end.

[6] In an account, quoted in the "Reliquary," July 1865, is the charge, on February 16, of "six shillings for a cravat for hur Vallentine."

[7] In the old Scotch song of Gilderoy, the famous highwayman, we have an instance :—

"For Gilderoy, that luve of mine,
  Gude faith, I freely bought
A wedding sark of Holland fine,
  Wi' silken flowers wrought."

[8] "Inv. après le decès de Mgr. C. de

Saint-Albin, Archevesque de Cambray" (son of the regent), 1764. Arch. Nat. M. M. 718.

Louis XVI. had 59 pairs the year before his death : 28 of point, 21 of Valenciennes, and 10 of Angleterre. "État des Effets subsistant et formant le fond de la garderobe du Roi au 1er Janvier 1792." Arch. Nat. K. 506, No. 30.

[9] "État d'un Trousseau," "Description des Arts et Métiers." Paris, 1777.

[10] "Deux aunes trois quarts d'Angleterre à bride pour deux paires de manchettes tournantes, à 45 livres l'aune." —Garderobe de S. A. S. Mgr. le Duc de Penthièvre, 1738. Arch. Nat. K. K. 390.

[11] Ibid. The laces for ruffles were of various kinds : point brodé, point à bride, point à raiseau, point à bride à écaille, point superfin, point brillant, Angleterre à bride à raiseau, and one pair of point d'Argentan ; "Valenciennes pour manchettes de nuit à 42 livres l'aune."

[The

exhibited in 1864 at Falaise, being carefully preserved in the family to whom they have descended.

Even, if a contemporary writer may be credited, "Monsieur de Paris," the executioner, mounted the scaffold in a velvet suit, powdered, with point lace jabot and ruffles.

" Les rubans, les miroirs, les dentelles sont trois choses sans lesquelles les François ne peuvent vivre. Le luxe démesuré a confondu le maître avec le valet,"[12] says an unknown writer, quoted by Dulaure.[13] The servants of the last century had on their state liveries lace equal in richness to those worn by their masters.[14] Speaking of a Prussian gentleman, we read, "His valets, who according to the reigning taste were the prettiest in the world, wore nothing but the most costly lace."[15] This custom was not confined, however, to France or the continent. " Our very footmen," writes the angry " World," " are adorned with gold and silver bags and lace ruffles. The valet is only distinguished from his master by being better dressed;" while the " Connoisseur" complains of " roast beef being banished from even

---

The duke's wardrobe accounts afford a good specimen of the extravagance in the decoration of night attire at this period :—

4 au. de point pour collet et manchettes de la chemise de nuit et garnir la coëffe, à 130 ll.	250 ll.
3 au. ¾ dito pour jabot et fourchettes de nuit et garnir le devant de la camisole, à 66 ll.	247 ll. 10s.
Sept douze de point pour plaquer sur les manches de camisolle, à 55 ll.	32 ll. 1s.

Then for his nightcaps :—

3 au. Toile fine pour Coëffes de Nuit	27 ll.
4 au. Dentelles de Malines pour les tours de Coëffes, à 20 ll. .	80 ll.
5 au. ½ Valenciennes, à 46 ll.	253 ll.
52 au. dito petit point, pour garnis les Tours, à 5 ll. 5s. .	273 ll.
Pour avoir monté un bonnet de nuit de point	1 l. 5s.
7 au. de campanne de point pour chamarrer la camisolle et le bonnet de nuit, à 10 ll. 10s.	73 ll. 10s.

The Marquise de Créquy speaks of a night-cap, "à grandes dentelles," offered, with "la robe de chambre," to the dauphin, son of Louis XV., by the people of the Duke de Grammont, on his having lost his way hunting, and wandered to the duke's château.

[12] " Le Parisien qui n'a pas dix mille livres de rente n'a ordinairement ni draps, ni lit, ni serviettes, ni chemises; mais il a une montre à répétition, des glaces, des bas de soie, des dentelles."—*Tableau de Paris.*

[13] " Histoire de Paris."

[14] " Ordinairement un laquais de bon ton prend le nom de son maître, quand il est avec d'autres laquais, il prend aussi ses mœurs, ses gestes, ses manières. . . . Le laquais d'un seigneur porte la montre d'or ciselée, des dentelles, des boucles à brillants," &c.—*Tableau de Paris.*

[15] " Amusemens des Eaux de Spa," Amsterdam, 1751.

'down stairs,' because the powdered footmen will not touch it for fear of daubing their lace ruffles."[16]

But the time, of all others, for a grand display of lace was at a visit to a Parisian lady on her "relevailles," or "uprising," as it was called, in the days of our third Edward. Reclining on a chaise longue, she is described as awaiting her visitors. Nothing is to be seen but the finest laces, arranged in artistic folds, and long bows of ribbon. An attendant stationed at the door asks of each new arrival, "Have you any perfumes?" She replies not, and passes on—an atmosphere of fragrance. The lady must not be spoken to, but, the usual compliments over, the visitors proceed to admire her lace. "Beautiful, exquisite!"—but, "Hist! speak low," and she who gave the caution is the first, in true French style, to speak the loudest.[17]

Lace "garnitures de lit" were general among great people as early as 1696. The "Mercure" speaks of "drap garnis d'une grande dentelle de point d'Angleterre." In 1738, the Duc de Luynes writes,[18] "Aujourd'hui Madame de Luynes s'est fait apporter les fournitures qu'elle avoit choisies pour la Reine, et qui regardent les dames d'honneur. Elles consistent en couvrepieds[19] garnis de dentelle pour le grand lit et pour les petits, en taies d'oreiller[20]

---

[16] "Les manches qu'à table on voit tâter la sauce."—*École des Maris.*

The state liveries of H. M. Queen Victoria are most richly embroidered in gold. They were made in the early part of George II.'s reign, since which t me they have been in use. In the year 1848, the servants appeared at the royal balls in gold and ruffles of the richest point of the same epoch as their dresses. In 1849 the lace no longer appeared—probably suppressed by order. Queen Anne, who was a great martinet in trifles, had her servants marshalled before her every day, that she might see if their ruffles were clean, and their periwigs dressed.

[17] "Tableau de Paris."

[18] "Mémoires."

[19] "1723. Un couvrepied de toile blanche, picqure de Marseille, garni autour d'un point en campane de demie aune de hauteur.'—*Inv. d'A. de Bavière, Princesse de Condé.*

"1743. Un couvrepied de toile picquée, brodée or et soye, bordé de trois côtés d'une grande dentelle d'Angleterre et du quatrième d'un moyen dentelle d'Angleterre à bords.

"Un autre, garni d'une grande et moyenne dentelle de point d'Alençon.

"Un autre, garni d'un grand point de demie aune de hauteur, brodé, garnie d'une campane en bas.

"Un autre, 'point à bride,'" and many others.—*Inv. de la Duchesse de Bourbon.*

[20] "1704. Deux taies d'oreiller garnies de dentelle, l'une à raiseau, et l'autre à bride."—*Inv. de F. P. Loisel.* Bib. Nat. MSS. F. Fr. 11,459.

"1723. Quatre taies d'oreiller, dont trois garnies de différentes dentelles, et l'autre de Point." — *Inv. d'Anne de Bavière, Princesse de Condé.*

"1755. Deux taies d'oreiller garnies de point d'Alençon."—*Inv. de Mademoiselle de Charollais.*

"1761. Trois taies d'oreiller de dentelle de point à brides."—*Inv. de la Duchesse de Modène.*

["1770.

garnies du même point d'Angleterre etc. Cette fourniture coûte environ 30,000 livres, quoique Madame de Luynes n'ait pas fait renouveler les beaux couvrepieds de la Reine." These garnitures were renewed every year, and Madame de Luynes inherited the old ones.

Madame de Créquy, describing her visit to the Duchesse Douairière de La Ferté, says, when that lady received her, she was lying in a state bed, under a coverlet made of point de Venise

Fig. 73.

Madame Sophie de France, daughter of Louis XV. By Drouais. 1782. Mus. Nat. Versailles.

in one piece. " I am persuaded," she adds, " that the trimming of her sheets, which were of point d'Argentan, were worth at least 40,000 crowns.[21] To such a pitch had the taste for lace-trimmed linen attained that, when, in 1739, Madame, eldest

---

" 1770. 7 au. 1/8 vraie Valenciennes pour garnir une taie d'oreiller, à 60 ll. 427 10."—*Comptes de Madame du Barry.*
" 1707. 7 au. tournante d'Angleterre pour garnir des plottes" (pincushions), " à 50 ll. 350 00."—*Ibid.*
" 1788. 12 Pelottes garnies de den-

telle."—*Ibid.*
" 6 trousses à peigne garnies de dentelle."—*Fourni pour Mgr. le Dauphin.* Arch. Nat.
" 1792. 6 Pelottes garnies de dentelle." —*Linge du çi-devant Roi.* Ibid.
[21] " Souvenirs."

daughter of Louis XV., espoused the Prince of Spain, the bill for these articles alone amounted to 25,000*l*.; and when Cardinal Fleury, a most economical prelate, saw the trousseau, he observed, " Qu'il croyait que c'était pour marier toutes les sept Mesdames." [22] (Figs. 73, 74.) Again, Swinburne writes from Paris: [23]—" The

Fig. 74.

Madame Adélaïde de France, daughter of Louis XV.   Mus. Nat. Versailles.

trousseau of Mademoiselle de Matignon will cost 100,000 crowns (25,000*l*.). The expense here of rigging [24] out a bride is equal

---

[22] " Mémoires du Duc de Luynes."

[23] 1786. " Courts of Europe."

[24] It may be amusing to the reader to learn the laces necessary for " l'état d'un trousseau," in 1777, as given in the "Description des Arts et Métiers:"—"Une toilette de ville en dentelle; 2 jupons garnis du même. Une coiffure avec tour de gorge, et le fichu plissé de point d'Alençon. Un idem de point d'Angleterre. 1 id. de vraie Valenciennes. Une coiffure dite ' Battant d'œil ' de Malines brodée, pour le négligé. 6 fichus simples en mousseline à mille fleurs garnis de dentelle pour le négligé. 12 grands bonnets garnis d'une petite dentelle pour la nuit. 12 à deux rangs, plus beaux, pour le jour, en cas d'indisposition. 12 serres-tête garnis d'une petite dentelle pour la nuit. 2 taies d'oreiller garnies en dentelle. 12 pièces d'estomach garnies d'une petite dentelle. 6 garnitures de corset. 12 tours de gorge. 12 paires de manchettes en dentelle. Une toilette; les volants, au nombre de deux, sont en dentelle; ils ont 5 aunes de tour. Dessus de pelotte, en toile garnie de dentelle etc. La Layette : 6 paires de manches

to a handsome portion in England. Five thousand pounds' worth
of lace, linen, &c., is a common thing among them."

The masks worn by the ladies at this period were of black
blonde lace [25] of the most exquisite fineness and design.[26] They
were trimmed round the eyes, like those described by Scarron :—

> " Dirai-je comme ces fantasques
> Qui portent dentelle à leurs masques,
> En chamarrent les trous des yeux,
> Croyant que le masque en est mieux."

In the reign of Louis XV., point de France was rivalled by

Fig 75.

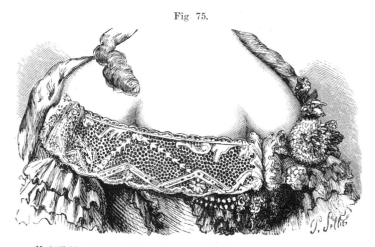

Marie Thérèse Ant. Raph., Infanta of Spain, first wife of Louis Dauphin, son of Louis XV.
By Tocqué.   Dated 1748.   Musée Nationale, Versailles.

Angleterre [27] and Malines. Argentan and Alençon (Fig. 75) were
declared by fashion to be "dentelles d'hiver" : each lace now

---

pour la mère, garnies de dentelle. 24
bonnets ronds de 3 âges en dentelle. 12
bavoirs de deux âges, garnis en dentelle."
The layette was furnished together with
the trousseau.

[25] "1787. Pour achat de 11 au. blonde
noire, à 6 10, 71 livres 10 sous."—*Comptes
de Monsieur Hergosse.* Bib. Nat. MSS.
F. Fr. 11,447.

[26] When the Empress Joséphine was
at Frankfort on the Main, a masked ball

was given on the occasion. The ladies,
says Mademoiselle Avrillion, wore short
dominoes with their faces covered with a
mask, "le tour des yeux garni d'une
petite dentelle noir."—*Mém. de Mademoiselle Avrillion, première femme de
chambre de l'Impératrice.* Paris, 1833.

[27] A few extracts from Madame du
Barry's lace accounts will furnish an
idea of her consumption of point d'Angleterre :—

had its appointed season.[28]   " On porte le point en hiver," says the Dictionary of the Academy.

There was much etiquette, too, in the court of France, as regards lace, which was never worn in mourning. Dangeau chronicles, on the death of the Princess of Baden, " Le roi qui avoit repris les dentelles. et les rubans d'or et d'argent, reprend demain le linge uni et les rubans unis aussi." [29]

" Madame" thus describes the " petit deuil" of the Margrave of Anspach : " Avec des dentelles blanches sur le noir, du beau ruban bleu, à dentelle blanches et noires. C'étoit une parure magnifique." [30]

" Une toilette d'Angleterre complette de . . . .   8823 livres.
" Une parure composée de deux barbes, rayon et fond, 6 rangs de
    manchettes, 1 1/2 au. de ruban fait exprès, 1/3 jabot pour le
    devant de tour. Le tout d'Angleterre superfin de   7000   „
" Un ajustement d'Angleterre complet de.   3216   „
" Une garniture de peignoir d'Angleterre de   2342   „
" Une garniture de fichu d'Angleterre.   388   „
" 8 au. d'Angleterre pour tayes d'oreiller . . . .   240 livres.
" 9 1/2 au. dito pour la tête   76   „
" 14 au. pied dito pour la tête   140   „
                                                          ————   456 livres."

CHAPTER XII.

LOUIS XVI. TO THE EMPIRE.

"Proud Versailles ! thy glory falls."
Pope.

In the reign of Louis XVI. society, tired out with ceremony and the stately manners of the old court, at last began to emancipate itself. Marie-Antoinette (Fig. 76) first gave the signal. Rid

Fig. 76.

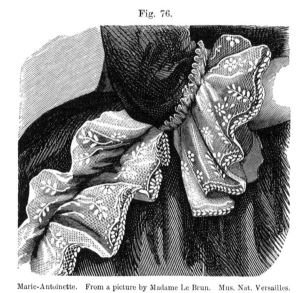

Marie-Antoinette. From a picture by Madame Le Brun. Mus. Nat. Versailles.

herself of the preachings of " Madame Étiquette " she could not on state occasions, so she did her best to amuse herself in private. The finest Indian muslin [1] now supplanted the heavy points of

---

[1] Madame du Barry, in her Memoirs, mentions the purchase of Indian muslin so fine that the piece did not weigh 15 oz., although sufficient to make four dresses.

the old court. "The ladies looked," indignantly observed the Maréchale de Luxembourg, "in their muslin aprons and handkerchiefs, like cooks and convent porters."[2] To signify her disapproval of this new-fangled custom, the Maréchale sent her granddaughter, the Duchesse de Lauzun, an apron of sailcloth, trimmed with fine point, and six fichus of the same material similarly decorated.

The arrangement of the lace lappets was still prescribed by rule. "Lappets to be pinned up"—lappets to be let down on grand occasions.[3] Later, Madame de Staël, like a true bas-bleu—without speaking of her curtsey to Marie-Antoinette, which was all wrong—on her first visit of ceremony to Madame de Polignac, in defiance of all etiquette, left her lace lappets in the carriage.

The democratic spirit of the age now first creeps out in the fashions. Among the rich parures of du Barry,[4] we find "barbes à la paysanne,"—everything now becomes "à coquille," "à papillon." Even the queen's hairdresser, Léonard, " qui

" Portait jusques au ciel l'audace de ses coiffures,"

did not venture to introduce much lace.

The affected phraseology of the day quite puts one out of all patience. We read of the toilette of Mademoiselle Duthé in which she appeared at the opera. She wore a robe " soupirs étouffés," trimmed with " regrets superflus ;" a point of " candeur parfaite, garnie en plaintes indiscrètes ;" ribbons " en attentions marquées ;" shoes " cheveux de la reine,"[5] embroidered with diamonds " en

---

[2] "Cuisinières et Tourières." The joke formed the subject of some clever verses from the Chevalier de Boufflers.

[3] The barbe or lappet, of whatever form it be, has always in all ages and all countries been a subject of etiquette. At the interment of Queen Mary Tudor, 1558, Dec. 14, it is told how the ladies in the first and second chariots were clad in mourning apparel, according to their estates, " their barbes above their chynes." " The 4 ladies on horseback in like manner had their barbes on their chynes." In the third chariot, " the ladies had their barbes under their chynes."—*State Papers, Domestic*, Eliz. vol. xxxii.

[4] Only in her last lace bill, 1773 : " Une paire de barbes plattes longues de 3/4 en blonde fine à fleurs fond d'Alençon, 36.

" Une blonde grande hauteur à bouquets détachés et à bordure riche.

" 6 au. de blonde de grande hauteur façon d'Alençon à coquilles à mille poix, à 18.

" Une paire de sabots de comtesse de deux rangs de tulle blonde à festons, fond d'Alençon."— *Comptes de la Comtesse du Barry.* Bib. Nat. F. Fr. 8157.

Madame du Barry went to the greatest extravagance in lace ajustements, barbes, collerettes, volants, quilles, coëffes, &c., of Argentan, Angleterre, and point à l'aiguille.

[5] The great fashion. The shoes were embroidered in diamonds, which were scarcely worn on other parts of the dress. The back seam, trimmed with emeralds, was called " venez-y-voir."

coups perfides" and "venez-y-voir" in emeralds. Her hair " en
sentiments soutenus," with a cap of " conquête assurée," trimmed
with ribbons of " œil abattu ;" a " chat[6] sur le col," the colour of
" gueux nouvellement arrivé," and upon her shoulders a Médicis
" en bienséance," and her muff of " agitation momentanée."

In the accounts of Mademoiselle Bertin, the queen's milliner,
known for her saying, " Il n'y a rien de nouveau dans ce monde
que ce qui est oublié," we have little mention of lace.[7]

" Blond à fond d'Alençon semé à poix, à mouches," now usurps
the place of the old points. Even one of the " grandes dames de
la vieille cour," Madame Adélaïde de France herself, is represented
in her picture by Madame Guiard with a spotted handkerchief,
probably of blonde (Fig. 77).

The church alone protects the ancient fabrics. The lace of the
Rohan family, almost hereditary prince-archbishops of Strasburg,
was of inestimable value. " We met," writes the Baroness de
Oberkirch, " the cardinal coming out of his chapel dressed in a
soutane of scarlet moire and rochet of English lace of inestimable
value. When on great occasions he officiates at Versailles, he
wears an alb of old lace 'en point à l'aiguille,' of such beauty that
his assistants were almost afraid to touch it. His arms and device
are worked in a medallion above the large flowers. This alb is
estimated at 100,000 livres. On the day of which I speak he
wore the rochet of English lace, one of his least beautiful, as his
secretary, the Abbé Georget, told me." [8]

On his elevation to the see of Bourges, 1859, Monseigneur de
La Tour d'Auvergne celebrated mass at Rome arrayed with all the
sacerdotal ornaments of point d'Alençon of the finest workmanship. This lace descended to him from his uncle, Cardinal de La
Tour d'Auvergne, who had inherited them from his mother, Madame
d'Aumale, so well known as the friend of Madame Maintenon.
Under the first empire a complete suit of lace was offered to the

---

[6] " Souvenirs du Marquis de Valfons,
1710-1786. A " chat," tippet or
palatine ; so named after the mother of
the regent.

[7] In the National Archives, formerly
preserved with the " Livre Rouge," in
the Armoire de Fer, is the " Gazette
pour l'anné 1782," of Marie-Antoinette,
consisting of a list of the dresses furnished
for the queen during the year, drawn up
by the Comtesse d'Ossune, her " dame

des atours." We find—" grands habits,
robes sur le grand panier, robes sur le
petit panier," with a pattern of the material affixed to each entry, and the name
of the " couturière" who made the dress.
One " Lévite" alone appears trimmed
with blonde. There is also the Gazette
of Madame Elizabeth, for 1792.

[8] " Mémoires sur la Cour de Louis
XVI.'

prelate for sale which had belonged to Marie-Antoinette. This lace is described as formed of squares of old point d'Angleterre or de Flandre, each representing a different subject. The beauty of the object and its derivation decided his eminence to speak of it to his colleague, Cardinal de Bonald, these two prelates united their resources, bought the lace, and divided it, thus consecrating to a pious use this relic, which had decorated the queen at the happy period of her life.[9]

Fig. 77.

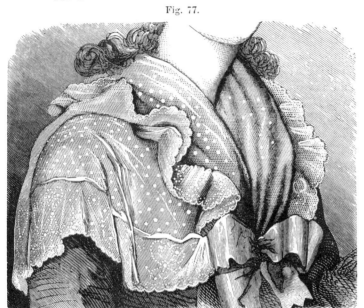

Madame Adélaïde de France. After a picture by Madame Guiard, dated 1787. Mus. Nat. Versailles.

But this extravagance and luxury were now soon to end. The years of '92 and '93 were approaching. The great nobility of France, who patronised the rich manufactures of the kingdom at the expense of a peasantry starving on estates they seldom, if ever, visited, were ere long outcasts in foreign climes, eking out a living as best they could, almost envying in their poverty the fate of those who, like their virtuous king and much maligned queen, had perished on the scaffold. The French Revolution was fatal to the lace trade. For twelve years the manufacture almost ceased, and more than thirty different manufactories entirely

---

[9] Note of the Comtesse de Clermont-Tonnerre, to the French translation of this work.

disappeared.[10] Its merits were, however, recognised by the États-Généraux in 1789, who, when previous to meeting they settled the costume of the three estates, decreed to the noblesse a lace cravat. It was not till 1801, when Napoleon wished to "faire revenir le luxe," that we again find it chronicled in the annals of the day: "How charming Caroline Murat looked in her white mantelet of 'point de Bruxelles et sa robe garnie des mêmes dentelles,'" &c. The old laces were the work of years, and transmitted as heirlooms [11] from generation to generation. They were often heavy and overloaded with ornament. The ancient style was now discarded, and a lighter description introduced. By an improvement in the point de raccroc several sections of lace were joined together so as to form one large piece; thus ten workers could now produce in a month what had formerly been the work of years.

Napoleon especially patronised the fabrics of Alençon, Brussels, and Chantilly. He endeavoured, too, without success, to raise that of Valenciennes. After the example of Louis XIV., he made the wearing of his two favourite points obligatory at the court of the Tuileries, and it is to his protection these towns owe the preservation of their manufactures. The lace-makers still speak of the rich orders received from the imperial court as the most remarkable epoch in their industrial career. Never was the beauty and costliness of the laces made for the marriage of Marie-Louise yet surpassed. To reproduce them now would, estimates M. Aubry, cost above a million of francs. Napoleon was a great lover of lace: he admired it as a work of art, and was proud of the proficiency of his subjects. Mademoiselle d'Avrillion relates the following anecdote. The Princess Pauline had given orders to the Empress Joséphine's lace-maker for a dress and various objects to the value of 30,000 francs. When the order was completed, and the lace brought home, the princess changed her mind, and refused to take them. Madame Lesœur, in despair,

---

[10] Among these were Sedan, Charleville, Mézières, Dieppe, Havre, Pont-l'Évêque, Honfleur, Eu, and more than ten neighbouring villages. The points of Aurillac, Bourgogne, and Murat disappeared; and worst of all was the loss of the manufacture of Valenciennes. Laces were also made in Champagne, at Troyes and Domchéry, &c.

[11] 1649. Anne Gohory leaves all her personals to Madame de Sévigné, except her " plus beau mouchoir, le col de point fin de Flandres, et une juppe de satin à fleurs fond vert, garnye de point fin d'or et de soie."

1764. Geneviève Laval bequeaths to her sister "une garniture de dentelle de raiseau à grandes dents, valant au

appealed to the empress. She thinking the price not unreasonable, considering the beauty of the points, showed them to Napoleon, and told him the circumstance. "I was in the room at the time," writes the authoress of the "Mémoires." The emperor examined minutely each carton, exclaiming at intervals, "Comme on travaille bien en France, je dois encourager un pareil commerce. Pauline a grand tort." He ended by paying the bill and distributing the laces among the ladies of the court.[12] Indeed, it may be said that never was lace more in vogue than during the early days of the empire.

The morning costume of a French duchess of that court is described in the following terms:—" Elle portait un peignoir brodé en mousseline garni d'une Angleterre très-belle, une fraise en point d'Angleterre. Sur sa tête la duchesse avait jeté en se levant une sorte de 'baigneuse,' comme nos mères l'auraient appelée, en point d'Angleterre, garnie de rubans de satin rose pâle."[13] The fair sister of Napoleon, the Princess Pauline Borghese, "s'est passionnée," as the term ran, "pour les dentelles."[14]

That Napoleon's example was quickly followed by the "élégantes" of the Directory, the following account, given to the brother of the author by an elderly lady who visited Paris during that very short period[15] when the English flocked to the continent, of a ball at Madame Récamier's, to which she had an invitation, will testify.

The First Consul was expected, and the élite of Paris early thronged the salons of the charming hostess — but where was Madame Récamier? "Souffrante," the murmur ran, retained to her bed by a sudden indisposition. She would, however, receive her guests "couchée."

The company passed to the bedroom of the lady, which, as still the custom in France, opened on one of the principal salons. There, in a gilded bed, lay Madame Récamier, the most beautiful woman in France. The bed-curtains were of the finest Brussels lace, bordered with garlands of honeysuckle, and lined with satin

moins quinze livres l'aune." Arch. Nat. Y. 58.

1764. Anne Challus leaves her "belle garniture de dentelle en plein, manchettes tour de gorge, palatine et fond." Ibid.

1764. Madame de Pompadour, in her will, says, "Je donne à mes deux femmes de chambre tout ce qui concerne ma garderobe . . . . y compris les dentelles."

[12] "Mém. de Mademoiselle d'Avrillion."

[13] "Mémoires sur la Restauration. Par Madame la Duchesse d'Abrantès."

[14] Ibid. t. v. p. 48.

[15] After the Peace of Amiens, 1801.

of the palest rose. The couvrepied was of the same material; from the pillow of embroidered cambric fell "des flots de Valenciennes."

The lady herself wore a peignoir trimmed with the most exquisite English point. Never had she looked more lovely— never had she done the honours of her hotel more gracefully. And so she received Napoleon—so she received the budding heroes of that great empire. All admired her "fortitude," her "dévouement," in thus sacrificing herself to society; and on the following day "tout Paris s'est fait inscrire chez elle." Never had such anxiety been expressed—never had woman gained such a triumph.

The Duchesse d'Abrantès, who married in the year 1800, describing her trousseau,[16] says she had "des mouchoirs, des jupons, des canezous du matin, des peignoirs de mousseline de l'Inde, des camisoles de nuit, des bonnets de nuit, des bonnets de matin, de toutes les couleurs, de toutes les formes, et tout cela brodé, garni de Valenciennes ou de Malines, ou de point d'Angleterre." In the "corbeille de mariage," with the cachemires were "les voiles de point d'Angleterre, les garnitures de robes en point à l'aiguille, et en point de Bruxelles, ainsi qu'en blonde pour l'été. Il y avait aussi des robes de blonde blanche et de dentelle noire," &c. When they go to the mairie, she describes her costume: "J'avais une robe de mousseline de l'Inde brodée au plumetis et en points à jour, comme c'était alors la mode. Cette robe était à queue, montante et avec de longues manches, le lé de devant entièrement brodé ainsi que le tour du corsage, le bout des manches, qu'on appelait alors amadis. La fraise était en magnifique point à l'aiguille, sur ma tête j'avais un bonnet en point de Bruxelles. . . . Au sommet du bonnet était attachée une petite couronne de fleurs d'oranger, d'où partait un long voile en point d'Angleterre qui tombait à mes pieds et dont je pouvais presque m'envelopper." Madame Junot winds up by saying that "Cette profusion de riches dentelles, si fines, si déliées ne semblaient être qu'un réseau nuageux autour de mon visage, où elles se jouaient dans les boucles de mes cheveux."

Hamlet always used to appear on the stage in lace cravat and ruffles, and Talma, the eminent French tragedian, was very proud of the beauty of his wardrobe of lace. Dr. Doran relates of him that

---

[16] "Mémoires de Madame la Duchesse d'Abrantes."

on one occasion, when stopped by the Belgian custom-house officers at the frontier, an official, turning over his wardrobe, his stage costumes, &c., contemptuously styled them "habits de Polichinelle." Talma, in a rage, exclaimed, "Habits de Polichinelle! Why, the lace of my jabot and ruffles alone is worth fifty louis a yard, and I wear it on my private costume." "And must pay for it accordingly," added the official. "Punch's clothes might pass untaxed, but Monsieur Talma's lace owes duty to our king." Talma was forced to submit.

The French lace manufacture felt the political events of 1813 to 1817, but experienced a more severe crisis in 1818, when bobbinnet was first made in France. Fashion at once adopted the new material, and pillow lace was for a time discarded. For fifteen years lace encountered a fearful competition. The manufacturers were forced to lower their prices and diminish the produce. The marts of Europe were inundated with tulle; but happily a new channel for exportation was opened in the United States of North America. In time a reaction took place, and in 1834, with the exception of Alençon, all the other fabrics were once more in full activity.[17] But a cheaper class of lace had been introduced. In 1832–33, cotton thread first began to be substituted for flax.[18] The lace-makers readily adopted the change; they found cotton more elastic and less expensive. It gives, too, a brilliant appearance, and breaks less easily in the working. All manufacturers now use the Scottish cotton, with the exception of Alençon, some choice pieces of Brussels, and the finer qualities of Mechlin and Valenciennes. The difference is not to be detected by the eye; both materials wash equally well.

We now turn to the various lace manufactures of France, taking each in its order.

---

[17] The revival first appeared in the towns which made the cheaper laces: Caen, Bayeux, Mirecourt, Le Puy, Arras, &c.   [18] Fil de mulquinerie.

CHAPTER XIII.

THE LACE MANUFACTURES OF FRANCE.

FRANCE is a lace-making, as well as a lace-wearing, country.

Of the half-million of lace-makers in Europe, nearly a quarter of a million are estimated as belonging to France.

Under the impulse of fashion and luxury, lace receives the stamp of the special style of each country. Italy furnished its points of Venice and Genoa; the Netherlands, its Brussels, Mechlin, and Valenciennes; Spain, its silk blondes; England, its Honiton; France, its sumptuous point d'Alençon, and its black lace of Bayeux. Now, each style is copied by every nation; and though France cannot compete with Belgium in the points of Brussels, or the Valenciennes of Ypres, she has no rival in her points of Alençon, or her black silk laces. To begin with Alençon, the only French lace not made on the pillow.

ALENÇON (Dép. de l'Orne), NORMANDY.

> " Alenchon est sous Sarthe assis,
> Il luic divise le pays."
> *Romant de Rou.*

The account given by the historian of Alençon of the establishment of the points de France in that town differs widely from that we have related (p. 128), but as it was the generally received version until the publication of the "Colbert Correspondence," we give it here.

In 1665, at the recommendation of the Sieur Ruel, Colbert selected Madame Gilbert, a native of Alençon, already acquainted with the manner of making Venice point, and making her an advance of 50,000 crowns, established her at his château of Lonray (Fig. 78), near Alençon, with thirty forewomen whom he had, at great expense, caused to be brought over from Venice.

In a short time, Madame Gilbert arrived at Paris with the

first specimens of her fabric: the king, inspired by Colbert with a desire to see the work, during supper at Versailles, announced to his courtiers he had just established a manufacture of point more beautiful than that of Venice, and appointed a day when he would inspect the specimens. The laces were artistically arranged over the walls of a room hung with crimson damask and shown to the best advantage. The king expressed himself delighted. He ordered a large sum to be given to Madame Gilbert, and desired that no other lace should appear at court except the new fabric, upon which he bestowed the name of " point de France."[1]

Fig. 78.

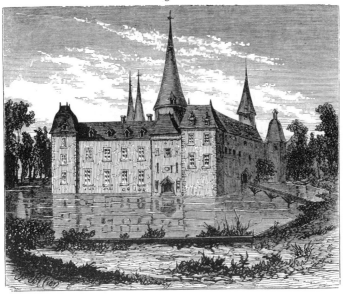

Château of Lonray, Dép. de l'Orne.

Scarcely had Louis retired than the courtiers eagerly stripped the room of its contents. The approval of the monarch was the fortune of Alençon; point de France adopted by court etiquette, the wearing of it became compulsory. All who had the privilege of the " casaque bleue,"—all who were received at Versailles, or were attached to the royal household, could only appear, the ladies in trimmings and head-dresses, the gentlemen in cravat and ruffles, of the royal manufacture.

---

[1] " Mémoires historiques sur la ville d'Alençon." M. Odillon Desnos. Alençon, 1787.

It is difficult to reconcile this with the previous statement; still, in the "Colbert Correspondence" and in the ordinances, there is no mention of Dame Gilbert and the château of Lonray;[2] and, in a letter from Catherine de Marcq, one of the "entrepreneurs," August 26, 1665, she asks leave to present to him the person she desires to send to Alençon, and her name is Marie Fillesac.

The "entrepreneurs" had found the lace industry flourishing at the time of the establishment of the point de France.

Point d'Alençon is mentioned in the "Révolte des Passemens," 1661, evidently as an advanced manufacture, but the monopoly of the privileged workmen—the new comers—displeased the old workwomen, and Colbert was too despotic in his orders prohibiting to make any kind of point except that of the royal manufactory,[3] and made the people so indignant that they revolted. The intendant, Dubourlay Favier, writes to Colbert, August 1665, that one named Le Prevost, of this town, having given suspicion to the people that he was about to form an establishment of "ouvrages de fil," the women to the number of above 1000 assembled and pursued him so that if he had not managed to escape their fury, he would assuredly have suffered from their violence. "He took refuge with me," he continues, "and I with difficulty appeased the multitude by assuring them that they would not be deprived of the liberty of working. It is a fact that for many years the town of Alençon subsists only by means of these small works of lace. That the same people make and sell, and in years of scarcity they subsist only by this little industry, and that wishing to take away their liberty, they were so incensed I had great difficulty in pacifying them."

The act, it appears, had come from the parliament of Paris, but as Alençon is in Normandy, it is necessary to have the assent of the parliament of Rouen.

"Point coupé," he adds, "has been long made here, which has a sale during its time, but a woman named Laperrière, skilled in these works, found some years since the means of imitating point de Venise in such perfection that she sold each collar she made at 1500 to 2000 francs. She has taught several girls this point because the work was very tedious, and she could not execute it

---

[2] Lonray belonged to Colbert's son, the Marquis de Seignelay, by his marriage (1671) with Mademoiselle Matignon.   [3] See p. 128.

alone. All these little girls are become mistresses, and finding that Laperrière gained a great deal, they determined to work for themselves and to their own profit, so that in their turn they employed others; this industry has thus by degrees so increased that above 8000 persons work in Alençon, Falaise, Séez, Argentan, and all the surrounding parishes of the Pays de Maine, at Fresnoy, Beaumont, and Menars. It is a real blessing of heaven sent into the country, by means of which little children of even seven years of age find the means of gaining a livelihood, and others of supporting their parents and their whole family. The old men work and find it answer. As soon as the work is finished, they are able to sell it, and are paid. It is this which makes them so miserable, because all sorts of persons are not fitted to work at the fine point they wish to make, and the children will be frustrated and sent away, because they cannot be sufficiently skilful to work at the fine point; and all those who gained their subsistence cannot succeed, being accustomed to a point of which they have now the sale.

"This it is which causes the resistance, thinking their trade is being taken away from them and the means of paying their taxes. The little shepherdesses of the fields even work. This is what in conscience I am obliged to represent to you, and to make you know all that they wished to do to a country favoured by heaven with this industry, which gives life and maintenance to so many thousand souls. This is the truth of the matter."

The remonstrance of the worthy intendant met with the attention it deserved.

On September 14 following, after a meeting headed by Prevost and the Marquis de Rasnes, intendant of the city, it was settled that after the king had found 200 girls, the rest were at liberty to work as they pleased; none had permission to make the fine point of the royal pattern except those who worked for the manufactory; and all girls must show to the authorities the patterns they intended working, "so that the king shall be satisfied and the people gain a livelihood."

The "maîtresse dentellière," Catherine du Marcq, writes to Colbert, November 30, 1665, complaining of the obstinacy of the people, who prefer the old work. "Out of 8000 women, we have got but 700, and I can only count on 250 who at least will have learnt to perfection the Venetian point, the remainder merely working a month and then leaving the establishment."

M

The productions of the infant manufacture are duly chronicled in the "Mercure." [4] In 1677 it announces:—"They make now many points de France without grounds, and 'picots en campannes' to all the fine handkerchiefs. We have seen some with little flowers over the large, which might be styled 'flying flowers,' being only attached in the centre."

In 1678, it says:—"The last points de France have no brides, the fleurons are closer together. The flowers, which are in higher relief in the centre, and lower at the edges, are united by small stalks and flowers, which keep them in their places, instead of brides. The manner of disposing the branches, called 'ordon-

Fig. 79.

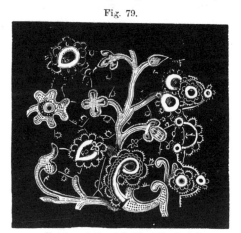

Venetian point in relief. "Dentelle volante."

nances,' is of two kinds: the one is a twirling stalk, which throws out flowers; the other is regular—a central flower, throwing out regular branches on each side." In October of the same year, the "Mercure" says, "There has been no change in the patterns," and it does not allude to them again. What can these be but Venice patterns? The flower upon flower—like "fleurs volantes" —exactly answers to the point in high relief. (Fig. 79.)

The Venetian point in relief, introduced by Colbert, was eminently successful, and he attained his object of making France independent of Venice, though the constant smuggling of Vene-

---

[4] In 1673, July, we read in the "Mercure:"—' On fait aussi des dentelles à grandes brides, comme aux points de fil sans raiseau, et des dentelles d'Espagne avec des brides claires sans picots; et l'on fait aux nouveaux points de France des brid s qui en sont remplies d'un nombre infini."

tian points into France formed a continual subject of correspondence between him and the French ambassador at Venice.
"The French," says Savary, "no longer purchase these articles,
having established themselves manufactures which rival those of
the Adriatic." And that the French exported largely their
products would appear from the same writer : " Russia and Poland
were its great marts." In 1680, in " Britannia Languens," a discourse upon trade,[5] it states that " the laces commonly called
points de Venice now come mostly from France, and amount to a
vast sum yearly."

Fig. 80.

Colbert.   From his portrait, Musée Nationale, Versailles.

January 6, 1673, Colbert writes to the Comte d'Avaux,
ambassador at Venice, thanking him for the "collet de point
rebrodé que vous m'avez envoyé que j'ai trouvé fort beau. Je le
confronterai avec ceux qui se font dans nos manufactures, mais je
dois vous dire à l'avance que l'on en a fait dans le royaume
d'aussi beaux." If the French manufacture attained such perfection, we may fairly infer that many of the fine points now
attributed to Venice are of French manufacture, Colbert's jabot
(Fig. 80), for instance, and probably Coloured Plate III., p. 44.

A memoir drawn up in 1698 by M. de Pommereu[6] is the next

---

[5] "Tracts on Trade of the Seventeenth Century," published by Mac-
Culloch, at the expense of Lord Montagu,
1856.

[6] " Mémoire concernant la Généralité
d'Alençon, dressé par M. de Pommereu."
1698. Bib. Nat. MSS. Fords Mortemart, No. 80.

mention we find of the lace of Alençon. "The manufacture of the points of France is also," he says, "one of the most considerable of the country. This fabric began at Alençon, where most of the women and girls work at it, to the number of more than eight to nine hundred, without counting those in the country, which are in considerable numbers. It is a commerce of about 500,000 livres per annum. This point is called 'vilain'[7] in the country; the principal sale was in Paris during the war, but the demand increases very much since the peace, in consequence of its exportation to foreign countries." The number of lace-workers given by M. Pommereu appears small, but the Alençon manufacture was then on the decline. The death of its protector Colbert (1683), the revocation of the Edict of Nantes (1685), which reduced the population of Alençon one-third, the industrial families retiring to other countries, the disastrous, long wars of Louis XIV., and finally his death (1715), all contributed to diminish the prosperity of this magnificent manufacture.[8]

In the eighteenth century, the réseau ground was introduced, and soon became universally adopted.

After carefully examining the engravings of the time, the collection of historic portraits at Versailles and other galleries, we find no traces of point d'Alençon with the réseau or network ground in the time of Louis XIV. The laces are all of the Venetian character, "à bride;" while, on the other hand, the daughters of Louis XV. (Mesdames de France), and the "Filles du Régent," all wear rich points of Alençon and Argentan, "à réseau."

The earlier patterns of the eighteenth century are flowery and undulating (Coloured Plate VII.), scarcely begun, never ending, into which are introduced haphazard patterns of a finer ground, much as the medallions of Boucher or Vanloo were inserted in the gilded panellings of a room. Twined among them appear a variety of "jours," filled up with patterns of endless variety, the whole wreathed and garlanded like the decoration of a theatre. Such was the taste of the day. "Après moi le déluge;" and the

---

[7] "Vilain," "velin," "vellum," from the parchment or vellum upon which it is made. The expression is still used. When the Author inquired at Alençon the way to the house of M. R., a lace manufacturer, she was asked in return if it was "Celui qui fait le velin?"

[8] In 1788 Arthur Young states the number of lace-makers at and about Alençon to be from 8000 to 9000. "Travels in France."

Plate VII.

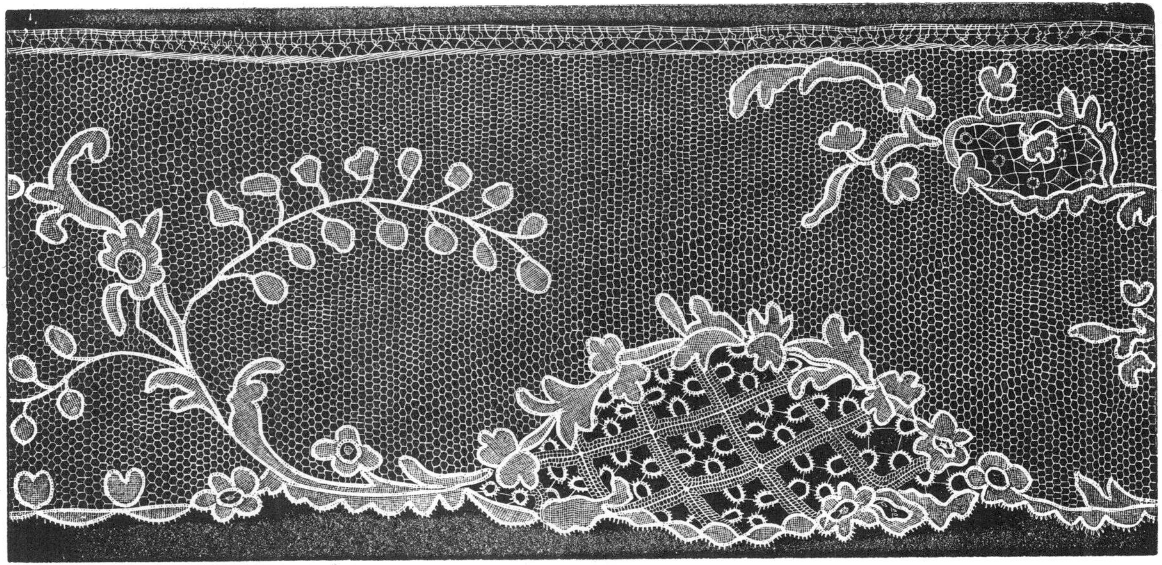

Point d'Alençon. 1750–1800.

precept of the favourite was carried out in the style of design : an insouciance and laisser-aller typical of a people regardless of the morrow.

Towards the latter end of the reign, a change came over the national taste. It appears in the architecture and domestic decoration. As the cabriole legs of the chairs are replaced by

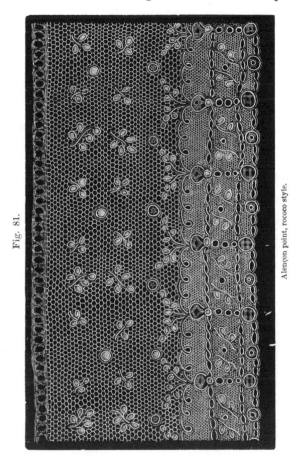

Fig. 81.

Alençon point, rococo style.

the " pieds de daim," so the running patterns of the lace give place to compact and more stiff designs. The flowers are rigid and angular, of the style called " bizarre," or rococo, of almost conventional form. With Louis XVI. began the ground semé with compact little bouquets, all intermixed with small patterns (Fig. 81), spots (pois), fleurons, rosettes, and tears (larmes), which towards the end of the century entirely expel the bouquets from the ground. Fig. 82, inadvertently placed here, is Brussels.[9]

Point d'Alençon is made entirely by hand, with a fine needle, upon a parchment pattern, in small pieces, afterwards united by invisible seams. Each part is executed by a special workwoman.

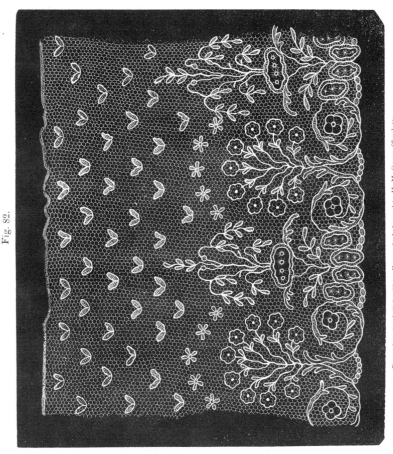

Fig. 82.

Brussels point à l'aiguille. Formerly belonged to H. M. Queen Charlotte.

Formerly it required eighteen [10] different hands to complete a

---

[9] Before the Revolution, Roland estimates the annual value of the manufacture at 11,000,000 to 12,000,000 livres.

Savary deducts 150,000 livres for the raw material, the Lille thread, which was used at prices ranging from 800 to 900 livres for good fine point; but Lille at that time fabricated thread as high as 1800 livres per lb.

[10] These were the "piqueuse," "tra-

piece of lace; the number, we believe, is now reduced to twelve. The design, engraved upon a copper plate, is printed off in divisions upon pieces of parchment 10 inches long, each numbered according to their order. Green parchment is now used, the worker being better able to detect any faults in her work than on white. The pattern is next pricked upon the parchment, which is stitched to a piece of very coarse linen folded double. The outline of the pattern is then formed by two flat threads, which are guided along the edge by the thumb of the left hand, and fixed by minute stitches, passed with another thread and needle, through the holes of the parchment. When the outline is finished, the work is given over to the "réseleuse" to make the ground, which is of two kinds, bride and réseau. The delicate réseau is worked backwards and forwards from the footing to the picot—of the bride, more hereafter. For the flowers the worker supplies herself with a long needle and a fine thread; with these she works the "point noué" (button-hole stitch) from left to right, and when arrived at the end of the flower, the thread is thrown back from the point of departure, and she works again from left to right over the thread. This gives a closeness and evenness to the work unequalled in any other point. Then follow the "modes," and other different operations, which completed, the threads which unite lace, parchment, and linen together are cut with a sharp razor passed between the two folds of linen, any little defects repaired, and then remains the great work of uniting all these segments imperceptibly together. This task devolves upon the head of the establishment, and is one requiring the greatest nicety. An ordinary pair of men's ruffles would be divided into ten pieces; but when the order must be executed quickly, the sub-divisions are even greater. The stitch by which these sections are worked is termed "assemblage," and differs from the "point de raccroc," where the segments are united by a fresh row of stitches. At Alençon, they are joined by a seam, following as much as possible the outlines of the pattern. When finished, a steel instrument, called "aficot," is passed into each flower, to polish it, and remove any inequalities in its surface. The more primitive lobster's claw was used until late years for the same purpose.

---

ceuse," "réseleuse," "remplisseuse," "toucheuse," "brideuse," "boucleuse," "fondeuse," "modeuse," "brodeuse," "gazeuse," "mignonneuse," "picoteuse," "abouleuse," "régaleuse," "assembleuse," "affineuse," "affiqueuse."

Point d'Alençon is of a solidity which defies time and washing, and has been justly called the Queen of Lace. It is the only lace in which horsehair is introduced along the edge, to give firmness and consistency to the cordonnet, rendered perhaps necessary to make the point stand up when exposed to wind, mounted on the towering fabrics then worn by the ladies. The objection to horsehair is that it shrinks in washing, and draws up the flower from the ground. In 1761, a writer, describing the point de France, says that it does not arrive at the taste and delicacy of Brussels, its chief defect consisting in the thickness of the cordonnet, which thickens when put into water. The horsehair edge also draws up the ground, and makes the lace rigid and heavy. He likewise finds fault with the "modes," or fancy stitches of Alençon, and states that much point is sent from there to Brussels to have the modes added, thereby giving it a borrowed beauty, but connoisseurs, he adds, easily detect the difference.[11]

When the points of Alençon and Argentan dropped the general designation of "points de France" is difficult to say. Probably at the expiration of the privilege, each manufacture began to adopt its own name. The last inventory in which we have found mention of "point de France" is one of 1723,[12] while point d'Argentan is noted in 1738,[13] and point d'Alençon in 1741, where it is specified to be "à réseau." [14]

'In the accounts of Madame du Barry, no point d'Alençon is mentioned—always point à l'aiguille—and "needle point" is the name by which point d'Alençon was alone known in England during the last century. The purchases of needle point of Madame du Barry were most extensive. Sleeves (engageantes) and lappets for 8400 livres; court ruffles at 1100; a mantelet at 2400; a veste at 6500; a grande coëffe, 1400; a garniture, 6010, &c.[15]

Coloured Plate VIII. represents a beautiful lappet which, in her former edition, the Author has placed under Genoa, as it was sent

---

[11] "Dictionnaire du Citoyen," Paris, 1761.

[12] "Inv. de Madame Anne Palatine, Princesse de Condé." See p. 131.

[13] In the inventory of the Duc de Penthièvre, 1738. See p. 143.

[14] "Une coiffure de point d'Alençon à raiseau."—*Inv. de decès de Mademoiselle de Clermont*, 1741. Again, 1743, *Inv. de la Duchesse de Bourbon*. Bib. Nat.

[15] Among the objects of religious art exhibited in 1864, at the General Assembly of the Catholics of Belgium, at Malines, was a "voile de bénédiction," the handkerchief used to cover the ciborium, of point d'Alençon, with figures of the Virgin, St. Catherine, St. Ursula, and St. Barbara. It belonged to the church of St. Christopher at Charleroi.

Plate VIII

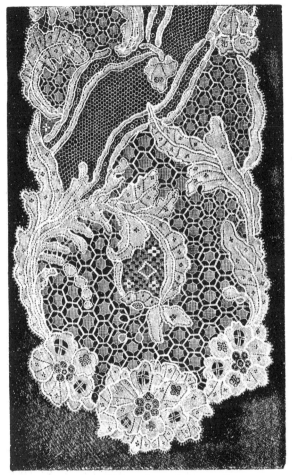

Argentella, or Point d'Alençon à réseau rosacé.

To face page 168

to her as having been made there, where it is styled " argentella,"
but M. Dupont-Auberville claims it as the product of Alençon, on
evidence, he states, that cannot be refuted.   The lovely diapered
ground, resembling the mayflower, or " œil de perdrix," of porcelain,
he has discovered in a piece of lace undoubtedly of Alençon make,
and has five other specimens which have been transmitted for
generations in a family of Normandy.   M. Dupont-Auberville
styles it " fond rosacé, " a term we shall adopt, with the name
" argentella," which it has always borne.

In the " Description of the Department of the Orne," drawn up
in 1801, it is stated, " Fifteen years back there were from 7000 to
8000 lace-workers at Alençon and its environs: the manufacture
of Argentan, whose productions are finer and more costly, had
about 2000."   Almost all these lace-makers passed into England,
Spain, Italy, Germany, and the courts of the North, especially to
Russia.   The two establishments produced to the annual value of
at least 1,800,000 francs, and when they had extraordinary orders,
such as " parures " for beds and other large works, it increased
to 2,000,000 francs (80,000l.).   But this commerce, subject to the
variable empire of fashion, had declined one-half even before the
Revolution.   " It supported three cities and their territory, for
that of Séez [16] bore its part.   Some black laces are still made at
Séez, but they are of little importance.   P.S.—These laces have
obtained a little favour at the last Leipsic fair." [17]

The manufacture of Alençon was nearly extinct when the
patronage of Napoleon caused it to return almost to its former
prosperity.   Among the orders executed for the emperor on his
marriage with the Empress Marie Louise was a bed furniture of
great richness; tester, curtains, coverlet, pillow-cases.   The
principal subject represented the arms of the empire surrounded
by bees.[18]   From its elaborate construction, point d'Alencon is
seldom met with in pieces of large size ; the amount of labour
therefore expended on this bed must have been marvellous.   The
Author, when at Alençon, was so fortunate as to meet with a piece
of the ground powdered with bees, bought from the ancient
manufacture of Mercier, at Lonray, when the stock many years

---

[16] Séez has now no records of its manufacture.
[17] "Descr du Dép. de l'Orne.   An
IX.   Publiée par ordre du ministre de
l'intérieur."
[18] "Illustrated News,' March 22,
1853.

back was sold off (Fig. 83). It is pillow-made, the réseau overcast. Part of the "équipage" of the King of Rome excited the admiration of all beholders at the exhibition of 1855.

Alençon again fell with the first empire. No new workers were trained, the old ones died off, and as it requires so many hands to execute even the most simple lace, the manufacture again nearly died out. In vain the Duchesse d'Angoulême endeavoured to revive the fabric, and gave large orders herself;

Fig. 83.

Bed made for Napoleon I.

but point lace had been replaced by blonde, and the consumption was so small, it was resumed on a very confined scale. So low had it fallen in 1830 that there were only between two and three hundred lace-workers, whose products did not exceed the value of 1200 francs (48l.). Again, in 1836, Baron Mercier, thinking by producing it at a lower price to procure a more favourable sale, set up a lace school, and caused the girls to work the patterns on bobbin-net, as bearing some resemblance to the old point de bride, but fashion did not favour point de bride, so the plan failed.

In 1840 fresh attempts were made to revive the manufacture. Two hundred aged women—all the lace-makers remaining of this once flourishing industry—were collected and again set to work. A new class of patterns was introduced, and the manufacture once more returned to favour and prosperity. But the difficulties were great. The old point was made by an hereditary set of workers, trained from their earliest infancy to the one special work they were to follow for life. Now new workers had to be procured from other lace districts, already taught the ground peculiar to their fabrics. The consequence was, their fingers never could acquire the art of making the pure Alençon réseau. They made a good ground, certainly, but it was mixed with their own early traditions: as the Alençon workers say, "Elles bâtardisent les fonds."

In the exhibition of 1851 were many fine specimens of the revived manufacture. One flounce, which was valued at 22,000 francs, and had taken thirty-six women eighteen months to complete, afterwards appeared in the "corbeille de mariage" of the Empress Eugénie.

In 1856 most magnificent orders were given for the imperial layette, a description of which is duly chronicled.[19] The young prince was "voué au blanc;" white, therefore, was the prevailing colour in the layette. The curtains of the imperial infant's cradle were of needle point, with Alençon coverlet lined with satin. The christening robe, mantle, and head-dress were all of Alençon; and the three corbeilles, bearing the imperial arms and cipher, were also covered with the same point. Twelve dozen embroidered frocks, each in itself a work of art, were all profusely trimmed with Alençon, as were also the aprons of the imperial nurses.

A magnificent work of Alençon point appeared in the exhibition of 18 5; a dress, purchased by the emperor for 70,000 francs (2800l.), and presented by him to the empress.

Costly orders for trousseaux are given not only in France, but from Russia and other countries. We saw one in progress which was to amount to 150,000 francs (6000l.); flounce, lappets and trimmings for the body, pockethandkerchief, fan, parasol, all en suite; and, moreover, there were a certain number of metres of

---

19 "Illustrated News," March 22, 1856.

" aunage," or border lace, for the layette. The making of point d'Alençon being so slow, it was impossible ever to execute it " to order " for this occasion.

Great as is the beauty of the workmanship of Alençon, it was never able to compete with Brussels in one respect: its designs were seldom copied from nature, while the fabric of Brabant sent forth roses and honeysuckles of a correctness worthy of a Dutch painter.

Alençon point is now successfully made at Bayeux, where the manufacture was introduced, in 1855, by M. Auguste Lefébure, a manufacturer of that town. Departing from the old custom of assigning to each lace-maker a special branch of the work, the lace is here executed through all its stages by the same worker. Perhaps the finest example of point d'Alençon, exhibited in 1867, was the produce of Bayeux; a dress consisting of two flounces, the pattern, flowers, and foliage of most artistic and harmonious design, relieved by the new introduction of shaded tints, giving to the lace the relief of a picture.[20]   The ground (réseau) was worked with the greatest smoothness and regularity, one of the great technical difficulties when such small pieces have to be joined together. The price of the dress was 85,000 francs, 3400*l.*   It took forty women seven years to complete.

---

[20] This effect is produced in the pillow-lace by varying the application of the two stitches used in making the flowers (see p. 26), the "toilé," which forms the close tissue, and the " grillé," the more open part of the pattern; in the needle point by threads of different coarseness. The system has been adopted in France, Belgium, and England, but with most success in France.

CHAPTER XIV.

ARGENTAN (Dép. de l'Orne).

" Vous qui voulez d'Argentan faire conte,
A sa grandeur arrêter ne faut ;
Petite elle est, mais en beauté surmonte
Maintes cités, car rien ne lui defaut ;
Elle est assise en lieu plaisant et haut,
De tout côté à prairie, à campaigne,
Un fleuve aussi, où maint poisson se baigne,
Des bois épais, suffisans pour nourrir
Biches et cerfs qui sont prompts à courir ;
Plus y trouvez, tant elle est bien garnie,
Plus au besoin nature secourir
Bon air, bon vin, et bonne compagnie ! "
Des Maisons, 1517.

THE name of the little town of Argentan, whose points long rivalled those of Alençon, is familiar to English ears as connected with our Norman kings. Argentan is mentioned by old Robert Wace as sending its sons to the conquest of England.[1] It was here the mother of Henry II. retired in 1130 ; and the imperial eagle borne as the arms of the town is said to be a memorial of her long sojourn. Here the first Plantagenet held the " cour plénière," in which the invasion of Ireland was arranged ; and it was here he uttered those rash words which prompted his servile adherents to leave Argentan to assassinate Thomas à Becket.[2]

But, apart from historic recollections, Argentan is celebrated for its point lace, which, though generally confounded in commerce with that of Alençon, essentially differs from it in character. No history of the establishment of this manufacture remains. The geographers and local historians of Argentan do not even allude to its existence, but it is mentioned in one of the letters of the

[1] " Li boen citean de Roem,
E la Jovante de Caem,
E de Falaise e d'Argentoen."
Romant de Rou.

[2] Henry founded a chapel at Argentan to St. Thomas of Canterbury.

"Colbert Correspondence," showing it to be coeval with Alençon. There still exists at Argentan an humble inn with "Le Point de France" as its sign. The two manufactures appear to have been distinct, though some lace-makers near Lignères-la-Doucelle worked for both establishments. Alençon made the finest réseau —Argentan specially excelled in the bride.

The bride, or we would rather call it the "grande bride," ground, to which we have before alluded in the notice on Alençon, belonged almost exclusively to Argentan. It was of very elaborate construction, and consists of a large six-sided mesh, worked over with the button-hole stitch. It was always printed on the parchment pattern, and the upper angle of the hexagon is pricked. After the hexagon is formed by passing the needle and thread round the pins in a way too complicated to be worth explaining, the six sides are worked over with seven or eight button-hole stitches in each side. The grande bride ground was consequently very strong. It was much affected in France; the réseau was more preferred abroad.[3]

The flowers of Argentan were bolder and larger in pattern, in higher relief, heavier and coarser than those of Alençon. (Coloured Plate IX., and Fig. 84.) The toilé was flatter, and more compact. The workmanship differed in character. On the clear grande bride ground this lace was more effective than the minuter workmanship of Alençon.

In 1708 the manufacture had almost fallen to decay, when it was raised by one Sieur Mathieu Guyard, merchant mercer at Paris, who states that "his ancestors and himself had for more than 120 years been occupied in fabricating black silk and white thread lace in the environs of Paris." He applies to the council of the king for permission to re-establish the fabric of Argentan, and to employ workwomen to the number of above 600. He asks for exemption from lodging soldiers, begs to have the royal arms placed over his door, and stipulates that Montulay, his draughtsman and engraver, shall be exempted from all taxes except the capitation. The arrêt obtained by Guyard is dated 24th July 1708.

Guyard's children continued the establishment. Montulay

---

[3] Indeed so little is the beautiful workmanship of this ground known or understood that the author has seen priceless flowers of Argentan relentlessly cut out, and transferred to bobbin-net, "to get rid of the ugly, coarse ground."

Plate IX.

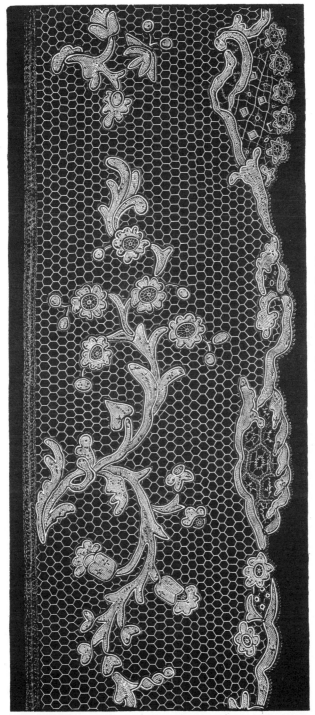

Point d'Argentan. Grande bride ground. Eighteenth century.

Fig. 84.

Point d'Argentan.

went over to another manufacturer, and was replaced by the Sieur James, who, in his turn, was succeeded by his daughter, and she took as her partner one Sieur De La Leu. Other manufactories were set up in competition with Guyard's; among others that of Madame Wyriot, whose factor, Du Ponchel, was in open warfare with the rival house.

The marriage of the dauphin, in 1744, was a signal for open hostilities. Du Ponchel asserted that Mademoiselle James enticed away his workwomen, and claimed protection, on the ground that he worked for the king and the court. But, on the other side, "It is I," writes De La Leu to the intendant, on behalf of Mademoiselle James, "that supply the 'Chambre du Roi' for this year, by order of the Duke de Richelieu. I too have the honour of furnishing the 'Garderobe du Roi,' by order of the grand master, the Duke de La Rochefoucault. Besides which, I furnish the King and Queen of Spain, and at this present moment am supplying lace for the marriage of the dauphin."[4] Du Ponchel rejoins "that he had to execute two 'toilettes et leurs suites, nombre de Bourgognes[5] et leurs suites,' for the queen, and also a cravat, all to be worn on the same occasion." Du Ponchel appears to have had the better interest with the controller-general; for the quarrel ended in a prohibition to the other manufacturers to molest the women working for Du Ponchel, though the Maison Guyard asked for reciprocity, and maintained that their opponents had suborned and carried off more than a hundred of their hands.[6]

The number of lace-makers in the town of Argentan and its environs at this period amounted to nearly 1200. In a list of 111 who worked for the Maison Guyard, appear the names of many of the good bourgeois families of the county of Alençon, and even some of noble birth, leading one to infer that making point lace was an occupation not disdained by ladies of poor but noble houses.

De La Leu, who, by virtue of an ordinance, had set up a

---

[4] Letter of the 19th of September 1744.

[5] "Burgoigne, the first part of the dress for the head next the hair."— *Mundus Muliebris*, 1690. "Burgoigin, the part of the head-dress that covers up the head."—*Ladies' Dictionary*, 1694. In Farquhar's comedy of "Sir Harry Wild-air," 1700, Parley, when asked what he had been about, answers, "Sir, I was coming to Mademoiselle Furbelow, the French milliner, for a new Burgundy for my lady's head."

[6] The offenders, manufacturers and workwomen, incurred considerable fines.

manufactory on his own account, applies, in 1745, to have 200 workwomen at Argentan, and 200 at Carrouges, delivered over to his factor, in order that he may execute works ordered for the king and the dauphin for the approaching fêtes of Christmas. This time the magistrate resists. "I have been forced to admit," he writes to the intendant, "that the workwomen cannot be transferred by force. We had an example when the layette of the dauphin was being made. You then gave me the order to furnish a certain number of women who worked at these points to the late Sieur de Montulay. A detachment of women and girls came to my house, with a female captain (capitaine femelle) at their head, and all with one accord declared that if forced to work they would make nothing but cobbling (bousillage). Partly by threats, and partly by entreaty, I succeeded in compelling about a dozen to go, but the Sieur de Montulay was obliged to discharge them the next day.[7] I am therefore of opinion that the only way is for M. De La Leu to endeavour to get some of the workwomen to suborn others to work for him under the promise of higher wages than they can earn elsewhere. M. De La Leu agrees with me there is no other course to pursue; and I have promised him that, in case any appeal is made to me, I shall answer that things must be so, as the work is doing for the king." From this period we have scarcely any notices concerning the fabric of Argentan.

In 1763 the widow Louvain endeavoured to establish at Mortagne (Orne) a manufacture of lace like that of Alençon and Argentan, and proposed to send workers from these two towns to teach the art gratuitously to the girls of Mortagne. We do not know what became of her project; but at the same period the Époux Malbiche de Boislaunay applied for permission to establish an office at Argentan, with the ordinary exemptions, under the title of Royal Manufacture. The title and exemptions were refused. There were then (1763) at Argentan three manufactories of point de France, without counting the general hospital of St. Louis, in which it was made for the profit of the institution, and evidently with success; for in 1764, a widow Roger was in treaty with the hospital to teach her two daughters the fabrication of point d'Argentan. They were to be boarded, and to give six years of their time. The fine on non-performance was 80 livres. In 1781, the Sieur Gravelle Desvallées made a fruitless application to

---

[7] 12 Nov 1745.

establish a manufactory at Argentan; nor could even the children of the widow Wyriot obtain a renewal of the privilege granted to their mother.[8] Gravelle was ruined by the Revolution, and died in 1830.

Arthur Young, in 1788, estimates the annual value of Argentan point at 500,000 livres.

Taking these data, we may fix the reigns of Louis XV. and Louis XVI. as the period when point d'Argentan was at its highest prosperity. It appears in the inventories of the personages of that time; most largely in the accounts of Madame du Barry (from 1769 to 1773), who patronised Argentan equally with point d'Angleterre and point à l'aiguille. In 1772, she pays 5740 francs for a complete garniture. Lappets, flounces, engageantes, colle-rettes, aunages, fichus, are all supplied to her of this costly fabric.[9]

One spécialité in the Argentan point is the "bride picotée," a remnant, perhaps, of the early Venetian teaching. It consists of the six-sided button-hole bride, fringed with a little row of three or four picots or pearls on each side. It was also called "bride épinglée," because pins were pricked in the parchment pattern, to form these picots or boucles[10] (loops); hence it was sometimes styled "bride bouclée."[11]

The "écaille de poisson" réseau was also much used at Alençon and Argentan.

The manner of making "bride picotée" was entirely lost. The old workwomen had died without leaving pupils, but through

---

[8] In 1765, under the name of Duponchel.

[9] "1772. Un ajustement de point d'Argentan—

"Les 6 rangs manchettes.

"1/3 pour devant de gorge.

"4 au. 1/3 festonné des deux costés, le fichu et une gar-
          niture de fichu de nuit . . . . 2500 livres.

" 1 au. 3/4 ruban de point d'Argentan, à 100 . . . 175 ,,

" Une collerette de point d'Argentan . . . . . . 360 ,,

          (*Comptes de Madame du Barry.*)

"1781. Une nappe d'autel garnie d'une très-belle dentelle de Point d'Argen-tan."—*Inv. de l'Église de St. Gervais.* Arch. Nat. L. 654.

See also p. 132, note [9], and p. 146.

"1789. Item, un parement de robe consistant en garniture, deux paires de manchettes, et fichu, le tout de point d'Argentan. (Dans la garderobe de Madame.)"—*Inv. de decès de Mgr. le Duc de Duras.* Bib. Nat. MSS. F. Fr. 11,440.

[10] "Une coiffure bride à picot com-plète."—*Inv. de decès de Mademoiselle de Clermont,* 1741.

[11] These details on the manufacture of Argentan have been furnished from the archives of Alençon, through the kindness of M. Léon de la Sicotière, the learned archæologist of the Department of the Orne.

the persevering exertions of M. Ernest Lefébure it is about to be reorganised in the original seat of its industry. In January 1874, with the assistance of the mayor, he made a search in the greniers of the Hôtel Dieu, and discovered three specimens of point d'Argentan, in progress on the parchment patterns. One was of bold pattern, with the " grande bride " ground, evidently a man's ruffle ; the other had the barette or bride ground of point de France ; the third bride picotée, showing that the three descriptions of lace were made contemporaneously at Argentan. M. Lefébure has set up in the convent of St. James, in the city, a workshop for making point de Argentan, the pupils under the direction of the most skilful lace-workers of Paris.

Some years since the nuns of the hospice offered to exchange a quantity of point d'Argentan and old guipure for a small sewing-machine, which proposal was rejected.

The author of a little pamphlet on point d'Argentan [12] remembers having seen in his youth in the Holy Week, in the churches of St. Martin and St. Germain, the statues of the apostles covered over from head to foot with this priceless point.

Point d'Argentan disappeared at the Revolution, though a few specimens were produced at the Exhibition of Industry in 1808. Embroidery has replaced this far-famed fabric among the workers of the town, and the hand-spinning of hemp among those of the country.

_____

[12] " Légende du Point d'Argentan," M. Eugène de Lonlay.

CHAPTER XV.

ISLE DE FRANCE.—PARIS (Dép. Seine).

> " Quelle heure est-il ?
> Passé midi.
> Qui vous l'a dit ?
> Une petite souris.
> Que fait-elle ?
> De la dentelle.
> Pour qui ?
> La reine de Paris."
>
> *Old Nursery Song.*

EARLY in the seventeenth century, lace was extensively made in the environs of Paris, at Louvres, Gisors, Villiers-le-Bel, Montmorency, and other localities. Of this we have confirmation in a work[1] published 1634, in which, after commenting upon the sums of money spent in Flanders for " ouvrages et passemens,[2] tant de point couppé que d'autres," which the king had put a stop to by the sumptuary law of 1633, the author says :—" Pour empescher icelle despence, il y a toute l'Isle de France et autres lieux qui sont remplis de plus de dix mille familles dans lesquels les enfans de l'un et l'autre sexe, dès l'âge de dix ans ne sont instruits qu'à la manufacture desdits ouvrages, dont il s'en trouve d'aussi beaux et biens faits que ceux des étrangers ; les Espagnols, qui le sçavent, ne s'en fournissent ailleurs."

Who first founded the lace-making of the Isle de France, it is difficult to say ; a great part of it was in the hands of the Huguenots, leading us to suppose it formed one of the numerous "industries" introduced or encouraged by Henry IV. and Sully.

---

[1] " Nouveau Réglement Général sur outres sortes de Marchandises et Manufactures qui sont utiles et necessaires dans ce Royaume etc., par M. le Marquis de la Gomberdière." Paris, 1634. In 8vo.

[2] M. Fournier says that France was at this time tributary to Flanders for " passemens de fil," very fine and delicately worked. Laffemas, in his " Réglement Général pour dresser les Manufactures du Royaume, 1597," estimates the annual cost of these " passemens " of every sort, silk stockings, &c., at 800,000 crowns ; Montchrestien, at above a million.

Plate X.

Point de France, pillow-made. Seventeenth century.

Point de Paris (Fig. 85), mignonette, bisette, and other narrow cheap laces were made, and common guipures were also fabricated at Saint-Denis, Écouen, and Groslay.   From 1665 to the French Revolution, the exigencies of fashion requiring a superior class of lace, the workwomen arrived gradually at making point of remarkable fineness and superior execution.

A branch manufactory of points de France had been established, as already mentioned, by Colbert at the Château de Madrid (p. 129), where they made, as well as at Aurillac, the

Fig. 85.

Point de Paris (reduced).   (By an error of the engraver, the point de Paris ground is not rendered.)

finest pillow lace in the style of the point d'Angleterre.   Some rich specimens of this period are occasionally met with, among which may be placed Coloured Plate X., in which is the crown of France, supporting medallion portraits of Louis XIV. and Maria Theresa.   The richness and elegance of this manufacture was sustained for many years, encouraged by the king and his court; and with distinguished artists at its disposal, the productions of the Château de Madrid were among the choicest of the points de France.[3]

[3] "Une chemisette de toile d'Hollande garnye de point de Paris."—*Inv. d'Anne d'Escoubleau, Baronne de Sourdis, veuve de François de Simiane,* 1681.   Arch. Nat. M. M. 802.

A second manufactory was established by the Comte de Marsan,[4] in Paris, towards the end of the same century. Having brought over from Brussels his nurse, named Dumont, with her four daughters, she asked him, as a reward for the care she had bestowed upon him in his infancy, to obtain for her the privilege of setting up in Paris a manufactory of point de France. Colbert granted the request: Dumont was established in the Faubourg Saint-Antoine—classic land of embroidery from early times—cited in the "Révolte des Passemens:"—"Telle Broderie qui n'avoit jamais esté plus loin que du Faubourg S.-Antoine au Louvre." A "cent Suisse" of the king's was appointed as guard before the door of her house. In a short time Dumont had collected more than 200 girls, among whom were several of good birth, and made beautiful lace called "point de France." Her manufactory was next transferred to the Rue Saint-Sauveur, and subsequently to the Hôtel Saint-Chaumont, near the Porte Saint-Denis. Dumont afterwards went to Portugal, leaving her establishment under the direction of Mademoiselle de Marsan. But, adds the historian, as fashion and taste often change in France, people became tired of this point. It proved difficult to wash; the flowers had to be raised each time it was cleaned; it was thick and unbecoming to the face. Points d'Espagne were now made instead, with small flowers, which, being very fine, was more suitable for a lady's dress. Lastly, the taste for Mechlin lace coming in, the manufacture of Dumont was entirely given up.[5]

In the time of Louis XIV. the commerce of lace was distributed in different localities of Paris, as we learn from the "Livre Commode,"[6] already quoted. The gold laces, forming of themselves a special commerce, had their shops in the "rue des Bourdonnais and the rue Sainte-Honoré, entre la place aux Chats et les piliers des Halles," while the Rue Bétizy retained for itself the spécialité of selling "points et dentelles."

The gold and silver laces of Paris, commonly known as points d'Espagne,[7] often embellished with pearls and other ornaments,

---

[4] Youngest son of the Comte d'Harcourt.

[5] "Vie de J.-Bap. Colbert." (Printed in the "Archives curieuses.")

[6] "Livre Commode ou les Adresses de la Ville de Paris," for 1692.

[7] For the introduction of the gold point of Spain into France, see Spain, p. 80. The manufacture of gold lace in Paris was, however, prior to Colbert.

"1732. Un bord de Point d'Espagne d'or de Paris, à fonds de réseau."—*Garderobe de S. A. S. Mgr. le Duc de Penthièvre.* Arch. Nat. K. K. 390–1.

were for years renowned throughout all Europe. Its importance is shown by the sumptuary edicts of the seventeenth century, forbidding its use, and also by its mention in the " Révolte des Passemens." It was made on the pillow. Until the revocation of the Edict of Nantes, it was an object of great commerce to France. Much was exported to Spain and the Indies. How those exiled workmen were received by the Protestant princes of Europe, and allowed to establish themselves in their dominions, to the loss of France and the enrichment of the lands of their adoption, will be told in due time, when we touch on the lace manufactures of Holland and Germany.

Since 1784, little lace has been made at Paris itself, but a large number of lace-makers are employed in applying the flowers of Binche and Mirecourt upon the bobbin-net grounds.

CHANTILLY (Dép. Oise).

" Dans sa pompe élégante admirez Chantilli,
De héros en héros, d'âge en âge embelli."
Delille, Les Jardins.

Although there long existed lace-makers in the environs of Paris, the establishment for which Chantilly was celebrated owes its formation to Catherine de Rohan, Duchesse de Longueville, who sent for workwomen from Dieppe and Havre to her château of Étrepagny, where she retired at the beginning of the seventeenth century, and established schools.

The town of Chantilly being the centre of a district of lace-makers, has given its name to the laces of the surrounding district, the trade being distributed over more than a hundred villages, the principal of which are Saint-Maximien, Viarmes, Méric, Luzarches, and Dammartin. The proximity to Paris affording a ready sale for its productions caused the manufacture to prosper, and the narrow laces which they first made were soon replaced by guipures, white thread and black silk lace.[8] Some twenty years since there dwelt

---

[8] In " Statistique de la France," 1800, the finest silk lace is said to be made at Fontenay, Puisieux, Morges, and Louvres-en-Parisis; the coarse and common kinds at Montmorency, Villiers-le-Bel, Sarcelles, Écouen, Saint-Brice, Groslay, Gisors, Saint-Pierre-les-Champs, Étre-pagny, &c. Peuchet adds : " Il s'y fait dans Paris et ces environs une grande quantité de dentelles noires dont il se fait des expéditions considérables.' It was this same black silk lace which raised to

at Chantilly an elderly lady, granddaughter of an old proprietor, who had in her possession one of the original pattern books of the fabric, with autograph letters of Marie-Antoinette, the Princesse de Lamballe, and other ladies of the court, giving their orders and expressing their opinion on the laces produced. We find in the inventories of the last century, "coëffure de cour de dentelle de soye noire," "mantelet garni de dentelles noires," a "petite duchesse et une respectueuse," and other "coëffes," all of "dentelle de soye noire." [9]

White blonde appears more sparingly. The Duchesse de Duras has "une paire de manchettes à trois rangs, deux fichus et deux paires de sabots en blonde;" [10] the latter to wear, probably, with her "robe en singe." Du Barry purchases more largely.[11]

Fig. 86.

Chantilly (reduced).   From one of the order books, temp. Louis XVI.

Fig. 86 is a specimen taken from the above-mentioned pattern book; the flowers and ground are of the same silk, the flowers worked "en grillé," or open stitch, instead of the compact tissue of the "blondes mates" of the Spanish style. This is essentially "Chantilly lace." Chantilly first created the black silk lace industry, and deservedly it retains her name, whether made there or in Calvados. Chantilly black lace has always been made of silk, but from its being a grenadine, not a shining silk, a

so high a reputation the fabrics of Chantilly.

[9] "Inv. de decès de la Duchesse de Modène," 1761.

[10] "Inv. de decès du Duc de Duras," 1789.

[11] "Une fraise à deux rangs de blonde très-fine, grande hauteur, 120 l.

"Une paire de sabots de la même blonde, 84 l.

"Un fichu en colonette, la fraise garnie à deux rangs d'une très-belle blonde fond d'Alençon, 120 l.

"Un pouff bordé d'un plissé de blonde tournante fond d'Alençon, à bouquets très-fins et des bouillons de même blonde." This wonderful coiffure being finished with "Un beau panache de quatre plumes couleurs impériales, 108 l."

common error prevails that it is of thread, whereas black thread lace has never been made either at Chantilly or Bayeux.

Chantilly fell with '93. Being considered a royal fabric, and its productions made for the nobility alone, its unfortunate lace-workers became the victims of revolutionary fury, and all perished, with their patrons, on the scaffold. We hear no more of the manu-facture until the empire, a period during which Chantilly enjoyed its greatest prosperity. In 1805, white blonde became the rage in Paris, and the workwomen were chiefly employed in its fabrication. The Chantilly laces were then in high repute, and much exported, the black, especially, to Spain and her American colonies; no other manufactories could produce mantillas, scarfs, and other large pieces of such great beauty. It was then they made those rich large-patterned blondes called by the French " blondes mates," by the Spaniards " trapeada," the prevailing style since the first empire.

About 1835 black lace again came into vogue, and the lace-makers were at once set to work at making black silk laces with double ground, and afterwards they revived the hexagonal ground of the last century, called " fond d'Alençon," [12] for the production of which they are celebrated.

The lace industry has been driven away of late years from Chantilly, by the increase in the price of labour consequent on its vicinity to the capital. The lace manufacturers, unable to pay such high salaries, retired to Gisors, where in 1851 there were from 8000 to 9000 lace-makers. They only make the extra fine lace. The black shawls, dresses, scarfs, now produced at Chantilly, are more objects of luxury than of commercial value. Specimens of the finest workmanship made at Viarmes were exhibited in 1867. The generally so-called Chantilly shawls are the production of Bayeux.

---

[12] See preceding note.

CHAPTER XVI.

NORMANDY.

"Dangling thy hands like bobbins before thee."
Congreve, Way of the World.

SEINE-INFÉRIEURE.

LACE forms an essential part of the costume of the Normandy peasants. The wondrous "bourgoin,"[1] with its long lappets of rich lace, descended from generation to generation, but little varied from the cornettes of the fourteenth and fifteenth centuries (Fig. 87). The countrywomen wore their lace at all times, when it was not replaced by the cotton nightcap, without much regard to the general effect of their daily clothes. "Madame the hostess," writes a traveller in 1739, "made her appearance in long lappets of bone lace, with a sack of linsey wolsey."

The manufactures of the Pays de Caux date from the beginning of the sixteenth century. Lace-making was the principal occupation of the wives and daughters of the mariners and fishermen. In 1692, M. de Sainte-Aignan, governor of Havre, found it employed 20,000 women.[2]

---

[1] "The bourgoin is formed of white, stiffly starched muslin, covering a pasteboard shape, and rises to a great height above the head, frequently diminishing in size towards the top, where it finishes in a circular form. Two long lappets hang from either side towards the back, composed often of the finest lace. The bourgoins throughout Normandy are not alike."—*Mrs. Stothard's Tour in Normandy.*

[2] This must have included Honfleur and other surrounding localities.

By a paper on the lace trade ("Mém. concernant le Commerce des Dentelles," 1704; Bib. Nat. MSS. F. Fr. 14,294), we find that the making of "dentelles de bas prix," employed at Rouen, Dieppe, Le Havre, and throughout the Pays de Caux, the Bailliage of Caen, at Lyons, Le Puy, and other parts of France, one quarter of the population of all classes and ages from six to seventy years. These laces were all made of Haarlem thread. See Holland.

"The lace-makers of Havre," writes Peuchet, "work both in black and white points, from 5 sous to 30 francs the ell. They are all employed by a certain number of dealers, who purchase the produce of their pillows. Much is transported to foreign countries, even to the East Indies, the Southern Seas, and the islands of America."

It was in the province of Normandy, as comprised in its ancient extent, that the lace trade made the most rapid increase in the eighteenth century. From Arras to St. Malo more than thirty

Fig. 87.

Cauchoise. From an engraving of the eighteenth century.

centres of manufacture established themselves, imitating with success the laces of Mechlin; the guipures of Flanders; the "fond clair," or single ground, then called point de Bruxelles; point de Paris; black thread laces, and also those guipures, enriched with gold and silver, so much esteemed for church ornament. The manufactures of Havre, Honfleur, Bolbec, Eu, Fécamp, and Dieppe, were most thriving. They made double and single grounds, guipure, and a kind of thick Valenciennes, such as is still made in the little town of Honfleur and its environs. In 1692, the number of lace-makers at Havre and its environs was not less than 22,000. Corneille,[3] 1707, declares the laces of Havre to be "très-recherchées;" and in an engraving, 1688, representing a "marchande lingère en sa boutique,"[4] among the stock in trade, together with the points of Spain and England, are certain "cartons" labelled "point du Havre." It appears also in the "Révolte des Passemens," and in the inventory of Colbert, who considered it worthy of trimming his pillow-cases and his camisoles;[5] and Madame de Simiane[6] had two "toilettes garnies de dentelle du Hâvre," with an "estuy à peigne," en suite.

Next in rank to the points du Havre came the laces of Dieppe and its environs, which, says an early writer of the eighteenth century, rivalled the "industrie" of Argentan and Caen. The city of Dieppe alone, with its little colony of Saint-Nicolas-d'Aliermont (a village of two leagues distant, descendants of a body of workmen who retired from the bombardment of Dieppe),[7] employed 4000 lace-makers. A writer in 1761[8] says : "A constant trade is that of laces, which yield only in precision of design and fineness to those of Mechlin ; but it has never been so considerable as it was at the end of the seventeenth century. Although it has slackened since about 1745 in the amount of its productions, which have diminished in value, it has not altogether fallen. As this work is the occupation of women and girls, a great number of whom have no other means of subsistence, there is also a large number of dealers who buy their laces, to send them into other parts of the kingdom, to Spain, and the islands of America. This trade is

[3] "Dictionnaire géographique," T. Corneille, 1707.

[4] "Gravures de Modes." Arch. Nat. M. 815–23.

[5] "1683. Deux housses de toille piquée avec dentelle du Havre deux camisolles de pareille toille et de dentelle du Havre."—*Inv. fait après le decedz de Monseigneur Colbert.* Bib. Nat. MSS. Suite de Mortemart, 34.

[6] "1851. Un tour d'autel de dentelle du Havre."—*Inv. des meubles de la Sacristie de l'Oratoire de Jésus à Paris.* Bib. Nat. MSS. F. F. 8621.

"1681. Une chemisette de toile de Marseille picquée garnye de dentelle du Havre."—*Inv. d'Anne d'Escoubleau de Sourdis, veuve de François de Simiane.* Arch. Nat. M. M. 802.

[7] "Les ouvriers n'étant apparemment rappelés par aucune possession dans cette ville, lorsqu'elle fut rétablie, ils s'y sont établis et ont transmis leur travail à la postérité."—*Peuchet.*

[8] Point de Dieppe appears among the tickets on the already quoted lace boxes of 1688.

free, without any corporation; but those who make lace without being mercers cannot sell lace thread, the sale of which is very lucrative."[9]

About twenty years later, we read: "The lace manufacture, which is very ancient, has much dimished since the points, embroidered muslins, and gauzes have gained the preference; yet good workers earn sufficient to live comfortably; but those who have not the requisite dexterity would do well to seek some other trade, as inferior lace-workers are unable to earn sufficient for a maintenance."[10] M. Feret writes in 1824:[11] "Dieppe laces are

Fig. 88.

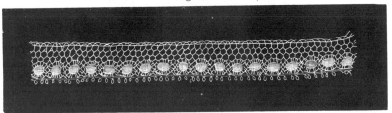

Petit poussin.

in little request; nevertheless there is a narrow kind, named 'poussin,' the habitual resource and work of the poor lace-makers of this town, and which recommends itself by its cheapness and

Fig. 89.

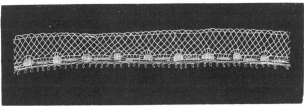

Ave Maria.

pleasing effect when used as a trimming to collars and morning dresses. Strangers who visit our town make an ample provision of this lace" (Fig. 88). The lace-makers of Dieppe love to give

---

[9] "Mémoires pour servir à l'Histoire de la Ville de Dieppe, composés en l'année 1761, par Michel-Claude Gurbert," p. 99.

[10] "Mémoires chronologiques pour servir à l'Histoire de Dieppe, par M. Desmarquets," 1785.

[11] "Notices sur Dieppe, Arques etc., par P. J. Ferret," 1824.

their own names to their different laces, Vierge, Ave Maria, &c.
(Fig. 89), and the designation of " poussin " (chicken) is given to
the lace in question from the delicacy of its workmanship.

Point de Dieppe (Fig. 90) much resembles Valenciennes, but

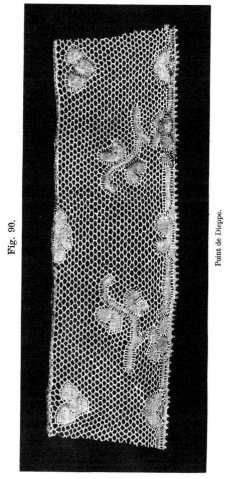

Fig. 90.

Point de Dieppe.

is less complicated in its make. The ground has three threads,
Valenciennes four ; and whereas Valenciennes can only be made in
lengths of 8 inches without detaching the lace from the pillow,
the Dieppe point is not taken off, but rolled.[12]   A few aged

---

[12] Peuchet, of Dieppe, says : " On ne fait pas la dentelle en roulant les fuseaux
sur le coussin, mais en l'y jetant."

workwomen, from 70 to 80 years of age, still make the ancient point, but it is now entirely superseded by Valenciennes. In 1826 a lace school was established at Dieppe, under the direction of two sisters from the convent of La Providence at Rouen, patron-

Fig. 91.

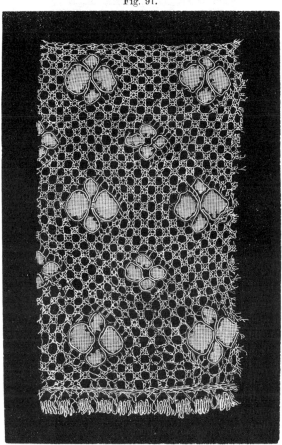
Dentelle à la Vierge.

ised by the Duchesse de Berri, the Queen of the French, and the Empress Eugénie. The exertions of the sisters have been most successful. In 1842 they received the gold medal for having, by the substitution of the Valenciennes for the old Dieppe stitch, introduced a new industry into the department. They make Valenciennes of every width, and are most expert in the square

grounds of the Belgian Valenciennes, made entirely of flax thread,
unmixed with cotton, and at most reasonable prices.[13]

A very pretty double-grounded old Normandy lace, greatly
used for caps, was locally known under the name of "dentelle
de la Vierge" (Fig. 91). We find only one mention of a lace so
designated, and that in the inventory made in 1785, after the
death of Louis-Philippe, Duke of Orleans, the father of Égalité,
where in his chapel at Villers-Cotterets is noted: "Une aube en
baptiste garnie en gros point de dentelle dite à la Vierge."[14]

The lace of Eu, resembling Valenciennes, was much esteemed.
Located on the site of a royal château, the property of the beloved
Duc de Penthièvre, himself a most enthusiastic lover of fine point,
as his wardrobe accounts testify, the lace-makers received, no

Fig. 92.

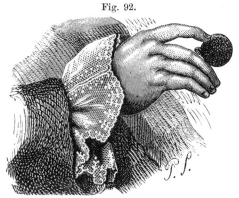

Duc de Penthièvre.   Vanloo.   Musée Nationale, Versailles.

doubt, much patronage and encouragement from the seigneur of
the domain. In the family picture by Vanloo, known as the "Tasse
de Chocolat," containing portraits of the Duc de Penthièvre, his
son, and the unfortunate Princesse de Lamballe, together with his
daughter, soon to be Duchess of Orleans, the duke, who is holding
in his hand a medal, enclosed in a case, wears a lace ruffle of
Valenciennes pattern, probably the production of his own people
(Fig. 92).

Arthur Young, in 1788, states the wages of the lace-makers
seldom exceed from seven or eight sous per day; some few, he

13 " Almanach de Dieppe pour 1847."
The Author has to express her thanks
to Sœur Hubert, of the École d'Appren-
tissage de Dentelle, and M. A. Morin,

librarian at Dieppe, for their communications.
14 Arch. Nat. X. 10,086.

adds, may earn fifteen. Previous to the Revolution the lace made
at Dieppe amounted to 400,000 francs annually. But Normandy
experienced the shock of 1790. Dieppe had already suffered from
the introduction of foreign lace when the Revolution broke out in
all its fury. The products of Havre, with the manufactures of
Pont-l'Évêque (Dép. Calvados), Harfleur, Eu, and more than ten
other neighbouring towns, entirely disappeared. Those of Dieppe
and Honfleur alone trailed on a precarious existence.

CALVADOS.

The principal lace centres in the Department of Calvados are
Caen and Bayeux.

From an early date white thread lace was made at Caen. It
was not until 1745 that the blondes or silk laces made their
appearance. The first silk used for the new production was of its
natural colour, " écrue," hence these laces were called " blondes." [15]
After a time silk was procured of a more suitable white, and those
beautiful laces produced which before long became of such commercial importance. A silk throwster, M. Duval, who died lately
at Caen, was in a great degree the originator of the success of the
Caen blondes, having been the first to prepare those brilliant
white silks which have made their reputation. The silk is procured from Bourg-Argental, in the Cevennes. The Caen workers
made the Chantilly lace, " grillé blanc," already described, and
also the " blonde de Caen," in which the flower is made with a
different silk from that which forms the réseau. It is this kind
of blonde which is so successfully imitated at Calais.

Lastly, the " blonde mate," or Spanish, already mentioned. In
no other place, except Chantilly, have the blondes attained so pure
a white, such perfect workmanship, such lightness, such brilliancy
as the " blondes de Caen." They had great success in France,
were extensively exported, and made the fortune of the surrounding country, where they were fabricated in every cottage. Not
every woman can work at the white lace. Those who have what
is locally termed the " haleine grasse " are obliged to confine

---

[15] " The silk came from Nankin, by
way of London or the East, the black
silk called ' grenadine ' was dyed and
prepared at Lyons, the thread was from
Haarlem."—*Roland de la Platière.*

O

themselves to black. In order to preserve purity of colour, the lacemakers work during the summer months in the open air, in winter in lofts over their cow-houses: warmed by the heat of the animals, they dispense with fire and its accompanying smoke.[16] Generally, it was only made in summer, and the black reserved for winter work. Peuchet speaks of white lace being made in Caen from the lowest price to 25 livres the ell.[17] The silk blonde trade did not suffer from the crisis of 1821 to 1832; when the thread-lace makers were reduced to the brink of ruin by the introduction of bobbin-net, the demand for blonde, on the contrary, had a rapid increase, and Caen exported great quantities, by smuggling, to England. The blonde-makers earning twenty-five per cent. more than the thread-lace makers, the province was in full prosperity. The competition with the machine-made blondes of Calais and Nottingham has caused the manufacture of the white blondes to be abandoned, and the Caen lace-makers now confine themselves to making black lace. Caen also produces gold and silver blondes, mixed sometimes with pearls. In 1847 the laces of Caen alone employed more than 50,000 persons, or one-eighth of the whole population of Calvados.

Bayeux formerly made only light thread laces—mignonettes, and what Peuchet calls [18] "point de Marli." "On ne voit dans ces dentelles," he writes, "que du réseau de diverses espèces, du fond et une canetille à gros fil, qu'on conduit autour de ces fonds." Marli, styled in the Dictionary of Napoléon Landais a "tissu à jour en fil et en soie fabriqué sur le métier à faire de la gaze," was in fact the predecessor of tulle. It was invented about 1765,[19] and for twenty years had great success. In the "Tableau de Paris," 1782, we read that marli employed a great number of workpeople, "et l'on a vu des soldats valides et invalides faire le marli, le promener, l'offrir, et le vendre eux-mêmes. Des soldats faire le

---

[16] Letter from Edgar McCulloch, Esq., Guernsey.

[17] Blondes appear also to have been made at Le Mans :—

"Cette manufacture qui étoit autrefois entretenue à l'hôpital du Mans, lui rapportoit un benefice de 4000 à 5000 fr. Elle est bien tombée par la dispersion des anciennes sœurs hospitalières."—*Stat. du Dép. de la Sarthe, par le Citoyen L.-M. Auvray.* An X.

[18] The handkerchief of "Paris net," mentioned by Goldsmith.

[19] In the Dép. du Nord, by Jean-Ph. Briatte. "Its fall was owing to the bad faith of imitators, who substituted a single thread of bad quality for the double twisted thread of the country."—*Dieudonné, Statistique du Dép. du Nord.*

In the "Mercure Galant" for June 1686, we find the ladies wear "cornettes à la jardinière 'de Marly.'"

marli!'' It was to this marli, or large pieces of white thread net, that Bayeux owes its reputation. No other manufactory could produce them at so low a price. Bayeux alone made albs, shawls, and other articles of large size.

Lace was first made at Bayeux in the convents and schools, under the direction of the nuns of La Providence. It was not until 1740 that a commercial house was established by M. Clément; from which period the manufacture has rapidly increased, and is now one of the most important in France. The black laces of Caen, Bayeux, and Chantilly, are alike; the design and mode of fabrication being identical, it is almost impossible, for even the most experienced eye, to detect the difference. They are mostly composed of "piece goods," shawls, dresses, flounces, and veils, made in small strips, united by the stitch already alluded to, the point de raccroc, to the invention of which Calvados owes her prosperity. This stitch, invented by a lace-maker named Cahanet, admits of putting a number of hands on the same piece, whereas, under the old system, not more than two could work at the same time. A scarf, which would formerly have taken two women six months to complete, divided into segments, can now be finished by ten women in one.

About 1827, Madame Carpentier caused silk blonde again to be made for French consumption, the fabric having died out. Two years later she was succeeded by M. Auguste Lefébure, by whom the making of "blondes mates" for exportation was introduced with such success that Caen, who had applied herself wholly to this manufacture, almost gave up the competition. Mantillas (Spanish, Havanese, and Mexican), in large quantities, were exported to Spain, Mexico, and the Southern Seas, and were superior to those made in Catalonia. This manufacture requires the greatest care, as it is necessary to throw aside the French taste, and adopt the heavy, overcharged patterns appropriate to the costumes and fashions of the countries for which they are destined. These mantillas have served as models for the imitations made at Nottingham.

To the exertions of M. Lefébure is due the great improvement in the teaching of the lace schools. Formerly the apprentices were consigned to the care of some aged lace-maker, probably of deficient eyesight; he, on the contrary, places them under young and skilful forewomen, and the result has been the rising up of a generation of workers who have given to Bayeux a reputation

superior to all in Calvados. It is the first manufactory for large
pieces of black lace (Fig. 93), of extra fine quality and rich design;
and as point d'Alençon (see p. 172) lace has also been introduced
into the city, Bayeux excels equally at the pillow and the
needle.

Fig. 93.

Black lace of Bayeux.

Messrs. Lefébure have also most successfully reproduced the
Venetian point in high relief; the raised flowers are executed with
great beauty, the picots rendered with the greatest precision
(Coloured Plate XI.). The discovery of the way in which this

Plate XI.

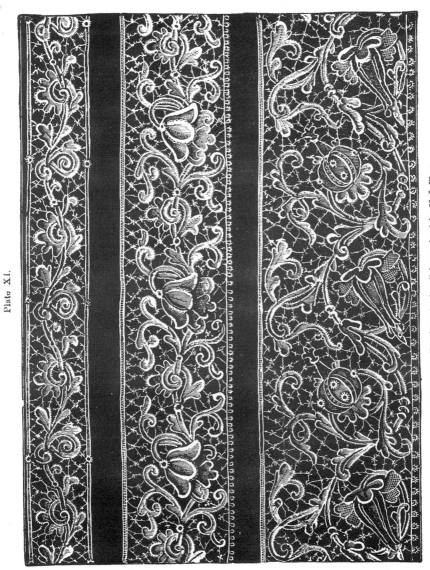

Point Colbert. Venetian point in relief, reproduced by M. Lefébure.

To face page 196.

richest and most complicated of point lace was made has been the work of great patience. It is called "point Colbert," after the minister to whom France owes the establishment of her lace industry.

In 1851 there were in Calvados 60,000 lace-workers, spread along the sea-coast to Cherbourg, where the nuns of La Providence have an establishment. It is only by visiting the district that an adequate idea can be formed of the resources this work affords to the labouring classes, thousands of women deriving from it their sole means of subsistence.[20]

---

[20] "L'Industrie française depuis la Révolution de Février et l'Exposition de 1848, par M. A. Audiganne."

M. Aubry, in his report, thus divides the lace-makers of Normandy:—

Department of Calvados	Arrondissement of Caen	. . . .	25,000
	„ „ Bayeux	. . . .	15,000
	„ „ Pont-l'Évêque, Falaise, and Lisieux	. . . . . .	10,000
Departments of La Manche and Seine-Inférieure	. . . .	10,000
			60,000

The women earn from 50 sous to 25 sous a day, an improvement on the wages of the last century, which, in the time of Arthur Young, seldom amounted to 24 sous. Their products are estimated at from 8 to 10 millions of francs (320,000l. to 400,000l.).

CHAPTER XVII.

VALENCIENNES (Dep. du Nord).

" Ils s'attachoient à considérer des tableaux de petit point de la manufacture de
Valencienne qui representoient des fleurs, et comme ils les trouvoient parfaitement
beaux, M. de Magelotte, leur hôte, vouloit les leur donner, mais ils ne les acceptèrent
point."—*Voyage des Ambassadeurs de Siam*, 1688.

PART of the ancient province of Hainault, Valenciennes, together
with Lille and Arras, is Flemish by birth, French only by conquest
and treaty.[1]   The date of its lace manufacture is unknown, but it
early made lace with straight edge and a ground of running pattern,
its first productions being attributed to a Pierre Chauvin and
Ignace Harent, who employed a three-thread twisted flax.   It
flourished under Louis XIV., and reached its climax from 1725
to 1780, when there were from 3000 to 4000 lace-makers in the
city alone.

Coloured Plate XII. shows the style of patterns till the
middle of the eighteenth century—flowers and scrolls of the
Renaissance, later replaced with the réseau ground.

From 1780 downwards, fashion changed.   The cheaper and
lighter laces of Brussels, Lille, and Arras, obtained the preference
over the costly and more substantial products of Valenciennes—
" les éternelles Valenciennes," as they were called—while the subsequent disappearance of ruffles from the costume of the men
greatly added to the evil.   Valenciennes fell with the monarchy.
During the war of liberty, foreign occupation decimated its population, and the art became nearly lost.   In 1790 the number of
lace-workers had diminished to 250; and though Napoleon used
every effort to revive the manufacture, he was unsuccessful.   In
1851 there were only two lace-makers remaining, and they both
upwards of eighty years of age.

---

[1] French Hainault, French Flanders
and Cambrésis (the present Dép. du
Nord), with Artois, were conquests of
Louis XIII. and Louis XIV., confirmed
to France by the treaties of Aix-la-
Chapelle (1668), and Nimeguen (1678).

Plate XII.

Valenciennes. 1650–1730.

The lace made in the city alone was termed "vraie Valenciennes," and attained a perfection unrivalled by the productions of the villages beyond the walls. In the lace accounts of Madame du Barry we find frequent mention of this term.[2] "Vraie Valenciennes" appears constantly in contradistinction to "bâtarde"[3] and "fausse."[4] M. Dieudonné writes:[5] "This beautiful manufacture is so inherent in the place that it is an established fact, if a piece of lace were begun at Valenciennes and finished outside the walls, the part which had not been made at Valenciennes would be visibly less beautiful and less perfect than the other, though continued by the same lace-maker with the same thread, and upon the same pillow."[6]

The extinction of the fabric and its transfer to Belgium has been a great commercial loss to France. Valenciennes being specially a "dentelle linge," is that of which the greatest quantity is consumed throughout the universe. Valenciennes lace is altogether made upon the pillow, of simple combination, with one kind of thread for the pattern and the ground (Fig. 94). No lace is so expensive to make from the number of bobbins required, and the flax used was of the finest quality. The city-made lace was remarkable for the beauty of its ground, the richness of its design, and evenness of its tissue. From their solidity, "les belles et éternelles Valenciennes" became an heirloom in each family. A mother bequeathed them to her daughter as she would now her jewels or her furs.[7] The lace-makers worked in underground cellars, from four in the morning till eight at night, scarcely earning their tenpence a day. The pattern was the especial

---

[2] "1772. 15 aunes 3–16ᵐᵉˢ jabot haut de vraie Valencienne, 3706 livres 17 sous;" and many other similar entries.

[3] "5/8 Bâtarde dito à bordure, à 60 ll., 37 ll. 10 s.'—*Comptes de Madame du Barry.*

[4] See Bailleul, p. 208.

[5] "Statistique du Dép. du Nord, par M. Dieudonné, Préfet en 1804."

[6] "Among the various lace fabrics having the same process of manufacture, there is not one which produces exactly the same style of lace. The same pattern, with the same material, whether executed in Belgium, Saxony, Lille, Arras, Mirecourt, or Le Puy, will always bear the stamp of the place where it is made. It has never

been possible to transfer any kind of manufacture from one city to another, without there being a marked difference between the productions."—*Aubry.*

May not this difference be rather attributed to mechanical causes, the different inclination of the pillow, the weight and size of the bobbins, the different way of pricking the pattern, and of twisting the bobbins? All these may influence the production.

[7] In the already quoted "Etat d'un Trousseau," 1771, among the necessary articles, are enumerated: "Une coëffure, tour de gorge et le fichu plissé de vraie Valencienne." The trimming of one of Madame du Barry's pillow-cases cost

property of the manufacturer; it was at the option of the worker
to pay for its use and retain her work, if not satisfied with the
price she received. This lace was generally made by young

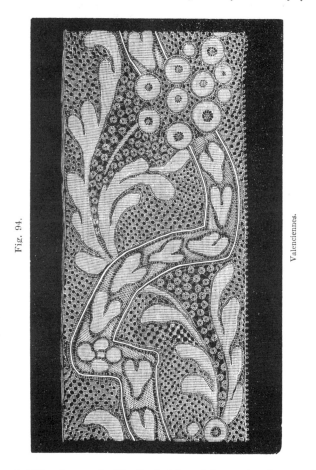

Fig. 94.

Valenciennes.

girls; it did not accord with the habits of the "mère bourgeoise"
either to abandon her household duties or to preserve the delicacy
of hand requisite for the work. It may be inferred, also, that no
eyes could support for a number of years the close confinement to

---

487 fr.; her lappets, 1030. The ruffles
of the Duchesse de Modène and Mademoiselle de Charollais are valued at 200

livres the pair. Du Barry, more extravagant, gives 770 for hers.

a cellar: many of the women are said to have become almost blind previous to attaining the age of thirty. It was a great point when the whole piece was executed by the same lace-worker. "All by the same hand," we find entered in the bills of the lace-sellers of the time.[8]

The labour of making "vraie Valenciennes" was so great that while the Lille lace-workers could produce from three to five ells

Fig. 95.

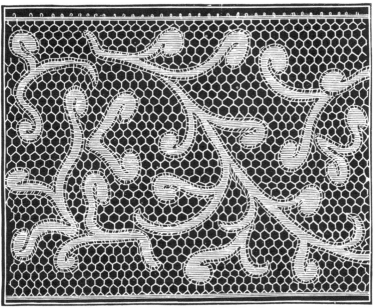

Valenciennes.

a day, those of Valenciennes could not complete more than an inch and a half in the same time. Some lace-workers only made half an ell (24 inches) in a year, and it took ten months, working fifteen hours a day, to finish a pair of men's ruffles—hence the costliness of the lace.[9] A pair of these now exploded articles of

---

[8] "2 barbes et rayon de vraie valen-cienne; 3 au. 3/4 collet grande hauteur; 4 au. grand jabot; le tout de la même main, de 2400 livres."— *Comptes de Madame du Barry.* 1770.

[9] Arthur Young, in 1788, says of Valenciennes: "Lace of 30 to 40 lines' breadth for gentlemen's ruffles is from 160 to 216 livres (9*l*. 9*s*.) an ell. The quantity for a lady's head-dress from 1000 to 24,000 livres. The women gain from 20 to 30 sous a day. 3600 persons are employed at Valenciennes, and are an object of 450,000 livres, of which the flax is not more than 1/30. The thread costs from 24 to 700 livres the pound."

dress would amount to 4000 livres, and the "barbes pleines,"[10] as a lady's cap was then termed, to 1200 livres and upwards.

The Valenciennes of 1780 was of a quality far superior to any made in the present century; much of it was still to be found a few years since in the market. The réseau was fine and compact, the flower resembling cambric in its texture; the designs still betraying the Flemish origin of the fabric—tulips, carnations, iris, or anemones—such as we see in the old Flemish flower-pieces, true to nature, executed with Dutch exactness (Coloured Plate XIII.). The city owed not its prosperity to the rich alone, the peasants themselves were great consumers of its produce. A woman laid by her earnings for years to purchase a "bonnet en vraie Valenciennes," some few of which still appear in the northern provinces of France at church festivals and holidays. These caps are formed of three pieces, "barbes, passe et fond." The Norman women also loved to trim the huge fabric with which they overcharge their heads with a real Valenciennes; and even in the present day of "bon marché," a peasant-woman will spend from 100 to 150 francs on a cap which is to last her for life (Fig. 95).

The last important piece made within the town walls was a head-dress of "vraie" Valenciennes presented by the town to the Duchesse de Nemours, on her marriage in 1840. It was furnished by Mademoiselle Ursule Glairo, herself an aged lady, who employed the few old lace-workers then living, with the patriotic wish of exhibiting the perfection of the ancient manufacture.[11]

LILLE (Dép. du Nord).

"Ces points couppés, passements et dentelles,
Las! qui venoient de l'Isle et de Bruxelles."
Consolation des Dames, 1620.

The manufactures of Lille and Arras are identical; both make white laces with single grounds (fond simple); but the productions of Lille are far superior to those of Arras in quality. The manufacture of the capital of French Flanders vies with those of the

---

[10] The "barbes pleines" consisted of a pair of lappets from 3 to 5 inches wide each, and ½ an ell (20 inches) long, with a double pattern of sprigged flowers and rounded at the ends. A narrow lace 1½ ell long, called the "papillon," with the

bande or passe, and the fond de bonnet, completed the suit.

[11] The fault of the old Valenciennes lace is its colour, never of a clear white, but inclining to a reddish cast.

Plate XIII.

Valenciennes lappet.   Eighteenth century.

To face page 232.

Netherlands in antiquity. As early as 1582 its lace-makers are described, at the entry of the Duke of Anjou into the city, " as wearing a special costume. A gown of striped stuff, with a cap of fine linen plaited in small flutes." A silver medal suspended from the neck by a black ribbon completed a dress which has descended to the present century.[12] The peace of Aix-la-Chapelle

Fig. 96.

Lille.

having transferred Lille to France, its artisans retired to Ghent ; they are described at that period as making both white and black lace.[13] The art, however, did not die out, for in 1713,[14] on the

---

[12] " Les dentelières avaient adopté un par-dessus de calamande rayée, un bonniquet de toile fine plissé à petits canons. Une médaille d'argent, pendue au cou par un petit liseré noir, complétait leur costume, qui est arrivé jusqu'à nous ; car nous l'avons vu, il n'y a pas trente ans."

—*Hist. de Lille, par V. Derode.* Paris et Lille, 1848.

[13] " Mémoires sur l'Intendance de Flandre." MS. Bib. de Lille.

[14] Period of the peace of Utrecht, when Lille, which had been retaken by Prince Eugène, was again restored to France.

marriage of the governor, young Boufflers, to Mademoiselle de Villeroi, the magistrates of Lille presented him with lace to the value of 4000 livres.[15]

The beauty of the Lille lace owes its celebrity to its ground, called "Lille ground," or "fond clair," "the finest, lightest, most transparent, and best made of all grounds."[16] The work is simple, consisting of the ground, with a thick thread to mark the pattern[17] (Fig. 96).

Fig. 97.

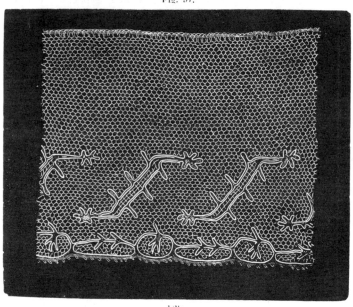

Lille.

In the eighteenth century more than two-thirds of the lace-making population of Europe made it under the name of "mignonettes et blondes de fil."

---

[15] "Histoire populaire de Lille," Henri Brunet, Lille, 1848; and "Histoire de Lille," V. Derode.

[16] "Report of the Commissioners for 1851."

[17] As late as 1761, Lille was considered as "foreign" with respect to France, and her laces made to pay duty according to the tariff of 1664.

In 1708 (31st of July) we have an "Arrest du Conseil d'Estat du Roy," relative to the seizure of seventeen cartons of lace belonging to one "Mathieu, marchand à l'Isle." Mathieu, in defence, pretends that "les dentelles avoient esté fabriquées à Haluin (near Lille), terre de la domination de Sa Majesté." Arch. Nat. Coll. Rondoneau.

The "treille"[18] was finer in the last century; but, in 1803, the price of thread having risen 30 per cent.,[19] the lace-makers, unwilling to raise the prices of their lace, adopted a larger treille, in order to diminish the quantity of thread required.

The straight edge and stiff pattern of the old Lille lace is well known (Fig. 97).

The laces of Lille, both black and white, have been much used in France: though Madame Junot speaks disparagingly of the fabric,[20] the light clear ground rendered them especially adapted for summer wear.

They found great favour also in England, into which country one-third of the lace manufactured throughout the Département du Nord was smuggled in 1789.[21] The broad black Lille lace has always been specially admired, and was extensively used to trim the long silk mantles of the last century.[22]

In 1788 there were above 16,000 lace-makers at Lille, and it made 120,000 pieces[23] of lace, representing a value of more than 160,000*l.* In 1851 the number of lace-makers was reduced to 1600; it is still gradually diminishing, from the competition of the fabric of Mirecourt and the numerous other manufactures established at Lille, which offers more lucrative wages than can be obtained by lace-making.

The old straight-edged is no longer made, but the rose pattern of the Mechlin is adopted, and the style of that lace copied: the semé of little square dots (points d'esprit) on the ground—one of the characteristics of Lille lace—is still retained. In 1862 the author saw at Lille a complete garniture of beautiful workmanship, ordered for a trousseau at Paris, but the commercial crisis and the revolutions of 1848 virtually put an end to the lace industry of Lille and Arras.

---

[18] See page 108, note [59].

[19] In 1782, thread was 192 francs the kilogramme.

[20] Describing her trousseau, every article of which was rimmed with Angle - terre, Malines, or Valenciennes, she adds: "A cette époque (1800), on ignorait même l'existence du tulle, les seules dentelles communes que l'on connût étaient les dentelles de Lille et d'Arras, qui n'étaient portées que par les femmes les plus ordinaires."—*Mém. de Madame la Duchesse d'Abrantès*, t. iii. Certainly the laces of Lille and Arras never appear in the inventories of the "grandes dames" of the last century.

[21] Dieudonné.

[22] Peuchet states much "fausse Valenciennes, très-rapprochée de la vraie," to have been fabricated in the hospital at Lille, in which institution there were, in 1723, 700 lace-workers.

[23] A piece of Lille lace contains from 10 to 12 ells.

ARRAS (Artois; Dép. Pas-de-Calais).

"Arras of ryche arraye,
Fresh as floures in Maye."
Skelton.

Arras, from the earliest ages, has been a working city. Her citizens were renowned for the tapestries which bore their name: the nuns of her convents excelled in all kinds of needlework. In the history of the Abbaye du Vivier,[24] we are told how the abbess, Madame Sainte, dite la Sauvage, set the sisters to work ornaments for the church :—

> " Les filles dans l'ouvroir tous les jours assemblées
> N'y paroissent pas moins que l'Abbesse zelées,
> Celle cÿ d'une aiguilie ajuste au petit point
> Un bel etuy d'autel que l'eglise n'a point,
> Broche d'or et de soÿe un voile de Calice ;
> L'autre fait un tapis du point de haute lice,
> Dont elle fait un riche et precieux frontal ;
> Une autre coud une aube, ou fait un corporal ;
> Une autre une chasuble, ou chappe nompareille,
> Où l'or, l'argent, la soÿe, arrangés à merveille,
> Representant des saints vestus plus richement
> Que leur eclat n'auroit souffert de leur vivant ;
> L'autre de son Carreau detachant la dentelle,
> En orne les surplis de quelque aube nouvelle."

Again, among the first rules of the institution of the " Filles de Sainte-Agnès," in the same city, it is ordained that the girls " aprendront a filer ou coudre, faire passement, tapisseries ou choses semblables." [25]

The Emperor Charles V. is said, however, to have first introduced the lace manufacture into Arras.[26] It flourished in the eighteenth century, when, writes Arthur Young, in 1788, were made " coarse thread laces, which find a good market in England.

---

[24] " L'Abbaye du Vivier, établie dans la Ville d'Arras, Poëme par le Père Dom Martin du Buisson," in "Mémoires et Pièces pour servir à l'Histoire de la Ville d'Arras." Bib. Nat. MSS. Fonds Français, 8936.

[25] Bib. Nat. MSS. Fonds Français, 8936.

[26] We find in the " Colbert Correspondence " (1669) the directors of the general hospital at Arras had enticed lace-workers of point de France, with a view to establish the manufacture in their hospital, but the jealousy of the other cities threatening to overthrow their commerce, they wrote to Colbert for protection.

The lace-workers earn from 12 to 15 sous." Pouchet corroborates this statement. " Arras," he says, "fait beaucoup de mignonette et entoilage, dont on consomme beaucoup en Angleterre." The fabric of Arras attained its climax during the empire (1804 to 1812), since which period it has declined. In 1851 there were 8000 lace-makers in a radius of eight miles round the city, their salary not exceeding 65 centimes a day.

There is little or, indeed, no variety in the pattern of Arras lace ; for years it has produced the same style and design ; as a

Fig. 98.

Arras (modern).

consequence of this sameness, the lace-makers, always executing the same pattern, acquire great rapidity. Though not so fine as that of Lille, the lace of Arras has three good qualities : it is very strong, firm to the touch, and perfectly white; hence the great demand for both home and foreign consumption; no other lace having this triple merit at so reasonable a price (Fig. 98).

The gold lace of Arras appears also to have had a reputation. We find among the coronation expenses of George I. a charge for 354 yards of Arras lace " atrebaticæ lacinæ." [27]

---

[27] Gt. Ward. Acc. Geo. I. 1714–15 (P. R. O.), and Acc. of John, Duke of Montagu, master of the great wardrobe, touching the expenses of the funeral of Queen Anne and the coronation of George I. P. R. O.

In 1761, an act was passed against its being counterfeited, and a vendor of " Orrice lace " (counterfeit, we suppose) forfeits her goods.

BAILLEUL (Dép. du Nord).

As already mentioned, up to 1790 the "vraie Valenciennes' was only made in the city of that name. The same lace manufactured at Lille, Bergues, Bailleul, Avesnes, Cassel, Armentières, as well as that of Belgium, was called "fausses Valenciennes." "Armentières et Bailleul ne font que de la Valencienne fausse, dans tous lex prix," writes Peuchet. "On nomme," states another author,[28] "fausses Valenciennes la dentelle de même espèce, inférieure en qualité, fabriquée moins serrée, dont le dessin est moins recherché et le toilé des fleurs moins marqué." Of such is the lace of Bailleul, whose manufacture is the most ancient and most important, extending to Hazebrouck, Bergues, Cassel, and the surrounding villages.[29]

Previous to 1830 Bailleul fabricated little besides straight edges for the Normandy market. In 1822 the scalloped edge was adopted, and from this period dates the progress and present prosperity of the manufacture. Its laces are not much esteemed in Paris. They have neither the finish nor lightness of the Belgian products, are soft to the touch, the mesh round, and the ground thick; but it is strong and cheap, and in general use for trimming lace. The lace, too, of Bailleul is the whitest and cleanest Valenciennes made; hence it is much sought after, for exportation to America and India. The patterns are varied and in good taste; and there is every reason to expect that in due time it may attain the perfection, if not of the Valenciennes of Ypres, at least to that of Bruges, which city alone annually sends to France lace to the value of from 120,000*l.* to 160,000*l.*

CHAMPAGNE.

The Ardennes lace was generally much esteemed, especially the "points de Sedan," which derived their name from the city where they were manufactured.[30] Not only were points made

---

[28] "Statistique des Gens de Lettres." 1803, Herbin, t. ii.

[29] In 1851, there were 8000 lace-makers

dispersed over the district.

[30] Savary. Sedan was ceded to Louis XIII. in 1642.

there, but, to infer from the Great Wardrobe Account of Charles I., the cutwork of Sedan had then reached our country, and was of great price. We find in one account,[31] a charge for "six handsome Sedan and Italian collars of cutwork, and for 62 yards of needlework purl for six pairs of linen ruffs," the enormous sum of 116*l*. 6*s*. And again, in the last year of his reign, he has " six handsome Pultenarian Sedan collars of cutwork, with the same accompaniment of 72 yards of needlework purl," amounting to 106*l*. 16*s*.[32] What these Pultenarian collars may have been, we cannot, at this distance of time, surmise; but the entries afford proof that the excellency of the Sedan cutwork was known in England. Lace was made in the seventeenth century at Sedan, Donchéry, Charleville, Mézières, and Troyes.

The thread manufacturers of Sedan furnished the material necessary for all the lace-workers of Champagne. Much point de Sedan was made at Charleville, and the laces of this last-named town[33] were valued at from four up to fifty livres the ell, and even sometimes at a higher rate. The greater part of the produce was sold in Paris, the rest found a ready market in England, Holland, Germany, and Poland.[34] Pignariol de la Force, writing later, says the manufacture of points and laces at Sedan, formerly so flourishing, is now of little value.[35]

The importance of the lace industry in Champagne, second only to that of Alençon, naturally pointed it out as a fitting site for the new manufacture of point de France; so we find Sedan, Rheims, and Château-Thierry among the towns mentioned in the declaration of 1665. In 1666, Colbert, by order of the king, writes to the governor of Sedan, enjoining him to take the greatest precautions against the malice of the dealers, who were in the habit of having work executed at Venice which they sold at court and in the kingdom as point de France, the work of Sedan.

Rheims, again, was the subject of a close correspondence.

General Hoguebert wrote to Colbert, on the 18th January 1665,

---

[31] "Eidem pro 6 divit Sedan et Italic̄ colaris opere sciss̄ et pro 62 purles opere acuo pro 6 par̄ maniē lintear̄ eisdem, 116*l*. 6*s*."—*Gt. Ward. Acc.* Car. I. ix. to xi. P. R. O.

[32] "Eidem pro 6 divit̄ Pultenarian Sedan de opere sciss̄ colaris et pro 72 purles divit̄ opere acuo pro maniē lintear̄ eisdem, 106*l*. 16*s*."—*Gt. Ward. Acc.* Car. I.

xi. to xii.

[33] In 1700, there were several lace manufacturers at Charleville, the principal of whom was named Vigoureux. "Hist. de Charleville," Charleville, 1854.

[34] Savary, ed. 1726.

[35] "Description de la France," ed. 1752.

P

assuring him that the establishment will not be wanting in assistance from the town and from himself. Again, on the 1st July of
the same year, he writes that the Sieur Pierre Chardin, a Frenchman, who has lived a long time in Venice, has arrived with his
wife, three sons, and two daughters, and has been made director
of the establishment. He has now in the house 5 Venetian
women, 22 Flemish and 30 girls of this town, without counting the
servants. There have also lately arrived 7 girls, sent from Paris.
So the director is sanguine of success; and, besides, the work has
the additional merit of being whiter than elsewhere. In three
months and a half the establishment had 120 workers.

In a previous letter to Colbert, from a nun who undertook
to watch the workgirls, she writes there has been a calamity
fallen upon the manufactory. Several girls had been attacked by
illness, which the grand vicaire attributes to witchcraft; but when
the house had been properly blessed, no more cases had occurred.
They now amount to 140 good workwomen, and they have sent
an " envoi " this week which the entrepreneurs will be satisfied
with.

Of the Château-Thierry manufacture, we hear nothing; and
Sens is incidentally mentioned by Colbert, 1670, in a letter to
Auxerre, in which he expresses his surprise to hear the lace-
workers diminish, while at Sens, a town in which he had not
the same interest, they are satisfied with the advantages it procures them.

Most of its lace-makers being Protestants, they emigrated after
the Edict of Revocation. Château-Renaud and Mézières were
chiefly employed in the manufacture of footings (engrêlures).[36] The
laces of Donchéry were similar to those of Charleville, but made
of the Holland thread. They were less esteemed than those of
Sedan. A large quantity were exported to Italy and Portugal;
some few found their way to England and Poland. Up to the
Revolution, Champagne employed from 5000 to 6000 lace-workers,
and their annual products were estimated at 200,000 fr. During
the twelve years of revolutionary anarchy, all the lace manufactories of this province disappeared.

---

[36] Savary.

CHAPTER XVIII.

AUVERGNE AND VÉLAY.

LE PUY (Dép. Haute-Loire).

As early as the fifteenth century, the countrywomen of the mountains of the Vélay would congregate together during the winter within the walls of the neighbouring cities, and there, forming themselves into companies, gain their subsistence by making coarse lace, to ornament the albs of the priests, the rochets of the bishops, and the petticoats of ladies of quality. And very coarse and tasteless were these early products, to judge from the specimens which remain tacked on to faded altar-cloths, still to be met with in the province, a mixture of netting and darning without design. They also made what was termed " dentelles de menage," with the coarse thread they used for weaving their cloth. They edged their linen with it, and both bleached together in the wearing.

This lace region of Central France, of which Le Puy is the chief place, is considered to be the most ancient and considerable in France. It is distributed over the four departments,[1] and employs from 125,000 to 130,000 women. It forms the sole industry of the Haute-Loire, in which department alone are 70,000 lace-makers.

The lace industry of Le Puy, like all others, has experienced various changes; it has had its trials[2] and its periods of great prosperity.[3] In the chronicles of Le Puy of the sixteenth century[4] we read that the merciers of Notre-Dame-des-Anges, " qui, suivant l'usage, faisaient dans notre ville le commerce des passementeries, broderies, dentelles etc., comptaient alors quarante boutiques, et

---

[1] Haut-Loire, Cantal, Puy-de-Dôme, and Loire.
[2] 1640.
[3] 1833 and 1848.
[4] By Medecis.

P 2

qu'ils figurent avec enseignes et torches au premier rang dans les solennités religieuses."

Judging from local documents, this manufacture has for more than two centuries back formed the chief occupation of the women of this province.

It suffered from the sumptuary edicts of 1629, 1635, and 1639, and in 1640 threatened to be annihilated altogether. In the month of January of that year, the seneschal of Le Puy published throughout the city a decree of the parliament of Toulouse, which forbade, under pain of heavy fine, all persons of whatever sex, quality, or condition, to wear upon their vestments any lace "tant de soie que de fil blanc, ensemble passement, clinquant d'or ni d'argent fin ou faux;" thus by one ordinance annihilating the industry of the province. The reasons assigned for this absurd edict were twofold: first, in consequence of the large number of women employed in the lace trade, there was great difficulty in obtaining domestic servants; secondly, the general custom of wearing lace among all classes caused the shades of distinction between the high and low to disappear. These ordinances, as may be imagined, created great consternation throughout Le Puy. Father Régis, a Jesuit, who was then in the province, did his best to console the sufferers thus reduced to beggary by the caprice of parliament. "Ayez confiance en Dieu," he said; "la dentelle ne perira pas." He set out to Toulouse, and by his remonstrances obtained a revocation of the edict. Nor did he rest satisfied with his good work. At his suggestion the Jesuits opened to the Auvergne laces a new market in Spain and the New World, which, until the year 1790, was the occasion of great prosperity to the province. The Jesuit father was later canonised for his good deeds; and under his new appellation of Saint François Régis,[5] is still held in the greatest veneration by the women of Auvergne—patron saint of the lace-makers.

Massillon, when bishop of Clermont (1717), greatly patronised the lace-makers of his diocese, and, anxious the province should itself furnish the thread used in the manufacture, he purchased a quantity of spinning-wheels which he distributed among the poor families of Beauregard, the village in which the summer palace of the bishop, previous to the Revolution, was situated.

The lace trade of this province frequently appears on the scene

---

[5] Died December 1640. The edict was promulgated the preceding January.

during the eighteenth century.   In 1707 the manufacturers demand a remission of the import duties of 1664 as unfair,[6] and with success.   Scarce ten years afterwards,[7] notwithstanding the privilege accorded, we again find them in trouble : whether their patterns did not advance with the fashions of the day, or the manufacturers deteriorated the quality of the thread—too often the effect of commercial prosperity—the magazines were filled with lace, " propres, les unes pour l'Italie, d'autres pour les mers du sud," which the merchants refused to buy.   To remedy this bad state of affairs, the commissioners assembled at Montpelier coolly decided that the diocese should borrow 60,000 livres to purchase the dead stock, and so clear the market.   After some arguments the lace was bought by the Sieur Jerphanion, syndic of the diocese.

Prosperity, however, was not restored, for in 1755 we again hear of a grant of 1000 livres, payable in ten years by the states of Vélay, for the relief of the distressed lace-makers, and again a fresh demand for exemption of the export duty.[8]   This is declared in a memorial of 1761 to be the chief cause of the distress, which memorial also states that, to employ the people in a more lucrative way, a manufacture of blondes and silk laces had been introduced.

Peuchet, with his predecessor, Savary, and other writers on statistics, describe the manufacture of Le Puy as the most flourishing in France.   " Her lace," writes Peuchet, " resembles greatly that of Flanders ; much is consumed in the French dominions, and a considerable quantity exported to Spain, Portugal, Germany, Italy, and England.   Much thread lace is also expedited by way of Cadiz to Peru and Mexico.   The ladies of these countries trim their petticoats and other parts of their dress with such a profusion of lace as to render the consumption ' prodigieuse.' "

" Les Anglois en donnent des commissions en contrebande pour l'Isthmus de Panama.   Les Hollandois en demandent aussi et

---

[6] They represent to the king that the laces of the " diocèse du Puy, du Vélay et de l'Auvergne, dont il se faisait un commerce très-considérable dans les pays étrangers, par les ports de Bordeaux, La Rochelle et Nantes," ought not to pay the import duties held by the " cinq grosses fermes."—*Arrest du Conseil*

d'Estat du Roy, 6 August 1707. Arch. Nat. Coll. Rond.   They ended by obtaining a duty of five sous per lb., instead of the 50 livres paid by Flanders and England, or the 10 livres paid by the laces of Comté, Liége, and Lorraine.

[7] 1715 and 1716.

[8] See p. 51.

faisaient expédier à Cadiz à leur compte." [9] It may indeed be said that, with the exception of the period of the French Revolution to 1801, the lace trade of Le Puy has been ever prosperous. [10]

Formerly, they only made at Le Puy laces to each of which was given a distinctive name—ave, pater, chapelets, mie, serpent, bonnet, scie, &c. [11]

Le Puy now produces every description of lace, white and coloured; silk, thread, and worsted; blondes of all kinds, black silk guipures, and others of the finest réseau grounds; application, double and single grounds; from gold and silver lace to edgings of a halfpenny a yard.

In 1847 more than 5000 women were employed in making Valenciennes. They have also succeeded in producing admirable needle-points, similar to the ancient Venetian. A dress of this lace, destined to adorn an image of the Virgin, was shown in the French Exhibition of 1855.

In 1848, commerce and the lace trade languished, and a cheaper lace was produced, made of worsted, for shawls and trimmings. This lace was not long in fashion, but it reappeared a few years after under the name of " lama," or " poil de chèvre," when it obtained a great success. The hair of the lama has never been used.

The finest collection of Auvergne lace in the International Exhibition was from the manufactory at Crâponne (Haute-Loire), [12] established in 1830 by M. Théodore Falcon, to whom Le Puy is indebted for her " musée de dentelles," containing specimens of the lace of all countries and all ages, a most useful and instructive collection for the centre of a lace district, and one which might to advantage be established in our own country. [13] Le Puy has also a lace school, numbering a hundred pupils, and a school of design for lace patterns, founded in 1859.

---

[9] Roland de la Platière.

[10] The thread used in Auvergne comes from Haarlem, purchased either from the merchants of Rouen or Lyons. In the palmy days of Le Puy her lace-workers consumed annually to the amount of 400,000 livres.

[11] Three-fourths of the Auvergne lace were consumed in Europe in time of peace:—Sardinia took 120,000 francs, purchased by the merchants of Turin, once a year, and then distributed through the country;

Florence and Spain, each 200,000; Guyenne exported by the merchants of Bordeaux 200,000; 500,000 went to the Spanish Indies. The rest was sold in France by means of colporteurs. Peuchet.

[12] In Auvergne, lace has preserved its ancient names of " passement " and " pointes," the latter applied especially to needle-made lace.

[13] We are happy to state that a lace museum has been opened in the Albert Memorial Museum of Exeter.

AURILLAC AND MURAT (Dép. Cantal)

The lace of Aurillac had an early reputation. The origin of the manufacture is assigned to the fourteenth century, when a company of emigrants established themselves at Cuença and Valcameos, and nearly all the points of Aurillac were exported into Spain through this company.[14]

It had an important commerce in the seventeenth century, where it is mentioned in the " Révolte des Passemens "; and in 1670, the author of the " Délices de la France " writes: " L'on fait à Orillac les dentelles qui ont vogue dans le royaume." [15]

Colbert established manufactories of points de France at Aurillac and Riom, and met with the usual resistance on the part of the lace-makers, who would not give up what the intendant terms " the wretched old point," which an historian of the department describes, on the contrary, as consisting of rich, flowered designs, as may be seen by studying the portraits of many Auvergnat noblemen of the period.[16] There are various letters on the subject in the " Colbert Correspondence; " in the last from Colbert, 1670, he writes that the point d'Aurillac is improving, and there are 8000 lace-women at work. It appears that he established at Aurillac a manufactory of lace, where they made, upon " des dessins flamands modifiés," a special article, then named " point Colbert," and, subsequently, " point d'Aurillac."

In the convent of the Visitation at Le Puy is shown the lace trimming of an alb, point d'Angleterre. It is 28 inches wide, of white thread, with brides picotées, of elegant scroll design. If, as tradition asserts, it was made in the country, it must be the produce of this manufactory.[17]

It appears that rich " passements," as they are still called in the country, of gold and silver were made long before the period of Colbert. We find abundant mention of them in the church

---

[14] Savary.

[15] Savinière d'Alquie.

[16] " Guide historique du Département de Cantal, par Henri Duref."

[17] Photographed in the " Album d'Archéologie religieuse," where it is styled " Valenciennes."

inventories of the province; and in the museum are pieces of
rich lace said to have belonged to Francis I. and his successors,
which, according to tradition, were the produce of Aurillac.
They are not of a wire, but consist of strips of metal twisted
round the silk.

In the inventory of the sacristy of the Benedictine monastery
at St.-Aligre, 1684, there is a great profusion of lace. " Voile de
brocard, fond d'or entouré d'un point d'Espagne d'or et argent; "
another, " garni de dentelles d'or et argent, enrichi de perles fines ;"
" 20 aubes à grandes dentelles, amicts, lavabos, surplis," &c., all
" à grandes ou petites dentelles." [18]

In the account of a masked ball, as given in the " Mercure
Galant " of 1679, these points find honourable mention. The
Prince de Conty is described as wearing a " mante de point
d'Aurillac or et argent; " the Comte de Vermandois, a veste
edged with the same; while Mademoiselle de Blois has " ses
voiles de point d'Aurillac d'argent;" and of the Duchesse de
Mortemart it is said, " On voyoit dessous ses plumes un voile de
point d'Aurillac or et argent qui tomboit sur ses épaules." The
Chevalier Colbert, who appeared in an African costume, had " des
manches pendantes " of the same material.

The same " Mercure," of April 1681, speaking of the dress of
the men, says : " La plupart portent des garnitures d'une richesse
qui empeschera que les particuliers ne les imitent, puisqu'elles
reviennent à 50 louis. Ces garnitures sont de point d'Espagne ou
d'Aurillac." From the above notices, as well as from the fact that
the greater part of these laces were sent into Spain, it appears
that the " passements," as they were still called, were a rich gold
and silver lace made at Aurillac, and similar to the point
d'Espagne.[19]

The laces of Murat (Dép. Haute-Garonne) were " façon de

---

[18] " Voile de toile d'argent, garni de
grandes dentelles d'or et argent fin, donné
en 1711 pour envelopper le chef de S.
Gaudence."—*Inventaire du Monastère des
Bénédictines de St.-Aligre.*.

In the inventory of Massillon's chapel
at Beauregard, 1742, are albs trimmed
with " point d'Aurillac," veils with " point
d'Espagne or et argent." In the convents
are constantly noted down " point

d'Espagne d'or et argent fin," while
in the cathedral of Clermont the chapter
contented itself with " dentelles d'or et
argent faux."

[19] The finest " points de France,"
writes Savary, were made at Aurillac
and Murat, the former alone at one time
producing to the annual value of 700,000
francs (28,000*l.*), and giving occupation
to from 3000 to 4000 lace-workers.

Malines et de Lille." They were also made at La Chaise-Dieu, Alenches, and Verceilles. These points were greatly esteemed, and purchased by the wholesale traders of Le Puy and Clermont, who distributed them over the kingdom through their colporteurs.

The manufacture of Aurillac and Murat ended with the Revolution. The women, finding they could earn more as domestic servants in the neighbouring towns, on the restoration of order, never again returned to their ancient occupation.

CHAPTER XIX.

LIMOUSIN.

In the seventeenth and eighteenth centuries, a kind of pillow net ("torchon entoilage," Mr. Ferguson calls it) [1] for women's sleeves was manufactured at Tulle (Corrèze), and also at Aurillac. From this circumstance many writers have derived "tulle," the French name for bobbin-net, from this town, where it has never, at any period, been made.

The first dictionary in which the word "tulle" occurs is the French Encyclopædia of 1765, where we find, "Tulle, une espèce de dentelle commune mais plus ordinairement ce qu'on appelait entoilage." [2] Entoilage, as we have already shown, is the plain net ground upon which the pattern is worked,[3] or a plain net used to widen points or laces, or worn as a plain border. In Louis XV.'s reign, Madame de Mailly is described after she had retired from the world as "sans rouge, sans poudre, et, qui plus est, sans dentelles, attendu qu'elle ne portait plus que de l'entoilage à bord plat." [4] We read in the "Tableau de Paris" how "le tul, la gaz et le marli ont occupés cent mille mains." Tulle was made on the pillow in Germany before lace was introduced. If tulle derived its name from any town, it would more probably be from Toul, celebrated, as all others in Lorraine, for its embroidery; and as net resembles the stitches made in embroidery by separating the threads (hemstitch, &c.), it may have taken its French name, tulle, German, Tüll, from the points de Tulle of the workwomen of the town of Toul, called in Latin, Tullum, or Tullo.[5]

---

[1] "1773. 6 au. de grande entoilage de belle blonde à poix."

[2] "16 au. entoilage à mouches à 11 l., 176 l."—*Comptes de Madame du Barry.*

[3] "7 au. de tulle pour hausser les manchettes, à 9 l., 63 l."—*Comptes de Madame du Barry,* 1770.

[4] "Souvenirs de la Marquise de Créquy."

[5] In an old geography, we find "Tulle, Tuille three hundred years ago."

The word Tule, or Tuly, occurs in an English inventory of 1315, and again, in "Sir Gawayn and the Green Knight;"

LORRAINE.

The lace manufacture of Lorraine passes for one of the oldest in France. It flourished in the seventeenth century. Mirecourt [6] and the villages of its environs, extending to the Department of the Meurthe, was the great centre of this trade, which formed the sole occupation of the countrywomen. For some centuries the lace-workers employed only hempen thread, spun in the environs of Épinal, and specially at Châtel-sur-Moselle.[7] From this they produced a species of coarse guipure termed " passament," or, in the patois of the province, " peussemot." [8]

As early as the seventeenth century, they set aside this coarse article, and soon produced a finer and more delicate lace, with various patterns: they now made double ground and mignonette; and at Luneville (Dép. Meurthe), " dentelles à l'instar de Flandre." In 1715, an edict of Duke Leopold regulates the manufacture at Mirecourt.[9] The lace was exported to Spain and the Indies. It found its way also to Holland, the German States, and England, where Randle Holme mentions "points of Lorraine, without raisings."[10]

The Lorraine laces were mostly known in commerce as " les dentelles de Saint-Mihiel," from the town of that name, one of the chief places of the fabric. These last named laces were much esteemed on their first appearance. Previous to the union of Lorraine to France, in 1766, there were scarcely 800 lace-makers in Mirecourt. The number now amounts to nearly 25,000.[11]

---

but in both cases, the word seems not to indicate a stuff, but rather a locality, probably Toulouse. Francisque Michel.

In Skelton's " Garland of Lawrell," we find, " A skein of tewly silk ;" which his commentator, the Rev. A. Dyce, considers to be " dyed of a red colour."

[6] Dép. Vosges.   [7] Neufchâteau.

[8] The trader who purchases the lace is called " peussemotier."

[9] The Lorraine laces could only enter France by the bureau of Chaumont, nor could they leave the country without a formal permit delivered at Monthureux-le-Sec.

[10] In a catalogue of the collection of objects of religious art exhibited at the General Assembly of the Catholics of Belgium, at Mechlin. We find noticed therein, " Dentelle pour rochet, point de Nancy," from the church of St. Charles at Antwerp, together with various "voiles de bénédiction," laces for rochets and altar-cloths, of " point de Paris."

[11] The " Tableau statistique du Dép. des Vosges," by Citoyen Desgoulles, An X, says : " Mirecourt is celebrated for its lace fabrics. There are twenty lace merchants; but the workers are not attached to any particular house. They buy their own thread, make the lace, and bring it to the merchants of Mirecourt

Early in the present century the export trade gave place to more extensive dealings with France. "Point de Flandre" was then very much made, the patterns imported by travelling merchants journeying on their way to Switzerland. Anxious to produce novelty, the manufacturers of Mirecourt wisely sent for draughtsmen and changed the old patterns. Their success was complete. They soon became formidable rivals to Lille, Geneva, and the Val de Travers (Switzerland). Lille now lowered her prices, and the Swiss lace trade sank in the contest.

Scarcely any but white lace is made, the patterns are varied and in excellent taste, the work similar to that of Lille and Arras.

Some few years since the making of application flowers was attempted with success at Mirecourt, and though it has not yet attained the perfection of the Brussels sprigs, yet it daily improves, and bids fair to supply France with a production for which she now pays Belgium 120,000*l.* annually. The Lorraine application possesses one advantage over those of Flanders: the flowers come from the hands of the lace-makers clean and white, and do not require bleaching.[12] The price, too, is most moderate. The production which of late years has been of the most commercial value is the Cluny lace, so called from the first patterns being copied from specimens of old lace of the sixteenth and seventeenth centuries, of Gothic geometric design, in the Musée de Cluny. The immense success of this lace has been highly profitable to Mirecourt and Le Puy.

Much of the Lorraine lace is consumed at Paris and in the interior of France; the rest is exported to America, the East Indies, and the different countries of Europe.

BURGUNDY.

Colbert was proprietor of the terre de Seignelay, three leagues from Auxerre, which caused him to interest himself in establishing manufactories in these countries, and especially that of point de

---

to purchase. The women follow this occupation when not engaged in field work; but they only earn from 25 to 40 centimes a day. Before the Revolution, 7/8 of the coarse lace was exported to Germany towards Swabia. Of the fine qualities, France consumed 2/3. The remainder went to the colonies."

[12] So are those of Courseulles (Calvados).

Fig. 99.

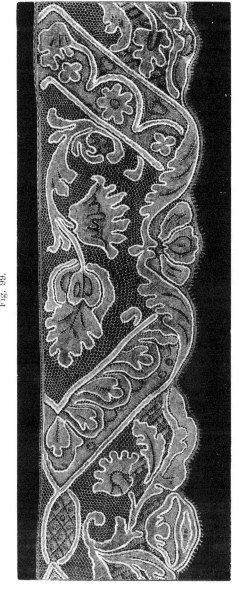

Point de Bourgogne (pillow-lace), façon Malines.

France. In his "Correspondence" are twelve letters relating to this manufacture for 1667–74, but it did not succeed.

At last worn out, he says "the mayor and aldermen will not avail themselves of the means of prosperity I offer, so I leave them to their bad conduct."

Specimens of a beautifully fine, well-finished pillow lace, resembling old Mechlin, are often to be met with in Belgium (Fig. 99), bearing the traditional name of "point de Bourgogne," but no record remains of its manufacture. In the census taken in 1571, giving the names of all strangers in the City of London, three are cited as natives of Burgundy, knitters and makers of lace.[13]

In the eighteenth century, a manufactory of Valenciennes was carried on in the hospital at Dijon, under the direction of the magistrates of the city. It fell towards the middle of the last century, and at the Revolution entirely disappeared.[14] "Les dentelles sont grosses," writes Savary, "mais il s'en débite beaucoup en Franche-Comté."

LYONNOIS.

Lyons, from the thirteenth century, made gold and silver laces enriched with ornaments similar to those of Paris. At the revocation of the Edict of Nantes, the trade, of an annual value of 4,000,000 francs, passed into Switzerland.

The laces of St.-Etienne resembled those of Valenciennes, and were much esteemed for their solidity. The finest productions were for men's ruffles, which they fabricated of exquisite beauty.

A considerable quantity of blonde was made at Meran, a village in the neighbourhood of Beauvoisin, but the commerce had fallen off at the end of the last century. These blondes go by the familiar name of "bisettes."

Lyons had great trade with Florence; and an author calls it "ville moitié florentine."

---

[13] John Roberts, of Burgundy, eight years in England, "a knitter of knotted wool."

Peter de Grue, Burgundian, "knitter of cauls and sleeves."

Callys de Hove, "maker of lace," and Jane his wife, born in Burgundy.—*State Papers, Dom.* Eliz. vol. lxxxiv. P. R. O.

[14] On referring to M. Joseph Garnier,

the learned archiviste of Dijon, he kindly informed the Author that "les archives de l'hospice Sainte-Anne n'ont conservé aucune trace de la manufacture de dentelles qui y fut établie. Tout ce qu'on sait, c'est qu'elle était sous la direction d'un sieur Helling, et qu'on y fabriquait le point d'Alençon."

ORLÉANOIS.

Colbert's attempts at establishing a manufactory of point de France at Montargis appears by his letters to have been unsuccessful.

BERRY.

Nor were the reports from Bourges more encouraging.

BRETAGNE.

No record of lace-making occurs in Bretagne, though probably the Normandy manufactures extended westward along the coast. At all events, the wearing of it was early adopted.

There is a popular ballad of the province, 1587, on " La Fontenelle le Ligueur," one of the most celebrated partisans of the League in Bretagne. He has been entrapped at Paris, and, while awaiting his doom, sends his page to his wife with these words (we spare our readers the Breton dialect) :—

" Page, mon page, petit page, va vite à Coadelan et dis à la pauvre héritière[15] de ne plus porter des dentelles.

" De ne plus porter des dentelles, parce que son pauvre époux est en peine. Toi, rapporte-moi une chemise à mettre, et un drap pour m'ensevelir."[16]

One singular custom prevails among the ancient families in Bretagne : a bride wears her lace-adorned dress but twice—once on her wedding-day, and only again at her death, when the corpse lies in state for a few hours before its placing in the coffin.

After the marriage ceremony the bride carefully folds away her dress[17] in linen of the finest homespun, intended for her winding-sheet, and each year, on the anniversary of the wedding-

---

[15] He had run away with the rich heiress of Coadelan.

[16] " Chants populaires de la Bretagne, par Th. Hersart de la Villemarqué."

[17] The bringing home of the wedding dress is an event of solemn importance. The family alone are admitted to see it.

and each of them sprinkles the orange blossoms with which it is trimmed with holy water placed at the foot of the bed whereon the dress is laid, and offers up a prayer for the future welfare of the wearer.

day, fresh sprigs of lavender and rosemary are laid upon it until the day of mourning comes, when the white marriage garment leaves its resting-place once more to deck the lifeless form of her who wore it in the hour of joy and hope.

POITOU.

Lace was made at Loudun in the seventeenth century, but the fabric has always been common.

"Mignonettes et dentelles à poignet de chemises, et de prix de toutes espèces," from one sol six deniers the ell, to forty sols the piece of twelve ells.

Children began lace-making at a very early age. "Loudun fournit quelques dentelles communes," says the government reporter of 1803.[18]

Peuchet speaks of lace manufactories at Perpignan, Aix, Cahors, Bordeaux, &c., but they do not appear to have been of any importance, and no longer exist.

With the exception of the Valenciennes-making town of Bailleul (Nord), the lace of industry of France is now concentrated in the provinces of Normandy, Auvergne, and Lorraine.

---

[18] " Descr. du Dép. de la Vienne, par le Citoyen Cochon.   An X."

CHAPTER XX.

HOLLAND, GERMANY, AND SWITZERLAND.

HOLLAND.

" A country that draws fifty feet of water,
In which men live as in the hold of nature,
And when the sea does in them break,
And drowns a province, does but spring a leak."
Hudibras.

WE know little of the early manufactures of this country. The laces of Holland, though made to a great extent, were overshadowed by the richer products of their Flemish neighbours. " The Netherlanders," writes Fynes Moryson, who visited Holland in 1589, " wear very little lace,[1] and no embroidery. Their gowns are mostly black, without lace or gards, and their neck-ruffs of very fine linen."

We read how, in 1667, France had become the rival of Holland in the trade with Spain, Portugal, and Italy ; but she laid such high duties on foreign merchandise, the Dutch themselves set up manufactures of lace and other articles, and found a market for their produce even in France." [2] A few years later, the revocation of the Edict of Nantes [3] caused 4000 lace-makers to leave the town of Alençon alone. Many took refuge in Holland, where, says a writer of the day, " they were treated like artists." Holland gained more than she lost by Louis XIV. The French

---

[1] In the census of 1571, giving the names of all strangers in the city of London, we find mention but of one Dutchman, Richard Thomas, "a worker of billament lace."

[2] In 1689 appears an "Arrest du Roi qui ordonne l'exécution d'une sentence du maître de poste de Rouen, portant confiscat n des dentelles venant d'Amsterdam. Arch. Nat. Coll. Rondoneau.

[3] 1685.

refugees founded a manufactory of that point lace called "dentelle à la reine"[4] in the Orphan House at Amsterdam.[5]

A few years later, another Huguenot, Zacharie Châtelain,[6] introduced into Holland the industry, at that time so important, of making gold and silver lace.

The Dutch possessed one advantage over most other nations, especially over England, in her far-famed Haarlem[7] thread, once considered the best adapted for lace in the world. "No place bleaches flax," says a writer of the day,[8] "like the meer of Haarlem."[9]

Still the points of Holland made little noise in the world. The Dutch strenuously forbade the entry of all foreign lace, and what they did not consume themselves, they exported to Italy, where the market was often deficient.[10] Once alone in England we hear tell of a considerable parcel of Dutch lace seized between Deptford and London from the Rotterdam hoy. England, however, according to Anderson, in 1764, received in return for her products from Holland "fine lace, but the balance was in England's favour."

In 1770, the empress queen (Maria Theresa) published a declaration prohibiting the importation of Dutch lace into any of her imperial majesty's hereditary dominions in Germany.[11]

---

[4] We have frequent mention of "dentelle à la reine," previous to its introduction into Holland.

1619. "Plus une aulne ung tiers de dentelle à la reyne."—*Trésorerie de Madame, Sœur du Roi.* Arch. Nat. K. K. 234.

1678. "Les dames mettent ordinairement deux cornettes de Point à la Reyne ou de soie écrue, rarement de Point de France, parce que le point clair sied mieux au visage."—*Mercure Galant.*

1683. "Deux Aubes de toille demie holande garnis de point à la Reyne."—*Inv. fait apres le decedz de Mgr. Colbert.* Bib. Nat. MSS. Suite de Mortemart, 34.

Among the articles to be taxed on their entry into Sweden, in 1691, are cravats and ruffles of "Poynte à la Reyne," together with those of "point de Venise" and "poynte d'Espagne."

[5] C. Weisse, "History of the French Protestant Refugees from the Edict of Nantes." Edinburgh, 1854.

[6] Grandson of Simon Châtelain. See p. 80.

[7] In the paper already referred to (see "Normandy"), on the lace trade, in 1704, it is stated the Flemish laces called "dentelles de haut prix" are made of Lille, Mons, and Mechlin thread, sent to bleach at Haarlem, "as they know not how to bleach them elsewhere." The "dentelles de bas prix" of Normandy and other parts of France being made entirely of the cheaper thread of Haarlem itself, an act, then just passed, excluding the Haarlem thread, would, if carried out, annihilate this branch of industry in France. "Commerce des Dentelles de Fil." Bib. Nat. MSS. F. Fr. 14,294.

[8] And. Yarranton, 1677.

[9] "Flax is improved by age. The saying was, 'Wool may be kept to dust, flax to silk.' I have seen flax twenty years old as fine as a hair."—*Ibid.*

[10] "Commerce de la Hollande," 1768.

[11] "Edinburgh Amusement."

As in other matters, the Dutch carried their love of lace to the extreme, tying up their knockers with rich point to announce the

Fig. 100.

Dutch pillow lace.

birth of an infant. A traveller who visited France in 1691 remarks of his hotel: "The warming-pans and brasses were not

here muffled up in point and cutwork, after the manner of Holland,
for there were no such things to be seen." [12]

The Dutch lace most in use was thick, strong, and serviceable.
Fig. 100 adorned a Dutchwoman's cap. That which has come
under our notice resembles the fine close Valenciennes, having a
pattern often of flowers or fruit strictly copied from nature. " The
ladies wear," remarks Mrs. Calderwood, " very good lace mobs."
The shirt worn by William the Silent when he fell by the assassin
is still preserved at the Hague; it is trimmed with a lace described as of thick linen stitches, drawn and worked over in a
style familiar to those acquainted with the earlier Dutch pictures.

SAXONY.

" Here unregarded lies the rich brocade,
   There Dresden lace in scatter'd heaps is laid;
   Here the gilt china vase bestrews the floor,
   While chidden Betty weeps without the door."
         Ecloque on the Death of Shock, a Pet Lapdog. Ladies'
                        Magazine, 1750.

" His olive-tann'd complexion graces
   With little dabs of Dresden laces;
   While for the body Mounseer Puff
   Would think e'en dowlas fine enough."
                    French Barber, 1756.

The honour of introducing pillow lace into Germany is accorded by common consent to Barbara Uttmann. She was born
in 1514, in the small town of Etterlein, which derives its name
from her family. Her parents, burghers of Nuremberg, had
removed to the Saxon Erzgebirge, for the purpose of working
some mines. Barbara Etterlein here married a rich master miner
named Christopher Uttmann, of Annaberg. It is said that she
learned lace-making from a native of Brabant, a Protestant, whom
the cruelties of the Spaniards had driven from her country
Barbara had observed the mountain girls occupied in making a
network for the miners to wear over their hair: she took great
interest in the work, and, profiting by the experience derived from
her Brabant teacher, succeeded in making her pupils produce a
kind of plain lace ground. In 1561, having procured aid from

---

[12] " Six Weeks in the Court and Country of France, "1691.

Flanders, she set up, in her own name of Barbara Uttmann, a workshop at Annaberg, and there began to make laces of various patterns. This branch of industry soon spread from the Bavarian frontier to Altenberg and Geissing, giving employment to 30,000 persons, and producing a revenue of 1,000,000 thalers. Barbara Uttmann died in 1575, leaving sixty-five children and grand-children, thus realising a prophecy made previous to her marriage, that her descendants would equal in number the stitches of the first lace ground she had made : such prophecies were common in

Fig. 101.

Tomb of Barbara Uttmann, at Annaberg.

those days. She sleeps in the churchyard of Annaberg, near the old lime-tree. On her tomb (Fig. 101) is inscribed : " Here lies Barbara Uttmann, died 14 January 1575, whose invention of lace in the year 1561 made her the benefactress of the Erz-gebirge."

" An active mind, a skilful hand,
Bring blessings down on the Fatherland."

In the Green Vault at Dresden is preserved an ivory statuette (Frontispiece) of Barbara Uttmann, 4½ inches high, beautifully executed by Koehler, a jeweller of Dresden, who worked at the beginning of the eighteenth century. It is richly ornamented with enamels and precious stones, such figures (of which there are many in the Green Vault) being favourite articles for birthday and Christmas gifts.[13]

Previous to the eighteenth century the nets of Germany had already found a market in Paris. "On vend," says the "Livre Commode des Adresses" of 1692, "le treillis d'Allemagne en plusieurs boutiques de la rue Béthizy." [14]

" Dresden," says Anderson, "makes very fine lace," a statement confirmed by nearly every traveller of the eighteenth century. We have every reason to believe the so-called Dresden lace was the drawn-work described p. 11, and which was carried to great perfection.

"Went to a shop at Spaw," writes Mrs. Calderwood, "and bought a pair of double Dresden ruffles, which are just like a sheaf, but not so open as yours, for two pounds two."

" La broderie de Dresde est très-connue et les ouvriers très-habiles," says Savary.

This drawn-work, for such it was, excited the emulation of other nations. The Anti-Gallican Society in 1753 leads the van, and awards three guineas as their second prize for ruffles of Saxony.[15]

Ireland, in 1755, gives a premium of 5l. for the best imitation of " Dresden point," while the Edinburgh Society, following in the wake, a year later, presents to Miss Jenny Dalrymple a gold medal for " the best imitation of Dresden work in a pair of ruffles."

In the " Fool of Quality," [16] and other works, from 1760 to 1770,

---

we have "Dresden aprons," "Dresden ruffles," showing that description of lace to have been in high fashion. Wraxall, too, 1778, describes a Polish beauty as wearing "a broad Medicis of Dresden lace." As early as 1760 "Dresden work" is advertised as taught to young ladies in a boarding-school at Kelso,[17] together with "shell-work in grottoes, flowers, catgut, working lace on bobbins or wires, and other useful accomplishments."

The lace of Saxony has sadly degenerated since the eighteenth century. The patterns are old and ungraceful, and the lace of inferior workmanship, but owing to the low price of labour, they have the great advantage of cheapness, which enables them to compete with France in the American and Russian markets. In all parts of Germany there are some few men who make lace. On the Saxon side of the Erzgebirge many boys are employed, and during the winter season men of all ages work at the pillow; and it is observed that the lace made by men is firmer and of a superior quality to that of the women. The lace is a dentelle torchon, of large pattern, much in the style of the old lace of Ischia.[18]

The Saxon lace of the present day is an imitation of old Brussels. This lace is costly, and is sold at Dresden and other large towns of Germany, and particularly at Paris, where the dealers pass it off for old lace. It employed, in 1851, 300 workers. A quantity of so-called Maltese lace is also made.

The new Museum for Art and Industry, lately opened at Vienna, contains several pattern books of the sixteenth century, and in it has been exhibited a fine collection of ancient lace belonging to General von Hauslaub, Master-General of the Ordnance.

GERMANY (NORTH AND SOUTH).

"Presque dans toutes sortes d'arts les plus habiles ouvriers, ainsi que les plus riches négociants, sont de la religion prétendue réformée," said the Chancellor d'Aguesseau:[19] and when his

---

aprons, silvered silks, and rich brocades." And again, "Your points of Spain, your ruffles of Dresden."—*Fool of Quality*, 1766.

[17] "Caledonian Mercury," 1760.
[18] Letter from Koestritz, 1863.
[19] In 1713.

master, Louïs XIV., whom he, in not too respectful terms, calls
"le roi trop crédule," signed the Act of Revocation (1685),
Europe was at once inundated with the most skilful workmen of
France. Hamburg alone of the Hanse Towns received the
wanderers. Lübeck and Bremen, in defiance of the remonstrances
of the Protestant princes, allowed no strangers to settle within
their precincts. The emigrants soon established considerable
manufactories of gold and silver lace, and also that now extinct
fabric known under the name of "Hamburg point,"[20] probably
a kind of drawn-work, like the Dresden point.

Miss Knight, in her "Autobiography," notes: "At Hamburg,
just before we embarked, Nelson purchased a magnificent lace
trimming for Lady Nelson, and a black lace cloak for another
lady, who, he said, had been very attentive to his wife during
his absence."

On the very year of the Revocation, Frederick William,
Elector of Brandenburg, anxious to attract the fugitive workmen
to his dominions, issued from Potsdam an edict[21] in their favour.
Crowds of French Protestants responded to the call, and before
many years had passed, Berlin alone boasted 450 lace manufactories.[22] Previous to this emigration she had none. These
"mangeurs d'haricots," as the Prussians styled the emigrants,
soon amassed large fortunes, and exported their laces to Poland
and to Russia. The tables were turned. France, who formerly
exported lace in large quantities to Germany, now received it
from the hands of her exiled workmen, and in 1723 and 1734, we
find "Arrêts du Conseil d'État," relative to the importation of
German laces.[23] Louis XV. having asked Frederick the Great
what he could do most agreeable to him, replied, "A second
Edict of Nantes."

The Landgrave of Hesse also received the refugees, publish-
ing an edict in their favour.[24] Two establishments of fine point
were set up at Hanover.[25] Leipzig, Anspach,[26] Elberfeld, all
profited by the migration. "On compte," writes Peuchet, "à
Leipsig cinq fabriques de dentelles et de galon d'or et d'argent."

---

[20] Weisse.

[21] Dated 29 Oct. 1685.

[22] Anderson.

[23] Arch. Nat. Col. Rondoneau.

[24] "Commissions and Privileges granted by Charles I., Landgrave of Hesse, to the French Protestants, dated Cassel, 12 Dec. 1685."

[25] Peuchet.

[26] Anderson.

A large colony settled at Halle, where they made "Hungarian" lace—"point de Hongrie,"[27] a term more generally applied to a stitch in tapestry.[28] The word, however, does occasionally occur:—

> "Your Hungerland [29] bands and Spanish quellio ruffs,
> Great Lords and Ladies feasted to survey." [30]

Fynes Moryson expresses surprise at the simplicity of the German costume—ruffs of coarse cloth, made at home. The Dantzickers, however, he adds, dress more richly. "Citizens' daughters of an inferior sort wear their hair woven with lace stitched up with a border of pearl. Citizens' wives wear much lace of silk on their petticoats." Dandyism began in Germany, says a writer,[31] about 1626, when the women first wore silver, which appeared very remarkable, and "at last indeed which lace." A century later luxury at the baths of Baden had reached an excess unparalleled in the present day. The bath mantles, "équipage de bain," of both sexes are described as trimmed with the richest point, and after the bath were spread out ostentatiously as a show on the baths before the windows of the rooms. Lords and ladies, princesses and margraves, loitered up and down, passing judgment on the laces of each new arrival.[32]

This love of dress, in some cases, extended too far, for Bishop Douglas[33] mentions how the Leipzig students "think it more honourable to beg, with a sword by their side, of all they meet than to gain their livelihood. I have often," he says, "given a few groschen to one finely powdered and dressed with sword and lace ruffles."

Concerning the manufactures of the once opulent cities of Nuremberg and Augsburg, we have no record. In the first-mentioned was published, in 1601, the model book, engraved on

---

[27] "La France Protestante, par M. M. Haag," Paris, 1846–59.

[28] "Item. Dix carrez de tapisserye a poinctz de Hongrye d'or, d'argent et soye de differends patrons."—*Inv. après le decès du Maréchal de Marillac*, 1632. Bib. Nat. MSS. F. Fr. 11,424.

[29] Hungary was so styled in the seventeenth century. In a "Relation of the most famous Kingdoms and Common Weales through the World," London, 1608, we find "Hungerland."

[30] "City Madam," Massinger.

[31] "Pictures of German Life, in the Fifteenth, Sixteenth, and Seventeenth Centuries," by Gustaf Freytag.

[32] "Merveilleux Amusements des Bains de Bade," Londres, 1739.

[33] Bishop of Salisbury, "Letters," 1748-9.

copper, of Sibmacher.[34]   On the frontispiece is depicted a garden
of the sixteenth century.   From the branches of a tree hangs a
label, informing the world "that she who loves the art of needlework, and desires to make herself skilful, can here have it in perfection, and she will acquire praise, honour, and reward."   At the
foot of the tree is seated a modest young lady, yclept Industria;
on the right a second, feather-fan in hand, called Ignavia—Idle-
ness; on the left, a respectable matron, named Sofia—Wisdom.
By way of a preface, the three hold a dialogue, reviewing, in most
flattering terms, the work.

A museum has been lately formed at Nuremberg for works
and objects connected with the lace manufacture and its history,
It contains some interesting specimens of Nuremberg lace, the
work of a certain Jungfrau Picklemann, in the year 1600, presented
by the widow of Pfarrer Michel, of Poppenreuth.[35]   The lace is
much of the Venetian character.   One specimen has the figures
of a knight and a lady, resembling the designs of Vecellio.   The
museum also possesses other curious examples of lace, together
with a collection of books relative to lace-making.

"In the chapel of St. Egidius at Nuremberg," writes one of
our correspondents, "we were led to make inquiries concerning
sundry ponderous-looking chairs, bearing some resemblance to
confessionals, but wanting the side compartments for the penitents.
We learned that they belonged to the several guilds (Innungen),
who had undertaken to collect money for the erection of a new
church after the destruction of the old by fire.   For this end the
last members sworn in of every trade sat in their respective
chairs at the church doors on every Sunday and holiday.   The
offerings were thrown into dishes placed on a raised stand on the
right of the chair, or into the hollow in front.   The devices of
each trade were painted or embossed on circular plates, said to
be of silver, on the back of each chair.   One "Handwerksstuhl"
in particular attracted our attention; it was that of the passe-
menterie-makers (in German, Portenmacher- or Posamentier-Hand-
werk), which, until the handicrafts became more divided, included the lace-makers.   An elegant scroll-pattern in rilievo
surrounds the plate, surmounted by a cherub's head, and various
designs, resembling those of the pattern-books, are embossed in a

---

[34] "Modelbuch in Kupfer gemacht," Nürnberg, 1601.
[35] Poppenreuth is about a German mile from Nuremberg.

most finished style upon the plate, together with an inscription dated 1718."

Misson, who visited Nuremberg in 1698, describes the dress of a newly married pair as rich in the extreme. That of the bridegroom as black, " fort chargé de dentelles ; " the bride as tricked out in the richest " dentelle antique," her petticoat trimmed with " des tresses d'or et de dentelle noire."

Perhaps the finest collection of old German point is preserved, or rather was so, five-and-thirty years since, in the palace of the ancient, but now extinct, prince-archbishops of Bamberg.

The modern laces of Bohemia are tasteless in design. The manufacture is of early date. " The Bohemian women," writes Moryson, " delight in black cloth with lace of light colours." In the beginning of the present century, upwards of 60,000 people, men, women, and children, were occupied in the Bohemian Erzgebirge alone in lace-making. Since the introduction of the bobbin-net machine into Austria, 1831, the number has decreased. There are now scarcely 8000 employed in the common laces, and about 4000 on Valenciennes and points.[36] Austria sent to the International Exhibition of 1874 specimens of needle point and point plat, made in the school of the Grand Duchess Sophie, and specimens of border laces in the style of those of Auvergne were exhibited from the Erzgebirge and Bohemia.

Countess Nako and Mr. Artaria, both of Vienna, possess fine collections of lace.

SWITZERLAND.

" Dans un vallon fort bien nommé Travers,
S'élève un mont, vrai séjour des hivers."—*Voltaire.*

In 1572, one Symphorien Thelusson, a merchant of Lyons, having escaped from the massacre of St. Bartholomew, concealed himself in a bale of goods, in which he reached Geneva, and was hospitably received by the inhabitants. When, after the lapse of near a hundred and twenty years, crowds of French emigrants arrived in the city, driven from their homes on the revocation of the Edict of Nantes, a descendant of this same Thelusson took a

---

[36] " Austria."—*Report of the International Exhibition of 1862.*

body of 2000 refugees into his service, and at once established a manufacture of lace,[37] especially gold lace made with false gold of Nuremberg, a cheap, strong production which was sent to Spain and the colonies. The produce of this industry was smuggled back into France, the goods conveyed across the Jura over passes known only to the bearers, by which they avoided the custom-house duties of Valence. " Every day," writes Jambonneau, himself a manufacturer, " they tell my wife what lace they want, and she takes their orders." Louis XIV. was furious.[38]

Though lace-making employed many women in various parts of the country, who made a common description while tending their flocks in the mountains, Neufchâtel has always been the " chef-lieu" of the trade. " In this town," says Savary, " they have carried their works to such a degree of perfection as to rival the laces of Flanders, not only in beauty but in quality." We have ourselves seen in Switzerland guipures of fine workmanship that were made in the country, belonging to old families, in which they have remained as heirlooms; and have now in our possession a pair of lappets, made in the last century at Neufchâtel, of such exquisite beauty as not to be surpassed by the richest productions of Brussels.

Formerly lace-making employed a large number of workmen in the Val-de-Travers, where, during his sojourn at Moutiers, Jean-Jacques Rousseau tells us he amused himself in handling the bobbins.

In 1780, the lace trade was an object of great profit to the country, producing laces valuing from 1 batz to upwards of 70 francs the ell, and exporting to the amount of 1,500,000 francs; on which the workwomen gained 800,000, averaging their labour at scarcely 8 sols per day. The villages of Fleurens and Connet were the centre of this once flourishing trade,[39] now ruined by competition with Mirecourt. In 1814 there were in the Neufchâtel district 5628 lace-makers; in 1844, a few aged women alone remained. The modern laces of Neufchâtel resemble those of Lille, but are apt to wash thick.

In 1840, a manufacture of " point plat de Bruxelles dite de Genève " was established at Geneva.

---

[37] Haag, " La France Protestante."

[38] The Neufchâtel trade extended through the Jura range from the valley of Lake Joux (Vaud) to Porentruy, near Bâle.

[39] " Statistique de la Suisse. Picot, de Genève." 1819.

By the sumptuary laws of Zurich, which[40] were most severe, women were especially forbidden to wear either blonde or thread lace, except upon their caps. This must have been a disadvantage to the native fabrics, "for Zurich," says Anderson, "makes much gold, silver, and thread lace."

Several pattern books for lace were published in Switzerland in the later years of the sixteenth century. One, without date, but evidently printed at Zürich about 1540, by C. Froschover, is entitled "Nüw Modelbüch allerley Gattungen Däntel," &c. We refer our reader to the Appendix for some interesting details relative to the introduction of lace given in the preface. Another one, entitled "New Model-Buch," printed by G. Strauben, 1593, at St. Gall, is but a reprint of the third book of Vecellio's "Corona." Another, called also "Sehr Newe Model-Buch," was published at Basle in 1599, at the printing-house of Ludwig Künigs.

_____

[40] A curious pattern book has been sent to us, belonging to the Antiquarian Society of Zurich, through the kindness of its president, Dr. Ferd. Keller. It contains specimens of a variety of narrow braids and edgings of a kind of knotted work; but only a few open-work edgings that could be called lace.

CHAPTER XXI.

DENMARK, SWEDEN, AND RUSSIA.

DENMARK.

" ERASTE.—Miss, how many parties have you been to this week?
" LADY.—I do not frequent such places; but if you want to know how much
lace I have made this fortnight, I might well tell you."

Holberg, The Inconstant Lady.

" The far-famed lace of Tönder."

" A CERTAIN kind of embroidery, or cutwork in linen, was much
used in Denmark before lace came in from Brabant," writes
Professor Thomsen. " This kind of work is still in use among the
peasants, and you will often have observed it on their bed-clothes."

The art of lace-making itself is supposed to have been first
brought over by the fugitive monks at the Reformation, or to have
been introduced by Queen Elizabeth,[1] sister of Charles V., and
wife of Christian II., that good queen who, had her husband been
more fortunate, would, says the chronicler, " have proved a second
Dagmar to Denmark."

Lace-making has never been practised as a means of livelihood
throughout Denmark. It is only in the province of North
Schleswig (or South Jutland, as it is also called) that a regular
manufacture was established. It is here that King Christian IV.
appears to have made his purchases; and while travelling in
Schleswig, entries constantly occur in his journal book, from 1619
to 1625, such as, " Paid to a female lace-worker 28 rixdollars—
71 specie to a lace-seller for lace for the use of the children," and
many similar notices.[2] It was one of those pieces of Tönder lace

---

[1] On her marriage, 1515.

[2] 1619. Sept. 11. Paid for a lace, 63 rixd. 11 skillings.
　1620. Oct. 11. Paid to a female lace-worker, 28 rixd.
　　„　Nov. 4. Paid 10 rixd. to a female lace-worker who received her dismissal

that King Christian sends to his chamberlain, with an autograph letter, ordering him to cut out of it four collars of the same size and manner as Prince Ulrik's Spanish. They must contrive also to get two pairs of manchettes of the same.

In the museum of the the palace at Rosenborg are still preserved some shirts of Christian IV., trimmed with Schleswig lace of great beauty (Fig. 102), evidently from a Brabant pattern, and in his portrait, which hangs in Hampton Court Palace, the lace on his shirt is of similar texture.

Fig. 102.

Shirt collar of Christian IV. Castle of Rosenborg, Copenhagen.

It was in the early part of this monarch's reign [3] that the celebrated Golden Horn, so long the chief treasure of the Scandinavian Museum at Copenhagen, was found by a young lace-maker on her way to her work. She carried her prize to the king, and with the money he so liberally bestowed on her she was enabled, says tradition, to marry the object of her choice.

1620. Nov. 11. Paid 71 specie dollars to a lace-seller for lace for the use of the children.

Paid 33 specie dollars and 18 skill. Lubeck money, to the same man for lace and cambric.

1625. May 19. Paid 21 rixd. for lace.

„ Dec. 20. Paid 25 specie dollars 15 skill. Lubeck money, for taffetas and lace.

[3] 1639.

The year 1647 was a great epoch in the lace-making of Jutland. A merchant named Steenbeck, taking a great interest in the fabric, engaged twelve persons from Dortmund, in Westphalia, to improve the trade, and settled them at Tönder, to teach the manufacture to both men and women, rich and poor. These twelve persons are described as aged men, with long beards, which, while making lace, they gathered into bags, to prevent the hair from becoming entangled among the bobbins. The manufacture soon made great progress under their guidance, and extended to the south-western part of Ribe, and to the island of Romö.[4] The lace was sold by means of " lace postmen," as they were termed, who carried their wares throughout all Scandinavia and part of Germany.

Christian IV. protected the native manufacture, and in the act of 1643,[5] " lace and such like pinwork " are described as luxurious articles, not allowed to be imported of a higher value than five shillings and sixpence the Danish ell.[6] A later ordinance, 1683, mentions " white and black lace which are manufactured in this country," and grants permission to the nobility to wear them.[7]

Christian IV. did not patronise foreign manufactures. " The King of Denmark," writes Moryson, " wears but little gold lace, and sends foreign apparel to the hangman to be disgraced, when brought in by gentlemen."

About the year 1712 the lace manufacture again was much improved by the arrival of a number of Brabant women, who accompanied the troops of King Frederick IV. on their return from the Netherlands,[8] and settled at Tönder. We have received from Jutland, through the kind exertions of Mr. Rudolf Bay, of Aalborg, a series of Tönder laces, taken from the pattern books of the manufacturers. The earlier specimens are all of Flemish character. There is the old Flanders lace, with its Dutch flowers and grounds in endless variety. The Brabant, with réseau ground, the flowers and "jours" well executed. Then follow the Mechlin grounds, the patterns worked with a coarser thread, in many,

---

[4] Rawert's "Report upon the Industry in the Kingdom of Denmark," 1848.

[5] "The Great Recess."

[6] Two-thirds of a yard.

[7] Dated 1643.

[8] "Tönder lace, fine and middling, made in the districts of Lygum Kloster, keeps all the peasant girls employed. Thereof is exported to the German markets and the Baltic, it is supposed, for more than 100,000 rixdollars (11,110l.), and the fine thread must be had from the Netherlands, and sometimes costs 100 rixdollars per lb."— Pontoppidan, Economical Balance, 1759.

apparently, run in with the needle. There is also a good specimen of that description of drawn muslin lace, commonly known under the name of " Indian work," but which appears to have been very generally made in various manners. The leaves and flowers formed of the muslin are worked round with a cordonnet, by way of relief to the thick double ground (Fig. 103).

In the Scandinavian Museum at Copenhagen is a pair of lappets of drawn muslin, a fine specimen of this work.

The modern laces are copied from French, Lille, and Saxon patterns; there are also imitations of the so-called Maltese. The Schleswig laces are all remarkable for their fine quality and excellent workmanship. Guipure after the manner of the Venice points was also fabricated. A fine example of this lace may be seen decorating the black velvet dress of the youthful daughter of Duke John of Holstein. She lies in her coffin within the mortuary chapel of her family, in the castle of Sonderborg. Lace was much used in burials in the seventeenth and eighteenth centuries, when it really appears people were arrayed in more costly clothing than in their lives. The author of " Jutland and the Danish Islands" has often seen mummies in the Danish churches exposed to view tricked out in points of great richness.

The lace industry continued to increase in value till the beginning of the present century. The year 1801 may be considered its culminating point. At that period the number of peasants employed in Tönder and its neighbourhood alone was 20,000. Even little boys were taught to make lace till strong enough to work in the fields, and there was scarcely a house without a lacemaker, who would sit before her cottage door, working from sunrise till midnight, singing the ballads handed down from their Brabant teachers.[9]

"My late father," [10] writes Mr. F. Wulff, of Brede, "who began the lace trade the end of the last century, first went on foot with his wares to Mecklenburg, Prussia, and Hanover: we con-

---

[9] " The lace fabric, in North Schleswig in 1840, was divided into two districts, that of Tönder and Lygum-Kloster, on the western coasts, and that of Hadersleben and Apenraade, on the east. The quality of the lace from these last localities is so bad that no Copenhagen dealers will have it in their shops."—*Report of the Royal Schleswig-Holstein Government,* 1840.

[10] Mr. Jens Wulff, an eminent lace dealer, knight of the Danebrog, who has made great exertions to revive the lace industry in Denmark.

signed lace to all parts of the world.　Soon he could afford to buy

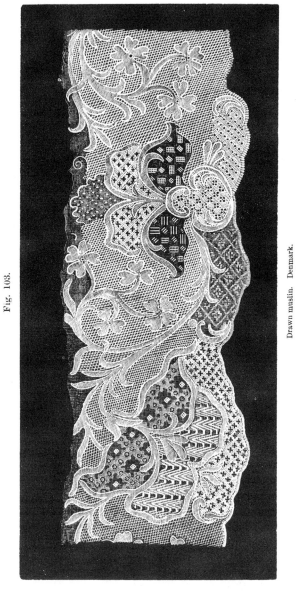

Fig. 103.

Drawn muslin.　Denmark.

a horse; and in his old age he calculated he had travelled on
horseback more than 75,000 English miles, or thrice round the

earth. In his youth the most durable and prettiest ground was the old Flemish, much used by the peasants in Germany. It was solid, and passed as an heirloom through several generations. Later, the fine needle ground came in, and lastly, the fond clair, or point de Lille, far less solid, but easier to work ; hence the lace-makers became less skilful than of old."

They had not many models, and the best workwomen were those who devoted their whole life to one special pattern. Few were found so persevering. One widow, however, is recorded who lived to the age of eighty, and brought up seven children on the produce of a narrow edging, which she sold at sixpence a yard.

Each pattern had its trivial name,—cock-eye, spider, lyre, chimney-pot, and feather.

The rich farmers' wives sat at their pillows daily, causing their household duties to be performed by hired servants from North Jutland. Ladies also, a century and a half ago, made it their occupation, as the motto of our chapter, from the drama of Holberg, will show. And this continued till the fashion of "hvidsom"— white seaming—the cutwork already alluded to, was for a time revived. This work was, however, looked upon as *infra dig.* for the wives of functionaries and such like, in whom it was unbecoming to waste on such employment time that should be devoted to household matters. Our informant tells of a lady in the north who thus embroidered the christening robe of her child by stealth in the kitchen, fearing to be caught by her visitors—cookery had in those days precedence over embroidery. Among the hoards of this child, born 1755, and who died not many years ago, was found a most exquisite collection of old Tönder lace, embracing all the varieties made by her mother and herself, from the thick Flemish to the finest needle-point.

The fashion of cutwork still prevails in Denmark, where collars and cuffs, decorated with stars, crosses, and other mediæval designs, are exposed in the shop-windows of Copenhagen for sale—the work of poor gentlewomen, who, by their needle, thus add a few dollars yearly to their income.

From 1830 dates the decline of the Tönder lace. Cotton thread was introduced, and the quality of the fabric was deteriorated.[11] The lace schools were given up ; and the flourishing state

---

[11] Tönder lace was celebrated for its durability, the best flax or silk thread only being used.

of agriculture rendered it no longer a profitable employment either for the boys or the women.[12] The trade passed from the manufacturers into the hands of the hawkers and petty dealers, who were too poor to purchase the finer points. The "lace postmen" once more travelled from house to house with their little leathern boxes, offering these inferior wares for sale.[13] The art died out. In 1840 there were not more than six lace manufactories in Schleswig.

The old people, however, still believe in a good time coming. "I have in my day," said an aged woman, "sold point at four thalers an ell, sir; and though I may never do so again, my daughter will. The lace trade slumbers, but it does not die."

SWEDEN.

At a very early period, the Scandinavian goldsmith had learned to draw out wires of gold, and twine them round threads either of silk or flax—in fact, to "guiper" them.

Wadstena, where repose the remains of Queen Philippa of Lancaster, daughter of Henry IV., has been considered from time immemorial as the cradle of lace-making in Sweden. The art, according to tradition, was introduced among the nuns of the convent by their foundress, St. Bridget, on her return from Italy. As St. Bridget died in 1335, we may be allowed to question the fact: certain it is, though, the funeral coif of the saintess, as depicted in an ancient portrait said to have been taken at Rome after death, is ornamented with a species of perforated needlework [14] By the rules of the convent, the nuns of Wadstena were forbidden to touch either gold or silver, save in their netting and embroidery.

---

[12] "A lace-maker earns from 3½d. to 4½d. per day of sixteen hours."—*Rawert's Report*, 1848.

[13] The Tönder lace traders enjoy the privilege of offering their wares for sale all over Denmark without a licence (concession), a privilege extended to no other industry.

[14] The early perfection of Bridget herself in this employment, which, if we may credit the chronicle of the Abbess Margaretha, 1440–46, may be ascribed to a miraculous origin.

When, at the age of twelve, she was employed at her knitted lace work, a fear came over her that she should not finish her work creditably to herself, and in her anxiety she raised her heart above. As her aunt came into the chamber, she beheld an unknown maiden sitting opposite to her niece, and aiding her in her task; she vanished immediately, and when the aunt asked Bridget who had helped her, she knew nothing about it, and assured her relation she had seen no one.

All were astonished at the fineness and perfection of the work, and kept the lace as of miraculous origin.

There exists an old journal of the Kloster, called "Diarium Vad-stenænse," in which are, however, no allusions to the art; but the letters of a Wadstena nun to her lover, extra muros, published from an old collection [15] of documents, somewhat helps us in our researches.

"I wish," she writes to her admirer, "I could send you a netted cap that I myself have made, but when Sister Karin Andersdotter saw that I had mingled gold and silver thread in it, she said, 'You must surely have some beloved.' 'Do not think so,' I answered. 'Here in the Kloster, you may easily see if any of the brethren has such a cap, and I dare not send it by any one to a sweetheart outside the walls.' 'You intend it for Axel Nilson,' answered Sister Karin. 'It is not for you to talk,' I replied. 'I have seen you net a long hood, and talk and prattle yourself with Brother Bertol.'"

From netted caps of thread, worked in with gold and silver, the transition to lace is easy, and history tells that in the middle ages the Wadstena nuns "knit their laces of gold and silk." We may therefore suppose the art to have flourished in the convents at an early date.

At the suppression of the monasteries, under Charles IX., a few of the nuns, too infirm to sail with their sisters for Poland, remained in Sweden. People took compassion on the outcasts, and gave them two rooms to dwell in, where they continued their occupation of making lace, and were able, for a season, to keep the secret of their art. After a time, however, lace-making became general throughout the town and neighbourhood, and was known to the laity previous to the dissolution of Wadstena—a favoured convent which survived the rest of the other monasteries of Sweden.

"Send up," writes Gustaf Vasa, in a familiar letter [16] to his queen, Margaret, "the lace passement made for me by Anne, the smith's daughter, at Upsala; I want it: don't neglect this." [17]

In an inventory of Eriksholm Castle, drawn up in 1548, are endless entries of "sheets seamed with cutwork, half worn-out

---

[15] "Wadstena Past and Present" (Förr och Nu).

[16] The letter is dated 20th March 1544.

[17] In the detailed account of the trousseau furnished to his daughter, there is no mention of lace; but the author of "One Year in Sweden" has seen the body of his little granddaughter, the Princess Isabella, daughter of John III., as it lies in the vault of Strengnäs, the child's dress and shoes literally covered with gold and silver lace of a Gothic pattern, fresh and untarnished as though made yesterday.

sheets with open border of cutwork, towels with cutwork and
with the king and queen's arms in each corner, blue curtains with
cutwork seams," &c.

The style of Wadstena lace changed with the times and fashion
of the national costume. Those made at present are of the single
or double ground, both black and white, fine, but wanting in
firmness. They also make much dentelle torchon, of the lozenge
pattern, for trimming the bed-linen they so elaborately embroider
in drawn-work.

In 1830, the products in value amounted to 30,000 rixdollars.
They were carried to every part of Sweden, and a small quantity
even to foreign parts. One dealer alone, a Madame Hartruide,
now sends her colporteurs hawking Wadstena lace round the
country. The manufacture, after much depression, has slightly
increased of late years, having received much encouragement from
her majesty Queen Louisa. Specimens of Wadstena lace were
sent to the great international exhibitions.

Hölesom, or cutwork, is a favourite employment of Swedish
women, and is generally taught in the schools. At the various
bathing-places you may see the young ladies working as indus-
triously as if for their daily sustenance ; they never purchase such
articles of decoration, but entirely adorn their houses by the
labours of their own hands. It was by a collar of this hölesom,
worked in silk and gold, that young Gustaf Erikson was nearly
betrayed when working as a labourer in the barn of Rankhytta,
the property of his old college friend, Anders Petersen. A servant
girl observed to her master, " The new farm-boy can be no peasant ;
for," says she, " his linen is far too fine, and I saw a collar wrought
in silk and gold beneath his kirtle."

Gold lace was much in vogue in the middle of the sixteenth
century. Entries of it abound in the inventory of Gustavus Vasa,
and his youngest son Magnus.

In an inventory of Eriksholm, 1536, is a pair of laced sheets. It
is the custom in Sweden to sew a broad border of seaming lace
between the breadths of the sheets, sometimes wove in the linen.
Directions, with patterns scarcely changed since the sixteenth
century, may be found in the " Weaving Book " published at
Stockholm in 1828.[18]

---

[18] Weber, " Bilderbuch," Leipzig, 1746. " Handbok for unga Fruntimmer," by
Ekenmark, Stockholm, 1826–28.

Towards the end of 1500, the term "passement" appears in general use, in an inventory of "Pontus de la Gardie."

In the neighbourhood of Wadstena, old soldiers, as well as women, may be seen of a summer's evening sitting at the cottage doors making lace. Though no other lace manufactory can be said to exist in Sweden beyond that of Wadstena, still much lace is made by the peasantry for home consumption. The author has received from the Countess Elizabeth Piper, late grande maîtresse to her majesty the Queen of Sweden, specimens of coarse pillow laces, worked by the Scanian peasant-women, which, she writes, "form a favourite occupation for the women of our province."

Fig. 104.

Dalecarlian lace.

Far more curious are the laces that have been sent to us, made by the peasants of Dalecarlia, still retaining the patterns used in the rest of Europe two hundred years since. The broader [19] kinds, of which we give a woodcut (Fig. 104), are from Gaguef, that part of Dalecarlia where laces are mostly made and used. Married women wear them on their summer caps, much starched, as a shelter against the sun. Others, of an unbleached thread, are from Orsa. This lace is never washed, as it is considered an elegance

---

[19] Some are twice the width of Fig. 104.

to preserve this coffee-coloured tint. The firmness and solidity of these last laces are wonderful.

The specimens from Rättwik are narrow "seaming" laces of the lozenge pattern.

There is also a sort of plaiting used as fringe, in the style of the Genoese macramè, from the ends of a small sheet which the peasants spread over their pillows. No improvement takes place in the designs. The Dalecarlian women do not make a trade of lace-making, they merely work to supply their own wants.[20]

Fig. 105 represents a lace collar worn by Gustavus Adolphus ; [21] a relic carefully preserved in the Northern Museum at Stockholm. In addition to this collar, there is preserved at the Royal Klads-kammar, at Stockholm, a blood-stained shirt worn by Gustavus at the battle of Dirschau, the collar and cuffs trimmed with lace of rich geometric pattern, the sleeves decorated with "seaming" lace.

In an adjoining case of the same collection are some splendid altar-cloths of ancient raised point, said to have been worked by the Swedish nuns previous to the suppression of the monasteries. A small escutcheon constantly repeated on the pattern of the oldest specimens has the semblance of a water-lily leaf, the emblem of the Stures, leading one to believe they may have been of Swedish fabrication, for many ladies of that illustrious house sought shelter from troublous times within the walls of the lace-making convent of Wadstena.

In the same cabinet is displayed, with others of more ordinary texture, a collar of raised Spanish guipure, worked by the princesses Catherine and Marie, daughters of Duke Johan Adolf (brother of Charles X.). Though a creditable performance, yet it is far inferior to the lace of convent make. The making of this Spanish point formed a favourite amusement of the Swedish ladies of the seventeenth century: bed-hangings, coverlets, and toilets of their handiwork may still be found in the remote castles of the provinces. We have received the photograph of a flower from an old bed of Swedish lace—an heirloom in a Smaland castle of Count Trolle Bonde.

---

[20] For this information, with a collection of specimens, the author has to thank Madame Petre, of Gefle.

[21] On it is inscribed, in Swedish, "This collar was work by Gustaf Adolf, King of Sweden, and presented, together with his portrait, as a remembrance, in 1632, to Miss Jacobina Lauber, of Augsburg, because she was the most beautiful damsel present."

Fig. 105.

Collar of Gustavus Adolphus.

To face page 248.

RUSSIA.

In Russia, lace-making and embroidery go hand in hand, as in our early examples of embroidery, drawn-work and cutwork combined. Lace-making was not a distinct industry; the peasants, especially in Eastern Russia, made it in their houses to decorate, in conjunction with embroidery, towels, table linen, shirts, and even the household linen, for which purpose it was purchased direct of the peasants by the inhabitants of the towns. All will have seen the Russian towels in the International Exhibition of 1874, and have admired their quaint design and bright colours, with the curious line of red and blue thread running through the pattern of the lace. Darned netting and drawn work appear, as elsewhere, to have been their earliest productions. The lace is loosely wrought on the pillow, the work simple, and requires few bobbins to execute the vermiculated pattern which is its characteristic (Fig. 106). In some, silks of various colours are employed, in others the network is formed of silver wire. The Eastern traditions are traceable in all the designs.

Peter the Great founded a manufactory of silk lace at Novogorod, which in the time of the Empress Elizabeth fell into decay.

The principal sites of modern pillow-lace making are Torjok, in the province of Tver, and Jetetz, in that of Orel.

A manufactory of needle-made lace, called " point de Moscou," has been successfully established by a lady of that city. In workmanship it resembles the old rose point, but retaining in design its Russian nationality.

Fig. 106.

CHAPTER XXII.

ENGLAND TO QUEEN ELIZABETH.

" We weare most fantastical fashions than any nation under the sun doth, the French only excepted."—*Coryat's Crudities*, 1611.

IT would be a difficult matter for antiquaries to decide at what precise time lace, as we now define the word, first appears as an article of commerce in the annals of our country.

As early as the reign of Edward III.[1] the excessive luxury of veils, worn even by servant girls, excited the indignation of the government, who, in an act, dated 1363, forbade them to be worn of silk, or of any other material, " mes soulement de fil fait deinz le Roialme," for which veils no one was to pay more than the sum of tenpence. Of what stuff these thread veils were composed, we have no record; probably they were a sort of network, similar to the caul of Queen Philippa, as we see represented on her tomb.[2] That a sort of crochet decoration used for edging was already made, we may infer from the monumental effigies of the day.[3] The purse of the carpenter is described, too, in Chaucer, as " purled with latoun," a kind of metal or wire lace, similar to that found at Herculaneum, and made in some parts of Europe to a recent period.

M. Aubry refers to a commercial treaty of 1390, between England and the city of Bruges, as the earliest mention of lace. This said treaty we cannot find in Rymer, Dumont, or anywhere else. We have, as before alluded to, constant edicts concerning the gold wires and threads of " Cipre, Venys, Luk, and Jeane,"

---

[1] Rot. Parl. 37 Edw. III. Printed p. 278, col. 2, No. 26.

[2] See her monument in Westminster Abbey. Sandford's " Genealogical Table."

[3] " Blanche, Duchess of Lancaster, wife of John of Gaunt, wears a quilted silk cap with a three-pointed border of broad lace network." (Sandford. St. Paul's monument, after Dugdale.) " Elizabeth, Duchess of Exeter, died 1425 (Sandford, p. 259), wore also a caul of network with a needlework edging."

of embroideries and such like, but no distinct allusion to "lace." [4]

According to Anderson, the first intimation of such an occupation being known in England is the complaint, made in 1454, by the women of the mystery of thread-working in London, in consequence of the importation of six foreign women, by which the manufacture of needlework [5] of thread and silk, not as yet understood, was introduced. These six women, probably Flemings, had brought over to England the cutwork or darning of the time, a work then unknown in this country.

All authors, up to the present period, refer to the well-known act of Edward IV.,[6] 1463, in which the entry of " laces, corses, ribans, fringes, de soie and de file, laces de file soie enfile," &c. are prohibited, as the first mention of " lace " in the public records.

The English edition of the " Fœdera," as well as the statutes at large, freely translate these words as laces of thread, silk, twined, laces of gold, &c. ; and the various writers on commerce and manufactures have accepted the definition as " lace," without troubling themselves to examine the question.[7] Some even go so far as to refer to a MS. in the Harleian Library,[8] giving " directions for making many sorts of laces,[9] which were in fashion in the times of King Henry VI. and Edward IV.," as a proof that lace was already well known, and formed the occupation of the " handcraftry "—as those who gained their livelihood by manual occupation were then

---

[4] In the statute 2 Rich. II. = 1378, merchant strangers are allowed to sell in gross and in retail " gold wire or silver wire," and " other such small ware.' Neither in this nor in the treaty 13 Rich. II. = 1390, between England, the Count of Flanders, and " les bonnes Gentz des Trois bonnes villes des Flandres, Gand, Brugges et Ipre" (see Rymer), is there any mention of lace, which, even if fabricated, was of too little importance, as an article of commerce, to deserve mention save as other " small wares."

[5] Pins not yet being in common use, any lace would be called " work of the needle."

[6] 3 Edw. IV. cap. iv.

[7] " 1463. John Barett bequeaths to 'My Lady Walgrave, my musk ball of gold with ple and lace.

" 'Item, to John Eden, my o gr. of tawny silk with poynts of needle work,—*opus punctatum.*'"— *Bury Will and Inventories.*

[8] Bib. Harl. 2320.

[9] Such as " Lace Bascon, Lace endented, Lace bordred on both syde, yn o syde, pykke Lace bordred, Lace Condrak, Lace Dawns, Lace Piol, Lace covert, Lace coverte doble, Lace compon coverte, Lace maskel, Lace cheyne brode, Las Cheveron, Lace Oundé, Grene dorge, Lace for Hattys," &c.

Another MS. of directions for making these same named laces is in the possession of the vicar of Ipsden, Oxfordshire, and has been examined by the author, through the kindness of the late Mr. W. Twopenny.

termed—of the country. Now the author has carefully examined this already quoted MS., in the principal letter of which is a damaged figure of a woman sitting and "making of lace," which is made by means of "bowys." [10] As regards the given directions, we defy any one, save the most inveterate lover of crochet-work, to understand one word of its contents, beyond that it relates to some sort of twisted threadwork, and perhaps we might, in utter confusion of mind, have accepted the definition as given, had not another MS. of similar tenor, bearing date 1651, been also preserved in the British Museum.[11]

This second MS. gives specimens of the laces, such as they were, stitched side by side with the directions; which at once establishes the fact that the laces of silk and gold, laces of thread, were nothing more than braids or cords—the laces used with tags, commonly called "poynts" (the "ferrets" of Anne of Austria)—for fastening the dresses, as well as for ornament, previous to the introduction of pins.

In the wardrobe accounts of the time we have frequent notice of these "laces" and corses. "Laces de quir" (cuir) also appear in the statutes,[12] which can only mean what we now term bootlaces, or something similar.

From the time of Edward IV. downwards, statute on apparel

---

[10] Bows, loops.

[11] Additional MSS. No. 6293, small quarto, ff. 38. It contains instructions for making various laces, letters, and "edges," such as "diamond stifl, fly, cross, long S, figure of 8, spider, hart," &c., and at the end :—

"Heare may you see in Letters New
The Love of her that honoreth you.
My love is this,
Presented is
The Love I owe
I cannot showe,
The fall of Kings
Confusion bringes
Not the vallyou but the Love.

When this you see
Remember me.

In the British Museum (Lansdowne Coll. No. 22) is a third MS. on the same subject, a parchment roll written about the time of Charles I., containing rules and directions for executing various kinds of sampler-work, to be wrought in letters, &c., by means of coloured strings or bows. It has a sort of title in these words, " To know the use of this Booke it is two folkes worke," meaning that the works are to be done by two persons.

Probably of this work was the "Brede (braid) of divers colours, woven by Four Ladies," the subject of some verses by Waller, beginning :—

"Twice twenty slender Virgins' Fingers twine
This curious web, where all their fancies shine.
As Nature them, so they this shade have wrought,
Soft as their Hands, and various as their Thoughts," &c.

[12] 1 Rich. III.=1483, act xii.

followed upon statute, renewed for a number of years, bearing
always the same expression, and nothing more definite.[13]

The Venetian galleys, at an early period, bore to England
"apes, sweet wines," and other articles of luxury. They brought
also the goldwork of "Luk," Florence, "Jeane," and Venice. In
our early parliamentary records are many statutes on the subject.
The Italians were in the habit of giving short lengths, gold thread
of bad quality, and were guilty of sundry other peccadilloes, which
greatly excited the wrath of the nation. The balance was not in
England's favour :—

> " Thei bare the gold out of this land
> And sowkethe the thrifte out of our hande
> As the waspe sowkethe the honey of the be."

It was these cheating Venetians who first brought over their
gold lace into England, but it is not till the reign of Henry VII.
that, according to Anderson, " Gold and thread lace came from
Florence, Venice, and Genoa, and became an article of commerce.
An act was then passed to prevent the buyers of such commodities
from selling for a pound weight a packet which does not contain
twelve ounces, and the inside of the said gold, silver, and thread
lace was to be of equal greatness of thread and goodness of colour
as the outside thereof." [14]

A warrant to the keeper of the great wardrobe, in the
eighteenth year of King Henry's reign,[15] contains an order for " a
mauntel lace of blewe silk and Venys gold, to be delivered for the
use of our right dere and well-beloved Cosyn the King of Romayne "
—Maximilian, who was made knight of the Garter.[16]

If lace was really worn in the days of Henry VII., it was
probably a braid or passement of gold or silk, as one of the last

---

[13] 1 Rich. III. renews 3 Edw. IV. for
ten years, and that of Richard is continued by 19 Henry VII. for twenty
years more.

[14] 4 Hen. VII. = 1488-9.

[15] P. R. O. The same warrant contains an order to deliver " for the use of
and wearing of our right dere daughter
the Lady Mary," together with a black
velvet gown, scarlet petticoat, &c., " a
nounce of lace for her kyrtel," and a
thousand " pynnes."

[16] In the list of the late King Henry's

plate, made 1543, we have some curious
entries in which the term lace appears:—

" Item, oone picture of a woman made
of erthe with a carnacion Roobe knitt
with a knott in the lefte shoulder and
bare hedid with her heere rowlid up
with a white lace sett in a boxe of
wodde.

" Item, oone picture of a woman made
of erthe with a carnacōn garment after
the Inglishe tyer and bareheddid with
her heare rowled up with a white lace
sett in a box of wodde." P. R. O.

acts of that monarch's reign—by which all foreign lace is prohibited, and " those who have it in their possession may keep it and wear it till Pentecost " [17]—was issued rather for the protection of the silk-women of the country than for the advantage of the ever-complaining " workers of the mysteries of thread-work.'

On the 3rd of October 1502, his queen, Elizabeth of York, pays to one " Master Bonner, at Langley, for laces, rybands," &c., 40s. ; and again, in the same year, 38s. 7d. to " Dame Margrette Cotton, for hosyn, laces, sope, and other necessaries for the Lords Henry Courtenay, Edward, and the Lady Margrette, their sister." A considerable sum is also paid to " Fryer Hercules for gold of Venys, gold of Danmarke, and making a lace for the King's mantell of the Garter." [18]

It is towards the early part of Henry VIII.'s reign that the " Actes of Apparell " [19] first mention the novel luxury of shirts and partlets, " garded and pynched," [20] in addition to clothes decorated in a similar manner, all of which are forbidden to be worn by any one under the degree of a knight.[21] In the year 1517 there had been a serious insurrection of the London apprentices against the numerous foreign tradesmen who already infested the land, which, followed up by the never-ending complaints of the workers of the mysteries of needlework, induced the king to ordain the wearing of such " myxte joyned, garded or browdered [22] articles of lynnen cloth be only allowed when the same be wrought within this realm of England, Wales, Berwick, Calais, or the Marches." [23]

The earliest record we find of laced linen is in the inventory of Sir Thomas L'Estrange, of Hunstanton, co. of Norfolk, 1519, where it is entered, " 3 elles of Holland cloth, for a shirte for hym, 6 shillings," with " a yard of lace for hym, 8d."

---

[17] 19 Hen. VII. = 1504.

[18] Sir H. Nicolas.

[19] Statute 1 Henry VIII. = 1509–10, 1514–15.

"An Act agaynst wearing of costly Apparell," and again, 6 Hen. VIII. = 1514–15.

[20] " Gard, to trim with lace."—Cotgrave.

" No lesse than crimson velvet did him grace,
All garded and regarded with gold lace."
        Samuel Rowlands, A Pair of Spy-Knaves.
" I do forsake these 'broidered gardes,
And all the fashions new."
        The Queen, in King Cambises, cir. 1561.

[21] Under forfeiture of the same shirt and a fine of 40s.

[22] 7 Hen. VIII. = 1515–16, " Thacte of Apparell."

[23] 24 Hen. VIII. = 1532–33, " An Act for Reformation of Excess in Apparel."

In a MS. called "The Boke of Curtasye"—a sort of treatise on etiquette, in which all grades of society are taught their duties —the chamberlain is commanded to provide for his master's up- rising, a "clene shirte," bordered with lace and curiously adorned with needlework.

The correspondence, too, of Honourable Lady Lisle, seized by Henry VIII.[24] as treasonous and dangerous to the state, embraces a hot correspondence with one Sœur Antoinette de Sevenges, a nun milliner of Dunkirk, on the important subject of nightcaps,[25] one half-dozen of which, she complains, are far too wide behind, and not of the lozenge (cut) work pattern she had selected. The nightcaps were in consequence to be changed.

Anne Basset, daughter of the said Lady Lisle, educated in a French convent, writes earnestly begging for an "edge of perle[26] for her coif and a tablete (tablier) to ware." Her sister Mary, too, gratefully expreses her thanks to her mother, in the same year,[27] for the "laced gloves you sent me by bearer." Calais was still an English possession, and her products, like those of the Scotch border fortresses, were held as such.[28]

Lace still appears but sparingly on the scene. Among the privy purse expenses of the king in 1530,[29] we find five shillings and eightpence paid to Richard Cecyll,[30] groom of the robes, for eight pieces of "yolowe lace, bought for the King's Grace." We

---

[24] In 1539.

[25] "Lisle Corr." vol. i. p. 64. P. R. O. Lord Lisle was governor of Calais, whence the letter is dated.

"Honor. Lylle to Madame Antoinette de Sevenges, à Dunkerke.

"Madame,—Je ne vous eusse vollu envoier ceste demi dousaine pour changier nestoit que tous celles que menvoiez dernierement sont trop larges, et une dousaine estoit de cestuy ouvrage dont jestis esmerveillé, veu que je vous avois escript que menvoissiez de louvrage aux lozenges, vous priant que la demy dousaine que menvoierez pour ceste demy dousaine soient du dict ouvrage de lozenge, et quil soient plus estroictes mesmement par devant noeobstant que lexemple est au contraire."

[26] Among the marriage clothes of

Mary Neville, who espoused George Clifton, 1536, is:—

"A neyge of perle, 1l. 4s. 0d."

In the pictures, at Hampton Court Palace, of Queens Mary and Elizabeth, and another of Francis II., all as children, their ruffs are edged with a very narrow purl.

[27] 1538. "Lisle Corr.' P. R. O.

[28] See p. 255.

[29] Privy Purse Ex. Hen. VIII. 1529- 1532. Sir H. Nicolas.

[30] Father of Lord Burleigh. There are other similar entries :—" 8 pieces of yellow silk, 9s. 4d." Also, "green silk lace."

1632, "green silk lace" occurs again, as trimming a pair of French shoes in a "Bill of shoes for Sir Francis Windebank and family."—State Papers, Dom. vol. ccxxi. P. R. O.

have, too, in the Harleian inventory,[31] a "coif laid over with passamyne of gold and silver."

These "Acts of Apparell," as regards foreign imports, are, however, somewhat set aside towards the year 1546, when Henry grants a licence in favour of two Florentine merchants to export for three years' time, together with other matters, "all manner of fryngys and passements wrought with gold or silver, or otherwise, and all other new gentillesses of what facyon or value soever they may be, for the pleasure of our dearest wyeff the Queen, our nobles, gentlemen, and others."[32] The king, however, reserves to himself the first view of their merchandise, with the privilege of selecting anything he may please for his own private use, previous to their being hawked about the country. The said "dearest wyeff," from the date of the act, must have been Katherine Parr; her predecessor, poor Katherine Howard, had for some four years slept headless in the vaults of the White Tower Chapel. Of these "gentillesses" the king now began to avail himself. He selects "trunk sleeves of redd cloth of gold with cutwork;" knitted gloves of silk, and "handkerchers" edged with gold and silver; his towels are of diaper, "with Stafford knots," or "knots and roses;" he has "coverpanes of fyne diaper of Adam and Eve garnished about with a narrow passamayne of Venice gold and silver; handkerchers of Holland, frynged with Venice gold, redd and white silk," others of "Flanders worke," and his shaving cloths trimmed in like fashion.[33] The merchandise of the two Florentines had found vast favour in the royal eyes. Though these articles were imported for our dear "wyeff's" sake, beyond a "perle edging" to the coif of the Duchess of Suffolk, and a similar adornment to the tucker of Jane Seymour,[34] lace seems to have been little employed for female decoration during the reign of King Henry VIII.

That lace was early used for the adornment of the ministers of the church, we have ample evidence. M. Aubry states having seen, in London, lace belonging to Cardinal Wolsey. On this matter we have no information; but we know the surplices were ornamented round the neck, shoulders, and sleeves, with "white work" and cutwork[35] at this period. The specimens we give (Figs. 107

---

[31] Inv. of Hen. VIII. and 4 Edw. VI. Harl. MS. 1419, A and B.

[32] 38 Hen. VIII. = 1546. Rymer's "Fœdera," vol. xv. p. 105.

[33] Harl. MS. 1419, *passim.*

[34] See Holbein's portraits.

[35] "The old cutwork cope."—*Beaumont and Fletcher, The Spanish Curate.*

and 108), are from a portrait formerly in the library of the
Sorbonne, now transferred to Versailles, of Fisher, Bishop of
Rochester, Cardinal Fisher, as he is styled—his cardinal's hat
arriving at Dover at the very moment the head that was to wear
it had fallen at Tower Hill.

Fig. 107.

Fisher, Bishop of Rochester. ✝ 1535. Musée Nationale, Versailles.

About this time, too, lace gradually dawns upon us in the
church inventories. Among the churchwardens' accounts of
St. Mary-at-Hill, date 1554, we find entered a charge of 3s. for
making "the Bishopp's (boy bishop) myter with stuff and lace."[36]

Fig. 108.

Fisher, Bishop of Rochester. Musée Nationale, Versailles.

The richly laced corporax cloths and church linen are sent to be
washed by the "Lady Ancress," an ecclesiastical washerwoman,
who is paid by the churchwardens of St. Margaret's, Westminster,

---

[36] We read too of "3 kyrcheys yᵗ was
given to the kyrk wash," large as a
woman's hood worn at a funeral, highly
ornamented with the needle by pious
women, and given to be sold for the good
of the impoverished church, for which the
churchwardens of St. Michael, Spurr
Gate, York, received the sum of 5s.

the sum of 8*d.*; this Lady Ancress, or Anchoress, being some worn-out old nun who, since the dissolution of the religious houses, eked out an existence by the art she had once practised within the walls of her convent.

At the burial of King Edward VI., Sir Edward Waldgrave enters on his account a charge of fifty yards of gold passemen lace for garnishing the pillars of the church.

The sumptuary laws of Henry VIII. were again renewed by Queen Mary:[37] in them, ruffles made or wrought out of England, commonly called cutwork, are forbidden to any one under the degree of a baron; while to women of a station beneath that of a knight's wife, all wreath lace or passement lace of gold and silver with sleeves, partlet or linen trimmed with purles of gold and silver, or whiteworks, alias cutworks, &c., made beyond the sea, is strictly prohibited. These articles were, it seems, of Flemish origin, for among the New Year's gifts presented to Queen Mary, 1556, we find enumerated, as given by Lady Jane Seymour, " a fair smock of white work,[38] Flanders making." Lace, too, is now in more general use, for on the same auspicious occasion, Mrs. Penne, King Edward's nurse, gave " six handkerchers edged with passamayne of golde and silke." [39] Two years previous to these New Year's gifts, Sir Thomas Wyatt is described as wearing, at his execution, " on his head a faire hat of velvet, with broad bone-work lace about it." [40]

Lace now seems to be called indifferently "purle," "passa-mayne," "bobbin-lace," or "bone-work," the two first-mentioned terms occurring most frequently. The origin of this last ap-pellation is generally stated to have been derived from the custom of using sheep's trotters previous to the invention of wooden bobbins. Fuller so explains it, and the various dictionaries have followed his theory.

The employing anything so heavy and cumbersome as sheeps' trotters for bobbins, of which some 300 to 400 are used on a pillow, is perfectly absurd. More simple to suppose the bobbins

[37] 1 & 2 Ph. & Mary.

[38] " White work " appears also among Queen Elizabeth's New Year's gifts:—

" 1578. Lady Ratcliff. A veil of white work, with spangles and small bone lace of silver. A swete bag, being of changeable silk, with a small bone lace of gold.

" 1589. Lady Shandowes (Chandos). A cushion cloth of lawne wrought with whitework of branches and trees, edged with bone work, wrought with crowns."— *Nichols' Royal Progresses.*

[39] Roll of New Year's Gifts, 1556.

[40] Stowe, " Queen Mary," an. 1554.

2 s

to have been made, as they are in the present day, of bone cut
into the prescribed form.

Shakespeare, in " Twelfth Night," speaks of

> " The spinsters and the knitters in the sun,
> And the free maids that weave their threads with bone."

The Devonshire lace-makers, on the other hand, deriving their
knowledge from tradition, consider the term as applying not to
bone bobbins, but the bone pins used in pricking out the lace.
When lace-making was first introduced into their county, pins,[41]
so indispensable to their art, being then sold at a price far beyond
their means, the lace-makers, mostly the wives of fishermen
living along the coast, adopted the bones of fish, which, pared
and cut into regular lengths, fully answered as a substitute. Even
at the present day pins made from chicken bones continue to be
employed in Spain; and bone pins are still used in Portugal.[42]

" Bone " lace [43] constantly appears in the wardrobe accounts;
while bobbin lace [44] is of less frequent occurrence.

----

[41] It is not known when brass wire
pins were first made in England, but it
must have been before 1543, in which
year a statute was passed (35 Hen.
VIII.), entitled, " An Act for the True
Making of Pynnes," in which the price is
fixed not to exceed 6s. 8d. per 1000. By an
act of Rich. III., the importation of pins
was prohibited. The early pins were of
boxwood, bone, bronze, or silver. In
1347 (" Liber Garderobæ," 12–16 Edw. III.
P. R. O.), we have a charge for 12,000
pins for the trousseau of Joanna, daughter
of Edward III., betrothed to Peter the
Cruel. The young princess probably
escaped a miserable married life by her
decease of the black death at Bordeaux,
when on her way to Castille.

The annual import of pins, in the time
of Elizabeth, amounted to 3297l. " State
Papers, Dom." Eliz. vol. viii. P. R. O.

In Eliz. Q. of Bohemia's Expenses, we
find : " Dix mille espingles dans un
papier, 4 florins."—Ger. Corr. No 41.
P. R. O.

" In Holland, pillow-lace is called Pinwork lace — Gespelde-werkte kant."—
Sewell's Eng. and Dutch Dict.

[42] Bone pins were in use until a recent period, and renounced only on account of their costliness. The author

purchased of a Devonshire lace-maker
one, bearing date 1829, with the name
tattooed into the bone, the gift of
some long-forgotten youth to her grandmother. These bone or wood bobbins,
some ornamented with glass beads—the
more ancient with silver let in—are the
calendar of a lace-worker's life. One
records her first appearance at a neighbouring fair, or May meeting; a second
was the first gift of her good man, long
cold in his grave ; a third, the first prize
brought home by her child from the
dame school, and proudly added to her
mother's cushion : one and all, as she sits
weaving her threads, are memories of
bygone days of hopes and fears, of joys
and sorrows; and though many a sigh it
calls forth, she cherishes her well-worn
cushion as an old friend, and works
away, her present labour lightened by
the memory of the past.

[43] " Surtees Wills and Inv."

" Hearing bone lace value 5s. 4d." is
mentioned " in ye shoppe of John Johnston, of Darlington, merchant."

[44] " 1578. James Backhouse, of Kirby in
Lonsdale. Bobbin lace, 6s. per ounce."

" 1597. John Farbeck, of Durham. In
ye Shoppe, 4 oz. & ½ of Bobbin lace,
6s. 4d."—Ibid.

Among the New Year's gifts presented to Queen Elizabeth, we have from the Lady Paget " a petticoat of cloth of gold stayned black and white, with a bone lace of gold and spangles, like the wayves of the sea;" a most astounding article, with other entries no less remarkable, but too numerous to cite.

In the marriage accounts of Prince Charles [45] we have charged 150 yards of bone lace [46] for six extraordinary ruffs and twelve pairs of cuffs, against the projected Spanish marriage. The lace was at 9s. a yard. Sum total, 67l. 10s.[47] Bone lace is mentioned in the catalogue of King Charles I.'s pictures, drawn up by Vanderdort,[48] where James I. is described " without a hat, in a bone lace falling band." [49]

Setting aside wardrobe accounts and inventories, the term constantly appears both in the literature and the plays of the seventeenth century.

> " Buy some quoifs, handkerchiefs, or very good bone lace, mistress,"

cries the pert sempstress when she enters with her basket of wares, in Green's " Tu Quoque," [50] showing it to have been at that time the usual designation.

> " You taught her to make shirts and bone lace,"

says some one in the " City Madam." [51]

Again, describing a thrifty wife, Loveless, in " The Scornful Lady," [52] exclaims—

> " She cuts cambric to a thread, weaves bone lace, and quilts balls admirably.

" Laqueo . . . fact. super les bobbins."—*G. W. A.* Eliz. 27 & 28. P. R. O.

" Three peces teniar bobbin."—*Ibid.* Car. I. vi.

" One pece of bobin lace, 2s.," occurs frequently in the accounts of Lord Compton, afterwards Earl of Northampton, master of the wardrobe of Prince Charles. Roll, 1622–23, Extraordinary Expenses, and others. P. R. O.

[45] In the Ward. Acc. of his brother Prince Henry, 1607, and the warrant to the G. Ward., on his sister's, the Princess Elizabeth's, marriage, 1612–13, " bone " lace is in endless quantities.

Bobbin lace appears invariably distinguished from bone lace, both being mentioned in the same inventory. It seems to have been sold by weight.

Would it specially refer to gold or silver wire and not to thread ?

[46] Randle Holme, in his enumeration of terms used in arts, gives: " Bone lace, wrought with pegs."

The materials used for bobbins in Italy have been already mentioned, p. 59, note [82].

[47] Lord Compton, " Extraordinary Expenses of the Wardrobe of K. Charles, before and after he was King."—*Roll*, 1622–26. P. R. O.

[48] An. 1635.

[49] A miniature of old Hilliard, now in the possession of his Grace the Duke of Hamilton.

[50] 1614.

[51] Massinger, 1612.

[52] Beaumont and Fletcher.

The same term is used in the " Tatler " [53] and " Spectator," [54] and in the list of prizes given, in 1752, by the Society of Anti-Gallicans, we find, " Six pieces of bone lace for men's ruffles." It continued to be applied in the acts of parliament and notices relative to lace, nearly to the end of the last century.[55] After a time, the sheep's trotters or bones having been universally replaced by bobbins of turned boxwood, the term fell into disuse, though it is still retained in Belgium and Germany.

But to return to Queen Mary Tudor. We have among the "late Queen Mary's clothes" an entry of "compas" lace; probably an early name for lace of geometric pattern. Openwork edging of gold and passamaine lace also occur; and on her gala robes, lace of " Venys gold," as well as " vales of black network," a fabric to which her sister, Queen Elizabeth, was most partial; "partlets, dressings, shadowes, and pynners 'de opere rete,'" appearing constantly in her accounts.[56]

We find in the entries from this period frequent mention of parchment lace.

From the privy purse expenses of the Princess Mary,[57] we find she gives to Lady Calthorpe a pair of sleeves of " gold, trimmed with parchment lace ;" a favourite donation of hers, it would appear, by the following anecdote :—

" A great man's daughter," relates Strype [58] (the Duke of Suffolk's daughter, the Lady Jane Grey), " receiving from Lady Mary, before she was queen, goodly apparel of tinsel, cloth of gold, and velvet, laid on with parchment lace of gold, when she saw it, said, ' What shall I do with it ? ' Mary said, ' Gentlewoman, wear it.' ' Nay,' quoth she, ' that were a shame to follow my Lady Mary against God's word, and leave my Lady Elizabeth, which followeth God's word.' "

---

[53] " The things you follow and make songs on now, should be sent to knit, or sit down to bobbins or bone-lace."— *Tatler.*

[54] " We destroy the symmetry of the human figure, and foolishly combine to call off the eye from great and real beauties, to childish gewgaw ribbands and bone-lace."—*Spectator.*

[55] It is used in Walpole's " New British Traveller," 1784.

[56] " Eidem pro 4 pec' de opera Rhet'

bon' florat' in forma oper' sciss' ad 24*s.*, 4*l.* 16*s.*"— *G. W. A. Eliz.* 43 to 44.

" 1578-79. New Year's Gifts. Baroness Shandowes. A vail of black network flourished with flowers of silver and a small bone-lace."—*Nichols.*

[57] 1536-44. Sir Fred. Madden.

" 2 payr of sleeves whereof one of gold w[h] p'chemene lace," &c.

" 2 prs. of sleves w[h] pchmyn lase, 8/6.'

[58] " Ecclesiastical Memoirs," iii. 2,' 167.

In the list of the Protestant refugees in England, 1563 to 1571,[59] among their trades, it is stated " some live by making matches of hempe stalks, and parchment lace."

Again, Sir Robert Bowes, " once ambassador to Scotland," in his inventory, 1553, has " One cassock of wrought velvet with p'chment lace of gold." [60]

" Parchment lace[61] of watchett and syllver at 7s. 8d. the ounce," appears also among the laces of Queen Elizabeth.[62]

King Charles I. has his carpet bag trimmed with " broad parchment gold lace,"[63] his satin nightcaps with gold and silver parchment laces,[64] and even the bag and comb case " for His Majesty's barber " is decorated with " silver purle and parchment lace." [65]

Again, Charles II. ornaments the seats on both sides the throne with silver parchment lace.[66]   In many of the inventories circa 1590, " sylke parchment lace " is noted down, and " red " and " green parchment lace," again, appear among the wares " in ye Stuffes." [67]

The term seems most generally associated with gold or silver, otherwise, we should consider it as merely referring to needle-made lace, which is made on a parchment pattern.

---

[59] " State Papers," vol. lxxxii. P. R. O.

[60] Surtees Society, Durham, " Wills and Inventories."

[61] 1572. Thynne, in his " Debate between Pride and Lowliness," describes a coat " layd upon with parchment lace withoute."

[62] B. M. Add. MSS. No. 5751.

[63] Roll, 1607.   P. R. O.

[64] Ibid. 1626. " 11 nightcaps of coloured satin, laid on thick, with gold and silver parchment lace, 41 . 9 . 9."

[65] Roll, 1630.

[66] " Eidem pro novemdecim virḡ et dīm aureæ et argenteæ pergameñ laciniæ pondent sexdecim unc̄ $\frac{2}{3}$ $\frac{1}{6}$ venet . . . pro consuat̄ ad ornand̄ duas sedes utroque latere thronæ in domo Parliament."—Gt. Ward. Acc. Car. II. 30 and 31 = 1678-9.

In 1672-73 is an entry for " 2 virgis teniæ pergameñ."

[67] " Surtees Inventories."

CHAPTER XXIII.

QUEEN ELIZABETH.

" By land and sea a Virgin Queen I reign,
  And spurn to dust both Antichrist and Spain."
                                    Old Masque.
" Tell me, Dorinda, why so gay ?
    Why such embroidery, fringe, and lace ?
  Can any dresses find a way
  To stop the approaches of decay,
    And mend a ruined face ? "
                                    Lord Dorset.

UP to the present time our mention of lace, both in the statutes
and the royal wardrobe accounts, has been but scanty. Suddenly,
in the days of the Virgin Queen, both the privy expenses and the
inventories of New Year's gifts overflow with notices of passements, drawn work, cutwork, crown lace,[1] bone lace for ruffs,
Spanish, chain, byas,[2] parchment, hollow,[3] billament,[4] and diamond

---

[1] Crown lace,—so called from the
pattern worked being a succession of
crowns sometimes intermixed with acorns
or roses. A relic of this lace may still be
found in the "faux galon" sold by the
German Jews, for the decoration of fancy
dresses and theatrical purposes. It is
frequently mentioned. We have :—
" 12 yards laquei, called crown lace of
black gold and silk."—*G. W. A.* Eliz.
4 & 5.
" 18 yards crown lace purled with one
wreath on one side."—*Ibid.* 5 & 6.

[2] " 11 virgis laquei Byas."—*Ibid.* 29
& 30.

[3] Hemming and edging 8 yards of ruff
of cambric with white lace called hollow
lace, and various entries of Spanish lace,
fringe, black chain, diamond, knotted,
hollow, and others, are scattered through

the earlier wardrobe accounts of Queen
Elizabeth.
The accounts of the keepers of the
great wardrobe, which we shall have
occasion so frequently to cite, are now
deposited in the Public Record Office, to
which place they were transferred from
the Audit Office, in 1859. They extend
from the 1 Elizabeth = 1558 to 10th Oct.
1781, and comprise 160 volumes, written
in Latin, until 1730–31, when the account
appears in English, and is continued so
to the end. 1743–49 is the last account
in which the items are given.

[4] Eliz. 30 & 31. Billament lace occurs
both in the "shoppes" and inventories of
the day. Among the list of foreigners
settled in the City of London in 1571
("State Papers, Dom." Eliz. vol. lxxxiv.
P. R. O.), are : William Crutall, "useth

lace,[5] in endless and to us, we must own, most incomprehensible variety.

The "Surtees Wills and Inventories" add to our list the laces of Waborne [6] and many others. Lace was no longer confined to the court and high nobility, but, as these inventories show, it had already found its way into the general shops and stores of the provincial towns. In that of John Johnston, merchant, of Darlington, already cited, we have 12 yards of "loom" lace, value 4s., black silk lace, "statute" lace, &c., all mixed up with entries of pepper, hornbooks, sugar-candy, and spangles. About the same date, in the inventory taken after the death of James Backhouse, of Kirby-in-Lonsdale, are found enumerated "In ye great shoppe," thread lace at 16s. per gross; 4 dozen and 4 "pyrled" lace, 4s.; 4 quarterns of "statching" (stitching or seaming?) lace; lace edging; crown lace; hollow lace; copper lace; gold and silver "chean" (chain) lace, &c. This last-mentioned merchant's store appears to have been one of the best-furnished provincial shops of the period. That of John Farbeck, of Durham, mercer, taken thirty years later, adds to our list 78 yards of velvet lace, coloured silk "chayne" lace, "coorld" lace, petticoat lace, all cheek by jowl with "Venys" gold and turpentine.

To follow the "stitches" and "works" quoted in the wardrobe accounts of Elizabeth—all made out in Latin, of which we sincerely trust, for the honour of Ascham, the queen herself was guiltless—would be but as the inventory of a haberdasher's shop.

We have white stitch, "opus ret' alb," of which she had a kirtle, "pro le hemmynge et edginge" of which, with "laqueo

---

the craft of making byllament lace;" Rich. Thomas, Dutch, "a worker of Billament lace."

In 1573, a country gentleman, by his will deposited in the Prerogative Court of Canterbury (Brayley and Britton's "Graphic Illustrations") bequeaths: "To my son Tyble my short gown faced with wolfskin and laid with Billements lace."

In John Johnston's shop, we have: "3 doz. of velvet Billemunt lace, 12s." In that of John Farbeck, 9 yards of the same. ("Surtees Wills and Inv.") Widow Chapman of Newcastle's inventory, 1533, contains: "One old cassock

of broad cloth, with billements lace, 10s." —*Ibid.*

[5] 95 dozen rich silver double diamond and cross laces occur also in the "Extraordinary Expenses for Prince Charles's Journey to Spain," 1623. P. R. O.

[6] "1571. In ye Great Shop, 8 peces of 'waborne' lace, 16d."—*Mr John Wilkinson's Goods, of Newcastle, Merchant.*

"1580. 100 Gross and a half of 'waborne' lace."— *Inv. of Cuthbert Ellyson.*

1549, John de Tronch, Abbot of Kilmainham Priory, is condemned to pay 100 marks fine for detaining 2 lbs. of Waborne thread, value 3s., and other articles, the property of W. Sacy.

coronat' de auro et arg'"—gold and silver crown lace—and
"laqueo alb' lat' bon' operat' super oss'"—broad white lace worked
upon bone—she pays the sum of 35s.[7]

Then there is the Spanish stitch, already mentioned as introduced by Queen Katherine, and true stitch,[8] laid-work,[9] net-work,
black work,[10] white work, and cutwork.

Of chain stitch we have many entries, such as " Six caules of
knotwork, worked with chain stitch and bound 'cum tapem' (tape),
of sister's (nun's) thread." [11] A scarf of white stitch-work appears
also among the New Year's gifts.

As regards the use, however, of these ornaments, the queen
stood no nonsense. Luxury for herself was quite a different affair
from that of the people; for, on finding that the London apprentices had adopted the white stitching and garding as a decoration
for their collars, she put a stop to all such finery by ordering [12] the
first transgressor to be publicly whipped in the hall of his company.

Laid-work, which, maybe, answers to our modern plumetis, or
simply signified a braidwork, adorned the royal garters, "Frauncie,"
which, worked " cum laidwork," stitched, and trimmed " in ambo-
bus lateribus " with gold and silver lace, from which hung silver
pendants, " tufted cum serico color," cost her majesty 33s. the
pair.[13]

The description of these right royal articles appears to have
given as much trouble to describe as it does ourselves to translate
the meaning of her accountant.

The drawn-work, " opus tract'," seems to have been but a

---

[7] G. W. A. Eliz. 16 & 17.

[8] " Eidem pro 6 manuterg' de camerick operat' cum serico nigra trustich," &c.—G. W. A. Eliz. 41 & 42, and, again, 44.

[9] 1572. Inventory of Thomas Swin-burne, of Ealingham, Esq.

" His Apparell."

" A wellwett cote layd with silver las.
" A satten doublet layd with silver las.
" A payr of wellwett sleeves layd with silver las."—Surtees Wills and Inv.

[10] New Year's gifts, Lady Mary Sydney : "A smock and two pillow beres of cameryck wrought with black-work and edged with a broad bone-lace of black sylke."

[11] " Eidem pro 6 caules alb' nodat opat' cu' le chainestich et ligat' cu' tape de filo soror, ad 14s., 4l. 4s."—G. W. A. Eliz. 41 & 42.

Also, in the last year of her reign (1602), we find :—

" Six fine net caules flourished with chaine stitch with sister's thread."—Wardrobe Accounts. B. M. Add. MSS. No. 5751.

[12] In 1583.

[13] G. W. A. Eliz. 38 & 39. We have it also on ruffs.

" Eidem pro 2 sutes de lez ruffs bon' de la lawne operat' in le laid work et edged cum ten' bon' ad 70s. per pec', 7l."—G. W. A. Eliz. 43 & 44.

drawing of thread worked over with silk. We have smocks thus wrought and decorated " cum lez ruffs et wrestbands." [14]

In addition to the already enumerated laces of Queen Elizabeth are the bride laces of Coventry blue,[15] worn and given to the guests at weddings, mentioned in the " Masques" of Ben Jonson : [16]—

" CLOD. And I have lost beside my purse, my best bride-lace I had at Joan Turnips' wedding.

" FRANCES. Ah, and I have lost my thimble and a skein of Coventry blue I had to work Gregory Litchfield a handkerchief."

When the queen visited Kenilworth, in 1577, a " Bridall " took place for the pastime of her Majesty. "First," writes the Chancellor, " came all the lusty lads and bold bachelors of the parish, every wight with his blue bridesman's bride lace upon a braunch of green broom." What these bride laces exactly were, we cannot now tell. They continued in fashion till the Puritans put down all festivals, ruined the commerce of Coventry, and the fabric of blue thread ceased for ever. It was probably a showy kind of coarse trimming, like that implied by Mopsa in the " Winter's Tale," when she says—

" You promised me a tawdry lace : " [17]

---

[14] G. W. A. Eliz., last year of her reign. Again—

1600. " Drawing and working with black silk drawne worke, five smocks of fine holland cloth."— *B. M. Add. MSS.* No. 5751.

" These Holland smocks as white as snow,
And gorgets brave with drawn-work wrought."
Pleasant Quippes for Upstart New-fangled Gentlewomen, 1596.

[15] As early as 1485, we have in the inventory of St. Mary-at-Hill, " An altar cloth of diaper, garnished with 3 blue Kays (St. Peter's) at each end." All the church linen seems to have been embroidered in blue thread, and so appears to have been the smocks and other linen.

Jenkin, speaking of his sweetheart, says: " She gave me a shirt collar, wrought over with no counterfeit stuff.

" GEORGE. What ! was it gold ?

" JENKIN. Nay, 'twas better than gold.

" GEORGE. What was it ?

" JENKIN. Right Coventry blue."— *Pinner of Wakefield,* 1599.

" It was a simple napkin wrought with Coventry blue."—*Laugh and Lie Downe,* or the *Worlde's Folly,* 1605.

" Though he perfume the table with rose cake or appropriate bone-lace and Coventry Blue," writes Stephens in his " Satirical Essays," 1615.

In the inventory of Mary Stuart, taken at Fotheringay, after her death, we have : " Furniture for a bedd of black velvet, garnished with Bleue lace. In the care of Rallay, *alias* Beauregard."

[16] The window of the famous clothier, called Jack of Newbury, is described when a bride as " led to church between two boys with bride laces and rosemary tied about their sleeves."

[17] " Tawdry. As Dr. Henshaw and Skinner suppose, of knots and ribbons,

articles which, judging from the song of Autolycus—

> " Will you buy any tape,
> Or lace for your cape ? "

were already hawked about among the pedlars' wares throughout the country : one of the " many laces " mentioned by Shakespeare.[18]

Dismissing, then, her stitches, her laces, and the 3000 gowns she left in her wardrobe behind her—for, as Shakespeare says, " Fashion wears out more apparel than the man "[19]—we must confine ourselves to those articles immediately under our notice, cutwork, bone lace, and purle.

Cutwork—" opus scissum," as it is termed by the keeper of the great wardrobe—was used by Queen Elizabeth to the greatest extent. She wore it on her ruffs, " with lilies of the like, set with small seed pearl ;" on her doublets, " flourished with squares of silver owes ; on her forepart of lawn, " flourished with silver and spangles ;"[20] on her cushion cloths,[21] her veils, her tooth-cloths,[22] her smocks, and her nightcaps.[23] All flourished, spangled, and edged in a manner so stupendous as to defy description. It was

---

bought at a fair held in St. Audrey's chapel ; fine, without grace or elegance." —*Bailey's Dict.* 1764.

Southey (" Omniana," vol. i. p. 8) says :—

" It was formerly the custom in England for women to wear a necklace of fine silk called Tawdry lace, from St. Audrey.

" She had in her youth been used to wear carcanets of jewels, and being afterwards tormented with violent pains in the neck, was wont to say, that Heaven, in his mercy, had thus punished her for her love of vanity. She died of a swelling in her neck. Audrey (the same as Ethelrede) was daughter of King Anna, who founded the Abbey of Ely."

Spenser, in the " Shepherd's Calendar," has :—

> " Bind your fillets faste
> And girde in your waste
> For more fineness with a tawdry lace ;"

and in the " Faithful Shepherdess " of Beaumont and Fletcher, Amaryllis speaks of

> " The primrose chaplet, tawdry lace
> and ring.

[18] A passage, already quoted, in " Much Ado about Nothing " shows us that, in Shakespeare's time, the term " to lace " was generally used as a verb, denoting to decorate with trimming. Margaret, the tiring woman, describes the Duchess of Milan's gown as of " Cloth o' gold, and cuts, and laced with silver."

[19] " Much Ado about Nothing."

[20] " New Year's Gifts of Mrs. Wyngfield, Lady Southwell, and Lady Willoughby."—*Nichols' Royal Progresses.*

[21] " Mrs. Edmonds. A cushion cloth of lawn cutwork like leaves, and a few owes of silver."—*New Year's Gifts.*

" Eidem pro le edginge unius panni vocat' a quishion cloth de lawne alb' operat' cum spaces de opere sciss' et pro vii. virg' de Laquei alb' lat' operat' sup' oss' 33s. 4d."—*G. A. W.* Eliz. 31 & 32.

[22] "Mistress Twist, the Court laundress. Four toothcloths of Holland wrought with black silk and edged with bone lace of silver and black silk."—*New Year's Gifts.*

[23] " Lady Ratcliffe. A night coyf of white cutwork flourished with silver and set with spangles."—*Ibid.*

dizened out in one of these last-named articles [24] that young Gilbert Talbot, son of Lord Shrewsbury, caught a sight of the queen while walking in the tilt-yard. Queen Elizabeth at the window in her nightcap! What a goodly sight! That evening she gave Talbot a good flap on the forehead, and told her chamberlain how the youth had seen her "unready and in her night stuff," and how ashamed she was thereof.

Cutwork first appears in the New Year's offerings of 1577-8, where, among the most distinguished of the givers, we find the name of Sir Philip Sidney, who on one occasion offers to his royal mistress a suit of ruffs of cutwork, on another a smock—strange presents according to our modern ideas. We read, however, that the offering of the youthful hero gave no offence, but was most graciously received. Singular enough, there is no entry of cutwork in the great wardrobe accounts before that of 1584-5, where there is a charge for mending, washing, and starching a bodice and cuffs of good white lawn, worked in divers places with broad spaces of Italian cutwork, 20 shillings,[25] and another for the same operation to a veil of white cutwork trimmed with needlework lace.[26] Cutwork was probably still a rarity; and really on reading the quantity offered to Elizabeth on each recurring new year there was scarcely any necessity for her to purchase it herself. By the year 1586-7 the queen's stock had apparently diminished. Now, for the first time, she invests the sum of sixty shillings in six yards of good ruff lawn, well worked, with cutwork, and edged with good white lace.[27] From this date the great wardrobe accounts swarm with entries such as a "sut' de lez ruffes de lawne," with spaces of "opre sciss',"[28] "un' caule de lawne alb' sciss' cum le edge," of similar work;[29] a "toga cum traine de opere sciss';"[30] all minutely detailed in the most excruciating gibberish. Sometimes the cutwork is of Italian [31] fabric, some-

---

[24] "Cropson. A night coyf of cameryk cutwork and spangles, with a forehead cloth, and a night border of cutwork with bone lace."—*Ibid.* 1577-8.

[25] "Eidem pro emendac̄ lavacione et starching unius par' corpor' (stays) et manic' de lawne alb' bon' deorsum operat' in diversis locis cum spaciis Lat' de operibus Italic' sciss̄ 20*sh*."—*G. W. A.* Eliz. 26-27.

[6] Ibid.

[27] Ibid. 28-29.

[28] Ibid. 29-30.

[29] Ibid. 35-36.

[30] Ibid. 43-44. "A round kyrtle of cutwork in lawne."—*B. M. Add. MSS.* No. 5751.

[31] "One yard of double Italian cutwork a quarter of a yard wide, 55*s.* 4*d.*"— *G. W. A.* Eliz. 33 & 34.

"Una virga de opere sciss' lat' de factura Italica, 26*s.* 8*d.*"—*Ibid.* 29 & 30.

times of Flanders ;[32] the ruffs edged with bone lace,[33] needle lace,[34] or purle.[35]

The needle lace is described as " curiously worked," " operat' cum acu curiose fact'," at 32s. the yard.[36] The dearest is specified as Italian.[37] We give a specimen (Coloured Plate XV.; see p. 334) of English workmanship, said to be of this period, which is very elaborate.[38]

The thread used for lace is termed " filo soror," or nun's thread, such as was fabricated in the convents of Flanders and Italy.[39] If, however, Lydgate, in his ballad of " London Lackpenny," is an authority, that of Paris was most prized :—

> " Another he taked me by his hand,
> Here is Paris thredde, the finest in the land."

Queen Elizabeth was not patriotic ; she got and wore her bone lace from whom she could, and from all countries. If she did not patronise English manufacture, on the other hand, she did not encourage foreign artisans ; for when, in 1572, the Flemish refugees desired an asylum in England, they were forcibly expelled from her shores. In the census of 1471, giving the names of all the strangers in the City of London,[40] including the two makers of billament lace already cited, we have but four foreigners of the lace craft : one described as " Mary Jurdaine, widow, of the French

---

[32] " For one yard of double Flanders cutwork worked with Italian purl, 33s. 4d."—*G. W. A.* Eliz. 33 & 34.

[33] " 3 suits of good lawn cutwork ruffs edged with good bone lace ' operat' super oss',' at 70s. 10l. 10s."—*Ibid.* 43 & 44.

[34] " 7 virg' Tenie lat' operis acui, ad 6s. 8d., 46s. 8d."—*Ibid.* 37–38.

[35] " Eidem pro 2 pectoral' de ope' sciss' fact' de Italic' et Flaundr' purle, ad 46s."—*Ibid.* 42 & 43.

" Eidem pro 1 virg' de Tenie de opere acuo cum le purle Italic' de cons' ope' acuo 20s."—*Ibid.* 40 & 41.

[36] Eliz. 44 = 1603.

[37] " 3 yards broad needlework lace of Italy, with the purls of similar work, at 50s. per yard, 8l. 15s."—*Ibid.* 41–42.

Bone lace varies in price from 40s. the dozen to 11s. 6d. the yard ; needle-made lace from 6s. 8d. to 50s. G. W. A. *passim.*

[38] Lace is always called " lacqueus "

in the great wardrobe accounts, up to 1595–6, after which it is rendered " tænia." Both terms seem, like our " lace," to have been equally applied to silk passements.

" Galons de soye, de l'espèce qui peuvent être dénominés par le terme latin de ' tæniola.' "

" Laqueus, enlassements de diverses couleurs, galons imitation de ces chaînes qui les Romains faisoient peindre, dorer et argenter, pour les rendre plus supportables aux illustres malheureux que le sort avoit réduit à les porter."—*Traité des Marques Nationales,* Paris, 1739.

[39] See p. 39.

From the G. W. accounts the price appears to have been half a crown an ounce.

" Eidem pro 2 li. 4 unc.' fili Sororis, and 2s. 6d. per unciam, 4l. 10s."—Eliz. 34 & 35.

[40] " State Papers, Domestic," Eliz. vol. lxxxiv. The sum total amounts to 4287.

nation, and maker of purled lace;" the other, the before-mentioned " Callys de Hove, of Burgundy." [41]

Various acts [42] were issued during the reign of Elizabeth in order to suppress the inordinate use of apparel. That of May 1562,[43] though corrected by Cecil himself, less summary than that framed against the "whitework" of the apprentice boys, was of little or no avail.

In 1568, a complaint was made to the queen against the frauds practised by the " 16 appointed waiters," in reference to the importation of haberdashery, &c., by which it appears that her majesty was a loser of " 5 or 600l. by yere at least " in the customs on " parsement, cap rebone bone lace, cheyne lace," &c.,[44] but with what effect we know not. The annual import of these articles is therein stated at 10,000l., an enormous increase since the year 1559, when, among the " necessary and unnecessary wares" brought into the port of London,[45] together with " babies " (dolls), " glasses to looke in," " glasses to drinke in," "pottes," gingerbread, cabbages, and other matters, we find enumerated, " Laces of all sortes, 775l. 6s. 8d.," just one-half less than the more necessary, though less refined, item of " eles fresh and salt." [46]

1573, Elizabeth again endeavoured to suppress "the silk glittering with silver and gold lace," but in vain.

The queen was a great lover of foreign novelties. All will call to mind how she overhauled the French finery of poor Mary Stuart [47] on its way to her prison, purloining and selecting for her own use any new-fashioned article she craved. We even find Cecil, on the sly, penning a letter to Sir Henry Norris, her Majesty's envoy to the court of France, " that the Queen's Majesty would fain have a tailor that has skill to make her apparel both after the French and Italian manner, and she thinketh you might use some means to obtain such one as suiteth the Queen without mentioning

---

[41] See p. 222, note [13]. " The naturalised French residing in this country are Normans of the district of Caux, a wicked sort of French, worse than all the English," writes, in 1553, Stephen Porlin, a French ecclesiastic, in his " Description of England and Scotland."

[42] "1559. Oct. 20. Proclamation against excess of apparel."—*State Papers, Dom.* Eliz. vol. vii.

1566. Feb. 12. Ibid. vol. xxxix.

1579. Star Chamber on apparel.

[43] " State Papers, Dom." Eliz. vol. xxiii. No 8.

[44] Ibid. vol. xlvii. No. 49.

[45] Ibid. vol. viii. No. 31.

[46] The value of thread imported amounts to 13,671l. 13s. 4d.

[47] Walsingham writes :—" In opening a coffer of the Queen of Scots, he found certain heades which so pleased certain ladies of his acquaintance, he had taken the liberty to detain a couple."

any manner of request in the Queen's Majesty's name." His lady
wife is to get one privately, without the knowledge coming to the
queen mother's ears, " as she does not want to be beholden to her."

It is not to be wondered at, then, that the New Year's gifts
and great wardrobe accounts [48] teem with entries of " doublets of
peche satten all over covered with cutwork and lyned with a lace
of Venyse gold,[49] kyrtells of white satten embroidered with purles
of gold-like clouds, and layed round about with a bone lace of
Venys gold." [50]   This gold lace appears upon her petticoats everywhere varied by bone lace of Venice silver.[51]

That the queen drew much fine thread point from the same
locality, her portraits testify, especially that preserved in the
royal gallery of Gripsholm, in Sweden, once the property of her
ill-fated admirer, Eric XIV. She wears a ruff, cuffs, tucker,
and apron of geometric lace, of exquisite fineness, stained of a pale
citron colour, similar to the liquid invented by Mrs. Turner, of
Overbury memory, or, maybe, adopted from the saffron-tinted
smocks of the Irish, the wearing of which she herself had prohibited.
We find among her entries laces of Jean [52] and Spanish lace ; she
did not even disdain bone lace of copper, and copper and silver at
18*d.* the ounce.[53]   Some of her furnishers are English.   One
Wylliam Bowll supplies the queen with " lace of crowne purle." [54]
Of her " sylkwoman," Alice Mountague, she has bone lace wrought
with silver and spangles, sold by the owner at nine shillings.[55]

The queen's smocks are entered as wrought with black work and

---

[48] " A mantel of lawn cutwork wrought
throughout with cutwork of ' pomegra-
nettes, roses, honeysuckles, cum crowns.' "
" A doublet of lawn cutwork worked
with ' lez rolls and true loves,' " &c.—
G. W. A. Eliz., last year.

[49] " New Year's Gifts.   By the Lady
Shandowes."   1577-8.

[50] Marquis of Northampton.

[51] Lady Carew.   " A cushyn of fine
cameryk edged with bone lace of Venice
sylver."

[52] " Laqueus de serico Jeano."—*G. W.
A.* Eliz. 30-31.

[53] 1571.   " Revels at Court."   Cun-
ningham.

Some curious entries occur on the occasion of a masque called " The Prince "
given at court, in 1600 :—

" For the tooth-drawer :
" To loope leace for his doublet and
cassacke, 8*s.*

" For leace for the corne-cutters suite, 7*s.*
" For green leace for the tinkers suite,
2*s.*

" For the mouse-trapp-man :
" 6 yards of copper leace to leace *is*
cloake, at 1*s.* 8*d.*, 10*s.*

" The Prophet merely wears fringe,
2 Ruffes and cuffes, 3*s.* 10*d.*"
The subject of the masque seems lost
to posterity.

[54] Lady Chandos, jun.   " A cushyn
cloth of lawne, wrought with white worke
of branches and trees edged with white
bone worke wrought with crownes."
New Year's Gifts, 1577-8.

[55] 1572.   " Revels at Court."

edged with bone lace of gold of various kinds. We have ourselves
seen a smock said to have been transmitted as an heirloom in one
family from generation to generation.[56] It is of linen cloth embroidered in red silk, with her favourite pattern of oak-leaves and
butterflies (Fig. 109). Many entries of these articles, besides that
of Sir Philip Sidney's, appear among the New Year's gifts.[57]

It was then the custom for the sponsors to give " christening
shirts," with little bands and cuffs edged with laces of gold and
various kinds—a relic of the ancient custom of presenting white
clothes to the neophytes when converted to Christianity.[58] The
" bearing cloth," as the mantle used to cover the child when
carried to baptism was called,[59] was also richly trimmed with lace

Fig. 109.

Queen Elizabeth's smock.

and cutwork, and the Tree of Knowledge, the Holy Dove (Fig.
110), or the Flowerpot of the Annunciation (Fig. 111), was worked
in " hollie-work " on the crown of the infant's cap or " biggin."

---

[56] In the possession of Mrs. Evans, of
Wimbledon.

[57] " Sir Gawine Carew. A smock of
cameryke wrought with black work and
edged with bone lace of gold."

" Lady Souche. A smock of cameryke, the ruffs and collar edged with a
bone lace of gold."

" The Lady Marquis of Winchester. A
smock of cameryke wrought with tanny
silk and black, the ruffs and collar edged
with a bone lace of silver."—*New Year's*

Gifts, 1578–9.

[58] " A bearing cloth," for the Squire's
child, is mentioned in the " Winter's
Tale."

[59] Many of these christening robes of
lace and point are preserved as heirlooms
in old families; some are of old guipure,
others of Flanders lace, and later of
Valenciennes, or needle-point. The bib
formed of guipure padded with tiny mittens of lace were also furnished to complete the suit.

T

Aprons, too, of lace appeared in this reign. The queen, as we have mentioned, wears one in her portrait at Gripsholm.[60]

> " Those aprons white, of finest thread,
>   So choicelie tied, so dearly bought ;
>   So finely fringed, so nicely spread ;
>   So quaintly cut, so richly wrought,"

writes the author of " Pleasant Quippes for Upstart Gentlewomen," in 1596. The fashion continued to the end of the eighteenth century.

Fig. 110.   Fig. 111.

Christening caps, needle-made Brussels, eighteenth century.

Laced handkerchiefs now came into fashion. " Maydes and gentlewomen," writes Stowe, " gave to their favourites, as tokens of their love, little handkerchiefs of about three or four inches square, wrought round about," with a button at each corner.[61] The best were edged with a small gold lace. Gentlemen wore them in their hats as favours of their mistresses. Some cost sixpence, some twelvepence, and the richest sixteenpence.

Of the difference between purles and true lace it is difficult now to decide. The former word is of frequent occurrence among the New Year's gifts, where we have " sleeves covered

---

[60] In 1584-5, Queen Elizabeth sends a most wonderful apron to be washed and starched, of cambric, edged with lace of gold, silver, and in-grain carnation silk, " operat' super oss'," with " pearl buttons pro ornatione dict' apron."—*G. W. A.* Eliz. 26 & 27.

[61] " A handkerchief she had,
    All wrought with silke and gold,
  Which she, to stay her trickling tears,
    Before her eyes did hold."
        Ballad of George Barnwell.

all over with purle," [62] and in one case the sleeves are offered un-made, with " a piece of purle upon a paper to edge them." [63] It was yet an article of great value and worthy almost of entail, for, in 1573, Elizabeth Sedgwicke, of Wathrape, widow, bequeaths to her daughter, Lassells, of Walbron, " an edge of perlle for a remembrance, desirying her to give it to one of her daughters." [64]

We now turn, before quitting the sixteenth century, to that most portentous of all fabrications, on which, breathless with awe, we have gazed in our childhood, before the waxwork figure of the Tower—Queen Elizabeth's ruff.

In the time of the Plantagenets, Flemish tastes prevailed. With the Tudors, Katherine of Aragon, on her marriage with Prince Arthur, introduced the Spanish fashions, and the inventories from Henry VIII. downwards are filled with Spanish work, Spanish stitch, and so forth. Queen Elizabeth leant to the French and Italian modes, and during the Stuarts they were universally adopted.

The ruff was first introduced into England about the reign of Philip and Mary. These sovereigns are both represented on the great seal of England with small ruffs about their necks, and with diminutive ones of the same form encircling the wrist.[65] This Spanish ruff was not ornamented with lace. On the accession of Queen Elizabeth the ruff had increased to a large size, as we see portrayed on her great seal.

The art of starching, though known to the manufacturers of Flanders, did not reach England until 1564, when the queen first set up a coach. Her coachman, named Gwyllam Boenen, was a Dutchman; his wife understood the art of starching, a secret she seems exclusively to have possessed, and of which the queen availed herself until the arrival, some time after, of Madame Dinghen van der Plasse, who, with her her husband, came from Flanders " for their better safeties," [66] and set up as a clear-starcher in London.

---

[62] New Year's Gift of Lady Radcliffe, 1561.

[63] New Year's Gift of Lady St. Lawrence.

[64] " Surtees Wills and Inv." " Though the luxury of the court was excessive, the nation at large were frugal in their habits. Our Argentine of Dorset was called ' Argentine the Golden,' in consequence of his

buckles, tags, and laces being of gold. Such an extravagance being looked on as a marvel in the remote hamlets of the southern counties."

[65] Hence ruffles, diminutive of ruffs. " Ruff cuffs " they are called in the G. W. A. of James I. 11 & 12.

[66] Stowe's " Chron."

"The most curious wives," says Stowe, "now made themselves
ruffs of cambric, and sent them to Madame Dinghen to be starched,
who charged high prices. After a time they made themselves ruffs
of lawn, and thereupon arose a general scoff, or by-word, that
shortly they would make their ruffs of spiders' webs." Mrs.
Dinghen at last took their daughters as her pupils. Her usual
terms were from four to five pounds for teaching them to starch,
and one pound for the art of seething starch.[67] The nobility
patronised her, but the commonalty looked on her as the evil one,
and called her famous liquid "devil's broth."

To keep the ruff erect, bewired[68] and starched though it be,
was a troublesome affair—its falling a cause of agony to the wearer.

"Not so close, thy breath will draw my ruff,"

exclaims the fop. The tools used in starching and fluting ruffs
were called setting-sticks, struts, and poking-sticks: the two first
were made of wood or bone, the poking-stick of iron, and heated
in the fire. By this heated tool the fold acquired that accurate
and seemly order which constituted the beauty of this very
preposterous attire. It was about the year 1576, according to
Stowe, the making of poking-sticks began. They figure in the
expenses of Elizabeth, who, in 1592, pays to her blacksmith, one
Thomas Larkin, "pro 2 de lez setting-stickes ad 2s. 6d.," the
sum of 5s.[69]

We have frequent allusion to the article in the plays of the
day :[70]—

"Your ruff must stand in print, and for that purpose, get poking-sticks with fair
long handles, lest they scorch your hands." [71]

---

[67] Endless are the entries in the Gt. W.
Acc. for washing, starching, and mending.
The court laundress can have had no
sinecure. We find "le Jup de lawne
operat' cum stellis et aristis tritici Anglice
wheateares" (Eliz. 42 & 43), sent to be
washed, starched, &c. A network vail
"sciss' totum desuper cum ragged staves"
(Leicester's device, ibid. 29 & 30). A
"diploid" (doublet) of cutwork flourished
"cum auro et spangles" (ibid.), and,
more wonderful still, in the last year of
her reign, she has washed and starched a
toga "cum traine de la lawne operat'
in auro et argento in forma cat. larum
pavorum," the identical dress in which

she is portrayed in one of her portraits.

[68] "Eidem pro un ruff bon pynned sup'
le wier Franc' cū rhet' aur' spangled,
70s."—Eliz. 42 & 43.

[69] Gt. W. Acc. Eliz. 33 & 34.

[70] "B. Where's my ruff and poker?

"R. There's your ruff, shall I poke it?

"B. So poke my ruff now."—Old Play,
by P. Dekker, 1602.

Autolycus, among his wares, has
"poking-sticks of steel."

"Poked her rebatoes and surveyed her
steel."—Law Tricks, 1608.

[71] Middleton's comedy of "Blurt,
Master Constable."

Again, in " Laugh and Lie Down " [72]—

"There she sat with her poking-stick, stiffening a fall."

When the use of starch and poking-sticks had rendered the arrangement of a ruff easy, the size began rapidly to increase. " Both men and women wore them intolerably large, being a quarter of a yard deep, and twelve lengths in a ruff." [73] In London this fashion was termed the French ruff; in France, on the other hand, it was called " the English monster." [74] Queen Elizabeth wore hers higher and stiffer than any one in Europe, save the Queen of Navarre, for she had a " yellow throat," and was desirous to conceal it. [75] Woe betide any fair lady of the court who dared let her white skin appear uncovered in the presence of majesty. Her ruffs were made of the finest cutwork, enriched with gold, silver, and even precious stones. Though she consumed endless yards of cutwork, purle, needlework lace, bone lace of gold, of silver, enriched with pearls, and bugles, and spangles in the fabrication of the " three-piled ruff," [76] she by no means extended such liberty to her subjects, for she selected grave citizens and placed them at every gate of the city to cut the ruffs if they exceeded the prescribed depth. These " pillars of pride " form a numerous item among the New Year's gifts. Each lady seems to have racked her brain to invent some novelty as yet unheard of to gratify the queen's vanity. On the New Year, 1559–60, the Countess of Worcester offers a ruff of lawn cutwork set with 20 small knots like mullets, garnished with small sparks of rubies and pearls. [77]

The cutwork ruff is decorated or enriched with ornament of every description. Nothing could be too gorgeous or too extravagant. [78] Great was the wrath of old Philip Stubbs [79] at these

---

[72] " Or the World's Folly," 1605.

[73] Stowe.

[74] Ibid.

[75] Therefore she wore " chin " ruffs.
" Eidem pro 2 sutes de lez chinne ruffs edged cu' arg., 10s.'—Eliz. 42 & 43.

[76] Ben Jonson, " Every Man Out of His Humour," 1599.

[77] Lady Cromwell. " Three sutes of ruffs of white cutwork edged with a passamayne of white."
Lady Mary Se'm'. " 3 ruffs of lawne cutwork of flowers."

[78] " They are either clogged with gold,

silver, or silk laces of stately price, wrought all over with needleworke, speckeled and sparkeled here and there with the sunne, the moone, the starres, and many other antiques strange to beholde. Some are wrought with open worke donne to the midst of the ruffe, and further some with close worke, some with purled lace so closed and other gewgawes so pestered, as the ruff is the leest parte of itself."—*Stubbs's Description of the Cutwork Ruff.*

[79] " Anatomie of Abuses," 1583.

monstrosities, which, standing out a quarter of a yard or more, " if Æolus with his blasts or Neptune with his stormes chaunce to hit upon the crazie bark or their bruised ruffes, then they goe flip flap in the winde like ragges that flew abroade, lying upon their shoulders like the dishclout of a slut. But wot ye what? the devill, as he, in the fulnesse of his malice, first invented these great ruffes," &c.; with a great deal more, which, as it comes rather under the head of costume than lace, we omit, as foreign to our subject.

Lace has always been made of human hair, and of this we have frequent mention in the expenses of Queen Elizabeth. We believe the invention to be far older than her reign, for there is frequent allusion to it in the early romances. In the "Chevalier aux ij Epées " (MS. Bib. Nat.), a lady requires of King Ris that he should present her with a mantle fringed with the beards of nine conquered kings, and hemmed with that of King Arthur, who was yet to conquer. The mantle is to have "de sa barbe le tassel." The entries of Elizabeth, however, are of a less heroic nature ; and though we are well aware it was the custom of old ladies to weave into lace their silver-grey locks, and much as the fashion of hair bracelets and chains prevails, in Queen Elizabeth's case, setting aside all sentiment, we cannot help fancying the "laquei fact' de crine brayded cum lez risinge puffs," [80] as well as the " devices fact' de crine similiter les scallop shells," [81] to have been nothing more than " stuffings,"—false additions, to swell the majesty of the royal " pirrywygge."

That " point tresse," as this hair lace is called, was known in her day, we have evidence in the Chartley inventory of Mary Stuart, in which is mentioned, "Un petit quarré fait à point tresse ouvré par la vieille Comtesse de Lennox elle estant à la Tour;" a tribute of affection the old countess would scarcely have offered to her daughter-in-law had she regarded her as

---

[80] "Eidem pro 3 dozin laquei fact' de crine braided cum lez rising puffs de crine, ad 36s. le dd., 5l. 8s."—Eliz. 31 & 32.

The entry occurs frequently.

In ibid. 37 & 38 is a charge "pro 4 pirrywigges de crine," at 16s. 8d. each.

[81] In the G. W. A. of the last year of her reign, Elizabeth had a variety of devices in false hair. We have :—

"Eidem pro 200 invencionibus factis de crine in forma lez lowpes et tuftes," at 6d. each ; the like number in the form of leaves at 12d.; 12 in form of " lez Peramides," at 3s. 4d.; 24 of globes, at 12d., with hair by the yard, made in " lowpes, crispat' curiose fact', curle rotund'," and other wonderful "inventions."

implicated in the murder of her son.   The writer saw at Chantilly
an aged lace-maker employed in making a lace ground of hair on
the pillow, used, she was informed, by wigmakers to give the
parting of the hair; but the fabric must be identical with the
point tresse sent by the mother of Darnley to the Queen of Scots.
Point tresse, when made out of the hair of aged people, was most
prized, as the silver grey colour gave great effect to the workmanship; it was occasionally to be met with, and, from its rarity, it
fetched a high price.   Some districts gained a reputation for this
work; according to Turner—

> " And Bedford's matrons wove their snowy locks."

It may be detected by the glittering of the hair when held up to
catch the sunbeams, or by frizzing when exposed to the test of fire,
instead of blazing.

With this casual mention of point tresse we conclude the reign
of Queen Elizabeth.

CHAPTER XXIV.

JAMES I. TO THE RESTORATION.

JAMES I.

" Now up aloft I mount unto the Ruffe,
Which into foolish mortals pride doth puffe ;
Yet Ruffe's antiquity is here but small :
Within these eighty years not one at all.
For the 8th Henry, as I understand,
Was the first king that ever wore a Band,
And but a falling band plaine with a hem,
All other people knew no use of them."

Taylor, *Water Poet*, 1640.

THE ruff single, double, three piled, and Dædalian,[1] to the delight
of the satirists, retained its sway during the early days of King
James I. It was the " commode " of the eighteenth—the crinoline
of the nineteenth century. Every play teems with allusions to
this monstrosity. One compares it to

" A pinched lanthorn
Which schoolboys made in winter ; "[2]

while a second[3] talks of a

" Starched ruff, like a new pigeon-house."

The lover, in the play of the " Antiquary,"[4] complains to his
mistress in pathetic terms—

" Do you not remember how you fooled me, and set me to pin pleats in your ruff
two hours together ? "

Mr. Stubbs stood not alone in his anathemas. The dignitaries

---

[1] " Your trebble-quadruple Dædalian ruffes, nor your stiffe necked Rebatoes that have more arches for pride to row under, than can stand under five London Bridges."—*The Gul's Horne-booke, by T. Deckar.* London, 1609.

[2] Beaumont and Fletcher, " Nice Valour."

[3] Ibid. " The Blind Lady," 1661.

[4] 1641.

of the Church of England waxed raging wroth, and violent were their pulpit invectives.

"Fashion," emphatically preached John King,[5] Bishop of London, "has brought in deep ruffs [6] and shallow ruffs, thick ruffs and thin ruffs, double ruffs and no ruffs. When the Judge of quick and dead shall appear, He will not know those who have so defaced the fashion He hath created." The Bishop of Exeter, too, Joseph Hall, a good man, but no prophet, little wotting how lace-making would furnish bread and comfort to the women of his own diocese for centuries to come, in a sermon preached at the Spitel, after a long vituperation against its profaneness, concludes with these words : "But if none of our persuasions can prevail, hear this ye garish popinjays of our time, if ye will not be ashamed to clothe yourselves after this shameless fashion, Heaven shall clothe you with shame and confusion. Hear this, ye plaister-faced Jezabels, if ye will not leave your daubs and your washes, Heaven will one day wash them off with fire and brimstone." Whether these denunciations had the effect of lessening the ruffs, we know not ; probably it only rendered them more exaggerated.

Of these offending adjuncts to the toilet of both sexes, we have fine illustrations in the paintings of the day, as well as in the monuments of our cathedrals and churches.[7] They were composed of the finest geometric lace, such as we see portrayed in the works of Vinciolo and others. The artists of the day took particular pleasure in depicting them with the most exquisite minuteness.

These ruffs must have proved expensive to the wearer, though in James I.'s time, as Ben Jonson has it, men thought little of "turning four or five hundred acres of their best land into two or three trunks of apparel." [8] According to the wardrobe

---

[5] Called by James I., "the King of Preachers." Ob. 1621.

[6] In the "Dumb Knight," 1608, a woman, speaking of her ruff, says:—

"This is but shallow. I have a ruff is a quarter deep, measured by the yard."

[7] See the portraits, in the National Portrait Gallery, of Sir Dudley and Lady Carleton, by Cornelius Janssens, of the Queen of Bohemia, by Mirevelt, and of the Countess of Pembroke, by Mark Geerards. In Westminster Abbey the effigies of Queen Elizabeth and Mary Queen of Scots, on their tombs.

[8] "Every Man Out of His Humour," 1599.

Again, in his "Silent Woman," he says :—

"She must have that
Rich gown for such a great day, a new one
For the next, a richer for the third ; have the chamber filled with
A succession of grooms, footmen, ushers,   [And

accounts,[9] " twenty-five yards of fyne bone lace " was required to edge a ruff, without counting the ground, composed either of lace squares or cutwork. Queen Anne, his consort, pays 5l. for her wrought ruff, for " shewing " which eighteen yards of fine lace are purchased at 5s. 8d.[10]

The ruffs of the City lady were kept down by the old sumptuary law of Elizabeth.

" See, now, that you have not your ' city ruff ' on, Mistress Sue," says Mistress Simple, in the " City Match." [11]

In 1620, the yellow starch of Mrs. Turner, supposed to give a rich hue to the lace and cutwork of which ruffs were " built," gave scandal to the clergy. The Dean of Westminster ordered no lady or gentleman wearing yellow ruffs to be admitted into any pew in his church ; but finding this " ill taken," and the king " moved in it," he ate his own words, and declared it to be all a mistake.[12] This fashion, again, gave great offence even in France.[13] Since the English[14] alliance, writes the " Courtisane à la Mode," 1625,[15] " cette mode Anglaise sera cause qu'il pourra advenir une cherté sur le safran qui fera que les Bretons et les Poitevins seront contraints de manger leur beurre blanc et non pas jaune, comme ils sont accoutumés." The Overbury murder (1613) and hanging

---

And other messengers; besides embroiderers,
Jewellers, tire-women, semsters, feather men,
Perfumers; whilst she feels not how the land
Drops away, nor the acres melt ; nor foresees
The change, when the mercer has your woods
For her velvets ; never weighs what her pride
Costs, Sir."

[9] " Second Acc. of Sir John Villiers, 1617-8." P. R. O.

" 150 yards of fyne bone lace for six extraordinary ruffs provided against his Majesty's marriage, at 9s., 67s. 10d."— Extraordinary Expenses, 1622-6. P. R. O.

[10] " State Papers, Dom." Jac. I. vol. iii. No. 89. P. R. O.

[11] Jasper Mayne, 1670.

[12] " State Papers, Dom." James I. vol. cxiii. No. 18.

[13] We read that in 1574 the Venetian ladies dyed their lace the colour of saffron. The fashion may therefore have been derived from them.

[14] " He is of England, by his yellow band."—Notes from Black Fryers, Henry Fitzgeffery, 1617.

" Now ten or twenty eggs will hardly suffice to starch one of these yellow bandes."— Barnaby Rich, The Irish Hubbub, or the English Hue and Cry, 1622.

Killigrew, in his play called " The Parson's Wedding," published in 1664, alludes to the time when ' yellow starch and wheel verdingales were cried down ;" and in " The Blind Lady," a play printed in 1661, a serving man says to the maid : " You had once better opinion of me, though now you wash every day your best handkerchief in yellow starch."

[15] " La Courtisane à la Mode, selon l'Usage de la Cour de ce Temps." Paris, 1625.

of Mrs. Turner at Tyburn, in 1615, are usually said, on the authority of Howel,[16] to have put an end to the fashion of yellow ruffs, but the above extracts show they were worn for some years later.

The bishops, who first denounced the ruff, themselves held to the fashion long after it had been set aside by all other professions. Folks were not patriotic in their tastes, as in more modern days ; they loved to go " as far as Paris to fetch over a fashion and come back again." [17]

The lace of Flanders, with the costly points and cutworks of Italy,[18] now became the rage, and continued so for nigh two centuries. Ben Jonson speaks of the "ruffs and cuffs of Flanders,"[19] while Lord Bacon, indignant at the female caprice of the day, writes to Sir George Villiers :—" Our English dames are much given to the wearing of costly laces, and if they be brought from Italy, or France, or Flanders, they are in much esteem ; whereas, if like laces were made by the English, so much thread would make a yard of lace, being put into that manufacture, would be five times, or perhaps ten or twenty times the value." [20] But Bacon had far better have looked at home, for he had himself, when chancellor, granted an exclusive patent to Sir Giles Mompesson, the original of Sir Giles Overreach, for the monopoly of the sale and manufacture of gold and silver thread, the abuses of which caused in part his fall.[21]

James had half ruined the commerce of England by the granting of monopolies, which, says Sir John Culpepper, are " as numerous as the frogs of Egypt. They have got possession of our dwellings, they sip in our cups, they dip in our dish. They sit by our fire. We find them in the dye-vat, wash-bowl, and powdering-tub, etc. ; they have marked and sealed us from head to foot." [22] The bone-lace trade suffered alike with other handicrafts.[23] In

---

[16] " Mistris Turner, the first inventresse of yellow starch, was executed in a cobweb lawn ruff of that colour at Tyburn, and with her I believe that yellow starch, which so much disfigured our nation and rendered them so ridiculous and fantastic, will receive its funerall."—*Howel's Letters*, 1645.

[17] Carlo, in " Every Man Out of His Humour," 1599.

[18] " Eidem pro 29 virg' de opere sciss' bon' Italic', ad 35*s*., 68*l*. 5*s*."—*Gt. W. A.*

Jac. I. 5 & 6.

[19] " The New Inn."

[20] " Advice to Sir George Villiers."

[21] See " Parliamentary History of England."

Sir Giles was proceeded against as " a monopolist and patentee," and sentenced to be degraded and banished for life.

[22] Speech in parliament. " Rushout Papers," vol. xi. p. 916.

[23] " The office or grant for sealing bone lace was quashed by the King's

1606 James had already given a licence to the Earl of Suffolk [24] for the import of gold and silver lace. In 1621, alarmed by the general complaints throughout the kingdom,[25] a proposition was made " for the erection of an Office of Pomp, to promote home manufactures," and to repress pride by levying taxes on all articles of luxury.[26] What became of the Pomp Office, we cannot pretend to say : the following year we are somewhat taken aback by a petition [27] from two Dutchmen, of Dort, showing " that the manufacture of gold and silver thread, purle, etc., in England," was " a great waste of bullion," the said Dutchmen being, we may infer, of opinion that it was more to their own advantage to import such articles themselves. After a lapse of three years, the petition is granted.[28] In the midst of all this granting and rescinding of monopolies, we hear in the month of April 1623 how the decay of the bone-lace trade at Great Marlow caused great poverty.[29]

Though the laces of Flanders and Italy were much patronised by the court and high nobility, Queen Anne of Denmark appears to have given some protection to the fabrics of the country. Poor Queen Anne! When, on the news of Elizabeth's death, James hurried off to England, a correspondence took place between the king and the English privy council regarding the queen's outfit, James considering, and wisely—for the Scotch court was always out of elbows—that his wife's wardrobe was totally unfit to be produced in London. To remedy the deficiency, the council forwarded to the queen, by the hands of her newly named ladies, a quantity of Elizabeth's old gowns and ruffs, wherewith to make a creditable appearance on her arrival in England. Elizabeth had died at the age of seventy, wizened, decayed, and yellow—Anne,

---

proclamation, 1639, dated from his manour of York."—*Verney Papers.*

[24] B. M. Bib. Lands. 172, No. 59.

[25] 1605. Sept. 27. Patent to Ric. Dike and others, to make Venice gold and silver thread for 21 years. " State Papers, Dom." Jas. I. vol. ix. 48.

1604. Dec. 30. Lease of the customs on gold and silver thread. Ibid. vol. x.

1605. Feb. 2. The same. Ibid. vol. xii.

1611. May 21. Patent to Ric. Dike renewed. Ibid. vol. lxiii. 9.

In the same year (June 30), we find a re-grant to the Earl of Suffolk of the moiety of all seizures of Venice gold and

silver, formerly granted in the fifth year of the king. Ibid. vol. lxiv. 66.

In 1622, a lease on the customs on gold and silver thread lace is given to Sir Edward Villiers. Ibid. vol. cxxxii. 34.

[26] Ibid. vol. cxxi. 64.

[27] Ibid. vol. cxxxii. 34.

[28] In 1624, King James renews his prohibition against the manufacture of "gold purles," as tending to the consumption of the coin and bullion of the kingdom. " Fœdera," vol. xvii. p. 605.

[29] Petition, April 8, 1623. " State Papers," vol. cxlii. 44. See Chap. XXX.

young and comely, had just attained her twenty-sixth year.
The rage of the high-spirited dame knew no bounds; she stormed
with indignation—wear the clothes she must, for there were no
others—so in revenge she refused to appoint any of the ladies,
save Lady Bedford, though nominated by the king, to serve about
her person in England. On her arrival she bought a considerable
quantity of linen, and as with the exception of one article,[30] purchased from a " French mann," her " nidell purle worke," her
" white worke," her " small nidell worke," her " pece of lawin to
bee a ruffe," with " eighteen yards of fine lace to shewe (sew) the
ruffe," the " Great Bone " lace, and " Little Bone " lace, were
purchased at Winchester and Basing, towns bordering on the lace-
making counties, leading us to infer them to have been of English
manufacture.[31]

The bill of laced linen purchased at the " Queen's lying down "
on the birth of the Princess Sophia, in 1606, amounts to the sum
of 614*l.* 5*s.* 8*d.*[32] In this we have no mention of any foreign-made
laces. The child lived but three days. Her little monument, of
cradle-form, with lace-trimmed coverlet and sheets (Fig. 112),
stands close to the recumbent effigy of her sister Mary [33] (Fig. 113),
with ruff, collar, and cap of geometric lace, in the north aisle of
Henry VII.'s Chapel.[34]

---

[30] " Twoe payer of hande rebayters,"
i.e. cuffs.

[31] In the P. R. O. ("State Papers, Dom."
James I. 1603, Sept. vol. iii. No. 89)
is " A Memorandum of that Misteris
Jane Drumonde her recyte from Ester
Littellye, the furnishinge of her Majesties
Linen Cloth," a long account, in which,
among numerous other entries, we find :—

" It. at Basinge. Twenty four yeardes of
small nidle worke, at 6*s.* the yearde, 7*l.* 4*s.*

" More at Basinge. One ruffe cloth,
cumbinge cloth and apron all shewed
with white worke, at 50*s.* the piece, 7*l.* 10*s.*

" It. one pece of fine lawin to bee a
ruffe, 5*l.*

" Item, for 18 yeards of fine lace to
shewe the ruffe, at 6*s.* the yearde, 5*l.* 8*s.*

" Item, 68 purle of fair needlework, at
20 pence the purle, 5*l.* 15*s.* 4*d.*

" Item, at Winchester, the 28th of
September, one piece of cambrick, 4*l.*

" Item, for 6 yards of fine purle, at
20*s.*, 6*l.*

" Item, for 5 yards of great bone lace,
at 9*s.* the yard, 36*s.*"

Queen Anne has also a fair wrought sark
costing 6*l.*, and a cutwork handkerchief,
12*l.*, and 2 pieces of cutwork, ell wide
and 2 yards long, at 2*l.* the length, &c.

[32] " Lady Audrye Walsingham's Account," 1606. P. R. O.

[33] Mary, her third daughter, died
1607, not two years of age. Mrs. Greene
quotes, from the P. R. O., a note of the
" necessaries to be provided for the child,"
among which are two large cambric handkerchiefs, whereof one is to be edged
with " fair cutwork to lay over the child's
face ;" six veils of lawn, edged with fair
bone lace; six " gathered bibs of fine
lawn with ruffles edged with bone lace,"
&c. The total value of the lace and
cambric required for the infant's garments is estimated at 300*l.* " Lives of
the Princesses of England," vol. vi. p. 90.

[34] England is rich in monumental effigies decorated with lace, too many to

Fig. 112.

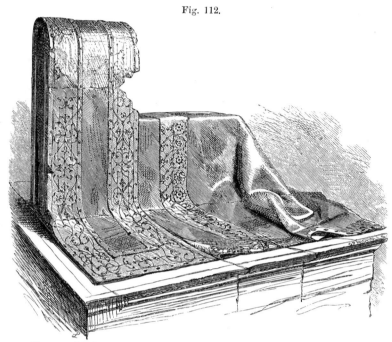

Monument of the Princess Sophia, fourth daughter of James I.   +   606.   Westminster Abbey.

Fig. 113.

Monument of the Princess Mary, third daughter of James I.   +   1607.   Westminster Abbey.

After a time—epoch of the Spanish marriage [35]—the ruff gave way to the "falling band," so familiar to us in the portraits of Rubens and Vandyke.

"There is such a deal of pinning these ruffs, when a fine clean fall is worth them all," says the "Malcontent." "If you should chance to take a nap in the afternoon, your falling band requires no poking-stick to recover it." [36] Cutwork still continued in high favour; it was worn on every article of linen, from the richly wrought collar to the nightcap. The Medicean ruff or gorget of the Countess of Pembroke ("Sidney's sister, Pembroke's mother"), with its elaborate border of swans (Fig. 114), is a good illustration of the fashion of her time.

Among the early entries of Prince Charles, we have four nightcaps of cutwork, 7*l.*,[37] for making two of which for his highness, garnished with gold and silver lace, Patrick Burke receives 15*l.*;[38] but these modest entries are quite put to shame by those of his royal father, who, for ten yards of needlework lace " pro le edginge " of his " galiriculis vulgo nightcaps," pays 16*l.* 13*s.* 4*d.*[39] Well might the Water Poet exclaim—

"A nightcap is a garment of high state." [40]

When Queen Anne died, in 1619, we have an elaborate account of her funeral,[41] and of the sum paid to Dorothy Speckart for dressing a hearse effigy with a large veil, wired and edged with peak lace and lawn, curiously cut in flowers, &c. Laced linen, however, was already discarded in mourning attire, for we find in

---

enumerate. Among them we would instance that of Alice, Countess of Derby, died 1636, in Harefield Church, Middlesex, in which the lace is very carefully sculptured. (Communicated by Mr. Albert Hartshorn.)

[35] 1620-1. We have entries of "falling bands" of good cambric, edged with beautiful bone lace, two dozen stitched and shagged, and cutwork nightcaps, purchased for James I., in the same account, with 28*s.* for "one load of hay to stuff the woolsacks for the Parliament House."—*G. W. Acc. Jac. I.* 18 to 19.
In the same year, 1620, an English company exported a large quantity of gold and silver lace to India, for the King of Golconda.

[36] "Malcontent," 1600.

[37] Extraordinary Expenses, 1622-6. P. R. O.

[38] "2nd Acc. of Sir J. Villiers, 1617-18." P. R. O.

[39] Gt. W. A. Jac. 6 to 7.

[40] Taylor, 1640 :—

"The beau would fain sickness
    To shew his nightcap fine,
And his wrought pillow overspread
    with lawn."
                Davies, Epigrams.

[41] "Acc. of Sir Lyonell Cranfield (now Earl of Middlesex), late Master of the Great Wardrobe, touching the funeral of Queen Anne, who died 2nd March 1618" (i.e. 1619, N. S.). P. R. O.

the charges for the king's mourning ruffs, an edging at 14*d*. the piece is alone recorded.[42]

Fig. 111.

Mary, Countess of Pembroke. + 1621. From her portrait in Walpole's "Royal and Noble Authors."

[42] About this time a complaint is made by the London tradesmen, of the influx of refugee artisans, "who keepe theire misteries to themselves, which hath made them bould of late to device engines for workinge lace, &c., and such wherein one man doth more among them than seven Englishmen can doe, soe as theire cheape sale of those commodities beggareth all our English artificers of that trade and enricheth them," which becomes "scarce tolleruble," they conclude. Cecil, in consequence, orders a census to be made in 1621. Among the traders appears "one satten lace maker."

Colchester is bitterly irate against the Dutch strangers, and complains of one "Jonas Snav, a Bay and Say maker, whose wife selleth blacke, browne, and white thredde, and all sorts of bone lace and vatuegardes, which they receive out of Holland. One Isaac Bowman, an Alyen born, a chirurgeon and merchant, selleth hoppes, bone lace, and such like, to the great grievance of the free burgesses."

A nest of refugee lace-makers, "who came out of France by reason of the late 'trobles' yet continuing," were congregated at Dover (1621–2). A list of about five-and-twenty "widows, being makers of Bone lace," is given, and then Mary

Towards the end of James I.'s reign a singular custom came into fashion, brought in by the Puritan ladies, that of representing religious subjects, both in lace, cutwork, and embroidery, a fashion hitherto confined to church vestments. We find constant allusions to it in the dramatists of the day. Thus, in the " City Match," [43] we read—

> " She works religious petticoats, for flowers
> She'll make church histories. Her needle doth
> So sanctify my cushionets, besides
> My smock sleeves have such holy embroideries,
> And are so learned, that I fear in time
> All my apparel will be quoted by
> Some pious instructor."

Again, in the " Custom of the Country " [44]—

> " Sure, you should not be
> Without a neat historical shirt."

We find in a Scotch inventory [45] of the seventeenth century : " Of Holland scheittes ii pair, quhairof i pair schewit (sewed) with hollie work." [46]

The entries of this reign, beyond the "hollie work," picked [47] and seaming [48] lace, contain little of any novelty ; all articles of the toilet were characterised by a most reckless extravagance.

Tanyer and Margarett Le Moyne, " maydens and makers of bone lace," wind up the catalogue of the Dover " Alyens."

The Maidstone authorities complain that the thread-makers' trade is much decayed by the importation of thread from Flanders. " List of Foreign Protestants resident in England," 1618–88. Printed by the Camden Society.

[43] Jasper Mayne.

[44] Beaumont and Fletcher.

[45] " Valuables of Glenurquhy,' 1640. Innes' " Sketches of Early Scotch History."

[46] Collars of " Hollie worke" appear in the inventories of Mary Stuart.

[47] " Thomas Hodges, for making ruffe and cuffes for his Highness of cuttworke edged with a fayre peake purle, 7l."— 2nd Acc. of Sir J. Villiers, Prince Charles, 1617–18. P. R. O.

" 40 yards broad peaked lace to edge 6 cupboard cloths, at 4s. per yard, 8l."— Ibid.

[48] " Seaming " lace and spacing lace appear to have been generally used at this period to unite the breadths of linen, instead of a seam sewed. We find them employed for cupboard cloths, cushion cloths, sheets, shirts, &c., throughout the accounts of King James and Prince Charles.

" At Stratford-upon-Avon is preserved, in the room where Shakspeare's wife, Anne Hathaway, was born, an oaken linen chest, containing a pillow case and a very large sheet made of homespun linen. Down the middle of the sheet is an ornamental open or cut work insertion, about an inch and a half deep, and the pillow case is similarly ornamented. They are marked E. H., and have always been used by the Hathaway family

U

"There is not a gentleman now in the fashion," says Peacham,[49] "whose band of Italian cutwork now standeth him not in the least three or four pounds. Yes, a semster in Holborn told me that there are of threescore pounds." We read how two-thirds of a woman's dower was often expended in the purchase of cutwork and Flanders lace.

In the warrant of the great wardrobe for the marriage expenses of the ill-fated princess Elizabeth, on which occasion it is recorded of poor Arabella Stuart, the "Lady Arabella, though still in the Tower, has shewn her joy by buying four new gowns, one of which cost 1500l.,"[50] in addition to "gold cheine laze, silver spangled, silver looped, myllen bone lace, drawneworke poynte, black silk Naples lace," &c., all in the most astonishing quantity, we have the astounding entry of 1692 ounces of silver bone lace.[51] No wonder, in after days, the princess caused so much anxiety to the palatine's privy purse, Colonel Schomberg, who in vain implores her to have her linen and lace bought beforehand, and paid at every fair.[52] "You brought," he writes, "3000l. worth of linen from England, and have bought 1000l. worth here," and yet "you are ill provided."[53]

---

on special occasions, such as births, deaths, and marriages. This is still a common custom in Warwickshire; and many families can proudly show embroidered bed linen, which has been used on state occasions, and carefully preserved in old carved chests for three centuries and more."—*A Shakspeare Memorial*, 1864.

[49] "The Truth of the Times," W. Peacham, 1638.

[50] "State Papers, Dom." Jas. I. vol. lxxii. No. 28.

[51] Warrant on the Great Wardrobe, 1612–13, Princess Elizabeth's marriage.

[52] Frankfort fair, at which most of the German princes made their purchases.

[53] "German Correspondence," 1614–15 P. R. O.

We find among the accounts of Col. Schomberg and others:—

"To a merchant of Strasbourg, for laces which she had sent from Italy, 288 rix-dollars." And in addition to numerous entries of silver and other laces :—

"Pour dentelle et linge karé pour Madame, 115 florins."

"Donné Madame de Caus pour des mouchoirs à point couppée pour Madame, 4l."

"Une petite dentelle à point couppé, 3l." &c.

Point coupé handkerchiefs seem to have been greatly in fashion. Ben Jonson, "Bartholomew Fair," 1614, mentions them :—

"A cutwork handkerchief she gave me."

CHARLES I.

"Embroider'd stockings, cutwork smocks and shirts."

Ben Jonson.

"Une mode a à peine détruit une autre mode, qu'elle est abolie par une plus nouvelle, qui cède elle-même à celle qui la suit et qui ne sera pas la dernière; telle est notre legèreté."—*La Bruyère.*

Ruffs may literally be said to have gone out with James I. His son Charles is represented on the coins of the two first years of his reign in a stiff starched ruff;[54] in the fourth and fifth we see

Fig. 115.

Falling collar of the seventeenth century.   After Abraham Bosse.

the ruff unstarched, falling down on his shoulders,[55] and afterwards, the falling band (Fig. 115) was generally adopted, and worn by all classes save the judges, who stuck to the ruff as a mark of dignity and decorum, till superseded by the peruke.[56]

Even loyal Oxford, conscientious to a hair's-breadth—always behind the rest of the world—when Whitelocke, in 1635, addresses

---

[54] See Snelling's "Coins," pl. ix. 8, 9, 10.

[55] Ibid. pl. ix. 5, 6, 11.

[56] Evelyn, describing a medal of King Charles I., struck in 1633, says he wears "a falling band, which new mode succeeded the cumbersome ruff; but neither did the bishops or the judges give it up so soon, the Lord Keeper Finch being, I think, the very first."

U 2

the quarter sessions arrayed in the new fashion, owned " one may speak as good sense in a falling band as in a ruff." The change did not, however, diminish the extravagance of the age. The bills for the king's lace and linen, which in the year 1625 amounted to 1000*l.*, in course of time rose to 1500*l.*[57] Falling bands of Flanders bone lace and cutwork appear constantly in the accounts.[58] As the foreign materials are carefully specified (it was one of the articles, then a novelty, that Queen Anne of Denmark " bought of the French Mann "), we may infer much of the bobbin or bone lace to have been of home produce. As Ben Jonson says, " Rich apparel has strong virtues." It is, he adds, " the birdlime of fools." There was, indeed, no article of toilet at this period which was not encircled with lace—towels, sheets, shirts, caps, cushions, boots

•Fig. 116.　　　　　　　　　Fig. 117.

From an engraving of Abraham Bosse.　　　From an engraving of Abraham Bosse.

(Fig. 116), cuffs (Fig. 117); and, as too often occurs in the case of excessive luxury, when the bills came in, money was wanting to discharge them; Julian Elliott, the royal lace merchant, seldom receiving more than half her account, and in 1630—nothing.[59] There were, as Shakespeare says,

" Bonds entered into
For gay apparel against the triumph day."[60]

---

[57] In 1633, the bills having risen to 1500*l.* a year, a project is made for reducing the charge for the king's fine linen and bone lace, " for his body," again to 1000*l.* per annum, for which sum it " may be very well done."—*State Papers,* Chas. I. vol. ccxxxiv. No. 83.

[58] " Paid to Smith Wilkinson, for 420 yards of good Flanders bone lace for 12

day ruffes and 6 night ruffes ' cum cuffes eisdem,' 87*l.* 15*s.*

" For 6 falling bands made of good broad Flanders lace and Cuttworks with cuffs of the same, 52*l.* 16*s.*"—*Gt. W. A.* Car. I. 6=1631.

[59] See G. W. A. Mich. 1629 to April 1630.

[60] " Twelfth Night."

The quantity of needlework purl consumed on the king's hunting collars, "colares pro venatione," scarcely appears credible. One entry alone makes 994 yards for 12 collars and 24 pairs of cuffs.[61] Again, 600 yards of fine bone lace is charged for trimming the ruffs of the king's night-clothes.[62]

The art of lace-making was now carried to great perfection in England; so much so that the lease of twenty-one years, granted in 1627 to Dame Barbara Villiers, of the duties on gold and silver thread, became a terrible loss to the holder, who, in 1629, petitions for a discharge of 437*l.* 10*s.* arrears due to the crown. The prayer is favourably received by the officers of the customs, to whom it was referred, who answer they "conceive those duties will decay, for the invention of making Venice gold and silver lace within the kingdom is come to that perfection that it will be made here more cheap than it can be brought from beyond seas." [63] The fancy for foreign articles still prevailed. "Among the goods brought in by Tristram Stephens," writes Sir John Hippisley, from Dover Castle, "are the bravest French bandes that ever I did see for ladies—they be fit for the Queen." [64]

Gold lace was exported in considerable quantities to India in the days of James I.;[65] and now, in 1631, we find the "riband roses," edged with lace, notified among the articles allowed to be exported. These lace rosette-trimmed shoes were in vogue in the time of James I., and when first brought to that monarch, he refused to adopt the fashion, asking "if they wanted to make a ruffe-footed dove of him." They were afterwards worn in all the

---

[61] G. W. A. Car. I. the Annunciation 9 to Mich. 11.

[62] Ibid. 8 and 9.

[63] "State Papers, Dom." Charles I. vol. cxlix. No. 31.

[64] In a letter to Mr. Edward Nicholas, Sec. of the Admiralty, 7 March 1627 (afterwards Sec. of State to Chas. II.). "State Papers, Dom." Charles I. vol. cxxiii. 62.

Among the "State Papers" (vol. cxxvi. 70) is a letter from Susan Nicholas to her "loveing Brother," 1628, about lace for his band. She writes :—" I have sent you your bootehose and could have sent your lase for your band, but that I did see these lasees which to my thought did do a greddcale better than that wh you did bespeake, and the best of them will cost

no more then that which is half a crowne a yard, and so the uppermost will cost you, and the other will cost 18 pence ; I did thinke you would rather staye something long for it then to pay so deare for that wh would make no better show; if you like either of these, you shall have it sone desptch, for I am promise to have it made in a fortnight. I haue received the monie from my consson Hunton. Heare is no news to wright of. Thus with my best love remembred unto you, I rest your very loving sister,

"SUSANNE NICHOLAS.

"I have sent ye the lase ye foyrst bespoke, to compare them togother, to see which ye like best."

[65] See p. 287, note [35].

extravagance of the French court (see Fig. 60, page 121). Mr. Brooks, in his speech in the House of Commons against costly apparel (18 James I.), says, " Nowadays, the roses worn by Members of the House on their shoes are more than their fathers' apparel." Peacham speaks of " shoe ties, that goe under the name of roses, from thirty shillings to three, four, and five pounds the pair. Yea, a gallant of the time, not long since, paid thirty pounds for a pair." [66] Well might Taylor say they

> " Wear a farm in shoe-strings edged with gold,
> And spangled garters worth a copyhold."

It was not till the year 1635 that an effort was made for the protection of our home manufactures, " at the request and for the benefit of the makers of those goods in and near London, and other parts of the realm, now brought to great want and necessity, occasioned by the excessive importation of these foreign wares." Foreign " Purles, Cutworks, or Bone-laces, or any commodities laced or edged therewith," are strictly prohibited. Orders are also given that " all purles, cutworks, and bone laces English made are to be taken to a house near the sign of the ' Red Hart,' in Fore Street, without Cripplegate, and there sealed by Thomas Smith or his deputy." [67]

An act the same year prohibits the use of " gold or silver purles " except manufactured in foreign parts, and especially forbids the melting down any coin of the realm.

The manufacture of bone lace in England had now much improved, and was held in high estimation in France. We hear of Henrietta Maria sending ribbons, lace, and other fashions from England, in 1636, as a present to her sister-in-law, Anne of Austria; [68] while, in a letter dated 7th February 1636, the Countess of Leicester writes to her husband, then in France, who

---

[66] W. Peacham, " Truth of the Times," 1638.

Hamlet says there are

> " Two Provençal roses on my regal shoes."

> " When roses in the gardens grow,
> And not in ribbons on a shoe:
> Now ribbon-roses take such place,
> That garden roses want their grace."
> *Friar Bacon's Prophesie*, 1604.

" I like," says Evelyn, " the boucle better than the formal rose."—*Tyrannus, or the Mode.*

[67] This proclamation is dated from " our Honour of Hampton Court, 30th April, 1635."—*Rymer's Fœdera*, t. xix. p. 690.

[68] When Anne of Austria was suspected of secret correspondence with Spain and England, Richelieu sent the chancellor to question the Abbess of the Val-de-Grâce with respect to the casket which had been

had requested her to procure him some fine bone lace of English make :—" The present for the Queen of France I will be careful to provide, but it cannot be handsome for that proportion of money which you do mention ; for these bone laces, if they be good, are dear, and I will send the best, for the honor of my nation and my own credit."

Referring to the same demand, the countess again writes to her lord, 18th May 1637:—" Leicester House.—All my present for the Queen of France is provided, which I have done with great care and some trouble; the expenses I cannot yet directly tell you, but I think it will be about 120*l.*, for the bone laces are extremely dear. I intend to send it by Monsieur Ruvigny, for most of the things are of new fashion, and I should keep them, they would be less acceptable, for what is new now will quickly grow common, such things being sent over almost every week."

We can have no better evidence of the improvement in the English lace manufacture than these two letters.

An act of 1638 for reforming abuses in the manufacture of lace, by which competent persons are appointed, whether natives or strangers, " who should be of the Church of England," can scarcely have been advantageous to the community.

Lace, since the Reformation, had disappeared from the garment of the Church. In the search warrants made after Jesuits and priests of the Roman faith, it now occasionally peeps out. In an inventory of goods seized at the house of some Jesuit priests at Clerkenwell, in 1627, we find—" One faire Alb of cambric, with needle worke purles about the skirt, necke, and bandes."

Smuggling, too, had appeared upon the scene. In 1621, information is laid how Nicholas Peeter, master of the " Greyhound, of Apsom," had landed at Dover sundry packets of " cutworkes " and bone laces without paying the customs.[69]

But the

> " Rebatoes, ribbands, cuffs, ruffs, falls,
> Scarfes, feathers, fans, maskes, muffs, laces, cauls," [70]

of King Charles's court were soon to disperse at the now outbreaking revolution. The Herrn Maior Frau (Lady Mayoress), the

---

secretly brought into the monastery. The Abbess (" Vie de la Mère d'Arbouse ") declared that this same casket came from the Queen of England, and that it only contained lace, ribbons, and other trimmings of English fashion, sent by Henrietta Maria as a present to the Queen. " Galerie de l'Ancienne Cour," 1791.

[69] " State Papers, Dom." vol. cxxiii. No. 65.

[70] " Rhodon and Iris, a Pastoral," 1631.

noble English lady depicted by Hollar,[71] must now lay aside her whisk, edged with broad lace of needle point, and no longer hie to St. Martin's for lace :[72] she must content herself with a plain attire.

> " Sempsters with ruffs and cuffs, and quoifs and caules,
>   And falls," [73]

must be dismissed. Smocks of three pounds a piece,[74] wrought smocks,[75] are no longer worn by all—much less those " seam'd thro' with cutwork." [76] " Lace to her smocks, broad seaming laces," [77] which, groans one of the Puritan writers, " is horrible to think of."

The ruff and cuffs of Flanders, gold lace cutwork and silver lace of curle,[78] needle point, and fine gartering with blown roses,[79] are now suppressed under Puritan rule.

The " fop, " whom Henry Fitz-Geoffrey describes as having

> " An attractive lace
> And whalebone bodies for the better grace,"

must now think twice before he wears it.[80]

The officer, whom the poor soldier apostrophises as shining—

> " One blaze of plate about you, which puts out
> Our eyes when we march 'gainst the sunne, and armes you
> Compleatly with your own gold lace, which is
> Laid on so thick, that your own trimmings due
> Render you engine proof, without more arms "—[81]

---

[71] " Ornatus Muliebris Anglicanus," 1645.

[72] " You must to the Pawn (Exchange) to buy lawn, to St. Martin for lace."—*Westward Ho*, 1607.

" A copper lace called St. Martin's lace."—*Strype*.

[73] Taylor, " Whip of Pride," 1640.

[74] In " Eastward Ho," 1605, proud Gertrude says : " Smocks of three pound a smock, are to be born with all."

[75] " Bartholomew Fair," 1614.

[76] " She shewed me gowns and head tires, Embroidered waistcoats, smocks seam'd thro' with cutworks."
    Beaumont and Fletcher, Four Plays in One, 1647.

[77] " Who would ha' thought a woman so well harness'd,
    Or rather well caparison'd, indeed,
    That wears such petticoats, and lace to her smocks,
    Broad seaming laces."
    Ben Jonson, The Devil is an Ass, 1616.

[78] A suite of russet " laced all over with silver curle lace." — *Expenses of Robt. Sidney, Earl of Leicester*, temp. Chas. I.

[79] " This comes of wearing
    Scarlet, gold lace and cutworks ; your fine gartering
    With your fine blown roses."   *The Devil is an Ass*.

[80] " Notes from Black Fryers."   [81] Jasper Mayne, " Amorous War," 1659.

must no longer boast of

> " This shirt five times victorious I have fought under,
> And cut through squadrons of your curious Cut-work,
> As I will do through mine." [82]

In the Roundhead army he will scarce deign to comb his cropped locks. All is now dingy, of a sad colour, soberly in character with the tone of the times.

THE COMMONWEALTH.

The rule of the Puritans was a sad time for lace-makers, as regards the middle and lower classes: every village festival, all amusement was put down, bride laces and Mayings—all were vanity.

With respect to the upper classes, the Puritan ladies, as well as the men of birth, had no fancy for exchanging the rich dress of the Stuart court for that of the Roundheads. Sir Thomas Fairfax, father of the general, is described as wearing a buff coat, richly ornamented with silver lace, his trunk hose trimmed with costly Flanders lace, his breastplate partly concealed by a falling collar of the same material. The foreign ambassadors of the parliament disdained the Puritan fashions. Lady Fanshaw describes her husband as wearing at the court of Madrid, on some state occasion, "his linen very fine, laced with very rich Flanders lace." [83]

Indeed, it was not till the arrival of the Spanish envoy, the first accredited to the Protectorate of Cromwell, that Harrison begged Colonel Hutchinson and Lord Warwick to set an example to other nations at the audience, and not appear in gold and silver lace. Colonel Hutchinson, though he saw no harm in a rich dress, yet not to appear offensive, came next day in a plain black suit, as did the other gentlemen, when, to the astonishment of all, Harrison appeared in a scarlet coat so laden with "clinquaint" and lace as to hide the material of which it was made, showing, remarks Mrs. Hutchinson, "his godly speeches were only made that he might appear braver above the rest in the eyes of the strangers."

Nor did the mother of Cromwell lay aside these adornments. She wore a handkerchief of which the broad point lace alone could

---

[82] " The Little French Lawyer." [83] " Memoirs."

be seen, and her green velvet cardinal was edged with broad gold lace.[84]   Cromwell himself, when once in power, became more particular in his dress; and if he lived as a Puritan, his body after death was more gorgeously attired than that of any deceased sovereign, with purple velvet, ermine, and the richest Flanders lace.[85]   His effigy, carved by one Symonds, was clad in a fine shirt of Holland, richly laced; he wore bands and cuffs of the same materials, and his clothes were covered with gold lace.[86]

The more we read the more we feel convinced that the dislike manifested by the Puritan leaders to lace and other luxuries was but a political necessity, in order to follow the spirit of the age.

As an illustration of this opinion we may cite that in the account of the disbursements of the Committee of Safety, 1660, a political jeu d'esprit which preceded the Restoration, we find entered for Lady Lambert—

"Item, for seven new whisks lac'd with Flanders lace of the last Edition, each whisk is valued at fifty pound, 350*l.*"

Followed up by—

"Six new Flanders lac'd smocks, 300*l.*"

The whisk, as the gorget was now termed, was as great an object of extravagance to the women as was the falling band to the men.   It continued in fashion during the reign of Charles II., and is often mentioned as lost or stolen among the advertisements in the public journals of the day.   In the "Mercurius Publicus," May 8, 1662, we find: "A cambric whisk with Flanders lace, about a quarter of a yard broad, and a lace turning up about an inch broad, with a stock in the neck, and a strap hanging down before, was lost between the new Palace and Whitehall.   Reward 30*s.*"   Again, in the "Newes," June 20, 1664: "Lost, a Tiffany whisk, with a great lace down, and a little one up, large Flowers, and open Work, with a Roul for the head and Peak."

---

84 "The Cromwell Family."
85 Sir Philip Warwick. 1640.
86 At the Restoration, it was removed from the Abbey and hung out of the window at Whitehall, and then broken up and destroyed.

CHAPTER XXV.

CHARLES II. TO THE HOUSE OF HANOVER.

CHARLES II.

" The dangling knee-fringe, and the bib-cravat."
Dryden, Prologue, 1674.

THE taste for luxury only required the restoration of the Stuarts to burst out in full vigour.

The following year Charles II. issued a proclamation[1] enforcing the act of his father prohibiting the entry of foreign bone lace; but, far from acting as he preached, he purchases Flanders lace at 18s. the yard, for the trimming of his fine lawn " collobium sindonis,"[2] a sort of surplice worn during the ceremony of the anointment at the coronation.

The hand-spinners of gold wire, thread lace, and spangles, of the City of London, no longer puritanically inclined, now speak out boldly. " Having heard a report the Parliament intend to pass an Act against the wearing of their manufacture, they hope it intends the reform, not the destruction of their craft, for by it many thousands would be ruined. Let every person," say they, " be prohibited from wearing gold, silver, and thread lace—that will encourage the gentry to do so." [3]

In 1662 is passed an act prohibiting the importation of foreign

---

[1] 1661. Nov. 20. " State Papers, Dom." Charles II. vol. xliv. P. R. O.

[2] " To William Briers, for making the Colobium Sindonis of fine lawn laced with fine Flanders lace, 33s. 4d.

" To Valentine Stucky, for 14 yards and a half of very fine Flanders lace for the same, at 18s. per yard, 12l. 6s. 6d."—*Acc. of the E. of Sandwich, Master of the G. W. for the Coronation of King Charles II.* 23 April 1661. P. R. O.

[3] In the G. W. A. for 29 and 30 occurs a curious entry by the master of the great wardrobe :—" I doo hereby charge myself with 5000 Livres by me received in the realm of France for gold and silver fringes by me there sold, belong to a rich embroidered Bed of his said Majesty, which at one shilling and sevenpence p lib. English, Being the value of the Exchange at that time, amounts to £395 16s. 8d.

" (Signed)   R. MONTAGUE.
" May 28, 1678."

bone lace, cutworks, &c., setting forth, "Whereas many poor children have attained great dexterity in the making thereof, the persons so employed have served most parts of the kingdom with bone lace, and for the carrying out of the same trade have caused much thread to be brought into the country, whereby the customs have been greatly advanced, until of late large quantities of bone lace, cutwork, &c., were brought into the kingdom and sold contrary to the former Statutes and the proclamation of November last; all such bone lace is to be forfeited, and a penalty of 100*l.* paid by the offender."[4]

This same act only occasioned the more smuggling of lace from Flanders, for the lace made in England had never attained the beauty of Brussels, and indeed, wherever fine lace is mentioned at this period, it is always of foreign fabric. That Charles himself was of this opinion, there can be no doubt, for in the very same year he grants to one John Eaton a licence to import such quantities of lace, "made beyond the seas, as may be for the wear of the Queen, our dear Mother the Queen, our dear brother James, Duke of York," and the rest of the royal family. The permission is softened down by the words, "And to the end the same may be patterns for the manufacture of these commodities here, notwithstanding the late Statute forbidding their importation."[5]   Charles had evidently received his lessons in the school of Mazarin. As the galleries of the cardinal were filled with sculptures, paintings, and maiolica—rich produce of Italian art, as patterns for France, " per mostra di farne in Francia "—so the king's " pilea nocturna," pillowberes, cravats, were trimmed with the points of Venice[6] and lace of Flanders, at the rate of 600*l.* per annum, for the sake of improving the lace manufacture of England.

The introduction of the flowing wig, with its long curls covering the shoulders, gave a final blow to the falling band; the ends floating and tied in front could alone be visible. In time they diminished in size, and the remains are still seen in the laced bands of the lawyer, when in full dress, and the homely bordered cambric

---

[4] 14 Car. II. c. 13.   Statutes at large. The acts of Charles II. date from the death of his father; so the year of the Restoration, 1660, is counted as the thirteenth of his reign.

[5] 1662. "State Papers, Dom." Charles II. vol. lv. No. 25.   P. R. O.

[6] He pays 149*l.* to his laceman (Teneatari) for 3 cravats " de poynt de Venez," and 24*s.* per yard for 57 yards of narrow point, " teniæ poynt augustæ," to trim his falling ruffles, " manicis cadentibus," &c.— *G. W. A.* Car. II. 24 & 25.

Later (1676-7) we find charged for " un par manicarum, le poynt, 14*l.*"

slips used by the clergy. The laced cravat now introduced continued in fashion until about the year 1735.[7]

It was at its height when Pepys writes in his diary : " Lord's Day, Oct. 19, 1662. Put on my new lace band, and so neat it is that I am resolved my great expense shall be lace bands, and it will set off anything else the more." The band was edged with the broadest lace. In the " Newes," 1663, January 7, we find : " Lost, a laced band, the lace a quarter of a yard deep, and the band marked in the stock with a B."

Mrs. Pepys—more thrifty soul—" wears her green petticoat of Florence satin, with white and black gimp lace of her own putting on (making), which is very pretty."

The custom, already common in France, of ladies making their own lace, excites the ire of the writer of " Britannia Languens," in his " Discourse upon Trade." [8] " The manfacture of linen," [9] he says, " was once the huswifery of English ladies, gentlewomen, and other women ; " now " the huswifery women of England employ themselves in making an ill sort of lace, which serves no national or natural necessity." [10]

The days of Puritan simplicity were at an end.

> " Instead of homespun coifs were seen
> Good pinners edged with Colberteen." [11]

The laced cravat succeeded the falling collar. Lace handkerchiefs [12] were the fashion, and

> " Gloves laced and trimmed as fine as Nell's." [13]

---

[7] When it was replaced by a black ribbon and a bow.

[8] London, 1680.

[9] Authors, however, disagree like the rest of the world. In a tract called " The Ancient Trades Decayed Repaired Again," by Sir Roger L'Estrange (1678), we read : " Nay, if the materials used in a trade be not of the growth of England yet, if the trade be to employ the poor, we should have it bought without money, and brought to us from beyond the seas where it is made as ' Bone lace.' "

[10] As early as 20th September 1675, Mrs. Rebecca Croxton advertises in the " London Gazette," informing the world in general that she has " lately found out a new way of making Point de Venise, and has obtained a patent from his Majesty for making the same ; that she

is now settled at Hammersmith, over against Lord Chief Justice Neville's house, where such as are willing to be instructed will find her all days save Tuesdays, on which day she will be spoken to at the Duke's Head, Henrietta Street, Covent Garden."

[11] Swift, " Baucis and Philemon."

[12] " Intelligencer," 1665, June 5: " Lost, six handkerchers wrapt up in a brown paper, two laced, one point-laced set on tiffany ; the two laced ones had been worn, the other four new."

" London Gazette," 1672, Dec. 5–9 : " Lost, a lawn pocket handkercher with a broad hem, laced round with a fine Point lace about four fingers broad, marked with an R in red silk."

[13] Evelyn. It was the custom, at a maiden assize, to present the judge with

Laced aprons, which even found their way to the homes of the Anglican clergy, and appear advertised as "Stolen from the vicarage house at Amersham in Oxfordshire: An apron of needle-work lace, the middle being Network, another Apron laced with cut and slash lace." [14]

The newspapers crowd with losses of lace, and rarer—finds. [15]

They give us, however, no clue to the home manufacture. "A pasteboard box full of laced linen, and a little portmanteau with some white and grey Bone lace," [16] would seem to signify a lace much made two hundred years ago, of which we have ourselves seen specimens from Dalecarlia, a sort of guipure, upon which the pattern is formed by the introduction of an unbleached thread, which comes out in full relief—a fancy more curious than pretty.

The petticoats of the ladies of King Charles's court have received due honour at the hands of Pepys, whose prying eyes seem to have been everywhere. On May 21 of the same year he so complacently admired himself in his new lace band, he writes down: "My wife and I to my Lord's lodging ; where she and I staid walking in White Hall Gardens. And in the Privy Garden saw the finest smocks and linen petticoats of my Lady Castlemaine's, laced with rich lace at the bottom, that ever I saw ; and it did me good to look at them."

Speaking of the ladies' attire of this age, Evelyn says :—

> "Another quilted white and red,
> With a broad Flanders lace below;
> Four pairs of bas de soye shot through

---

a pair of "laced gloves." Lord Campbell, in 1856, at the Lincoln Lent assizes, received from the sheriff a pair of white gloves richly trimmed with Brussels lace and embroidered, the city arms embossed in frosted silver on the back.

[14] "London Gazette," 1677, Jan. 28–31 ; again, Oct. 4–8, in the same year: "Stolen or lost out of the Petworth waggon, a deal box directed to the Lady Young of Burton in Sussex ; there was in it a fine Point Apron, a suit of thin laced Night clothes," &c.

[15] "London Gazette," 1675, June 14–17: "A right Point lace with a long musling neck laced at the ends with a

narrow Point about three fingers broad, and a pair of Point cuffs of the same, worn foul and never washt, was lost on Monday last."

Ibid. 1677, Oct 22-25 : "Found in a ditch, Four laced forehead cloths. One laced Pinner, one laced Quoif, one pair of laced ruffels. . . . Two point aprons and other laced linen."

"Intelligencer," 1664, Oct. 3 : "Lost, A needle work point without a border, with a great part of the loups cut out, and a quarter of it new loupt with the needle. £5 reward."

[16] "London Gazette," 1677, Oct. 8–11.

> With silver; diamond buckles too,
> For garters, and as rich for shoe.
> Twice twelve day smocks of Holland fine,
> With cambric sleeves rich Point to joyn
> (For she despises Colbertine);
> Twelve more for night, all Flanders lac'd,
> Or else she'll think herself disgrac'd.
> The same her night gown must adorn,
> With two Point waistcoats for the morn;
> Of pocket mouchoirs, nose to drain,
> A dozen laced, a dozen plain;
> Three night gowns of rich Indian stuff;
> Four cushion-cloths are scarce enough
> Of Point and Flanders," [17] &c.

It is difficult now to ascertain what description of lace was that styled Colbertine.[18] It is constantly alluded to by the writers of the period. Randle Holme (1688) styles it, " A kind of open lace with a square grounding." [19] Evelyn himself, in his " Fop's Dictionary " (1690), gives, " Colbertine, a lace resembling net-work of the fabric of Monsieur Colbert, superintendent of the French King's manufactures ;" and the " Ladies' Dictionary," 1694, repeats his definition. This is more incomprehensible still, point d'Alençon being the lace that can be specially styled of " the fabric " of Colbert, and Colbertine appears to have been a coarse production.[20] Swift talks of knowing

> " The difference between
> Rich Flanders lace and Colberteen." [21]

Congreve makes Lady Westport say—[22]

> " Go hang out an old Frisonier gorget with a yard of yellow Colberteen."

And a traveller, in 1691,[23] speaking of Paris, writes :—" You shall see here the finer sort of people flaunting it in tawdry gauze or Colbertine, a parcel of coarse staring ribbons; but ten of their holyday habits shall not amount to what a citizen's wife of London wears on her head every day."

---

[17] " Tyrannus, or the Mode," 1661.

[18] It is written Colberteen, Colbertain, Golbertain, Colbertine.

[19] Colberteen, a lace resembling net-work, being of the manufacture of M. Colbert, a French statesman.

[20] A writer, in " Notes and Queries," says : " I recollect this lace worn as a ruffle fifty years ago. The ground was square and coarse, it had a fine edge, with a round mesh, on which the pattern was woven. It was an inferior lace and in every-day wear."

[21] " Cadenus and Vanessa." See also Young, p. 111.

[22] " Way of the World."

[23] " Six Weeks in France," 1691.

JAMES II.

" To know the age and pedigrees
Of points of Flanders and Venise."
Hudibras.

The reign of James II., short and troubled, brought but little change in the fashion of the day.

Charles II., in the last year of his reign, spends 20*l*. 12*s*. for a new cravat to be worn " on the birthday of his dear brother," [24] and James expends 29*l*. upon one of Venice point to appear in on that of his queen. Frequent entries of lace for the attendants of the Chapel Royal form items in the royal wardrobe accounts.

Ruffles, night-rails, and cravats of point d'Espagne and de Venise now figure in gazettes,[25] but " Flanders lace is still in high estimation," writes somebody, in 1668, " and even fans are made of it."

Then James II. fled, and years after we find him dying at Saint-Germain in—a laced nightcap. " This cap was called a ' toquet,' and put on when the king was in extremis, as a compliment to Louis XIV." " It was the court etiquette for all the Royals," writes Madame, in her " Memoirs," " to die with a nightcap on." The toquet of King James may still be seen by the curious, adorning a wax model of the king's head, preserved as a relic in the Museum of Dunkirk.[26]

Out of mingled gratitude, we suppose, for the hospitality she had received at the French court, and the protection of the angels,

---

[24] Gt. W. A. Car. II. 35-36 = 1683-4.

[25] " Gazette," July 20, 1682. Lost, a portmanteau full of women's clothes, among which are enumerated " two pairs of Point d'Espagne ruffles, a laced night rail and waistcoat, a pair of Point de Venise ruffles, a black laced scarf," &c.— *Malcolm's Anecdotes of London.*

The lace of James II.'s cravats and ruffles are of point de Venise.

" Sex prælant cravatts de lacinia Venetiarum " are charged 141*l*., and 9 yards lace, for six more cravats, 45*l*.

3 *l*. 10*s*. for the cravat of Venice lace to wear on the day of his coronation, &c. G. W. A Jac. II. 1685-6.

[26] A writer in the " Gentleman's Magazine " (October 1745) mentions : " In the parlour of the monastery of English Benedictines at Paris, I was shown the mask of the king's face, taken off immediately after he was dead, together with the fine laced nightcap he died in." The cap at Dunkirk is trimmed with Flemish lace (old Mechlin). It must have passed from Paris to the convent of English Benedictines at Dunkirk, who left that city in 1793. There is no record how it became deposited in the Museum. Communicated by M. de la Forçade, Conservator of the Museum, Dunkirk.

which, she writes, " I experienced once when I set fire to my lace night cornet, which was burned to the very head without singeing a single hair "—good Queen Mary of Modena, who shone so brightly in her days of adversity, died, " selon les règles," coeffed in like fashion.

With this notice we finish the Saint-Germain reign of King James II.

WILLIAM III.

> " Long wigs,
> Steinkirk cravats."
>> *Congreve, Love for Love.*

In 1698, the English parliament passed another act " for rendering the laws more effectual for preventing the importation of foreign Bone lace, Loom lace, Needlework Point, and Cutwork," [27] with a penalty of 20s. per yard, and forfeiture. This act caused such excitement among the convents and béguinages of Flanders that the government, at that time under the dominion of Spain, prohibited, by way of retaliation, the importation of English wool. In consequence of the general distress occasioned by this edict among the woolstaplers of England, the act prohibiting the importation of foreign lace into England was repealed,[28] so far as related to the Spanish Low Countries. England was the loser by this custom-house war.[29]

Dress, after the Revolution, partook of the stately sobriety of the house of Nassau, but lace was extensively worn. Queen Mary favoured that wonderful erection, already spoken of in our chapter on France,[30] the tower or fontange, more generally called, certainly not from its convenience, the " commode," with its piled tiers of lace and ribbon, and the long hanging pinners, celebrated by Prior in his " Tale of the Widow and her Cat :"—

> " He scratch'd the maid, he stole the cream,
> He tore her best lac'd pinner."

Their Flanders lace heads, with the engageantes [31] or ruffles, and

---

[27] 9 & 10 Will. III.=1697–8.
[28] 11 & 12 Will. III. =1698–9.
[29] Smith's " Wealth of Nations."

[30] See p. 138.
[31] See p. 139.

X

the dress covered with lace frills and flounces—"every part of the garment in curl"—caused a lady, says the "Spectator," to resemble "a Friesland hen."[32]

Never yet were such sums expended on lace as in the days of William and Mary. The lace bill of the queen, signed by Lady Derby, mistress of the robes, for the year 1694, amounts to the enormous sum of 1918*l*.[33] Among the most extravagant entries we find :—

	£.	s.	d.
21 yards of lace for 12 pillow beres, at 52s.	54	12	0
16 yards of lace for 2 toylights (toilets), at 12*l*.	192	0	0
24 yards for 6 handkerchiefs, at 4*l*. 10s.	108	0	0
30 yards for 6 night shifts, at 62s.	93	0	0
6 yards for 2 combing cloths, at 14*l*.	84	0	0
3½ yards for a do. do. at 17*l*.	53	2	6
3⅛ do. at 14*l*.	42	0	0
An apron of lace .	17	0	0

None of the lace furnished by Mr. Bampton, thread lace provider and milliner to the court, for the queen's engageantes and ruffles, however, seems to have exceeded 5*l*. 10s. the yard. There is little new in this account. The lace is entered as scalloped,[34] ruffled, "loopt;" lace "purle"[35] still lingers on; catgut, too, appears for the first time,[36] as well as raised point,[37] and needlework.[38]

---

[32] "Spectator," No. 129, 1711.

"Lost, from behind a Hackney coach, Lombard Street, a grounded lace night rail."—*London Gazette*, 1695, Aug. 8.

"Lost, two loopt lace Pinners and a pair of double laced ruffles, bundled up together."—*Ibid.* 1697, Jan. 6–10.

"Taken out of two boxes in Mr. Drouth's waggon. . . six cards of piece lace looped and purled, scolopt heads to most of them . . . a fine Flanders lace head and ruffles, groundwork set on a wier," &c.—*Ibid.* 1698, April 11–14.

"Furbelows are not confined to scarfs, but they must have furbelow'd gowns and furbelow'd petticoats, and furbelow'd aprons; and, as I have heard, furbelow'd smocks too."— *Pleasant Art of Money-catching*, 1730.

[33] B. M. Add. MSS. No. 5751.

[34] "Bought of John Bishop & Jer. Peirie, att yᵉ Golden Ball, in Ludgate Hill, 26 April, 1693 :

"3 yards 1/2 of Rich silver ruff'd scollop lace falbala, with a Rich broad silver Tire Orris at the head, at 7s. 3*d*. a yard, 25*l*. 0s. 6*d*.

"8 yards of broad scollopped thread lace, at 25s.

"3 yards rich Paigning (?) Lace, 48s. 8*d*., 8*l*. 14s."

[35] "9 1/2 Fine purle to set on the pinner, at 3s."

[36] "5 3/4 of fine broad cattgutt border, at 20s."

[37] "1 yard 7/16 Raised Point to put on the top of a pair of sleeves, at 30s."

[38] "8 yards of Broad Needlework Lace, at 30s."

The queen's pinners are mentioned as Mazzarined;[39] some fashion named in honour of the once fair Hortense, who ended her exiled life in England.

> " What do you lack, ladies fair,
> Mazzarine hoods, Fontanges, girdles ? " [40]

King William himself, stern and morose in private life, early imbued with the Dutch taste for lace, exceeded, we may say, his wife in the extravagance of his lace bills; for though the lace account for 1690 is noted only at 1603*l.*, it increases annually until the year 1695-6, when the entries amount to the astonishing sum of 2459*l.* 19*s.*[41] Among the items charged will be found—

	£.	s.	d.
To six point cravats	158	0	0
To eight do. for hunting	85	0	0
54 yds. for 6 barbing cloths . . .	270	0	0
63 yds. for 6 combing cloths	283	10	0
117 yds. of " scissæ teniæ " (cutwork) for trimming 12 pockethandfs.	485	14	3
78 yds. for 24 cravats, at 8*l.* 10*s.* . .	663	0	0

In this right royal account of expenditure we find mention of "cockscombe laciniæ," of which the king consumes 341 yards.[42] What this may be, we cannot say, as it is described as " green and white ;" otherwise we might have supposed it some kind of Venice point, the little pearl-edged raised patterns of which are designated by Randle Holme as " cockscombs." More coquet than a woman, we find an exchange effected with Henry Furness, " Mercatori," of various laces, purchased for his handkerchiefs and razor cloths which, laid by during the two years of "lugubris " for his beloved consort, the queen—during which period he had used razor cloths with broad hems and no lace—had become " obsolete "—quite out of fashion. To effect this exchange the king pays the sum of 178*l.* 12*s.* 6*d.*, the lace purchased for the six new razor cloths

---

[39] " 3 yards of lace to Mazzarine yᵉ pinners, at 25*s.*"

Probably the same as the French "campanner." See p. 104.

[40] The Milliner, in Shadwell's " Bury Fair," 1720.

[41] G. W. A. Will. III. 1688 to 1702. P. R. O.

[42] Ibid. vii. & viii.

x 2

amounting to 270*l*. In the same page we find him, now out of mourning, expending 499*l*. 10*s*. for lace to trim his 24 new nightshirts, " indusiis nocturnis."

With such royal patronage, no wonder the lace trade prospered, and that, within ten years of William's death, Defoe should quote the point lace of Blandford as selling at 30*l*. the yard.

We have already told how the fashion of the laced Steinkirk found as much favour in England [43] as in France. Many people still possess, among their family relics, long oval-shaped brooches of topaz or Bristol stones, and wonder what they were used for. These old-fashioned articles of jewellery were worn to fasten (when not passed through the button-hole) the lace Steinkirk, so prevalent not only among the nobility, but worn by all classes. If the dialogue between Sir Nicholas Dainty and Major-General Blunt, as given in Shadwell's play, be correct, the volunteers of King William's day were not behind the military in elegance :—

" SIR NICHOLAS. I must make great haste, I shall ne'er get my Points and Laces done up time enough.

" MAJ. GEN. B. What say'st, young fellow ? Points and Laces for camps ?

" SIR NICH. Yes, Points and Laces ; why, I carry two laundresses on purpose. . . . Would you have a gentleman go undress'd in a camp ? Do you think I would see a camp if there were no dressing ? Why, I have two campaign suits, one trimmed with Flanders lace, and the other with rich Point.

" MAJ. GEN. B. Campaign suits with lace and Point !" [44]

---

[43] " I hope your Lordship is pleased with your Steinkerk."
Sir John Vanbrugh, The Relapse

In Colley Cibber's "Careless Husband," Lady Easy takes the Steinkirk off her neck and lays it on Sir Charles's head when he is asleep.

In "Love's Last Shift," by the same author (1695), the hero speaks of being " Strangled in my own Steinkerk."

In "Love for Love," by Congreve, Sir Novelty enumerates the Steinkirk, the large button, with other fashions, as created by him

" I have heard the Steenkirk arrived but two months ago."—*Spectator*, No. 129.

The " modish spark " wears " a huge Steinkirk, twisted to the waist."—*Prologue to First Part of Don Quixote*, 1694.

Frank Osbaldeston, in " Rob Roy," is deprived by the Highlanders of his cravat, " a Steinkirke richly laced."

At Ham House was the portrait of a Countess of Dysart, temp. Anne, in threecornered cocked hat, long coat, flapped waistcoat, and Mechlin Steinkirk.

In the account book of Isabella, Duchess of Grafton, daughter of Lord Arlington, Evelyn's " sweet child "—her portrait hangs in Queen Mary's Room, Hampton Court—we have : " 1709. To a Stinkirk, 1*l*. 12*s*. 3*d*."

They appear to have been made of other stuffs than lace, for in the same account, 1708, we have entered : " To a green Steenkirk, 1*l*. 1*s*. 6*d*."

[44] " The Volunteers, or the Stock Jobbers."

In Westminster Abbey, where, as somewhat disrespectfully say the Brothers Popplewell,[45] the images of William and Mary

> " Stand upright in a press, with their bodies made of wax,
> A globe and a wand in either hand and their robes upon their backs "—

the lace tucker and double sleeves of Queen Mary are of the finest raised Venice point, resembling Fig. 25, p. 43; King William likewise wears a rich lace cravat and ruffles.[46] We have already alluded to a memorandnm (carta d' informazione) given to the Venetian ambassadors about to proceed to England, 1696, in which they are directed to be provided with very handsome collars of the finest Venetian point.[47]

Before concluding the subject of the lace-bearing heroes, we may as well state here that the English soldiers rivalled the cavaliers of France in the richness of their points till the extinction of hair-powder (the wearing of which in the army consumes, says some indignant writer, flour enough to feed 00,000 persons per annum), when the lace cravat was replaced by the now happily expiring stock. Speaking of these military dandies, writes the " World :"—" Nor can I behold the lace and the waste of finery in their clothing but in the same light as the silver plates and ornaments on a coffin ; indeed I am apt to impute their going to battle so trimmed and adorned to the same reason a once fine lady painted her cheeks just before she expired, that she might not look frightful when she was dead.

> " To war the troops advance,
> Adorned and trim like females for the dance.
> Down sinks Lothario, sent by one dire blow
> A well-dress'd hero to the shades below."

As the justice's daughter says to her mamma, in Sheridan's " St. Patrick's Day :"—

> " Dear; to think how the sweet fellows sleep on the ground, and fight in silk stockings and lace ruffles."

Lace had now become an article worthy the attention of the

---

[45] "The Tombs in Westminster Abbey," sung by the Brothers Popplewell. Broadside, 1775. B. M. Roxburgh Coll.

[46] King Charles II.'s lace is the same as that of Queen Mary. The Duchess of Buckingham (the " mad " Duchess, daughter of James II.) has also very fine raised lace.

[47] See page 45.

light-fingered gentry. The jewels worn by our great-grandmothers
of the eighteenth century, though mounted in the most exquisite
taste, were for the most part false—Bristol or Alençon " diamonds,"
paste, or " Strass." Lace, on the other hand, was a sure commodity
and easily disposed of. At the robbery of Lady Anderson's house
in Red Lion Square during a fire, in 1700, the family of George
Heneage, Esq., on a visit, are recorded to have lost—" A head with
fine loopt lace, of very great value; a Flanders lace hood; a pair
of double ruffles and tuckers; two laced aprons, one point, the
other Flanders lace; and a large black lace scarf embroidered in
gold."

Again, at an opera row some years later, the number of caps,
ruffles, and heads enumerated as stolen by the pickpockets is quite
fabulous. So expert had they become that, when first the ladies
took to wearing powdered wigs, they dexterously cut open the
leather backs of the hack coaches and carried off wig, head and all,
before the rifled occupant had the slightest idea of their attack.[48]
To remedy the evil, the police request all ladies for the future to
sit with their backs to the horses.[49]

QUEEN ANNE.

" PARLEY.—Oh, Sir, there's the prettiest fashion lately come over! so airy, so
French, and all that! The Pinners are double ruffled with twelve plaits of a side,
and open all from the face ; the hair is frizzled up all round head, and stands as stiff
as a bodkin. Then the Favourites hang loose upon the temple with a languishing
lock in the middle. Then the Caule is extremely wide, and over all is a Cornet rais'd
very high and all the Lappets behind."—*Farquhar, Sir Harry Wildair.*

Queen Anne, though less extravagant than her sister, was
scarcely more patriotic. The point purchased for her coronation,[50]
though it cost but 64l. 13s. 9d., was of Flanders growth. The bill
is made out to the royal laceman of King William's day, now Sir
Henry Furnesse, knight and merchant.

The queen, too, in her gratitude, conferred a pension of 100l.
upon one Mrs. Abrahat, the royal clear-starcher; " because," writes
the Duchess of Marlborough, " she had washed the queen's heads
for twenty pounds a year when she was a princess."

---

[48] " Weekly Journal," March 1717.   Master of the G. W., touching the Fu-
[49] " The Modern Warrior," 1756.   neral of William III. and Coronation of
[50] " Acc. of Ralph, Earl of Montague, Queen Anne." P. R. O.

In 1706, Anne again repeals the acts which prohibit Flanders lace, with the clear understanding that nothing be construed into allowing the importation of lace made in "the dominions of the French King ; " [51] an edict in itself sufficient to bring the laces of France into the highest fashion.[52]

"France," writes an essayist, "is the wardrobe of the world ; " nay, "the English have so great an esteem for the workmanship of the French refugees, that hardly a thing vends without a Gallic name." [53]

To these refugees from Alençon and elsewhere, expelled by the cruel edict of Louis XIV., we owe the visible improvement of our lace in the eighteenth century.

Up to the present time we have had mention only of "Flanders lace" in general. In the reign of Queen Anne the points of " Macklin" and Brussels are first noted down in the royal wardrobe accounts. In 1710, her majesty pays for 26 yards of fine edged Brussels lace 151l.[54] "Mais, l'appétit vient en mangeant." The bill of Margareta Jolly, for the year 1712, for the furnishing of Mechlin and Brussels lace alone, amounts to the somewhat extravagant sum of 1418l. 14s. Taking the average price of the "Lace chanter on Ludgate Hill," articles of daily use were costly enough. "One Brussels head is valued at 40l.; a grounded Brussels head, 30l.; one looped Brussels, 30l." These objects, high as the price may seem, lasted a woman's life. People in the last century did not care for variety, they contented themselves with a few good articles; hence among the objects given in 1719, as necessary to a lady of fashion, we merely find :—

	£	s.	d.
A French point or Flanders head and ruffles .	80	0	0
A ditto handkerchief	10	0	0
A black French laced hood . . .	5	5	0

When the Princess Mary, daughter of George II., married, she

---

[51] Statutes at large, Anne 5 & 6.

[52] This edict greatly injured the lace trade of France. In the " Atlas Maritime et Commercial" of 1727, it states: " I might mention several other articles of French manufacture which, for want of a market in England, where their chief consumption was, are so much decayed and in a manner quite sunk. I mean as to exportation, the English having now set up the same among themselves, such as bone lace."

[53] " History of Trade," London, 1702.

[54] " Pro 14 virgis lautæ Fimbr' Bruxell' laciniæ et 12 virgis dict' laciniæ pro Reginæ persona, £151."—G. W. A. 1710–11.

had but four fine laced Brussels heads, two loopt and two grounded, two extremely fine point ones, with ruffles and lappets, six French caps and ruffles.[55]

Two point lace cravats were considered as a full supply for any gentleman. Even young extravagant Lord Bedford, who, at eighteen years of age, found he could not spend less than 6000*l.* a year at Rome, when on the grand tour, only charges his mother, Rachel Lady Russell, with that number.[56]

The high commode,[57] with its lace rising tier upon tier, which made the wits about town declare the ladies " carried Bow steeple upon their heads, " of a sudden collapsed in Queen Anne's reign. It had shot up to a most extravagant height, " insomuch that the female part of our species were much taller than the men. We appeared," says the " Spectator,"[58] " as grasshoppers before them."[59]

In 1711, Anne forbade the entry of gold and silver lace,[60] of which the consumption had become most preposterous,[61] under pain of forfeiture and the fine of 100*l.* Ladies wore even cherry-coloured stays trimmed with the forbidden fabric.[62] The point of Spain had the preference over thread lace for state garments, heads and ruffles excepted ; and as late as 1763, when the Dowager Lady Effingham was robbed of her coronation robes, among the wonderful finery detailed there is no mention of thread lace.

The commerce of Flanders, notwithstanding the French taste, seemed now on a comfortable footing. " The Flanderkins, "writes the " British Merchant, " in 1713, " are gone off from wool, which we have got, to lace and linen. . . . We have learned better, I hope, by our unsuccessful attempt to prohibit the Flanders laces, which made the Flemings retaliate upon us, and lessened our

---

[55] " Letters of the Countess of Hartford to the Countess of Pomfret," 1740.

[56] " Memoirs of Lady R. Russell."

[57] " My high commode, my damask gown,
    My laced shoes of Spanish leather."
    D'Urfey, The Young Maid's Portion.

[58] No. 98, 1711.

[59] After fifteen years' discontinuance it shot up again. Swift, on meeting the Duchess of Grafton, dining at Sir Thomas Hanmer's, thus attired, declared she

" looked liked a mad woman."

[60] Statutes at large.

[61] In 1712, Mrs. Beale had stolen from her " a green silk knit waistcoat with gold and silver flowers all over it, and about 14 yards of gold and silver thick lace on it ;" while another lady was robbed of " a scarlet cloth coat so overlaid with the same lace, it might have been of any other colour."—*Malcolm's Anecdotes of the Manners and Customs of London in the Eighteenth Century.*

[62] " Post Boy," Nov. 15, 1709. Articles Lost.

exportation of woollen manufactures by several 100,000*l.* per annum." [63]

Men looked upon lace as a necessary article to their wives' equipment. Addison declares that when the china mania first came in, women exchanged their Flanders lace for punch-bowls and mandarins, thus picking their husbands' pockets, who is often purchasing a huge china vase when he fancies that he is buying a fine head for his wife.[64] Indeed, they could scarcely grumble, as a good wig cost from forty to fifty guineas—to say nothing of their own lace ties and ruffles. Only an old antiquary like Sir Thomas Clayton could note down in his accounts:—"Lace and fal-lalls,[65] and a large looking-glass to see her old ugly face in—frivolous expenses to please my proud lady."

---

[63] "A Discourse on Trade," by John Cary, merchant of Bristol, 1717.

Again : "What injury was done by the Act 9–10 Will. III. for the more effectual preventing of importation of foreign bone lace, doth sufficiently appear by the preamble to that made 10–12 of the same reign for repealing it three months after the prohibition of our woollen manufactures in Flanders (which was occasioned by it) should be taken off; but I don't understand it to be yet done, and it may prove an inevitable loss to the nation."

[64] "Lover," No. 10, 1714.

[65] The ornamental ribbons worn about the dress : "His dress has bows, and fine fallals."—*Evelyn.* Sometimes the term appears applied to the fontanges or commode. We read (1691) of "her three-storied Fladdal."

CHAPTER XXVI.

GEORGE I. AND II.

GEORGE I.

" Wisdom with periwigs, with cassocks grace,
Courage with swords, gentility with lace."
Connoisseur.

" Les fols donnent cours aux modes; les sages n'affectent pas de s'en écarter. Si
ridicule que puisse être certaine mode, il est encore plus ridicule de s'en écarter."
Alleaume.

THE accession of the house of Hanover brought but little change
either in the fashions or the fabrics. In 1717 the king published
an edict regarding the hawking of lace, but the world was too
much taken up with the old Pretender and the court of Saint-
Germain; the king, too, was often absent, preferring greatly his
German dominions.

We now hear a great deal of lace ruffles; they were worn long
and falling. Lord Bolingbroke, who enraged Queen Anne by his
untidy dress—" she supposed, forsooth, he would some day come
to court in his nightcap "—is described as having his cravat of
point lace, and his hands hidden by exaggerated ruffles of the
same material. In good old Jacobite times, these weeping ruffles
served as well to conceal notes— " poulets "—passed from one
wary politician to another, as they did the French sharpers to
juggle and cheat at cards.

Lace continued the mania of the day. " Since your fantastical
geers came in with wires, ribbons, and laces, and your furbelows
with three hundred yards in a gown and petticoat, there has not
been a good housewife in the nation," [1] writes an indignant dramatist. The lover was made to bribe the Abigail of his mistress

---

[1] " Tunbridge Wells," 1727.

with a piece of Flanders lace [2]—an offering not to be resisted. Lace appeared at baptisms,[3] at marriages, as well as at burials, of which more hereafter—even at the Old Bailey, where one Miss Margaret Caroline Rudd, a beauty of the day, tried for forgery, quite moved her jurors to tears, and nigh gained her acquittal by the taste of her elegantly laced stomacher, the lace robings of her dress, and single lace flounce, her long pendulous ruffles, hanging from the elbow, heard, fluttering in her agitation, by the court; but, in spite of these allurements, Margaret Caroline Rudd was hanged.

Every woman, writes Swift,[4] is

> " In choosing lace a critic nice,
> Knows to a groat the lowest price."

Together, they

> " Of caps and ruffles hold the grave debate,
> As of their lives they would decide the fate."

Again, he says :—

" And when you are among yourselves, how naturally, after the first compliments, do you entertain yourselves with the price and choice of lace, apply your hands to each other's lappets and ruffles, as if the whole business of your life and the public concern depended on the cut of your petticoats. " [5]

Even wise Mrs. Elizabeth Montague, who wrote epistles about the ancients, and, instead of going to a ball, sat at home and read

---

[2] In " The Recruiting Officer " (1781), Lucy the maid says: " Indeed, Madam, the last bribe I had from the Captain was only a small piece of Flanders lace for a cap." Melinda answers: " Ay, Flanders lace is a constant present from officers. . . . They every year bring over a cargo of lace, to cheat the king of his duty and his subjects of their honesty." Again, Silvio, in the bill of costs he sends in to the widow Zelinda, at the termination of his unsuccessful suit, makes a charge for " a piece of Flanders lace " to Mrs. Abigail, her woman. Addison, in " Guardian," No. 17, 1713.

[3] " In the next reign, George III. and Queen Charlotte often condescended to become sponsors to the children of the aristocracy. To one child their presence was fatal. In 1778 they ' stood' to the infant daughter of the last Duke and Duchess of Chandos. Cornwallis, Archbishop of Canterbury, officiated. The baby, overwhelmed by whole mountains of lace, lay in a dead faint. Her mother was so tender on the point of etiquette that she would not let the little incident trouble a ceremony at which a king and queen were about to endow her child with the names of Georgiana Charlotte. As Cornwallis gave back the infant to her nurse, he remarked that it was the quietest baby he had ever held. Poor victim of ceremony! It was not quite dead, but dying; in a few unconscious hours it calmly slept away."—*A Gossip on Royal Christenings, Cornhill Magazine*, April 1864.

[4] " Furniture of a Woman's Mind."
[5] " Dean Swift to a Young Lady."

Sophocles, exclaims to her sister—"Surely your heroic spirit will prefer a beau's hand in Brussels lace to a stubborn Scævola without an arm."

No young lady of the nineteenth century wears, or should wear, lace previous to her marriage. In the reign of George II. etiquette was different, for we find the Duchess of Portland presenting Mrs. Montague, then a girl, with a lace head and ruffles.

Wrathfully do the satirists of the day rail against the expense of

> " The powder, patches, and the pins,
> The ribbon, jewels, and the rings,
> The lace, the paint, and warlike things
> That make up all their magazines," [6]

and the consequent distress of the lace merchants, to whom ladies are indebted for thousands. After a drawing-room, in which the fair population appeared in "borrowed," i. e. unpaid, lace,[7] one of the chief lacemen became well-nigh bankrupt. Duns besieged the houses of the great :—

> " By mercers, lacemen, mantua-makers press'd ;
> But most for ready cash, for play distress'd,
> Where can she turn ?"[8]

The "Connoisseur," describing the reckless extravagance of one of these ladies, writes :—"The lady played till all her ready money was gone, staked her cap and lost it, afterwards, her handkerchief. He then staked both cap and handkerchief against her tucker, which, to his pique, she gained." When enumerating the various causes of suicide, he proposes "that an annual bill or report should be made out, giving the different causes which have led to the act." Among others, in his proposed "Bill of Suicide," he gives French claret, French lace, French cooks, &c.

The men, though scarcely coming up to the standard of Sir Courtly Nice,[9] who has all his bands and linen made in Holland and washed at Haarlem, were just as extravagant as the ladies.

---

[6] Cowley.

[7] 1731. "Simile for the Ladies, alluding to the laces worn at the last Birthday and not paid for."

" In Evening fair you may behold
  The Clouds are fringed with borrowed gold,

And this is many a lady's case
  Who flaunts about in borrowed lace."

[8] Jenyns, "The Modern Fine Lady."

[9] Crown, "Sir Courtly Nice, or It Cannot Be," a Comedy, 1731.

GEORGE II.

" ' How well this ribband's glass becomes your face,'
She cries in rapture ; ' then so sweet a lace !
How charmingly you look ! ' "
Lady M. W. Montagu, Town Eclogues.

For court and state occasions Brussels lace still held its sway.

In the reign of George II. we read how at the drawing-room of 1735 fine escalloped Brussels laced heads, triple ditto laced ruffles,[10] lappets hooked up with diamond solitaires, found favour. At the next the ladies wore heads dressed English, i. e. bows of fine Brussels lace of exceeding rich patterns, with the same amount of laced ruffles and lappets. Gold flounces were also worn.

Speaking of the passion for Brussels lace, Postlethwait indignantly observes :—" 'Tis but a few years since England expended upon foreign lace and linen not less than two millions yearly. As lace in particular is the manufacture of nuns, our British ladies may as well endow monasteries as wear Flanders lace, for these Popish nuns are maintained by Protestant contributions." [11]

Patriotism, it would appear, did come into vogue in the year 1736, when at the marriage of Frederick, Prince of Wales, the bride is described as wearing a night-dress of superb lace, the bridegroom a cap of similar material. All the lace worn by the court on this occasion is announced to have been of English manufacture, with the exception of that of the Duke of Marlborough, who appeared in point d'Espagne. The bride, however, does not profit by this high example, for shortly after we read, in the " Memoirs of Madame Palatine," of the secretary of Sir Luke Schaub being drugged at Paris by an impostor, and robbed of some money sent to defray the purchase of some French lace ruffles for the Princess of Wales.

It was of native-made lace, we may infer, Mrs. Delany writes in the same year :—" Thanks for your apron. Brussels nor Mechlin ever produced anything prettier."

---

[10] " 1748. Ruffles of twelve pounds a yard."—*Apology for Mrs. T. C. Philips,* 1748.

Lace, however, might be had at a more reasonable rate :—

" ' I have a fine lac'd suit of pinners,' says Mrs. Thomas, ' that was my great grandmother's ! that has been worn but twice these forty years, and my mother told me cost almost four pounds when it was new, and reaches down hither.' "— *Miss Lucy in Town, Fielding.*

[11] " Dictionary of Commerce," 1766.

It appears somewhat strange that patriotism, as regards native manufactures, should have received an impulse during the reign of that most uninteresting though gallant little monarch, the second George of Brunswick.[12]   But patriotism has its evils, for, writes an essayist, "some ladies now squander away all their money in fine laces, because it sets a great many poor people to work."[13]

Ten years previous to the death of King George II. was founded, with a view to correct the prevalent taste for foreign manufactures,[14] the Society of the Anti-Gallicans, who held their quarterly meetings, and distributed prizes for bone, point lace, and other articles of English manufacture.[15]

This society, which continued in great activity for many years, proved most beneficial to the lace-making trade.   It excited also a spirit of emulation among gentlewomen of the middle class, who were glad in the course of the year to add to a small income by making the finer kinds of needle-point, which, on account of their elaborate workmanship, could be produced only in foreign convents, or by persons whose maintenance did not entirely depend upon the work of their hands.

Towards the year 1756, certain changes in the fashion of the day now again mark the period, for—

"Dress still varying, most to form confined,
Shifts like the sands, the sport of every wind."

---

[12] He was a martinet about his own dress, for his biographer relates during the last illness of Queen Caroline (1737), though the king was "visibly affected," remembering he had to meet the foreign ministers next day, he gave particular directions to his pages "to see that new ruffles were sewn on his old shirt sleeves, whereby he might wear a decent air in the eyes of the representatives of foreign majesty."

[13] "By a list of linen furnished to the Princesses Louisa and Mary, we find their night-dresses were trimmed with lace at 10s. per yard, and while their Royal Highnesses were in bibs, they had six suits of broad lace for aprons at from 50l. to 60l. each suit."—*Corr. of the Countess of Suffolk, Lady of the Bedchamber to Queen Caroline.*

Observe also the lace-trimmed aprons, ruffles, tuckers, &c., in the pretty picture of the family of Frederick, Prince of Wales, at Hampton Court Palace.

[14] The laws regarding the introduction of lace during this reign continued much the same until 1749, when the royal assent was given to an act preventing the importation or wear of gold, silver, and thread lace manufactured in foreign parts.

[15] In the meeting of Nov. 10, 1752, at the "Crown, behind the Royal Exchange," the Hon. Edward Vernon, grand president, in the chair, it was agreed that the following premiums should be awarded: "For the best pair of men's needlework ruffles, to be produced to the committee in the first week of May next, five guineas; to the second, three guineas; to the third, two guineas   And for the best pair of English bone lace for ladies' lappets, to be produced to the committee in August next, fifteen guineas; to the second, ten guineas; to the third, five guineas."—*Gentleman's Magazine.*

" Long lappets, the horse-shoe cap, the Brussels head, and the prudish mob pinned under the chin, have all had their day," says the " Connoisseur," in 1754. Now we have first mention of lace cardinals ; trollopies or slammerkins [16] come in at the same period, with treble ruffles to the cuffs ; writers talk, too, of a " gentle dame in blonde lace," blonde being as yet a newly introduced manufacture.

Though history may only be all false,[17] as Sir Robert Walpole said to that " cynic in lace ruffles," his son Horace, yet the newspapers are to be depended upon for the fashion of the day, or, as Lady Mary would say, " for what new whim adorns the ruffle." [18]

The lace apron,[19] worn since the days of Queen Elizabeth, continued to hold its own till the end of the eighteenth century, though some considered it an appendage scarcely consistent with the dignity of polite society. The anecdote of Beau Nash, who held these articles in the strongest aversion, has been often related. " He absolutely excluded," says his biographer, " all who ventured to appear at the Assembly Room, at Bath, so attired. I have known him at a ball night strip the Duchess of Queensberry, and throw her apron on one of the hinder benches among the ladies' women, observing that none but Abigails appeared in white aprons ; though that apron was of the costliest point, and cost two hundred guineas." [20]

George II. did his best to promote the fabrics of his country, but at this period smuggling increased with fearful rapidity. It was a war to the knife between the revenue officer and society at large : all classes combined, town ladies of high degree, with waiting-maids and the common sailor, to avoid the obnoxious duties and cheat the government. To this subject we devote the following chapter.

---

[16] Slammerkin, a sort of loose dress. This ugly word, in course of time, was used as an adjective, to signify untidy. The author recollects to have heard it so applied in her youth. Fortunately it is now obsolete.

[17] " Don't read history to me, for that I know to be false," said Sir R. Walpole to his son Horace, when he offered to read to him in his last illness.

[18] Lady M. W. Montagu, " Letter to Lord Harvey on the King's Birthday."

[19] " The working apron, too, from France,
With all its trim appurtenance."
Mundus Muliebris.

[20] Goldsmith, " Life of Richard Nash, of Bath," London, 1762.

CHAPTER XXVII.

SMUGGLING.

" May that mistaken taste be starv'd to reason,
That does not think French fashions—English treason.
Souse their cook's talent, and cut short their tailors ;
Wear your own lace; eat beef like Vernon's sailors."
Aaron Hill, 1754.

WE have had occasional mention of this kindly looked upon offence, in the carrying out of which many a reckless seaman paid the penalty of his life in the latter part of the eighteenth century.

From 1700 downwards, though the edicts prohibiting the entry of Flanders lace were repealed, the points of France, Spain, and Venice, with other fabrics of note, were still excluded from the ports. (Coloured Plate XIV.) " England," writes Anderson,[1] " brings home in a smuggling way from France much fine lace and other prohibited fopperies." Prohibition went for nothing ; foreign lace ladies would have, and if they could not smuggle it themselves, the smuggler brought it to them. It was not till 1751 that the customs appear to have used undue severity as regards the entries, prying into people's houses, and exercising a surveillance of so strict a nature as to render the chance to evade their watchfulness a very madness on the part of all degrees. In short, there was not a female within ten miles of a seaport, writes an essayist, that was in possession of a Mechlin lace cap or pinner but they examined her title to it.

Lord Chesterfield, whose opinion, that " dress is a very silly thing, but it is much more silly not to be dressed according to your station," was more than acted up to, referring to the strictness of the customs, writes to his son in 1751, when coming over on a

---

[1] 1764.

Plate XIV.

short visit : "Bring only two or three of your laced shirts, and the rest plain ones."

The revenue officers made frequent visits to the tailors' shops and confiscated whatever articles they found of foreign manufacture.

On the 19th January 1752, a considerable quantity of foreign lace, gold and silver, seized at a tailor's, who paid the penalty of 100l., was publicly burnt.[2]

George III., who really from his coming to the throne endeavoured to protect English manufactures, ordered, in 1764, all the stuffs and laces worn at the marriage of his sister, the Princess Augusta, to the Duke of Brunswick, to be of English make. To this decree the nobility paid little attention. Three days previous to the marriage, a descent was made by the customs on the court milliner of the day, and nearly the whole of the clothes, silver, gold stuffs and lace, carried off, to the dismay of the modiste, as well as of the ladies thus deprived of their finery. The disgusted French milliner retired with a fortune of 11,000l. to Versailles, where she purchased a villa, which, in base ingratitude to the English court, she called "La Folie des Dames Anglaises." In May of the same year, three wedding garments, together with a large seizure of French lace, weighing nearly 100 lbs., were burnt at Mr. Coxe's refinery, conformably to the act of parliament. The following birthday, warned by the foregoing mischances, the nobility appeared in clothes and laces entirely of British manufacture.

Every paper tells how lace and ruffles of great value, sold on the previous day, had been seized in a hackney coach, between St. Paul's and Covent Garden ; how a lady of rank was stopped in her chair, and relieved of French lace to a large amount ; or how a poor woman, carelessly picking a quartern loaf as she walked along, was arrested, and the loaf found to contain 200l. worth of lace. Even ladies, when walking, had their black lace mittens cut off their hands, the officers supposing them to be of French manufacture; and lastly, a Turk's turban, of most Mameluke dimensions, was found, containing a stuffing of 90l. worth of lace. Books, bottles, babies, false-bottomed boxes, umbrellas, daily poured out their treasures to the lynx-eyed officers.

In May 1765, the lace-makers joined the procession of the silk-workers of Spitalfields to Westminster, bearing flags and banners,

---

[2] "Gentleman's Magazine."

to which were attached long floating pieces of French lace, demanding of the Lords redress, and the total exclusion of foreign goods. On receiving an answer that it was too late, they must wait till next session, the assemblage declared they would not be put off by promises ; they broke the Duke of Bedford's palings on their way home, and threatened to burn the premises of Mr. Carr, an obnoxious draper. At the next levée they once more assembled before St. James's, but, finding the dresses of the nobility to be all of right English stuff, retired satisfied, without further clamour.

The papers of the year 1764 teem with accounts of seizures made by the customs. Among the confiscated effects of a person of the highest quality are enumerated: " 16 black à-la-mode cloaks, trimmed with lace; 44 French lace caps; 11 black laced handkerchiefs; 6 lace hats; 6 ditto aprons; 10 pairs of ruffles; 6 pairs of ladies' blonde ditto, and 25 gentlemen's. " Eleven yards of edging and 6 pairs of ruffles are extracted from the pocket of the footman. Everybody smuggled. A gentleman attached to the Spanish embassy is unloaded of 36 dozen shirts, with fine Dresden ruffles and jabots, and endless lace in pieces for ladies' wear. These articles had escaped the vigilance of the officers at Dover, but were seized on his arrival by the coach at Southwark. Though prime ministers in those days accepted bribes, the custom-house officers seem to have done their duty.[3]

When the body of his grace the Duke of Devonshire was brought over from France, where he died, the officers, to the anger of his servants, not content with opening and searching the coffin, poked the corpse with a stick to ascertain if it was a real body ; but the trick of smuggling in coffins was too old to be attempted. Forty years before, when a deceased clergyman was conveyed from the Low Countries for interment, the body of the corpse was found to have disappeared, and to have been replaced by Flanders lace of immense value—the head and hands and feet alone remaining. This discovery did not, however, prevent the high sheriff of Westminister from running—and that successfully—6000l. worth of French lace in the coffin of Bishop

---

[3] " 1767. An officer of the customs seized nearly 400l. worth of Flanders lace, artfully concealed in the hollow of a ship's buoy, on board a French trader, lying off Iron Gate."—*Annual Register.*

" 1772. 27,000 ells of French (Blois?) lace were seized in the port of Leigh alone."—*Gentleman's Magazine.*

Atterbury,[4] when his body was brought over from Calais for interment.

One of the greatest frauds on record against the custom-house authorities, however, was perpetrated by a man named John Wilkes, who, on one occasion, as he afterwards boasted, when apprehended on another charge, brought from Calais to Dover 1000*l.* worth of lace wrapped round the limbs of a corpse! A woman for years made a trade of taking forty or fifty females across from Dover to Calais, who on their return journey wore upon their heads bonnets trimmed with the most elaborate and valuable lace. Of course the custom-house officers could not legally stop her, and after a time she retired upon a fortune. All were not equally successful, however, for in the reign of George II. we read about one Ann Warner being sentenced to ten years' penal servitude for smuggling laces, hidden in the insides of Normandy poultry, which she professed to be bringing to the English market.

Towards the close of the French war, in the present century, smuggling of lace again became more rife than ever. It was in vain the authorities stopped the travelling carriages on their road from seaport towns to London, rifled the baggage of the unfortunate passengers by the mail at Rochester and Canterbury; they were generally outwitted, though spies in the pay of the customs were ever on the watch.

The writer has in her possession a Brussels veil of great beauty, which narrowly escaped seizure. It belonged to a lady who was in the habit of accompanying her husband, for many years member for one of the Cinque Ports. The day after the election she was about to leave for London, somewhat nervous as to the fate of a Brussels veil she had purchased of a smuggler for a hundred guineas; when, at a dinner party, it was announced that Lady Ellenborough, wife of the Lord Chief Justice, had been stopped near Dover, and a large quantity of valuable lace seized concealed in the lining of her carriage. Dismayed at the news, the lady imparted her trouble to a gentleman at her side, who immediately offered to take charge of the lace and convey it to London, remarking that "no one would suspect him, as he was a bachelor." Turning round suddenly, she observed one of the hired waiters to

---

[4] The turbulent bishop of Rochester, who was arraigned for his Jacobite intrigues, and died in exile at Paris, 1731.

smile, and at once settling him to be a spy, she loudly accepted the offer; but that night, before going to bed, secretly caused the veil to be sewn up in the waistcoat of the newly elected M.P., in such a manner that it filled the hollow of his back. Next morning they started, and reached London in safety, while her friend, who remained two days later, was stopped, and underwent a rigorous but unsuccessful examination from the custom-house officers.

The free trade principles of the nineteenth century have put a more effectual stop to smuggling than all the activity of revenue officers, spies, and informers, or even laws framed for the punishment of the offenders.

CHAPTER XXVIII.

GEORGE III.

" In clothes, cheap handsomeness doth bear the bell,
Wisdome's a trimmer thing than shop e'er gave.
Say not then, This with that lace will do well;
But, This with my discretion will be brave.
Much curiousnesse is a perpetual wooing,
Nothing with labour, fully long a doing."
Herbert, The Church Porch.

In 1760 commences the reign of George III. The king was patriotic, and did his best to encourage the fabrics of his country.

From the year 1761, various acts were passed for the benefit of the lace-makers : the last, that of 1806, " increases the duties on foreign laces." [1]

Queen Charlotte, on her first landing in England, wore, in compliment to the subjects of her royal consort, a fly cap richly trimmed with lappets of British lace, and a dress of similar manufacture.

The Englishman, however, regardless of the Anti-Gallicans, preferred his " Macklin " and his Brussels to all the finest productions of Devonshire or Newport Pagnel.

Ruffles,[2] according to the fashion of Tavistock Street and St. James's, in May 1773, still continued long, dipped in the sauce alike by clown and cavalier.[3]

"The beau,
A critic styled in point of dress,
Harangues on fashion, point, and lace."

A man was known by his " points ; he collected lace, as, in these more athletic days, a gentleman prides himself on his

---

[1] If imported in smaller quantities than twelve yards, the duty imposed was 2*l.* per yard.

[2] " Let the ruffle grace his hand,
Ruffle, pride of Gallic land."
The Beau, 1755.

[3] " And dip your wristbands
(For cuffs you've none) as comely in the sauce
As any courtier." *Beaumont and Fletcher.*

pointers or his horses. We read in the journals of the time how on the day after Lord George Gordon's riots, a report ran through London that the Earl of Effingham, having joined the rioters, had been mortally wounded, and his body thrown into the Thames. He had been recognised, folks declared, by his point lace ruffles.[4]

Mr. Damer, less known than his wife, the talented sculptor and friend of Horace Walpole, appeared three times a day in a new suit, and at his death [5] left a wardrobe which sold for 15,000*l.*[6] Well might have been said of him—

> " We sacrifice to dress, till household joys
>   And comforts cease. Dress drains our cellars dry,
>   And keeps our larder bare ; puts out our fires,
>   And introduces hunger, frost, and woe,
>   Where peace and hospitality might reign."[7]

There was " no difference between the nobleman and city 'prentice, except that the latter was sometimes the greater beau," writes the " Female Spectator." [8]

> " His hands must be covered with fine Brussels lace." [9]

Our painters of the last century loved to adorn their portraits with the finest productions of Venice and Flanders ; modern artists consider such decorations as far too much trouble. " Over the chimney-piece," writes one of the essayists, describing a citizen's country box, " was my friend's portrait, which was drawn bolt upright in a full-bottomed periwig, a laced cravat, with the fringed ends appearing through the button-hole (Steinkirk fashion). Indeed, one would almost wonder how and where people managed to afford so rich a selection of laces in their days, did it not call to mind the demand of the Vicaress of Wakefield ' to have as many pearls and diamonds put into her picture as could be given for the money.' "

Ruffles were equally worn by the ladies : —[10]

> " Frizzle your elbows with ruffles sixteen :
>   Furl off your lawn apron with flounces in rows." [11]

---

[4] He had retired to the country to be out of the way.

[5] August 1776.

[6] The wardrobe of George IV. was estimated at the same sum.

[7] Cowper.

[8] 1757.

[9] " Monsieur à la Mode," 1753.

[10] " Let of ruffles many a row
     Guard your elbows white as snow."
                    The Belle, 1755.
" Gone to a lady of distinction with a Brussels head and ruffles."
                    The Fool of Quality, 1766.

[11] " Receipt for Modern Dress," 1753.

Indeed, if we may judge by the intellectual conversation over-heard and accurately noted down by Miss Burney,[12] at Miss Monckton's (Lady Cork) party, court ruffles were inconvenient to wear :—

" ' You can't think how I am encumbered with these nasty ruffles,' said Mrs. Hampden.

" ' And I dined in them,' says the other.   ' Only think ! '

" ' Oh ! ' answered Mrs. Hampden, ' it really puts me out of spirits.' "

Both ladies were dressed for a party at Cumberland House, and ill at ease in the costume prescribed by etiquette.   If this con-versation was considered worth noting down, we may be excused for repeating it.

Our history of English lace is now drawing to a close ; but before quitting the subject, we must, however, make some allusion to the custom prevalent here, as in all countries, of using lace as a decoration to grave-clothes.   In the chapter devoted to Greece, we have mentioned how much lace is still taken from the tombs of the Ionian Islands, washed, mended, or, more often, as a proof of its authenticity, sold in a most disgusting state to the purchaser. The custom was prevalent at Malta, as the lines of the dramatist testify :—

> " In her best habit, as the custom is,
> You know, in Malta, with all ceremonies
> She's buried in the family monument,
> I' the temple of St. John." [13]

At Palermo you may see the mummies thus adorned in the celebrated catacombs of the Capuchin convent.[14]

In Denmark,[15] Sweden, and the north of Europe,[16] the custom was general.   The mass of lace in the tomb of the once fair Aurora Königsmarck, at Quedlinburg, would in itself be a fortune.   She sleeps clad in the richest point d'Angleterre, Malines, and guipure.

---

[12] " Recollections of Madame d'Ar-blay."

[13] Beaumont and Fletcher, " The Knight of Malta."

[14] In coffins with glass tops.   Some of them date from 1700.

[15] In the vault of the Schleswig-Hol-stein family, at Sonderburg.

[16] In the church of Revel lies the Duc de Croÿ, a general of Charles XII., ar-rayed in full costume, with a rich flowing tie of fine guipure; not that he was ever interred—his body had been seized by his creditors for debt, and there it still remains.

The author of " Letters from a Lady in Russia " (1775), describing the funeral of a daughter of Prince Menzikoff, states she was dressed in a night-gown of silver tissue, on her head a fine laced mob, and a coronet; round her forehead, a ribbon embroidered with her name and age, &c.

Setting aside the jewels which still glitter around her parchment form, no daughter of Pharaoh was ever so richly swathed.[17]

In Spain, it is related as the privilege of a grandee : all people of a lower rank are interred in the habit of some religious order.[18]

Taking the grave-clothes of St. Cuthbert as an example, we believe the same custom to have prevailed in England from the earliest times.[19]

Mrs. Oldfield, the celebrated actress, who died in 1730, caused herself to be thus interred. The lines of Pope have long since immortalised the story :—

> " Odious ! in woollen ! 'twould a saint provoke !
> (Were the last words that poor Narcissa spoke.)
> No, let a charming chintz and Brussels lace
> Wrap my cold limbs, and shade my lifeless face ;
> One would not, sure, be frightful when one's dead—
> And—Betty—give this cheek a little red."

" She was laid in her coffin," says her maid, " in a very fine Brussels lace head, a Holland shift with a tucker of double ruffles, and a pair of new kid gloves." Previous to her interment in Westminster Abbey, she lay in state in the Jerusalem Chamber.[20] For

---

[17] Alluding to this custom of interring ladies of rank in full dress, Madame de Sévigné writes to her daughter :—" Mon Dieu, ma chère enfant, que vos femmes sont sottes, vivantes et mortes ! Vous me faites horreur de cette fontange ; quelle profanation ! cela sent le paganisme, ho ! cela me dégoûteroit bien de mourir en Provence ; il faudroit que du moins je fusse assuré qu'on ne m'iroit pas chercher une coëffeuse en même temps qu'un plombier. Ah ! vraiment ! fi ! ne parlez plus de cela."—*Lettre* 627. Paris, 13 Dec. 1688.

[18] Laborde, " Itin. de l'Espagne." Again, the Duc de Luynes says : " The Curé of St. Sulpice related to me the fashion in which the Duke of Alva, who died in Paris in 1739, was by his own will interred. A shirt of the finest Holland, trimmed with new point lace, the finest to be had for money ; a new coat of Vardez cloth, embroidered in silver ; a new wig ; his cane on the right, his sword on the left of his coffin."—*Mémoires.*

[19] That grave-clothes were lace-trimmed we infer by the following strange announcement in the " London Gazette "

for August 12 to 15, 1678 :—" Whereas decent and fashionable lace shifts and Dressings for the dead, made of woollen, have been presented to his Majesty by Amy Potter, widow (the first that put the making of such things in practice), and his Majesty well liking the same, hath upon her humble Petition, been graciously pleased to give her leave to insert this advertisement, that it may be known she now wholly applies herself in making both lace and plain of all sorts, at reasonable prices, and lives in Crane Court in the Old Change, near St. Paul's Church Yard." Again, in November of the same year, we find another advertisement :—" His Majesty, to increase the woollen manufacture and to encourage obedience to the late act for burying in woollen, has granted to Amy Potter the sole privilege of making all sorts of woollen laces for the decent burial of the dead or otherwise, for fourteen years, being the first inventor thereof."

[20] Betterton's " History of the English Stage." Her kindness to the poet Savage is well known.

Mrs. Oldfield in her lifetime was a great judge of lace, and treasured a statuette of the Earl of Strafford, finely carved in ivory by Grinling Gibbons, more, it is supposed, for the beauty of its lace Vandyke collar [21] than any other sentiment.

In 1763, another instance is recorded in the " London Magazine," of a young lady buried in her wedding clothes, point lace tucker, handkerchief, ruffles, and apron; also, a fine point lappet head. From this period, we happily hear no more of such extravagances.

Passing from interments and shrouds to more lively matters we must quote the opinion of that Colossus of the last century, Dr. Johnson, who, instead of sticking to his Dictionary, was too apt to talk on matters of taste and art, of which he was no competent judge. " A Brussels trimming," declaims he to Mrs. Piozzi, " is like bread sauce; it takes away the glow of colour from the gown, and gives you nothing instead of it: but sauce was invented to heighten the flavour of our food, and trimming is an ornament to the manteau or it is nothing." [22] A man whose culinary ideas did not soar higher than bread sauce could scarcely pronounce on the relative effect and beauty of point lace.

If England had leant towards the products of France, in 1788, an Anglomania ran riot at Paris. Ladies wore a cap of mixed lace, English and French, which they styled the " Union of France and England." On the appearance of the French Revolution, the classic style of dress—its India muslins and transparent gauzes—caused the ancient points to fall into neglect. From this time dates the decline of the lace manufacture throughout Europe.

Point still appeared at court and on state occasions, such as on the marriage of the Princess Caroline of Wales, 1795, but as an article of daily use, it gradually disappeared from the wardrobes of all classes. A scrupulous feeling also arose in ladies' minds as to the propriety of wearing articles of so costly a nature, forgetting how many thousands of women gained a livelihood by its manufacture. Mrs. Hannah More, among the first, in her " Cœlebs in Search of a Wife," alludes to the frivolity of the taste, when the little child exclaimed " at the beautiful lace with which the frock of another was trimmed, and which she was sure her mamma had

[21] This seems to have been a spécialité of Gibbons; for we find among the treasures of Strawberry Hill: " A beautiful cravat, in imitation of lace, carved by Gibbons, very masterly."— *Hist. and Antiquities of Twickenham.* London, 1797.

[22] Mrs. Piozzi's " Memoirs.'

given her for being good," remarks, " A profitable and, doubtless,
lasting and inseparable association was thus formed in the child's
mind between lace and goodness."

Whether in consequence of the French Revolution, or from
the caprice of fashion, " real " lace—worse off than the passements
and points of 1634, when in revolt—now underwent the most
degrading vicissitudes. Indeed, so thoroughly was the taste for
lace at this epoch gone by that in many families collections of
great value were, at the death of their respective owners, handed
over as rubbish to the waiting-maid.[23] Many ladies recollect in
their youth to have tricked out their dolls in the finest Alençon
point, which now would sell at a price far beyond their purses.
Among the few who, in England, unseduced by frippery blonde,
never neglected to preserve their collections entire, was her late
royal highness the Duchess of Gloucester, whose lace was
esteemed among the most magnificent in Europe.

When the taste of the age again turned towards the rich
productions of the preceding centuries, much lace, both black and
white, was found in the country farm-houses, preserved as remem-
brances of deceased patrons by old family dependents. Sometimes
the hoard had been forgotten, and was again routed out from old
wardrobes and chests, where it had lain unheeded for years.
Much was recovered from theatric wardrobes and the masquerade
shops, and the church, no longer in its temporal glory, both in
Italy, Spain, and Germany, gladly parted with what, to them, was
of small value, compared with the high price given for it by
amateurs. In Italy perhaps the fine fabrics of Milan, Genoa, and
Venice, had fared best, from the custom which prevailed of sewing
up family lace in rolls of linen to insure its preservation.

After years of neglect, lace became a "mania." In England
the literary ladies were the first to take it up. Sydney Lady
Morgan and Lady Stepney quarrelled weekly on the respective

---

[23] A lady, who had very fine old lace,
bequeathed her "wardrobe and lace" to
some young friends, who, going after her
death to take possession of their legacy,
were surprised to find nothing but new
lace. On inquiring of the old faithful
Scotch servant what had become of the
old needle points, she said: "Deed it's
aw there, 'cept a wheen auld Dudds,
black and ragged, I flinged on the fire."

Another collection of old lace met with
an equally melancholy fate. The maid,
not liking to give it over to the legatees in
its coffee-coloured hue, sewed it carefully
together, and put it in a strong soap lye
on the fire, to simmer all night. When
she took it out in the morning, it was
reduced to a jelly. Medea's caldron had
not been more effectual!

value and richness of their points. The former at one time commenced a history of lace, though what was the ultimate fate of the MS. the author is unable to state. The Countess of Blessington, at her death, left several chests filled with the finest antique lace of all descriptions.

The "dames du grande monde," both in England and France, now began to wear lace. But, strange as it may seem, never at any period did they appear to so little advantage as during the counter-revolution of the lace period. Lace was the fashion, and wear it somehow they would; though that somehow often gave them an appearance, as the French say, "du dernier ridicule," simply from an ignorance displayed in the manner of arranging it. That lace was old seemed sufficient to satisfy all parties. They covered their dresses with odds and ends of all fabrics, without attention either to date or texture. We recollect one English lady appearing at a ball given by the French embassy at Rome, boasting that she wore on the tablier of her dress every description of lace, from point coupé, of the sixteenth, to Alençon, of the eighteenth century. H. R. H. the Count of Syracuse was accustomed to say : "The English ladies buy a scrap of lace as a souvenir of every town they pass through, till they reach Naples, they sew it on their dresses, and make one grand toilette of the whole to honour our first ball at the Academia Nobile."

The taste for lace has again become universal, and the quality now produced renders it within the reach of all classes of society ; and though by some the taste may be condemned, it gives employment to thousands and ten thousands of women, who find it more profitable and better adapted to their strength than the field labour which forms the occupation of the women in agricultural districts. To these last, in a general point of view, the lace-maker of our southern counties, who works at home in her own cottage, is superior, both in education, refinement, and morality :—

> " Here the needle plies its busy task ;
> The pattern grows, the well-depicted flower,
> Wrought patiently into the snowy lawn,
> Unfolds its bosom ; buds, and leaves, and sprigs,
> And curling tendrils, gracefully dispos'd,
> Follow the nimble fingers of the fair—
> A wreath that cannot fade, of flowers that blow
> With most success when all besides decay." [24]

---

[24] Cowper, "The Winter Evening."

CHAPTER XXIX.

THE LACE MANUFACTURES OF ENGLAND.

> " Yon cottager, who weaves at her own door,
>   Pillow and bobbins all her little store;
>   Content though mean, and cheerful if not gay,
>   Shuffling her threads about the livelong day :
>   Just earns a scanty pittance, and at night
>   Lies down secure, her heart and pocket light."
>
> Cowper.

THE bone lace manufactures of England in the sixteenth and seventeenth centuries appear to have extended over a much wider area than they occupy in the present day. From Cambridge to the adjacent counties of Northampton and Hertfordshire, by Buckinghamshire, Bedfordshire, and Oxfordshire, the trade spread over the southern counties of Wiltshire, Somersetshire,[1] Hampshire, and Dorset, to the more secluded valleys of Devon—the county which still sustains the ancient reputation of " English point "—terminating at Launceston, on the Cornish coast.

Various offsets from these fabrics were established in Wales.[2] Ripon,[3] an isolated manufactory, represented the lace industry of

---

[1] " Wells, bone lace and knitting stockings."—*Anderson.*

[2] " Launceston, where are two schools for forty-eight children of both sexes. The girls are taught to read, sew, and make bone lace, and they are to have their earnings for encouragement."—*Magna Britannia,* 1720.

Welsh lace was made at Swansea, Pont-Ardawe, Llanwrtyd, Dufynock, and Brecon, but never of any beauty, some not unlike a coarse Valenciennes. " It was much made and worn," said an aged Wesleyan lady, " by our ' connexion,' and as a child I had all my frocks and pinafores trimmed with it. It was made in the cottages; each lace-maker had her own pattern, and carried it out for sale in the country."

[3] At what period, and by whom, the lace manufactory of Ripon was founded, we have been unable to ascertain. It was probably a relic of conventual days, which, after having followed the fashion of each time, has now gradually died out. Twenty years since, broad trolly laces of French design and fair workmanship were fabricated in the old cathedral city; where, in the poorer localities near the Bond and Blossomgate, young women might be seen working their intricate patterns, with pillows, bobbins, and pins. Now, one old woman alone, says our informant, sustains the memory of the

York; while the dependent islands of Man,[4] Wight,[5] and Jersey,[6] may be supposed to have derived their learning from the smugglers who frequented their coast, rather than from the teaching of the Protestant refugees[7] who sought an asylum on the peaceful shores of Britain.

craft, her produce a lace of a small lozenge-shaped pattern (Fig. 118), that earliest of all designs, and a narrow edging, known in local parlance by the name of " fourpenny spot."

Fig. 118.

Ripon.

[4] Till its annexation to the crown, the Isle of Man was the great smuggling depot for French laces. The traders then removed *en masse* to the Channel Isles, there to carry on their traffic. An idiot called " Peg the Fly," in Castletown, was some years since seen working at her pillow, on a summer's evening, the last lace-maker of the island. Isle of Man lace was a simple Valenciennes edging.

[5] The so-called lace of the Isle of Wight has been honoured by the patronage of Her Majesty. The Princess Royal, reports the " Illustrated News " of May 1856, at the drawing-room, on her first presentation, wore a dress of Newport lace, her train trimmed with the same.

The weariness of incarceration, when at Carisbrook, did not bring on the king any distaste for rich apparel. Among the charges of 1648, Sept. and Nov., we find a sum of nigh 800*l.* for suits and cloaks of black brocade tabby, black unshorn velvet, and black satin, all lined with plush and trimmed with rich bone lace.

[6] Lace-making was never the staple manufacture of the Channel Islands; stockings and garments of knitted wool afforded a livelihood to the natives. We have early mention of these articles in the inventories of James V. of Scotland, and of Mary Stuart; also in those of Henry VIII. and Queen Elizabeth, in which last we find (Gt. Ward. Acc. 28 & 29) the charge of 20*s.* for a pair of " Caligarum nexat' de factura Garneseie." the upper part and " lez clocks " worked in silk. At the beginning of the present century, when the island was inundated with French refugees, lace-making was introduced, with much success, into the poor-house of St. Heliers. It formed the favourite occupation of the ladies of the island, some of whom still retain the patterns and pillows of their mothers. Of late years, many of the old raised points have been imitated in " Jersey crochet work."

[7] The Puritans again, on their part, transferred the fabric to the other side of the Atlantic, where, says a writer of the last century, " very much fine lace was made in Long Island by the Protestant settlers."

Many of these fabrics now belong to the past, consigned to oblivion even in the very counties where they once flourished. In describing, therefore, the lace manufactures of the United Kingdom, we shall confine ourselves to those which still remain, alluding only slightly to such as were once of note, and of which the existence is confirmed by the testimony of contemporary writers.

The " women of the mystery of thread-working " would appear to have made lace in London,[8] and of their complaints and grievances our public records bear goodly evidence. Of the products of their needle we know little or nothing.

Various Flemings and Burgundians established themselves in the City ; and though the emigrants, for the most part, betook themselves to the adjoining counties, the craft, till the end of the eighteenth century, may be said to have held fair commerce in the capital.

The London fabric can scarcely be looked upon as a staple trade in itself, mixed up as it was with lace-cleaning and lace-washing— an occupation first established by the ejected nuns.[9] Much point, too, was made by poor gentlewomen, as the records of the Anti-Gallican Society testify. "A strange infatuation," says a writer of the last century, "prevailed in the capital for many years, among the class called demi-fashionables, of sending their daughters to convents in France for education, if that could be so termed which amounted to a learning to work in lace. The Revolution, however, put an end to this practice." It is owing to this French education that the fine needle points were so extensively made in England ; though this occupation, however, did not seem to belong to any one county in particular ; for the reader who runs his eye over the proceedings of the Anti-Gallican Society will find prizes to have been awarded to gentlewomen from all parts—from the town of Leominster in Herefordshire to Broughton in Leicestershire, or Stourton in Gloucester.[10] Needle point, in contradistinction to bone lace, was an occupation confined to no special locality. (Coloured Plate XV.)

In 1764, the attention of the nobility seems to have been first directed towards the employment of the indigent poor, and,

---

[8] See p. 252.
[9] See p. 259.
[10] In 1753, prizes varying from two to five guineas were awarded for fourteen pairs of curious needlework point ruffles.

Plate XV.

English needle-made lace.   Late eighteenth century.

indeed, the better classes in the metropolis, in the making of bone lace and point; and in 1775, sanctioned by the patronage of H. M. Queen Charlotte, the princesses, the Princess Amelia, and various members of the aristocracy, an institution was formed in Marylebone Lane, and also in James Street, Westminster, "for employing the female infants of the poor in the blonde and black silk lacemaking and thread laces." More than 300 girls attended the school. "They gave," says the "Annual Register," "such a proof of their capacity that many who had not been there more than six months carried home to their parents from 5s. to 7s. a month, with expectation of getting more as they improve."

From this time we hear no more of the making of lace, either point or bone, in the metropolis.

CHAPTER XXX.

BEDFORDSHIRE, BUCKINGHAMSHIRE, AND NORTHAMPTONSHIRE.

BEDFORDSHIRE.

> " He wears a stuff whose thread is coarse and round,
> But trimm'd with curious lace."
>
> *Herbert.*

IT would be a difficult matter now to determine when and by whom lace-making was first introduced into the counties of Bedfordshire and Buckingham. Authors, for the most part, have been glad to assign its introduction to the Flemings,[1] a nation to whose successive emigrations England owes much of her manufacturing greatness.

On the other hand, certain traditions handed down in the county villages of a good queen who protected their craft, the annual festival of the workers—in the palmy days of the trade a matter of great moment—combined with the residence of that unhappy queen, for the space of two years, at her jointure manor of Ampthill,[2] lead us rather to infer that the art of lace-working, as it then existed, was first imparted to the peasantry of Bedfordshire, as a means of subsistence, through the charity of Queen Katherine of Aragon. In our chapter devoted to needlework we have already alluded to the proficiency of this queen in all arts connected with the needle, to the "trials of needlework" established by her mother, Queen Isabella, at which she, as a girl, had

---

[1] Who fled from the Alva persecutions, and settled, in 1568, first at Cranfield, in Bedfordshire, then at Buckingham, Stoney Stratford, and Newport Pagnel; whence the manufacture extended gradually over Oxford, Northampton, and Cambridge. Many Flemish names are still to be found in the villages of Bedfordshire.

[2] She retired to Ampthill early in 1531, while her appeal to Rome was pending, and remained there till the summer of 1533.

assisted. It is related, also, that during her sojourn at Ampthill " she passed her time, when not at her devotions, with her gentle-women, working with her own hands something wrought in needlework, costly and artificially, which she intended for the honour of God to bestow on some of the churches." [3]

" The country people," continues her contemporary, " began to love her exceedingly. They visited her out of pure respect, and she received the tokens of regard they daily showed her most sweetly and graciously." The love borne by the peasantry to the queen, the sympathy shown to her in her days of trouble and disgrace, most likely met with its reward; and we believe Katherine to have taught them an art which, aided, no doubt, by the later introduction of the pillow and the improvements of the refugees, has now, for the space of nigh three centuries, been the staple employment of the female population of Bedfordshire and the adjoining counties.[4] To this very day—though, like all such festivals in the present utilitarian age, gradually dying out, the lace-makers still hold " Cattern's day,"[5] the 25th November, as the holiday of their craft, kept, they say, " in memory of good Queen Katherine, who, when the trade was dull, burnt all her lace and ordered new to be made. The ladies of the court followed her example, and the fabric once more revived." " Ainsi s'écrit l'histoire," as the French say; and this garbled version may rest on as much foundation as most of the folk-lore current throughout the provinces.

Speaking of Bedfordshire, Defoe writes: " Thro' the whole south part of this country, as far as the borders of Buckingham-shire and Hertfordshire, the people are taken up with the manu-facture of bone lace, in which they are wonderfully exercised and improved within these few years past," [6]—probably since the

---

[3] Dr. Nicolas Harpsfield. Douay, 1622. (In Latin.)

Again we read that at Kimbolton " she plied her needle, drank her potions, and told her beads."—*Duke of Manchester, Kimbolton Papers.*

[4] Queen Katherine died 1536.

[5] A lady from Ampthill writes : " The feast of St. Katherine is no longer kept. In the palmy days of the trade, both old and young used to subscribe a sum of money and enjoy a good cup of Bohea and cake, which they called ' Cattern ' cake. After tea, they danced and made merry, and finished the evening with a supper of boiled stuffed rabbits smothered with onion sauce." The custom of send-ing about Cattern cakes was also ob-served at Kettering, in Northampton-shire, but the lace trade there is nearly extinct.

[6] " Tour through the whole Island of Great Britain," by a Gentleman. 3 vols. 1724–27. Several subsequent editions of

arrival of the French settlers after the revocation of the Edict of
Nantes. At the same period, the author of the " Magna Britannia "[7] states that, at Woburn, " lace of a high price is made in
considerable quantities." Savary and Peuchet both declare the
town of Bedford alone to have contained 500 lace-workers.

The lace schools of Bedfordshire are far more considerable
than those in Devonshire. Four or five may frequently be found
in the same village, numbering from twenty to thirty children
each, and they are considered sufficiently important to be visited
by government inspectors. Their work is mostly purchased by
large dealers, who make their arrangements with the instructress :
the children are not bound for a term, as in the southern counties.
Boys formerly attended the lace schools, but now they go at an
early age to the fields.

The wages of a lace-worker average a shilling a day ; under
press of business, caused by the demand for some fashionable
article, they sometimes rise to one shilling and sixpence.

BUCKINGHAMSHIRE.

Though the first establishment of the manufacture may have
been in the sister county, the workers of Buckingham appear
early to have gained the lion's share of public estimation for the
produce of their pillows, and the manufacture flourished, till,
suffering from the monopolies of James I., we read how in the
year 1623, April 8th, a petition was addressed from Great Marlow
to the high sheriff of Bucks, representing the distress of the
people from " the bone-lace making being much decayed." [8]

Three years later, 1626, Sir Henry Borlase founds and endows
the free school of Great Marlow, for twenty-four boys, to read,
write, and cast accounts ; and for twenty-four girls, " to knit, spin,
and make bone lace ; " and here at Great Marlow the trade

Defoe were published, with additions, by
Richardson the novelist, in 1732, '42, '62,
'69, and '78 : The last is " brought down
to the present time by a gentleman of
eminence in the literary world."

[7] " Magna Britannia et Hibernia, or a

New Survey of Great Britain, collected
and composed by an impartial hand,
by the Rev. Thos. Owen." Lond.
1720-31.

[8] "State Papers, Dom." Jas. I. vol. cxlii.
P. R. O.

flourished, all English, and even French authors,[9] citing its "manufactures de dentelles au fuseau" as the staple produce of the town and its surrounding villages, which said lace, however, they pronounce as "inférieure à celle de Flandre."

During the seventeenth century the trade continued to advance, and Fuller testifies to its once more prosperous condition in Bucks, towards the year 1640. "No handicrafts of note," he writes, "(save what are common to other countries), are used therein, except any will instance in bone lace, much thereof being made about Owldney, in this county, though more, I believe, in Devonshire, where we shall meet more properly therewith."[10] Olney, as it is now written, a small market town, for many years the residence of Cowper, known by its twenty-four-arched bridge, now no more, "of wearisome but needful length," spanning the Ouse— Olney, together with its fellow towns of Newport Pagnel and Aylesbury, are much quoted by the authorities of the last century, though, as is too often the case in books of travels and statistics, one writer copies from another the information derived from a preceding author. Defoe, however, who really did solace the pains of pillory and ear-cropping by visiting each county in detail, quotes "Ouldney as possessing a considerable manufacture of bone lace;" while a letter from the poet Cowper to the Rev. John Newton, in 1780, enclosing a petition to Lord Dartmouth in favour of the lace-makers, declares that "hundreds in this little town are upon the point of starving, and that the most unremitting industry is barely sufficient to keep them from it." A distress caused, we may infer, by some caprice of fashion.

"The lace manufacture is still carried on," says Lysons,[11] "to a great extent in and about Olney, where veils and other lace of the finer sort are made, and great fortunes are said to be acquired by the factors. Lace-making is in no part of the country so general as at Hanslape and in its immediate vicinity; but it prevails from fifteen to twenty miles round in every direction. At Hanslape not fewer than 800, out of a population of 1275, were employed in it in the year 1801. Children are there put to the lace schools at, or soon after, five years of age. At eleven or twelve years of age they are all able to maintain themselves without any assistance: both girls and boys are taught to make

---

[9] Savary and Peuchet.
[10] "Worthies," vol. i. p. 134.

[11] "Magna Britannia," Daniel and Samuel Lysons, 1806-22.

it, and some men when grown up follow no other employment; others, when out of work, find it a good resource, and can earn as much as the generality of day labourers. The lace made in Hanslape is from sixpence to two guineas a yard in value. It is calculated that from 8000*l.* to 9000*l.* net profit is annually brought into the parish by the lace manufacture."

The bone lace of Stoney Stratford [12] and Aylesbury are both quoted by Defoe, and the produce of the latter city is mentioned with praise. He writes: "Many of the poor here are employed in making lace for edgings, not much inferior to those from Flanders; but it is some pleasure to us to observe that the English are not the only nation in the world which admires foreign manufactures above its own, since the French, who give fashions to most nations, buy and sell the finest laces at Paris under the name of 'dentelles d'Angleterre,' or English laces." [13]

But Newport Pagnel, whether from its more central position, or being of greater commercial importance, is the town which receives most praise from all contemporary authors. "This town," says the "Magna Britannia," in 1720, "is a sort of staple for bone lace, of which more is thought to be made here than any town in England; that commodity is brought to as great perfection almost as in Flanders." "Newport Pagnel," writes Defoe, "carries on a great trade in bone lace, and this same manufacture employs all the neighbouring villages;" while Don Manuel Gonzales, in 1730, speaks of its lace as little inferior to that of Flanders,[14] which assertion he may probably have copied from previous writers.

At one of the earliest meetings of the Anti-Gallican Society, 1752, Admiral Vernon in the chair, the first prize to the maker of the best piece of English bone lace was awarded to Mr. William Marriott, of Newport Pagnel, Bucks. The principal lace dealers in London were invited to give their opinion, and they allowed it to be the best ever made in England. Emboldened by this success, we read how, in 1761, Earl Temple, lord-lieutenant of Bucks, having been requested by Richard Lowndes, Esq., one of

---

[12] Describing the "lace and edgings" of the tradesman's wife, she has "from Stoney Stratford the first, and Great Marlow the last."—*The Complete English Tradesman, Dan. Defoe,* 1726.

[13] Edition 1762.

[14] "The Voyage to Great Britain of Don Manuel Gonzales, late Merchant of the City of Lisbon." "Some say Defoe wrote this book himself: it is evidently from the pen of an Englishman."—*Lowndes' Bibliographer's Manual,* Bohn's edition.

the knights of the shire, on behalf of the lace-makers, to present
to the king a pair of fine lace ruffles, made by Messrs. Milward and

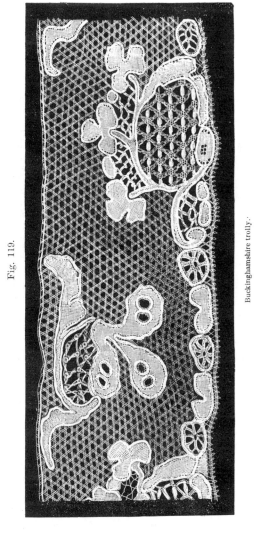

Fig. 119.

Buckinghamshire trolly.

Company, at Newport Pagnel, in the same county, his majesty,
after looking at them, and asking many questions respecting this
branch of trade, was most graciously pleased to express himself
that the inclination of his own heart naturally led him to set a

high value on every endeavour to further English manufactures, and whatever had such recommendation would be preferred by him to works of possibly higher perfection made in any other country.[15] From this period Newport Pagnel is cited as one of the most noted towns in the kingdom for making bone lace.[16]

At the end of the last century, the Revolution again drove

Fig. 120.

Buckinghamshire "point."

many of the poorer French to seek refuge on our shores, as they had done a century before; and we find stated in the "Annual Register" of 1794: "A number of ingenious French emigrants have found employment in Bucks, Bedfordshire, and the adjacent counties, in the manufacturing of lace, and it is expected through, the means of these artificers considerable improvements will be introduced into the method of making English lace."

Fig. 119 (see p. 341) represents the Buckinghamshire trolly; the designation given to lace in which the pattern is outlined by a thicker thread. The bobbins that hold the trolly threads are

---

[15] "Annual Register."
[16] See "Britannia Depicta," by John Owen, Gent. (Lond. 1764), and others.

longer and heavier than the others. Figs. 120 and 121 represent the "point" ground, from the beauty of which the laces of the midland counties derived their reputation.

Fig. 121.

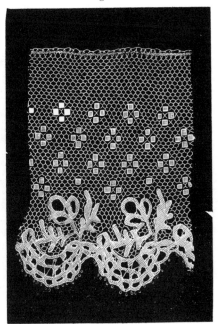

Buckinghamshire "point."

NORTHAMPTONSHIRE.

The laces of Northampton do not appear to have attracted the notice of the writers of the last century so much as those of the sister counties.

Anderson mentions that Kettering has "a considerable trade in lace;" and Lysons, later, observes that lace is made at Cheney. Certainly, the productions of this county a century back were of exquisite beauty, as we can bear testimony from the specimens in a pattern book inherited by Mr. Cardwell, the well-known lace merchant of Northampton, from his predecessor in the trade, which we have had an opportunity of examining. We have also received examples from various localities in Bedfordshire and Buckinghamshire, and as there is much similarity in the products of the three counties, we shall, perhaps, better describe them by treating of them all collectively.

The earliest English lace was naturally the old Flemish, the pattern wavy and graceful, the ground well executed. Fig. 122,

Fig. 122.

Old Flemish.   Newport Pagnel.

which we select as an example, is a specimen we received, with many others, of old Newport Pagnel lace, given by Mrs. Bell, of that town, where her family has been established from time immemorial.   Mrs. Bell herself can carry these laces back to the

Fig. 123.

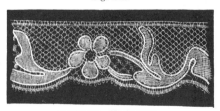

Old Brussels.   Northampton.

year 1780, when they were bequeathed to her father by an aged relative who had long been in the lace trade.   The packets remain for the most part entire.   The custom of "storing" lace was common among the country-people.

Next in antiquity is Fig. 123, a lace of Flemish design, with the fine Brussels ground.   This is among the Northamptonshire laces already alluded to.

Many of the early patterns appear to have been run or worked in with the needle on the net ground (Fig. 124).

In 1778, according to M'Culloch,[17] was introduced the " point "

Fig. 124.

"Run" lace. Newport Pagnel.

ground, as it is locally termed, from which period dates the staple pillow lace trade of these counties. This ground is beautifully clear, the patterns well executed : we doubt if Fig. 125 could be

Fig. 125.

English ' point.'' Northampton.

surpassed in beauty by lace of any foreign manufacture. Much of this point ground was made by men.

[17] " Dict. of Commerce."

The principal branch of the lace trade was the making of "baby lace," as those narrow laces were called, most specially employed for the adorning of infants' caps (Figs. 126, 127, 128). The "point" ground was used, the patterns taken from those of Lille and Arras—hence the laces of Buckingham and Bedford-

Fig. 126.

"Baby" lace. Northampton.

Fig. 127.   Fig. 128.

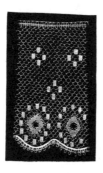   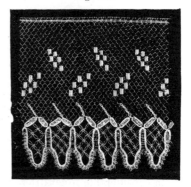

"Baby" lace. Beds.   "Baby" lace. Bucks.

shire have often been styled "English Lille." Though the fashion in the mother-country has passed away, the American ladies still hold to the gorgeously trimmed infant's cap ; and till the breaking out of the Civil War, large quantities of "baby lace" were exported to America, the finer sorts varying from five shillings to

seven shillings and sixpence a yard, still retaining their ancient
name of " points."

Many other descriptions of grounds were made. Wire
(Fig. 129), double, and trolly, in every kind of quality and width.
In the making of the finer sorts of edging as many as 200 threads
would be employed.

Fig. 129.

Wire ground. Northampton.

On the breaking out of the war with France, the closing of
our ports to French goods gave an impetus to the trade, and the
manufacturers undertook to supply the English market with lace
similar to that of Normandy and the sea-coast villages of France ;
hence a sort of " fausse " Valenciennes, called the " French
ground." But true Valenciennes was also fabricated so fine
(Fig. 130) as to rival the products of French Hainault. It was

Fig. 130.

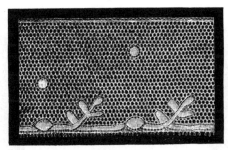

Valenciennes. Northampton.

made in considerable quantities, until the expertness of the
smuggler and the cessation of the war caused it to be laid aside.

One-third of the lace-workers of Northampton were employed,
previous to the introduction of machine-made net, in making
quillings on the pillow.

A " point " lace, with the " cloth " or " toilé " on the edge,
for many years was in fashion, and, in compliment to the prince,

was named by the loyal manufacturers " Regency point." It was
a durable and handsome lace. (Fig. 131.)

Fig. 131.

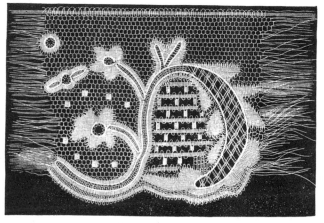

Regency point. Bedford.

Towards the year 1830, insertions found their way to the
public taste (Fig. 132).

Fig. 132.

Insertion. Bedford.

The exhibition of 1851 gave a sudden impulse to the traders,
and from that period the lace industry rapidly developed. At
this time were introduced the Maltese guipures and the "plaited"
laces, a variety grafted on the old Maltese (Fig. 133). Five
years later appears the first specimen of the raised plait, now so
thoroughly established in the market.

The exhibition of 1862 showed an astonishing progress in both design and execution; leaves in strict imitation of nature

Fig. 133.

Plaited lace. Bedford.

being mingled with the Oriental arabesque of the so-called Maltese (Fig. 134) in the fabrics of Bedfordshire, which may now be dis-

Fig. 134.

Raised plait. Bedford.

tinguished by this characteristic from those of her sister county. The Buckinghamshire stick to the old Maltese designs, their laces unrelieved by the introduction of either flowers or foliage.

The imitations of the guipures of Malta and Le Puy unfit the lace-workers for the more delicate white laces with the Lille ground. Mr. Lester, of Bedford, is making most spirited endeavours to sustain the old industry, and in the international exhibition of 1874 he produced a collection of specimens remarkable for their excellent workmanship, for the even " clothing " of the leaves, and the firmness of the raised cord.

Buckingham produces black lace of great beauty. Her lace-makers have also succeeded in making pieces of considerable width, showing great skill and artistic design. They formerly could only produce lace 8 inches wide ; some they exhibited measured 38 inches ; the English lace-makers having acquired the art of " fine joining," a knowledge until of late confined to France and Belgium. But since this period the lace industry of Buckingham has to sustain a powerful competition in the narrow laces of Normandy and the " piece goods " of Grammont. The number of lace-makers in the counties of Buckingham, Northampton, Bedford, and Oxford, is estimated at 25,000.

Pillow lace was also made to some extent in Derbyshire.

CHAPTER XXXI.

WILTSHIRE AND DORSETSHIRE.

From Wiltshire and Dorset, counties in the last century renowned for their lace, the trade has now passed away ; a few workers may yet be found in the retired sea-side village of Charmouth, and these are diminishing fast.

Of the Wiltshire manufactures we know but little, even from tradition, save that the art did once prevail. Peuchet alludes to it. When Sir Edward Hungerford attacked Wardour Castle, in Wiltshire, Lady Arundel, describing the destruction of the leaden pipes by the soldiers, says, " They cut up the pipe and sold it, as these men's wives in North Wiltshire do bone lace, at sixpence a yard."

One Mary Hurdle, of Marlborough, in the time of Charles II., tells us in her " Memoirs " [1] that, being left an orphan, she was apprenticed by the chief magistrate to a maker of bone lace for eight years, and after that period of servitude she apprenticed herself for five years more.

Again, at the time of the Great Plague, cautions are issued by the mayor of Marlborough to all parents and masters how they send their children and servants to school or abroad in making bone lace or otherwise, in any public house, place, or school used for that purpose. [2]

In the proceedings of the Anti-Gallican Society it is recorded that the second prize for needle point ruffles was, in 1751, awarded to Mrs. Elizabeth Waterman, of the episcopal city of Salisbury. Such are the scanty notices we have been able to glean of the once flourishing lace trade in Wiltshire.

Dorset, on the other hand, holds high her head in the annals

---

[1] " The Conversion and Experience of Mary Hurll', or Hurdle, of Marlborough, a maker of bone lace in this town, by   the Rev. — Hughes, of that town."
[2] Waylem's "History of Marlborough."

of lace-making; three separate towns, in their day—Blandford, Sherborne, and Lyme Regis—disputing the palm of excellence for their productions.

Of Blandford the earliest mention we find is in Owen's " Magna Britannia" of 1720, where he states : " The manufacture of this town was heretofore 'band-strings,' which were once risen to a great price, but now times hath brought both bands themselves and their strings out of use, and so the inhabitants have turned their hands to making straw works and bone lace, which perhaps may come to nothing, if the fickle humour of fashionmongers take to wearing Flanders lace."

Only four years later, Defoe writes of Blandford :—" This city is chiefly famous for making the finest bone lace in England, and where they showed us some so exquisitely fine as I think I never saw better in Flanders, France, or Italy, and which, they said, they rated above 30l. sterling a yard ; but it is most certain that they make exceeding rich lace in this county, such as no part of England can equal." In the edition of 1762, Defoe adds, " This was the state and trade of the town when I was there in my first journey ; but on June 4, 1731, the whole town, except twenty-six houses, was consumed by fire, together with the church."

Postlethwayt,[3] Hutchins,[4] Lysons, and Knight (" Imperial Cyclopædia "), all tell the same story. Peuchet cites the Blandford laces as " comparables à celles qu'on fait en Flandre (excepté Bruxelles), en France et même dans les États de Venise ; " and Anderson mentions Blandford as " a well-built town, surpassing all England in fine lace." More reliance is to be placed on the two last-named authorities than the former, who have evidently copied Defoe without troubling themselves to inquire more deeply into the matter.

It is generally supposed that the trade gradually declined after the great fire of 1731, when it was replaced by the manufacture of buttons, and no record of its former existence can be found among the present inhabitants of the place.[5]

---

[3] "At Bland, on the Stour, between Salisbury and Dorchester, they made the finest lace in England, valued at 30l. per yard."— *Universal Dict. of Trade and Commerce*, 1774.

[4] " Much bone lace was made here, and the finest point in England, equal, if not superior, to that of Flanders, and valued

at 30l. per yard, till the beginning of this century."—*Hutchins' Hist. of the County of Dorset*, 2nd edit. 1796.

[5] What this celebrated point was, we cannot ascertain. Two samplers sent to us as Blandford point were of geometric pattern, resembling the sampler, Coloured Plate I , p. 19.

Fig. 135 represents a curious piece of lace, preserved as an

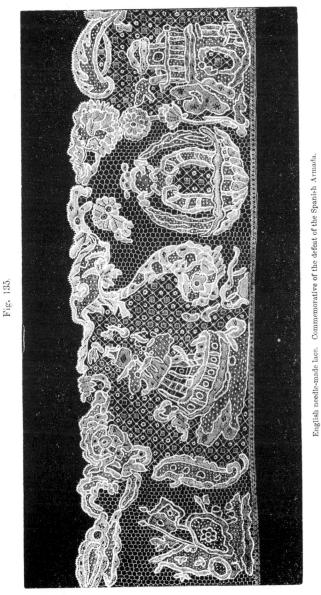

Fig. 135.

English needle-made lace. Commemorative of the defeat of the Spanish Armada.

heirloom in a family in Dorsetshire. It formerly belonged to her
majesty Queen Charlotte, and, when purchased by the present

owner, had a label attached to it, "Queen Elizabeth's lace," with the tradition that it was made in commemoration of the defeat of the Spanish Armada. At this we beg to demur, as no similar lace was made at that period; but we do not doubt its having been made in honour of that victory, for the building is decidedly old Tilbury Fort, familiar to all by the pencil of Stanfield. The lace is point d'Argentan, and was probably the handiwork of some English lady, sent as a present to Queen Charlotte.

"Since the Reformation the clothing trade declined," writes Defoe, of Sherborne. "Before 1700, making buttons, haberdashery wares, and bone laces employed a great many hands." Other authors, such as Anderson, declare, at a far later date, Sherborne to carry on a good trade in lace, and how, up to 1780, much blonde, both white and black, and of various colours, was made there, of which a supply was sent to all markets.

The points of Lyme Regis rivalled, in the last century, those of Honiton and Blandford, and when the trade of the last-named town passed away, Lyme and Honiton laces held their own, side by side, in the London market. The fabric of Lyme Regis, for a period, came more before the public eye, for that old, deserted, and half forgotten mercantile city, in the eighteenth century, once more raised its head as a fashionable watering-place. Prizes were awarded by the Anti-Gallican Society [6] to its townswomen for ruffles of needle point and bone lace, and the reputation of the fabric reached even the court; for when Queen Charlotte first set foot on English ground, she wore a head and lappets of Dorset manufacture. Some years later, a splendid lace dress was made for her Majesty by the workers of Lyme.[7]

The laces of Lyme, like all good articles, were expensive. A narrow piece set quite plain round a cap would cost four guineas, nor were five guineas a yard considered an exorbitant price.

The making of such expensive lace being scarcely found remunerative, the trade gradually expired; and when the order for the marriage lace of H. M. Queen Victoria reached the southern counties, not one lace-maker was to be found to aid in the work in the once flourishing town of Lyme Regis.

---

[6] In 1752.   [7] Roberts' "Hist. of Lyme Regis."

CHAPTER XXXII.

DEVONSHIRE.

" Bone lace and Cyder."

Anderson.

" At Axminster, you may be furnished with fyne flax thread there spunne. At Honyton and Braduinch with bone lace much in request."—*Westcote.*

HONITON.

LACE-MAKING is said to have been introduced into Devonshire by sundry Flemings who took refuge in England during the persecutions of the Duke of Alva (1567–73). Whether the art was first made known to the inhabitants of the county at that period, it is impossible now to say.

We may rather infer that laces of silk and coarse thread were already manufactured in Devonshire, as elsewhere; and that the Flemings, on their arrival, having introduced the fine thread, spun almost exclusively in their own country, from that period the trade of bone-lace making flourished in the southern as in the midland counties of England.

Although the earliest known MS.,[1] giving an account of the different towns of Devon, makes no mention of lace, we find from it that Mrs. Minifie, one of the earliest named lace-makers, was an Englishwoman.[2]

Towards the latter end of the sixteenth century, various and, indeed, numerous patronymics of Flemish origin appear among the

---

[1] Ker's " Synopsis," written about the year 1561. Two copies of this MS. exist, one in the library of Sir Lawrence Palk, at Halden House (Co. Devon), the other in the British Museum. This MS. was never printed, but served as an authority for Westcote and others.

[2] " She was a daughter of John Flay, Vicar of Buckrell. near Honiton, who by will, in 1614, bequeaths certain lands to Jerom Minify (*sic*), son of Jerom Minify, of Burwash, Sussex, who married his only daughter."—*Prince's Worthies of Devon,* 1701.

entries of the church registers still preserved at Honiton,[3] names all handed down to their descendants in the present generation,[4] and in these families the fabric has continued for a long lapse of years.

That the trade was already flourishing in the days of our first James, the oft cited brass inscription, let into a raised tombstone near the wall of old Honiton church, fully testifies :—

" Here lieth ye Body of James Rodge, of Honiton, in ye County of Devonshire, Bone lace seller, who hath given unto the poor of Honiton P'ishe the benyfite of 100l. for ever, who deceased ye 27 July, A.D. 1617, ætatis suæ 50. Remember the Poore."

If any credit may be attached to the folk-lore of the lace-making trade, this James Rodge[5] was a valet, who, escaping from Brussels, first brought over the secret of the finer stitches as used in the Flanders laces of that period, Having made his fortune at Honiton, he, in gratitude, bequeathed a sum of money to the poor of his adopted city.

Westcote, too, who wrote about the year 1620, when noticing " Honitoun," says :—" Here is made abundance of bone lace, a pretty toy now greatly in request."[6] He does not speak of it as a new manufacture ; the trade had already taken root and flourished, for, including the above-mentioned Rodge, the three earliest bone-lace-makers of the seventeenth century on record all at their decease bequeathed sums of money for the benefit of their indigent townspeople, viz. Mrs. Minifie,[7] before mentioned, who died in 1617, and Thomas Humphrey of Honiton, laceman, who willed, in the year 1658, 20l. towards the purchase of certain tenements, a notice of which benefaction is recorded on a painted board above the gallery in the old parish church.

---

[3] Burd, Genest, Raymunds, Brock, Couch, Gerard, Murck, Stocker, Maynard, Trump, Groot, &c.

[4] Up to a recent date, the Honiton lace-makers were mostly of Flemish origin. Mrs. Stocker, ob. 1769; Mr. J. Stocker, + 1783, and four daughters; Mrs. Mary Stocker, + 179–; Mr. Gerard + 1799, and daughter; Mrs. Lydia Maynard (of Anti-Gallican celebrity), + 1786; Mrs. Ann Brock, + 1815; Mrs. Elizabeth Humphrey, + 1790, whose family had been in the lace manufacture one hundred and fifty years and more. The above list has been furnished to the author by Mrs. Frank Aberdein, whose grandfather was for many years in the trade. ·Mrs. Treadwin, of Exeter, found an old lace-worker using a lace "Turn" for winding sticks, having the date 1678 rudely carved on the foot, showing how the trade was continued in the same families from generation to generation.

[5] Rodge, or Ridge, with all due deference to Devonshire tradition, does not sound like a name of Flemish extraction.

[6] " View of Devon," T. Westcote.

[7] Her bequest is called " Minifie's Gift."

By this time English lace had advanced in public estimation. In the year 1660, a royal ordinance of France provided that a mark should be affixed to thread lace imported from England, as well as on that of Flanders; and we have already told elsewhere [8] how the Earl of Leicester procures, through his countess, bone lace to a considerable amount, as a present to Queen Anne of Austria.

Speaking of bone lace, writes Fuller in his "Worthies:" "Much of this is made in and about Honyton, and weekly returned to London. . . . . Modern is the use thereof in England, and not exceeding the middle of the reign of Queen Elizabeth. Let it not be condemned for a superfluous wearing because it doth neither hide, nor heat, seeing it doth adorn. Besides, though private persons pay for it, it stands the State in nothing; not expensive of bullion like other lace, costing nothing save a little thread descanted on by art and industry. Hereby many children, who otherwise would be burthensome to the parish, prove beneficial to their parents. Yea, many lame in their limbs and impotent in their arms, if able in their fingers, gain a livelihood thereby; not to say that it saveth some thousands of pounds yearly, formerly sent over seas to fetch lace from Flanders."

Even in 1655, when the variety of points furnished matter for a letter from the members of the Baptist church assembled at Bridgewater, the "Beleeven men," unwilling to injure so flourishing a commerce, merely censure "points and more laces than are required on garments," and these they desired might be proceeded against " with all sweetness and tenderness and long-suffering." [9] The conciliatory measures of the Puritans, maybe, affected the trade less than the doings of Lord Cambury and Lord Churchill's dragoons in the suppression of Monmouth's rebellion in 1680, by which time the lace-making art was carried on in many small country places in Devon. They pillaged the lace-makers right and left, and when quartered at Colyton,[10] these unruly soldiers

---

[8] See p. 294.
[9] Church Book of the Baptist Chapel of Lyme Regis.
[10] Colyton and Ottery St. Mary were among the first. Wherever the say or serge fabric decayed, the lace trade planted itself.

In the church of Colyton, under a fine canopied tomb, repose back to back, in most unsociable fashion, the recumbent figures of Sir John and Lady Pole. "Dame Elizabeth, daughter of Roger How, merchant of London, ob. 1623," wears a splendid cape of three rows of bone lace descending to the waist. Her cap is trimmed with the same material. As this lace may be of Devonshire fabric, we give a woodcut of the pattern (Fig. 136).

Sundry Flemish names may still be

broke into the house of one William Burd, a dealer in bone lace, and there stole merchandise to the amount of 325*l.* 17*s.* 9*d.*[11]

"The valuable manufactures of lace, for which the inhabitants of Devon have long been conspicuous, are extending now from Exmouth to Torbay,"[12] writes Defoe in 1724. These must, however, have received a check as regards the export trade, for, says Savary, who wrote about the same date:—"Depuis qu'on imite les dentelles nommées point d'Angleterre en Flandre, Picardie et Champagne, on n'en tire plus de Londres pour la France."

Great distress, too, is said to have existed among the Honiton lace-makers after the two great fires of 1756 and 1767, which consumed a considerable part of their town. Three years previous to this calamity, among a number of premiums awarded by the Anti-Gallican Society[13] for the encouragement of our lace trade, the first prize of fifteen guineas is bestowed upon Mrs. Lydia Maynard, of Honiton, "in token of six pairs of ladies' lappets of unprecedented beauty, exhibited by her." About this time we read in Bowen's "Geography"[14] that at Honiton "the people are chiefly

seen above the shop-windows of Colyton, similar to those of Honiton: Stocker, Murch, Spiller, Rochett, Boatch, Kettel, Woram, and others.

Fig. 136.

Monument of Lady Pole. + 1623. Colyton Church.

[11] Don Manuel Gonzales mentions "bone lace" among the commodities of Devon.

[12] The lace manufacture now extends along the coast, from the small watering-place of Seaton, by Beer, Branscombe, Salcombe, Sidmouth, and Ollerton, to Exmouth, including the Vale of Honiton and the towns above mentioned.

[13] 1753.

[14] "Complete System of Geography," Emanuel Bowen, 1747.

This extract is repeated verbatim in "England's Gazetteer," by Philip Luckombe. London, 1790.

employed in the manufactory of lace, the broadest sort that is made in England, of which great quantities are sent to London." "It acquired," says Lysons, "some years since, the name of Bath Brussels lace."

To give a precise description of the earliest Devonshire lace would now be impossible. Though many heirlooms, carefully hoarded in the old Devonshire families, are supposed to be of native produce, the author has met with no specimen which can really be authenticated as of the old bone lace manufacture of the county.

In Exeter Cathedral is the monument of Bishop Stafford.[15] His collar appears to be of a network, embroidered in patterns of graceful design (Fig. 137).

Fig. 137.

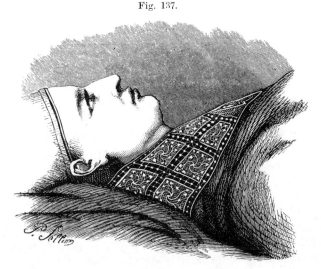

Monument of Bishop Stafford, Exeter Cathedral.

In the same cathedral lies the recumbent effigy of Lady Doddridge, a member of the Bampfylde family, her cuffs and tucker adorned with geometric lace of simple pattern (Fig. 138). These, with the monument of Lady Pole, at Colyton, are the sole accredited examples, either in painting or sculpture, of lace-adorned figures that have come under the author's notice in the county.

Honiton lace long preserved its Flemish character. Specimens

---

[15] Died 1398.

Fig. 138.

Monument of Lady Doddridge. + 1614. Exeter Cathedral.

Fig. 139.

Old Devonshire lace.

produced as the work of James Rodge, or his contemporaries,

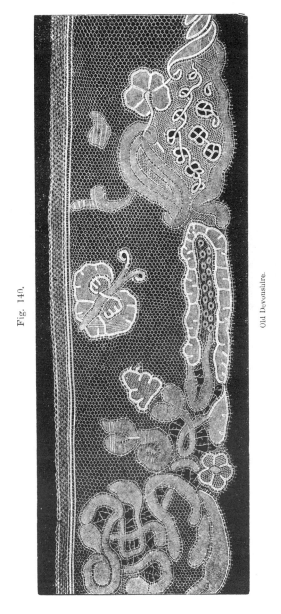

Fig. 140.

Old Devonshire.

consist of large flowing guipure patterns, united by brides, and later worked in with the Brussels ground.

The Flemish character of Fig. 139 is unmistakable ; the design of the flower vase being that of Angleterre à bride. If really of English make, we should place its fabrication at the beginning of the last century, for it was long before the Devonshire lace-makers could rival in beauty the " cordonnet " of the Flemish workers.

Fig. 140 is an example of the pattern worked into the réseau ground, the favourite design of the butterfly and the acorn, already familiar to us in the old point d'Angleterre of Fig. 52 (p. 99), and in the smock of Queen Elizabeth (Fig. 109, p. 273).

It is to its sprigs that Honiton owes its great reputation. Like the Brussels, they were made separately. At first they were worked in with the pillow, afterwards " appliqué " or sewn on a réseau ground.

Fig. 141.

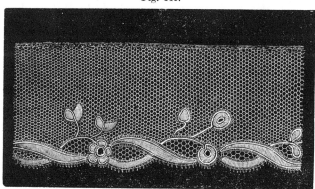

Old Honiton application.

The pattern in Fig. 141 is sewn on the plain pillow ground, the making of which formed an extensive branch of the Honiton trade in the last century. This net was very beautiful and regular, but very expensive. It was made of the finest thread produced from Antwerp, the market price of which, in 1790, was 70l. per pound ; [16] and an old lace-maker told the author her father had, during the war, paid a hundred guineas a pound to the smugglers for this highly prized and then almost unattainable commodity.

Nor were the lace-worker's gains less remunerative. She would receive as much as eighteen shillings a yard for the work-

---

[16] Mrs. Aberdein, of Honiton, informs us her father has often paid ninety-five guineas per pound for the thread at Antwerp.

manship alone of a piece of this elaborate net, measuring scarce 2 inches in width ;[17] and one of the old lace-dealers showed Mrs. Treadwin, some years since, a piece of ground, 18 inches square, for the making of which she had paid 15l., shortly before the establishment of the machine-net manufacture.[18] The price of the lace was proportionably high. A Honiton veil would often cost a hundred guineas.

The invention of Heathcoat [19] dealt a fatal blow to the Honiton net-makers. A hopeless struggle ensued between manual labour and the results of science : human industry yielded to the pressure. Young women, in large numbers, forsook the pillow and went to service, and but few children were trained to succeed them.

The lappet (Coloured Plate VI. p. 101) has been shown to the author, purchased from a Devonshire gentlewoman in reduced circumstances, to whose great-grandmother it had belonged, which she at once pronounced to be Brussels needle point; but it has been shown to four different lace-makers, who all recognise the open-work or " finishings " peculiar to the Honiton fabric, and claim it as English ; but it is of such decidedly Brussels character we have place l it under that head, with this explanation.

To return to our history. For twenty years the lace trade suffered the greatest depression,[20] and the Honiton lace-workers, forsaking the designs of their forefathers, introduced a most hideous set of patterns, designed, as they said, " out of their own heads." " Turkey tails," " frying-pans," " bullocks' hearts," and the most senseless sprigs and borderings took the place of the graceful compositions of the old school; not a leaf, not a flower, was copied from nature. Anxious to introduce a purer taste, Queen Adelaide,

---

[17] The manner of payment was somewhat Phœnician, reminding one of Queen Dido and her bargain. The lace ground was spread out on the counter, and the worker herself desired to cover it with shillings ; and as many coins as found place on her work, she carried away as the fruit of her labour. The author once calculated the cost, after this fashion, of a small lace veil on real ground, said to be one of the first ever fabricated : it was 12 inches wide and 30 long, and, making allowance for the shrinking caused by washing, the value amounted to 20l., which proved to be exactly the sum originally paid for the veil. The ground of this veil, though perfect in its workmanship, is of a much wider mesh than was made in the last days of the fabric. It was the property of Mrs. Chick.

[18] The last specimen of " real " ground made in Devon was the marriage veil of the late Mrs. Marwood Tucker, about forty years since. It was with the greatest difficulty workers could be procured to make it. The price paid for the ground alone was 30 guineas.   [19] 1839.

[20] In 1822, Lysons remarks that " some years ago the manufacture of Honiton employed 2400 hands in the town and neighbouring villages. They do not now employ 300."

to whom a petition had been sent on behalf of the distressed lace-makers, gave the order for a dress to be made of Honiton sprigs, sewn on machine net, and commanded that the flowers should all be copied from nature. The order was executed by Mrs. Davey, of Honiton ; the skirt was encircled with a wreath of elegantly designed sprigs, the initial of each flower forming the name of her majesty.[21]

The example of the amiable queen found few followers ; and when, in the progress of time, the wedding lace was required for her present majesty, it was with difficulty the necessary number of workers could be obtained to make it. The work was executed in the small fishing hamlet of Beer,[22] and its environs. The dress cost 100l. ; it was composed entirely of Honiton sprigs, connected on the pillow by a variety of open-work stitches.

The bridal dresses of their royal highnesses the Princess Royal, the Princess Alice, and the Princess of Wales, were all of Honiton lace, the patterns consisted of the national flowers, the latter with prince's feathers, intermixed with ferns, and introduced with the most happy effect.

The application of Honiton sprigs upon bobbin-net has been of late years almost entirely superseded by the modern guipure (Coloured Plate XVI.). The sprigs, when made, are tacked upon a piece of blue paper, and then united either on the pillow by " cut-works " or " purlings," or else joined with the needle by various stitches—lacet point, réseau, cutwork, and button-hole stitch (the most effective of all) ; purling is made by the yard. The Honiton guipure has an original character almost unique. The large pieces surpass in richness and perfection the point duchesse of Belgium. The reliefs are embroidered with the greatest delicacy, and the beauty of the workmanship is exquisite ; and whereas the guipure applications of Belgium require to be whitened with lead, the Honiton workers give up their lace in all its original brilliancy and whiteness.[23] The fault in the Honiton lace has been its crowded and spiritless designs.

The author's brother took much pains, during a residence at Sidmouth, to procure for the lace-makers new patterns of flowers,

---

[21] AMARANTH.   AURICULA.
DAPHNE.   IVY.
EGLANTINE.   DAHLIA.
LILAC.   EGLANTINE.
[22] The workers of Beer, Axmouth, and

Branscombe, have always been considered the best in the trade.
[23] " Exposition Universelle de 1867; Rapport du Jury International, ' Dentelles,' par Felix Aubry."

Plate XVI.

Honiton guipure.

To face page 364.

insects, and other natural objects. The younger members of the
community accepted with gratitude these new patterns, and one
even reproduced a piece of a collar from Vecellio's book, in a
manner most creditable to her ingenuity. In consequence of this
movement, some gentlemen connected with the Bath and West of

Fig. 142.

Honeysuckle sprig of modern Honiton.

England Society [24] proposed that an exhibition should take place
at the annual agricultural show, held at Clifton, of Honiton lace,
"designs strictly after nature." Prizes to the amount of 100*l.*
were given. Her Majesty the Queen expressed a desire that the
articles exhibited should be sent to Windsor for her inspection,
and graciously commanded that two flounces, with a corresponding
length of trimming lace, after a design by Miss Cecilia Marryat,

---

[24] For the Encouragement of Agriculture, Arts, Manufactures, and Commerce.

Fig. 143.

Lappet made by Mrs. Treadwin, of Exeter. 1864.

should be made for her. The order was given to Mrs. Hayman, of Sidmouth. Fig. 142 is one of the honeysuckle sprigs selected.

The Honiton lace-makers show great aptitude in imitating the Brussels designs, and, through the skill and perseverance of Mrs. Treadwin, have succeeded in reproducing the ancient laces in the most wonderful manner. Fig. 143 is a lappet in the Brussels style, and in the International Exhibition of 1874 Mrs. Treadwin [25] produced admirable specimens after the pillow-made lace of Genoa and Flanders, and also a most successful reproduction (Fig. 144) of the Venetian point in relief, thus opening to the lace-workers a new branch of industry, which will probably prove more remunerative than their own guipures.

Much trolly [26] lace was made in Devonshire until thirty years back. Trolly lace, before its downfall, has been sold at five guineas the yard.[27] Unlike the Honiton, it was made of English thread, at first of a coarse quality; the ground generally double, similar to that of the Flanders laces, from which country it doubtless derives its name.

Trolly lace was not the work of women alone. In the flourishing days of its manufacture, every boy, until he had attained the age of fifteen, and was competent to work in the fields, attended the lace schools daily. A lace-maker of Sidmouth, now verging on forty-five, learned her craft at the village dame school,[28] in company with many boys. The men, especially the sailor returned from sea, would again resume the employment of their boyhood, in their hours of leisure, and the labourer, seated at his pillow on a summer's evening, would add to his weekly gains.

Mrs. Treadwin recollects in her younger days some twenty-four men lace-makers in her native village of Woodbury, one of whom worked at his pillow so late as 1820.

The writer's brother succeeded in finding out a man of sixty, dwelling in Salcombe parish, near Sidmouth, who had, in his day, been a lace-maker of some reputation. " I have made hundreds of yards in my time," he said, " both wide and narrow, but never

---

[25] " Honiton Lace," by Mrs. Treadwin. London, 1874. " Honiton Lace-making," by Devonia. London, 1874.

[26] We have this year seen at Paris the needle-made laces of Mademoiselle Dugrenot, the best reproductions of the Italian reticella that have been executed.

The firmness and precision of the work is most remarkable, and of exceptional beauty.

[27] See p. 342. Mrs. Delany, in one of her letters, dated 1756, speaks of a " trolly head."

[28] Of Ollerton.

Fig. 144.

Venetian point in relief, reproduced by Mrs. Treadwin.

worked regularly at my pillow after sixteen years of age."
Delighted to exhibit the craft of his boyhood, he hunted out his
patterns, and, setting to work, produced a piece of trolly edging,
which soon found a place in the albums of sundry lace-collecting
ladies, the last specimen of man-worked lace likely to be
fabricated in the county of Devon.

In Woodbury will be found a small colony of lace-makers who
are employed in making Maltese or Greek lace, an industry introduced into Devon by order of her late majesty the queen dowager,
on her return from Malta. The workers copy these coarse geometric laces with great facility and precision. Among the various
cheap articles to which the Devonshire workers have of late
directed their labours is the tape or braid lace.

A good lace-maker easily gains her shilling a day, but in most
parts of Devonshire the work is paid by the truck system; many
of the more respectable shops giving one half in money, the
remaining sixpence to be taken out in tea or clothing, sold often
considerably above their value. Other manufacturers—to their
shame be it told—pay their workers altogether in grocery, and
should the lace-maker, from illness or any other cause, require an
advance in cash, she is compelled to give work to the value of
fourteenpence for every shilling she receives. Some few houses,
such as that of Mrs. Treadwin, of Exeter, and others of London,
pay their workers in money.

When we consider that well-nigh the whole female population
of Devon is employed in lace-making, it is a matter of surprise
that its staple manufacture should receive but little encouragement from the resident gentry of the county, and that (so different
from the energy of the ladies of Ireland) not one should have been
found to improve by her taste the artistic combination of the
fabric. But the air is soft and balmy, and the inhabitants an
apathetic generation, alone to be roused by famine, or some like
calamity, from the natural somnolence of their existence.

CHAPTER XXXIII.

SCOTLAND.

" With the pearlin above her brow."
                                        Old Scotch Song.

" Pearlin-lace as fine as spiders' webs."
                                        Heart of Midlothian.

FROM her constant intercourse with France, lace must have been early known in Scotland.

Of its use for ecclesiastical purposes, at a period when it was still unknown to the laity, we have evidence in the mutilated effigy of a crosiered ecclesiastic which once stood in a niche of the now ruined abbey church of Arbroath. The lace which adorns the robes of this figure is very elaborately and sharply chiselled, and, when first discovered, still preserved some remains of the gold leaf with which it had been ornamented.

In the inventories of King James V.—that handsome but ill-fated monarch—we find constant mention of " pasment " of gold and silver,[1] as well as an entry of—" Ane gown of fresit clayth of gold, with pasment of perle of gold smyth wark lynit with cramasy sating." [2] And we have other proofs,[3] in addition to the testimony of Sir Walter Scott, as given in the " Monastery," [4] that

---

[1] " 1539. Ane uther gowne of purpour satyne with ane braid pasment of gold and silver," &c.

" Twa Spanye cloikis of black freis with ane braid pasment of gold and silver."

" 1542. Three peces of braid pasmenttes of gold and silver."—*Inventories of the Royal Wardrobe and Jewel House,* 1488-1606. Edinb. 1815.

[2] 1542. Same Inv.

[3] In the Inv. of the Earl of Huntley, 1511-12, there is mention of dresses

" passamenté d'or."

[4] Chap. X., note.

1537. James V. and Lord Somerville at Holyrood :—" Where are all your men and attendants, my Lord ? "

" Please your Majesty, they are here," pointing to the lace which was on his son's and two pages' dress. The king laughed heartily and surveyed the finery, and bade him " Away with it all, and let him have his stout band of spears again."

"pasments" of gold and silver, as well as "purle," were already in daily use during King James's reign.

Indeed, as early as 1575, the General Assembly of Scotland found necessary, as did the bishops in Denmark, to express its mind as to the style of dress befitting the clergy, and prohibit "all begares (gardes) of velvet on gown, hose, or coat, all superfluous cut-out work, all sewing on of pasments and laces."

A parchment, too, found in the cabinet of the Countess of Mar,[5] entitled "The Passement Bond," signed by the Duke of Lennox and other nobles, by which they engaged themselves to leave off wearing "passement," as a matter of expense and superfluity, shows that luxury in dress had early found its way into Scotland.

Notwithstanding these entries, it was not until the arrival of Mary Stuart in her northern dominions that lace in all its varieties appears. The inventory of the queen's effects in 1567, printed by the Bannatyne Club, gives entries of "passements, guimpeure d'or, and guimpeure d'argent,"[6] with which her "robes de satin blanc et jaune" were "bordées" and "chamarées." Each style of embroidery and lace is designated by its special name. There is the "natte d'argent faite par entrelatz, passement d'or et d'argent fait à jour, chamarré de bisette,"[7] &c.

The word dentelle, as told elsewhere,[8] occurs but once.

We have also alluded to the will made by the queen previous to the birth of James VI., and her bequest of her "ouvrages maschés."[9] A relic of this expression is yet found in the word

[5] Croft's "Excerpta Antiqua."

The Countess of Mar, daughter of the first Duke of Lennox, and granddaughter by her mother's side to Marie Touchet. She was daughter-in-law to the preceptress of James VI., and in 1593 had the honour, at the baptism of Prince Henry, of lifting the child from his bed and delivering him to the Duke of Lennox. A portrait of this lady, in the high Elizabethan ruff, and with a "forepart" and tucker of exquisite raised Venice point, hung, when last we were in Edinburgh, in the drawing-room of the late Miss Katherine Sinclair, so well known by her literary attainments and her widely spread philanthropy.

[6] "Une robe de velours vert couverte de Broderies, gimpeures, et cordons d'or et d'argent, et bordée d'un passement de même.

"Une robe veluat cramoisi bandée de broderie de guimpeure d'argent.

"Une robe de satin blanc chamarrée de broderie faite de guimpeure d'or.

"Id. de satin jaune toute couverte de broderye gumpeure, &c.

"Robe de weloux noyr semée de geynpeurs d'or."—Inv. of Lillebourg, 1561.

[7] "Chamarrée de bisette."—Inv. of Lillebourg, 1561.

"Ane rabbat of wolvin thread with passmentet with silver."

[8] Page 23.

[9] Page 18.

" mawsch," or " masch," as the pinking of silk and muslin is termed
in Scotland, an advertisement of which accomplishment " done
here " may frequently be seen in the shop-windows of the old town
of Edinburgh.

In the palace of Holyrood is still exhibited a small basket
lined with blue silk, and trimmed with a bone lace of rudely spun
flax, run on with a ribbon of the same colour, recorded to be an
offering sent by Queen Elizabeth to her cousin previous to the
birth of her godchild. Antiquaries assert the story to be a fable.
Whether the lace be of the time or not, as a work of art it is of
no credit to any country.

How Queen Mary, in her youth, was instructed in the arts of
point coupé and lacis, according to the works of Vinciolo, has been
already related.[10] Of her talents as a needlewoman there is ample
proof in the numerous beds, screens, &c., treasured as relics in the
houses of the nobles where she was held captive. She knitted
head-dresses of gold " réseille," with cuffs and collars [11] en suite,[12]
to say nothing of nightcaps, and sent them as presents to Elizabeth,[13] all of which, we are told, the queen received most graciously. Mary, in her early portraits as daupnine of France,
wears no thread lace. Much fine gold embroidered with passament enriches her dresses; her sleeves are of gold réseuil. In
those of a later date, like that taken when in Lochleven Castle,
her veil is bordered with a narrow bone lace—as yet a rarity ; may
be one of the same noted in the inventory of 1578, as " Fyve litell
vaills of wovin rasour (réseau) of threde, ane meekle twa of thame,
passmentit with perle and black silk." [14]

---

[10] Page 7.

[11] Her lace ruffs Mary appears to have
had from France, as we may infer from a
letter written by Walsingham, at Paris,
to Burleigh, when the queen was captive
at Sheffield Castle, 1578: " I have of late
granted a passport to one that conveyeth
a box of linen to the queen of Scots, who
leaveth not this town for three or four
days. I think your Lordship shall see
somewhat written on some of the linen
contained in the same, that shall be worth
the reading. Her Majesty, under colour
of seeing the fashion of the *ruffes*, may
cause the several parcels of the linen to
be held to the fire, whereby the writing
may appear ; for I judge there will be

some such matter discovered, which was
the cause why I did the more willingly
grant the passport."

[12] In 1575.

[13] There was some demur about receiving the nightcaps, for Elizabeth declared
" that great commotions had taken place
in the Privy Council, because she had
accepted the gifts of the Queen of Scots.
They therefore remained for some time in
the hands of La Mothe, the ambassador,
but were finally accepted."—*Miss Strickland.*

[14] " Inventaire of our Soveraine Lord
and his dearest moder, 1578." Record
Office, Edinburgh.

When the Queen of Scots ascended the scaffold, "she wore on her head," writes Burleigh's reporter, "a dressing of lawn edged with bone lace," and "a vest of lawn fastened to her caul," edged with the same material. This lace-edged veil was long preserved as a relic in the exiled Stuart family, until Cardinal York bequeathed it to Sir John Cox Hippisley. Miss Pigott [15] describes it of "transparent zephyr gauze, with a light check or plaid pattern interwoven with gold; the form as that of a long scarf." [16] Sir John, when exhibiting the veil at Baden, had the indiscretion to throw it over the Queen of Bavaria's head. The queen shuddered at the omen, threw off the veil, and retired precipitately from the apartment, evidently in great alarm.

"Cuttit out werk," collars of "hollie crisp," "quaiffs of woven thread," [17] "cornettes of layn (linen) sewit with cuttit out werk of gold," "wovin collars of threde," follow in quick succession. The "cuttit out werk" is mostly wrought in gold, silver, cramoisi, or black silk. [18] The queen's "towell claiths" are adorned in similar manner. [19]

The Chartley Inventory of 1568 [20] is rich in works of point coupé and réseuil, in which are portrayed with the needle figures of birds, fishes, beasts, and flowers, "couppés chascune en son carré." The queen exercised much ingenuity in her labours, varying the pattern according to her taste. In the list are noted fifty-two specimens of flowers designed after nature, "tirés au naturel;" 124 birds; as well as sixteen sorts of four-footed beasts, "entre

---

[15] "Records of Life," by Miss H. Pigott. 1839.

[16] Similar to the New Year's gift of the Baroness Aletti to Queen Elizabeth :—

"A veil of lawn cutwork flourished with silver and divers colours."—*Nichols' Royal Progresses.*

[17] "Twa quaiffs ane of layn and uther of woving thread.

"Ane quaiff of layn with twa cornettes sewitt with cuttit out werk of gold and silver.

"Twa pair of cornettes of layn sewitt with cuttit out werk of gold.

"Ane wovin collar of thread passementit with incarnit and blew silk and silver."—*Inv. of 1578.*

[18] "Ane rabbat of cuttit out werk and gold and cramoisie silk with the handis (cuffs) thereof.

"Ane rabbat of cuttit out werk of gold and black silk.

"Ane rabbat of cuttit out werk with purpure silk with the handis of the same."—*Ibid.*

[19] "Twa towell claiths of holane claith sewitt with cuttit out werk and gold.

"Four napkinnes of holane claith and cammaraye sewitt with cuttit out werk of gold and silver and divers cullours of silk."—*Ibid.*

[20] Published by Prince Labanoff. "Recueil de Lettres de Marie Stuart," t. vii. p. 247.

lesquelles y ha un lyon assailant un sanglier ;" with fifty-two fishes, all of divers sorts—giving good proofs of the poor prisoner's industry. As to the designs after nature, with all respect to the memory of Queen Mary, the lions, cocks, and fishes of the six-teenth century which have come under our notice require a student of mediæval needlework, rather than a naturalist, to pro-nounce upon their identity.

James VI. of Scotland, reared in a hotbed of Calvinism, had not the means, even if he had the inclination, to indulge in much luxury in dress. Certain necessary entries of " braid pasmentis " of gold, " gold clinquant," " braid pasmentis," " cramoisi," for the ornamenting of " clokkis," " coittis," " breikis," and "roobes " of the king, with " Twa unce and ane half pasmentis of gold and silver to werk the headis of the fokkis," make up the amount of expense sanctioned for the royal wedding ;[21] while " 34 ells braid pasmentis " of gold to trim a robe for " his Majesties darrest bedfellow the Quene for her coronation," [22] gives but a poor idea of the luxury of the Scottish court.

Various enactments [23] were passed during the reign of James VI. against " unnecessary sumptuousness in men's apparel," by which no one except noblemen, lords of session, prelates, &c. were allowed to wear silver or gold lace. Provosts were permitted to wear silk, but no " lace pearlin " or " pasmenterie," only a " watling silk lace " on the seams.[24] No one but the above same privileged persons were to have pearlin on their ruffles, " sarkis," napkins, and " sokkis," and that pearlin to be made in the kingdom of Scotland. This act, dated 1621, is the first mention we have found of Scottish-made lace.

James VI. having granted to one James Bannatyne of Leith a patent for the " importing of foraine pearlin " into the country, in consequence of great complaint of the embroiderers in 1639, this patent is rescinded, and the king forbids the entry of all " foraine pearlin."

The word lace does not exist in the Scotch language. " Pearlin " is the term used in old documents, defined in the dictionaries to

---

[21] " Marriage Expenses of James VI., 1589." Published by the Bannatyne Club.

[22] " Accounts of the Great Chamber-lain of Scotland, 1590." Bannatyne Club.

[23] In 1581, 1597, and 1621.

[24] The same privilege was extended to their wives, their eldest sons with their wives, and their eldest daughters, but not to the younger children.

be " a species of lace made with thread." In the old Scotch songs it frequently occurs :— [25]

> " Then round the ring she dealt them ane by ane,
> Clean in her pearlin keck, and gown alane."
>
> *Ross Helonora.*

Again—

> " We maun hae pearlins and mabbies and cocks,
> And some other things that ladies call smocks."

As the latter articles may appear more familiar to the world in general than " kecks," and " mabbies," and " cocks," we may as well explain a " pearlin keck " to signify a linen cap with a lace border ; a " mabbie," a mob ; a " cock," or cock-up, no more eccentric head-dress than the lofty fontanges or commode of the last century.

Again, in " Rob Roy," we have the term " pearlin " : when Bailie Nicol Jarvie piteously pleads to his kinswoman, Helen Macgregor, he says—

" I hae been serviceable to Rob before now, forbye a set of pearlins I sent yoursell when you were gaun to be married."

The recollection of these delicate attentions, however, has little effect on the Highland chieftainess, who threatens to have him chopped up, if ill befalls her lord, into as many square pieces as compose the Macgregor tartan, or throw him neck and heels into the Highland loch.

The brave Montrose, we read, sent his lace ruffles to be starched and dressed before they were sewn on the embroidered sark he had made only to wear at his execution. " Pearlin " was provided for him which cost above 10*l.* an ell.

The close-fitting velvet cap, enriched with lace, appears in the seventeenth century to have been adopted by the lawyers of the Scotch courts. An example may be seen in the portrait of Sir Thomas Hope, Lord Advocate of Scotland, who died in 1646, which hangs in the Hall of the Advocates of Edinburgh. Another (Fig. 145) appears in the engraving of Sir Alexander Gibson, Bart., Lord Durie, one of the lords of session, who died two years previously.

In 1672, when lace—" point lace made of thread "—came

---

[25] 1633. In the " Account of Expenses for the young Lord of Lorne," we find :—

" 2 ells Cambridg' at 8*s.* the ell for ruffles, 16*s.*

" 2 ells of Perling at 30*s.*, the uther at 33*s.* 4*d.*, 3*l.* 3*s.* 4*d.*"—*Innes' Sketches of Early Scotch History.*

under the ban of the Covenanters, with a penalty of " 500 merks toties quoties," the wearing such vanities on liveries is strictly forbidden ; servants, however, are allowed to wear out their masters' and mistresses' old clothes.

In 1674, his majesty, understanding that the manufacture of " pearlin and whyt lace made of thread (whereby many people gain their livelihood) was thereby much prejudiced and impaired, declares that from henceforth it shall be free to all and every person within this kingdom to wear ' whyt lace,' as well as the privileged persons above mentioned." Finding these exclusions

Fig. 145.

Sir Alexander Gibson, Bart., Lord Durie, Lord of Session. + 1644.

of little or no avail, in January 1685 the act remits the wearing of lace, both native and foreign, to all folks living.

The dead now came under the scrutiny of the Scotch parliament, who ordered all lace or " poynt," gold or silver, to be disused at interments, under the penalty of 300 pounds Scots.[26]

From the united effects of poverty, Covenanters, and legislation, after the departure of the court for England, luxury, small though it was, declined in Edinburgh.

It was not till 1680, when James II., as Duke of York, accom-

------

[26] January 1686.

panied by Mary of Modena and his " duteous " daughter Anne, visited the Scotch capital, that anything like gaiety or dress can be said to have appalled the eyes of the strait-laced population.

Dryden, sneering at the barbarism of the Scotch capital, writes, in the prologue to a play delivered at Oxford, referring to a portion of the troop that accompanied the court to Scotland—

> " Laced linen there would be a dangerous thing ;
> It might perhaps a new rebellion bring—
> The Scot who wore it would be chosen king."

The Highlander, however, when in full dress, did not disdain to adopt the falling band and ruffles of guipure or Flanders lace.

A curious relic of this ancient mode may still be found in the long white crinkled sugar-plums familiar to most people in the Dundee mixtures, which, from their fancied resemblance to the guipure of the old falls, still bear the name of " band-ties."

The advertisements and inventories of the first years of the eighteenth century give us little reason to imagine any change had been effected in the homely habits of the people.

At the marriage of a daughter of Thomas Smythe, of Methuen, in 1701, to Sir Thomas Moncrieffe, the bride had a head-suit and ruffles of cutwork which cost nearly six pounds ten shillings.[27] Few and scanty advertisements of roups of " white thread lace " appear in the journals of the day.[28]

---

[27] " In 1701, when Mistress Margaret, daughter of the Baron of Kilravock, married, ' flounced muslin and lace for combing cloths,' appear in her outfit."— *Innes' Sketches.*

[28] In a pamphlet published 1702, entitled " An Accompt carried between England and Scotland," alluding to the encouragement of the yarn trade, the author says : " This great improvement can be attested by the industry of many young gentlewomen that have little or no portion, by spinning one pound of fine lint, and then breaking it into fine flax and whitening it. One gentlewoman told me herself that, by making an ounce or two of it into fine bone lace, it was worth, or she got, twenty pounds Scots for that part of it ; and might, after same manner, five or eight pounds sterling out of a pound of lint, that cost her not one

shilling sterling. Now if a law were made not to import any muslin (her Grace the Duchess of Hamilton still wears our finest Scots muslin as a pattern to others—she who may wear the finest apparel) and Holland lace, it would induce and stir up many of all ranks to wear more fine ' Scots lace,' which would encourage and give bread to many young gentlewomen and help their fortunes." Then, among the products of Scotland by which " we may balance any nation," the same writer mentions " our white thread, and making laces."

" On Tuesday, the 16th inst., will begin the roup of several sort of merchants' goods, in the first story of the Turnpyke, above the head of Bells Wynd, from 9 to 12 and 2 till 5. ' White thread lace.' "—*Edinburgh Courant,* 1706.

And in such a state matters continued till the Jacobites,
going and coming from Saint-Germain, introduced French
fashions and luxuries as yet unheard of in the then aristocratic
Canongate.

It sounds strange to a traveller, as he wanders among these
now deserted closes of Edinburgh, to read of the gay doings and
of the grand people who, in the last century, dwelt within these
poor-looking abodes. A difficult matter it must have been to the
Jacobite beauties, whose hoop (from 1725–8) measured nine yards
in circumference, to mount the narrow winding staircases of their
dwellings ; and this very difficulty gave rise to a luxury of under-
clothing almost unknown in England or elsewhere. Every lady
wore a petticoat trimmed with the richest point lace, which, when
her hooped dress was raised, lay exhibited to her admiring follower.
Nor did this terminate with the jupe ; independent of

" Twa lappets at her head, that flaunted gallantlie,"

ladies extended the luxury to finely laced garters.

In 1720, the bubble company "for the trading in Flanders
laces" appears advertised in the Scotch papers in large and
attractive letters. We strongly doubt, however, it having gained
any shareholders among the prudent population of Auld Reekie.

The prohibition of lace made in the dominions of the French
king [29] was a boon to the Jacobites, and many a lady, and gentleman too, became wondrous loyal to the exiled family, bribed by a
packet from Saint-Germain. In the first year of George II., says
the " Gazette," [30] a parcel of rich lace was secretly brought to the
Duke of Devonshire, by a mistake in the similarity of the title.
On being opened, hidden among the folds, was found a miniature
portrait of the Pretender, set round with large diamonds. The
packet was addressed to a noble lord high in office, one of the
most zealous converts to loyalty.[31]

---

[29] See p. 311.

[30] " Edinburgh Advertiser," 1764.

[31] 1745. The following description of
Lady Lovat, wife of the rebel Simon, is a
charming picture of a Scotch gentlewoman of the last century :—
" When at home her dress was a red
silk gown with ruffled cuffs and sleeves
puckered like a man's shirt, a fly cap of
lace encircling her head, with a mob cap

laid across it, falling down on her cheeks ;
her hair dressed and powdered ; a lace
handkerchief round the neck and bosom
(termed by the Scotch a *Befong*) ; a white
apron edged with lace. . . . Any one
who saw her sitting on her chair, so neat,
fresh, and clean, would have taken her
for a queen in wax-work, placed in a
glass case."—*Heart of Midlothian.*

Sir Walter Scott describes the dressing-

Smuggling was universal in Scotland in the reigns of George I.
and George II., for the people, unaccustomed to imposts, and
regarding them as an unjust aggression upon their ancient
liberties, made no scruple to elude the customs whenever it was
possible so to do.

It was smuggling that originated the Porteous riots of 1736;
and in his description of the excited mob, Sir Walter Scott makes
Miss Grizel Dalmahoy exclaim—" They hae ta'en awa' our
Parliament. They hae oppressed our trade. Our gentles will
hardly allow that a Scots needle can sew ruffles on a sark or lace
on an owerlay." [32]

To enliven this chapter, we give in a note the legend of
" Pearlin' Jean," [33] so called from the profusion of lace in which

---

room of Mrs. Bethune Balliol, as exhibiting a superb mirror framed in silver
filigree-work, with a toilet cover of
Flanders lace.

[32] " Heart of Midlothian."

[33] Pearlin' Jean was a Frenchwoman,
whom the first baronet, then Mr. Robert
Stuart, met at Paris, when making the
grand tour to finish his education. Some
said she was a nun, probably a sister
of charity, as she does not appear to
have been confined in a cloister. After
some time, Mr. Stuart either became
faithless to the lady or was suddenly re-
called to Scotland by his parents, and had
got into his carriage at the door of his
hotel, about to start from Paris, when
the lady unexpectedly made her appearance, and, stepping on the forewheel of
the coach to address her lover, he ordered
the postillion to drive on; the consequence of which was that the lady fell,
and one of the wheels passing over her
forehead, killed her on the spot. In a
dusky autumnal evening, when Mr.
Stuart arrived at Allenbank, and drove
under the arched gateway, he perceived
Pearlin' Jean sitting on the top, awaiting
his arrival, her head and shoulders
covered with blood. After this, for
many years, the house was haunted,
doors shut and opened with great noise
at midnight; the rustling of silks and
the pattering of high-heeled shoes in the
passage were constantly heard. Seven

ministers were called together at one
time to lay the spirit, but the family nurse
Jenny, said " they did no muckle good "
Jean still wandered about in silk attire,
adorned with the richest lace. Nurse
Jenny relates of herself, that on one
occasion, when she made an assignation
with her lover to meet her one moonlight
night in the orchard, the impatient
swain was the first at the trysting-place,
and seeing a female figure at some distance, he ran forward to embrace, as he
thought, his Jenny, when, lo! the figure
vanished, and he ran home in a fright.

In despair, the portrait of Pearlin' Jean
was hung up in the picture gallery between
those of Sir Robert and his wife, and this
appeared to propitiate her for a time,
and kept her comparatively quiet, but
when her portrait was taken away, she
became worse than ever.

The housekeeper, who lived many years
at Allenbank, declared that she and many
others had often seen Jean, but they
became so accustomed to her visits as to
be no longer alarmed at her noises.

The last time she was seen was about
1790, when two ladies paid a visit to
Allenbank, and passed the night there.
They had never heard a word about the
ghost, but declared next morning they had
been disturbed all night by some person
walking backwards and forwards in their
bedchamber.

At length the place was sold, the old

she always appeared, and whose persevering annoyance at Allenbank, the seat of the Stuart family, on the Blackadder River, was so thoroughly believed and established as to have prevented at various times the habitation of the place; as the popular rhyme in Berwickshire runs :—

> " O Pearlin' Jean, O Pearlin' Jean,
> She haunts the house, she haunts the green,
> And glowers on us a' wi' her wullcat e'en."

house at Allenbank was taken down, and another built by the new possessor in its stead. Its inmates are no more disturbed by the visits of Pearlin' Jean, whose troubled spirit has ceased from wandering, and is at last, we hope, at rest.

The story of Pearlin' Jean was originally given by Mr. Kirkpatrick Sharpe, from whom it has been copied by Mrs. Crowe and others.

CHAPTER XXXIV.

LACE MANUFACTURES OF SCOTLAND.

" Sae put on your pearlins, Marion,
And kirtle o' the cramasie."
Scottish Song.

DURING the treasonable year of '45, Scotland was far too occupied with her risings and executions to give much attention to her national industry. Up to that time considerable pains had been taken to improve the spinning of fine thread, prizes had been awarded, and the art taught in schools and other charitable institutions.

It was not till the middle of the eighteenth century that Anne, Duchess of Hamilton, known to society by tradition as " one of the beautiful Miss Gunnings, " seeing lace-makers at work when travelling on the continent, thought employment might be given to the women of her own country by introducing the art into Scotland. The duchess therefore brought over women from France, and caused them to teach the girls in her schools how to make " bunt lace, " as it was termed.

Sir John Sinclair thus notices the school :—" A small manufacture of thread lace has long been carried on here. At an early period it was the occupation of a good many women, but, from the fluctuation of fashion, it has fallen greatly into disuse. Fashion again revived the demand, and the late Duchess of Hamilton, afterwards of Argyle, found still some lace-workers remaining, to whom her own demand, and that of those who followed her example, gave employment To these her Grace added twelve orphan girls, who were clothed, maintained, and taught at her expense. Others learned the art, and while the demand lasted, the manufacture employed a good many hands. Though the number is again diminished, there are still above forty at the business, who make handsome laces of different patterns, besides those who work occasionally for themselves or their friends. Perhaps, under the patronage of the present respectable duchess, the manufacture of Hamilton lace may again become as flourishing as ever." [1]

"The Duchess of Hamilton," says the "Edinburgh Amusement" of 1752, "has ordered a home to be set up in Hamilton for the reception of twelve poor girls and a mistress. The girls are to be taken in at the age of seven, clothed, fed, taught to spin, make lace, etc., and dismissed at fourteen."

The work of the fair duchess throve, for, in 1754, we read how—"The Duchess of Hamilton has now the pleasure to see the good effects of her charity. Her Grace's small orphan family have, by spinning, gained a sum of money, and lately presented the duke and duchess with a double piece of Holland, and some suits of exceeding fine lace ruffles, of their own manufacture, which their Graces did them the honour to wear on the duke's birthday, July 14, and which vied with anything worn on the occasion, though there was a splendid company present. The yarn of which the ruffles were made weighed only ten drops each hank." [2]

It was probably owing to the influence of this impulsive Irishwoman that, in the year 1754, was founded the Select Society of Edinburgh for encouraging the arts and manufactures of Scotland, headed by the Duke of Hamilton. This society was contemporary with the Anti-Gallican in England and the Dublin Society, though we believe, in this case, Dublin can claim precedence over the capital of North Britain.

At a meeting of the society it was moved that "The annual importation of worked ruffles and of bone lace and edging into this country is considerable. By proper encouragement we might be supplied at home with these ornaments. It was therefore resolved—

"That a premium be assigned to all superior merit in such work; such a one as may be a mark of respect to women of fashion, and may also be of some solid advantage to those whose laudable industry contributes to their own support.

"For the best imitation of Dresden work, or a pair of men's ruffles, a prize of 5*l.* 5*s.*

"For the best bone lace, not under twenty yards, 5*l.* 5*s.* The gainers of these two best articles may have the money or a gold medal, at their option."

---

[1] "Statistical Account of Scotland." Sir John Sinclair. Edinburgh, 1792. Vol. ii. 198.   [2] "Edinburgh Amusement."

As may be supposed, the newly founded fabric of the duchess was not passed over by a society of which the duke himself was the patron. In the year 1757, we have, among the prizes adjudged, one of two guineas to Anne Henderson, of Hamilton, "for the whitest, and best, and finest lace, commonly called Hamilton lace, not under two yards." A prize had already been offered in 1755,[3] but, as stated the following year, "no lace was given in." Prizes continued in 1758 and 1759 to be given for the produce of Hamilton; in the last year to the value of four gineas.[4]

The early death of the Duke of Hamilton, and the second marriage of the Duchess, did not in any way impede the progress of Hamilton lace, for, as late as 1778, we read in Locke's "Essays on the Scotch Commerce:"—"The lace manufactory, under the patronage of the amiable Duchess of Hamilton (now Argyle), goes on with success and spirit."

Fig. 146.

Hamilton lace.

With respect to the quality of this Hamilton lace, laudable as were the efforts of the duchess, she succeeded in producing but a very coarse fabric. The specimens which have come under our notice are edgings of the commonest description, of a coarse thread, always of the lozenge pattern (Fig. 146); being strong and firm, it was used for nightcaps, never for dresses, and justified the

---

[3] 1755. Premium 2l. offered. "For the whitest, best, and finest lace, commonly called Hamilton lace, and of the best pattern, not under two yards in length and not under three inches in breadth."

[4] The Edinburgh Society did not confine their rewards to Hamilton lace; imitation of Dresden, catgut lace, gold, silver, and even livery lace, each met with its due reward.

1758. For imitation of lace done on catgut, for ruffles, a gold medal to Miss Anne Cant, Edinburgh.

For a piece of livery lace done to perfection to J. Bowie, 2 guineas.

To W. Bowie for a piece of gold and silver lace, 2 guineas.

description of a lady, now in her ninety-fifth year, who told the authoress it was of little account, and spoke of it as "only Hamilton."

It appears that the Edinburgh Society died a natural death, about 1764, but, notwithstanding the untimely demise of this patriotic club, a strong impetus had been given to the lace-makers of Scotland.[5]   Lace-making was introduced into the schools, and, what was better far, many daughters of the smaller gentry and scions of noble Jacobite houses, ruined by the catastrophe of '45, either added to their incomes or supported themselves wholly by the making of the finer lace.   This custom seems to have been general, and in alluding to it, Mrs. Calderwood speaks of the "helplessness" of the English women in comparison to the Scotch.

In the journals of the day we have constant advertisements, informing the public of the advantages to be gained by the useful arts imparted to their offspring in their establishments, inserted by ladies of gentle blood—for the Scotchwomen for the last century no more disdained to employ themselves in the training of youth than does now a French dame de qualité to place herself at the head of the Sacré Cœur or some other convent devoted to educational purposes.[6]

The entry of all foreign laces was excluded by law.   The Scotch nation—Hanoverian-way inclined—were sadly wrath at the frivolity of the Jacobite party.   "400,000l. have been sent out of the country during the last year," writes the "Edinburgh Adver-

---

[5] 1769. Pennant, in his "Tour," mentions among the manufactures of Scotland, thread laces at Leith, Hamilton, and Dalkeith.

[6] In 1762, Dec. 9, a schoolmistress in Dundee, among thirty-one accomplishments in which she professes to instruct her pupils, such as "waxwork, boning fowls without cutting the back," &c., enumerates, No. 21, "True point or tape lace," as well as "washing Flanders lace and point."

Again, in 1764, Mr. and Mrs. Mitchell advertise in their boarding school, "lace-work and the washing of blonde laces; the pupils' own laces washed and got up at home. Terms 24l."

At Miss Glen's boarding-school in the Trunk Close, 1768, young ladies are taught "white and coloured seam and washing of lace"—gratis.   And the writer is acquainted with an aged gentle-woman, still living at Edinburgh, who recollects being well whipped, in good old Covenanting style, when at school, by a teacher, for carelessly "running the 'guse' (iron) through her Hamilton."

These lady teachers were not appointed in Scotland without giving due proofs of their capacity.   In 1758, the magistrates and council of Aberdeen, being unanimous as to the "strict morality, Dresden work, modesty, and catgut lace-making," &c. of Miss Betsey Forbes, elected her to the office of schoolmistress of the city.

In "The Cottagers of Glenburnie," a lady, Mrs. Mason, tells a long story of the young laird having torn a suit of lace she was busied in getting up.

tiser" of 1764, "to support our exiled countrymen in France, where they learn nothing but folly and extravagance." English laces were not included in the prohibition. In 1763, that "neat shop near the Stinking Style, in the Lukenbooths," held by Mr. James Baillie, advertises "Trollies, English laces, and pearl edgings." Four years later, black silk lace and guipure are added to the stock, "mennuet," and very cheap bone lace.[7]

Great efforts, and with success, were made for the improvement of the thread manufacture, for the purchase of which article at Lille 200,000*l.* were annually sent from Scotland to France. Badly spun yarn was seized and burned by the stamp master; of this we have frequent mention.[8]

Peuchet, speaking of Scotland, says:—"Il s'est formé près d'Édimbourg une manufacture de fil de dentelle. On prétend que le fil de cette manufacture sert à faire des dentelles qui non-seulement égalent en beauté celles qui sont fabriquées avec le fil de l'étranger, mais encore les surpassent en durée. Cet avantage serait d'autant plus grand que l'importation de ce fil de l'étranger occasionne aux habitans de ce royaume une perte annuelle de 100,000*l.*"[9]

Whether about the year 1775 any change had taken place in the legislation of the customs of Scotland, and they had become regulated by English law, we cannot say, but suddenly constant advertisements of Brussels lace and fine point appear in the "Gazette," and this at the very time Loch was doing his best to stir up once more Scotch patriotism with regard to manufactures.[10]

The Scotch Foresters set the example at their meeting in 1766, and then—we hear nothing more on the matter.

---

[7] "Edinburgh Advertiser."

[8] 1774. "Several punds of badly spun yarn was burnt by the stamp master in Montrose." This announcement constantly occurs.

[9] About this period, a Mr. Brotherton, of Leith, seems to have made a discovery which was but a prelude to the bobbin-net. It is thus described in the "Weekly Magazine" of 1772:—"A new invention has lately been discovered by Mr. Brotherton, in Leith, for working black silk lace or white thread lace on a loom, to imitate any pattern whatever, and the lace done in this way looks fully as well as if sewed, and comes much cheaper. It is done any breadth, from three inches to three-quarters of a yard wide."

[10] In 1775, Dallas, Barclay, and Co., advertise a selling off of fine point, Brussels thread, blonde, and black laces of all kinds, silver double-edged lace, &c. "Edinburgh Advertiser."

1775. "Black blonde and thread laces, catguts of all sorts, just arrived from the India House in London in the Canongate."—*Caledonian Mercury.*

"Fashions for January : dresses trimmed with Brussels point or Mignonette." —*Ibid.* same year.

2 c

The "Weekly Magazine" of 1776 strongly recommends the art of lace-making as one calculated to flourish in Scotland; young girls beginning to learn at eight years of age, adding: "The directors of the hospital of Glasgow have already sent twenty-three girls to be taught by Madame Puteau,[11] a native of Lisle, now residing at Renfrew; you will find the lace of Renfrew cheaper, as good and as neat as those imported from Brussels, Lisle, and Antwerp." David Loch also mentions the success of the young Glasgow lace-makers, who made lace, he says, from 10d. to 4s. 6d. per yard. He adds: "It is a pleasure to see them at work. I saw them ten days ago." He recommends the managers of the workhouse of the Canongate to adopt the same plan: adding, they need not send to Glasgow for teachers, as there are plenty at the orphan hospital at Edinburgh capable of undertaking the office. Of the lace fabricated at Glasgow, we know nothing, save from an advertisement in the "Caledonian Mercury" of 1778, where one William Smith, "Lace-maker," at the Greenhead, Glasgow, informs the public he has for some years "made and bleached candlewicks." Anderson and Loch did not agree on the subject of lace-making; the former considering it an unstable fabric, too easily affected by the caprices of fashion.[12]

Be that as it may, the manufacture of thread for lace alone employed five hundred machines, each machine occupying thirty-six persons: the value of the thread produced annually 175,000l. Loch adds that, in consequence of the cheapness of provisions, Scotland, as a country, is better adapted for lace-making than England. In consequence of Loch's remarks, his Majesty's Board of Trustees for the Fisheries and Manufactures, after asking a number of questions, determined to give proper encouragement

---

[11] "Madame Puteau carries on a lace manufacture after the manner of Mechlin and Brussels. She had lately twenty-two apprentices from the Glasgow Hospital. . . . . Mrs. Puteau has as much merit in this branch as has her husband in the making of fine thread. This he manufactures of such a fineness as to be valued at 10l. the pound weight."— *Essays on the Trade, Commerce, Manufactures, Fisheries, &c. of Scotland, David Loch*, 1778.

[12] "If you look at the wardrobes of your grandmother, you will perceive what revolutions have happened in taste of mankind for laces and other fineries of that sort. How many suits of this kind do you meet with that cost amazing sums, which are now and have long since been entirely useless. In our own day, did we not see that in one year Brussels laces are most in fashion and purchased at any price, while the next perhaps they are entirely laid aside, and French or other thread laces, or fine sewings, the names of which I know not, highly prized."— *Observations on the National Industry of Scotland, Anderson*, 1778.

and have mistresses for teaching the different kinds of lace made in England and France, and oblige them to take girls of the poorer class, some from the hospitals, and the mistress for five years to have the benefit of their work. A girl might earn from 10*d.* to 1*s.* per day. They gave a salary to an experienced person from Lisle for the purpose of teaching the making of thread; his wife to instruct in lace-making. With the records of 1788 end all mention of lace-making in Scotland.

Lace-making at Hamilton is now a thing of the past, replaced by a tambour network for veils, scarfs, and flounces. At Glasgow and elsewhere, the sewing of muslin and embroidery occupies the women of all classes, and, though less patronised, fully equals in beauty the productions of Switzerland or Lorraine. The fishwife at her door scolds the small bare-legged urchin while sewing the strip of muslin in her hand. The shepherd girl on the mountain's brow, while tending her flock, stitches away, the ever watchful colly by her side; and the employment, though scarcely more lucrative, is at any rate more healthy than the art, now forgotten in Scotland, of lace-making.

CHAPTER XXXV.

IRELAND.

"The undoubted aptitude for lace-making of the women of Ireland."

Jurors' Report, International Exhibition, 1862.

LITTLE is known of the early state of manufactures in Ireland, save that the art of needlework was held in high estimation.

By the sumptuary laws of King Mogha Nuadhad, killed at the battle of Maylean, A.D. 192, we learn that the value of a queen's raiment, should she bring a suitable dowry, ought to amount to the cost of six cows ; but of what the said raiment consisted, history is dark.

The same record, however, informs us that the price of a mantle, wrought with the needle, should be " a young bullock or steer." [1] This hooded mantle is described by Giraldus Cambrensis as composed of various pieces of cloth, striped, and worked in squares by the needle ; may be a species of cutwork.

Morgan, who wrote in 1588, declares the saffron-tinted shirts of the Irish to contain from 20 to 30 ells of linen. No wonder they are described—

> " With pleates on pleates they pleated are,
> As thick as pleates may lie." [2]

It was in such guise the Irish appeared at court before Queen Elizabeth,[3] and from them the yellow starch of Mrs. Turner may have derived its origin. The Irish, however, produced the dye not from saffron, but from a lichen gathered on the rocks. Be that as it may, the government prohibited its use, and the shirts were reduced in quantity to six ells,[4] for the making of which " new-

---

[1] " Essay on the Dress of the Early Irish," J. C. Walker, 1788.

[2] " The Image of Irelande," by Jhon Derricke, 1578.

[3] In 1562. See Camden, " Hist Eliz."

[4] Henry VIII. 1537. Against Irish fashions. Not " to weare any shirt, smock,

fangled pair of Gally-cushes," i. e. English shirts, as we find by the Corporation Book of Kilkenny (1573), eighteenpence was charged if done with silk or cutwork. Ninepence extra was charged for every ounce of silk worked in.

An Irish smock wrought with silk and gold was considered an object worthy of a king's wardrobe, as the inventory of King Edward IV.[5] attests:—" Item, one Irishe smocke wrought with gold and silke."

The Rebellion at an end, a friendly intercourse, as regards fashion, was kept up between the English and the Irish. The ruff of geometric design, falling band, and cravat of Flanders lace, all appeared in due succession. The Irish, always lovers of pomp and show, early used lace at the interments of the great, as appears from an anecdote related in a letter of Mr. O'Halloran :—" The late Lord Glandore told me," he writes, " that when a boy, under a spacious tomb in the ruined monastery at his seat, Ardfert Abbey (Co. Kerry), he perceived something white. He drew it forth, and it proved to be a shroud of Flanders lace, the covering of some person long since deceased."

In the beginning of the eighteenth century a patriotic feeling arose among the Irish, who joined hand in hand to encourage the productions of their own country. Swift was among the first to support the movement, and in a prologue he composed, in 1721, to a play acted for the benefit of the Irish weavers, he says :—

> " Since waiting-women, like exacting jades,
> Hold up the prices of their old brocades,
> We'll dress in manufactures made at home."

Shortly afterwards, at a meeting, he proposed the following resolution :—

" That the ladies wear Irish manufactures. There is brought annually into this kingdom near 90,000*l.* worth of silk, whereof the greater part is manufactured ; 30,000*l.* more is expended in muslin, holland, cambric, and calico. What the price of lace amounts to is not easy to be collected from the custom-house book, being a kind of goods that, taking up little room, is easily run ; but, considering the prodigious price of a woman's head-dress at ten, twelve, twenty pounds a yard, it must be very great."

---

kerchor, bendel, neckerchour, mocket, or linen cappe colored or dyed with saffron," and not to use more than seven yards of linen in their shirts or smocks.

[5] 4 Edw. IV. Harl. MSS. No. 1419. *b.-g.* 494.

Though a club of patriots had been formed in Ireland since the beginning of the eighteenth century, called the Dublin Society, they were not incorporated by charter until the year 1749; hence many of their records are lost, and we are unable to ascertain the precise period at which they took upon themselves the encouragement of the bone lace trade in Ireland. From their "Transactions" we learn that, so early as the year 1743, the annual value of the bone lace manufactured by the children of the workhouses of the city of Dublin amounted to 164*l*. 14*s*. 10½*d*.[6] In consequence of this success, the society ordain that 34*l*. 2*s*. 6*d*. be given to the Lady Arabella Denny, to distribute among the children, for their encouragement in making bone lace. Indeed, to such a pitch were the productions of the needle already brought in Ireland that in the same year, 1743, the Dublin Society gave Robert Baker, of Rollin Street, Dublin, a prize of 10*l*. for his imitation of Brussels lace ruffles, which are described as being most exquisite both in design and workmanship. This Brussels lace of Irish growth was much prized by the patriots.[7] From this time the Dublin Society acted under their good genius, the Lady Arabella Denny. The prizes they awarded were liberal, and success attended their efforts.

In 1755, we find a prize of 2*l*. 15*s*. 6*d*. awarded to Susanna Hunt, of Fishamble Street, aged eleven, for a piece of lace most extraordinarily well wrought. Miss Elinor Brereton, of Raheenduff, Queen's County, for the best imitation of Brussels lace with the needle, 7*l*. On the same occasion, Miss Martha M'Cullow, of Cork Bridge, gains the prize of 5*l*. for "Dresden point." Miss Mary Gibson has 2*l*. for "Cheyne Lace,"[8] of which we have scarcely heard mention since the days of Queen Elizabeth.

---

[6] That lace ruffs soon appeared in Ireland may be proved by the effigy on a tomb still extant in the Abbey of Clonard, in which the Dillon arms are conspicuous, and also by paintings of the St. Lawrence family, cir. 1521, preserved at Howth Castle.

In the portrait at Muckruss of the Countess of Desmond, she is represented with a lace collar. It was taken, as stated at the back of the portrait, "as she appeared at the court of King James, 1614, and in yᵉ 140th year of her age." Thither she went to endeavour to reverse the attainder of her house.

[7] At the end of the last century there lived at Creaden, near Waterford, a lady of the name of Power, lineal descendant of the kings of Munster, and called the Queen of Creaden. She affected the dress of the ancient Irish. The border of her coif was of the finest Irish-made Brussels lace; her jacket of the finest brown cloth, trimmed with gold lace; her petticoat of the finest scarlet cloth, bordered with a row of broad gold lace; all her dress was of Irish manufacture.

[8] "Gentleman's and Citizen's Almanack," by G. Watson, Dublin, 1757.

Bone lace had never in any quantity been imported from England. In 1703, but 2333 yards, valuing only 116*l.* 13*s.*, or 1*s.* per yard, passed through the Irish custom-house. Ireland, like the rest of the United Kingdom, received her lace either from France or Flanders.

The thread used in the Irish fabric was derived from Hamburg, of which, in 1765, 2573 lbs. were imported.

It was in this same year the Irish club of young gentlemen refused, by unanimous consent, to toast or consider beautiful any lady who should wear French lace or indulge in foreign fopperies.

During the two succeeding years the lace of various kinds exhibited by the workhouse children was greatly approved of, and the thanks of the Society were offered to the Lady Arabella Denny.[9]

Prizes were given to the children to the amount of 34*l.* 2*s.* 6*d.* ; the same for bone lace made by other manufacturers; and one half the sum is also to be applied to "thread lace made with knitting needles."

A certain Mrs. Rachel Armstrong, of Inistioge (Co. Kilkenny), is also awarded a prize of 11*l.* 7*s.* 6*d.*, "for having caused a considerable quantity of bone lace to be made by girls whom she has instructed and employed in the work." Among the premiums granted to "poor gentlewomen," we find: "To Miss Jane Knox, for an apron of elegant pattern, and curiously wrought, 6*l.* 16*s.* 6*d.*," and silver medals to two ladies who, we suppose, are above receiving money as a reward. The society recommended that the bone lace made be exposed for sale in the warehouses of the Irish Silk Company. In consequence of the emulation excited among all classes, advertisements appear in the "Dublin News" of ladies "very capable of instructing young misses in fine lace-making, needlework point, broderie en tambour, all in the genteelest taste."

Lady Arabella stood not alone as a patroness of the art. In 1770, we read how "a considerable quantity of bone lace of extraordinary fineness and elegance of pattern, made at Castlebar, in the Co. of Mayo, being produced to the society, and it appearing that the manufacture of bone lace was founded, and is at

[9] "The freedom of the city of Dublin was also conferred upon her, presented in due form in a silver box, as a mark of esteem for her great charities and constant care of the Foundling children in the city workhouse."— *Dublin Freeman's Journal,* July 30, 1765.

present supported there by Lady Bingham, it was ordered that
the sum of 25*l.* be paid into the hands of her Ladyship, to be
disposed of in such encouragements as she shall judge will most
effectually conduce to the carrying on and improvement of the
said manufacture at Castlebar." The thanks of the society are,
at the same time, voted to her ladyship. In consequence of the
large quantity fabricated, after the lapse of a few years, the
society, in 1773, found themselves compelled to put some bounds
to their liberality. No prizes are given for any lace exhibited at
less than 11*s.* 4½*d.* the yard, and that only to those not resident in
the city of Dublin, or within five miles of it. Twenty per cent.
will be given on the value of the lace, provided it shall not exceed
500*l.* in value. The society do not, however, withdraw the annual
premium of 30*l.* for the products of the " famishing children " of
the city of Dublin workhouse,[10] always directed by the indefati-
gable Lady Arabella Denny.[11] From this period we hear no more
of the Dublin Society, and its prizes awarded for point, Dresden,
Brussels, or bone lace.

The manufacture of gold and silver lace having met with
considerable success, the Irish parliament, in 1778, gave it their
protection by passing an act prohibiting the entry of all such
commodities either from England or foreign parts.

And now, for fifty years and more, history is silent on the
subject of lace-making by the " famishing children " of the
Emerald Isle.[12]

In the year 1829 the manufacture of Limerick lace was first
established in Ireland. Lace, in the strictest sense of the word,
it cannot be termed; it consists entirely of tambour-work upon
what is commonly known as Nottingham net. This fabric was
first introduced by one Charles Walker,[13] a native of Oxfordshire,

---

[10] " Gentleman's and Citizen's Almanack." by Samuel Watson, 1773.

[11] " The Lady Arabella Denny died
1792, aged 85; she was second daughter
of Thos. Fitzmaurice, Earl of Kerry.
The Irish Academy, in acknowledgment
of her patriotic exertions, offered a prize
of 100 guineas for the best monody on
her death. It was gained by John
Macaulay, Esq." — *Dublin Freeman's
Journal,* July 20, 1766.

[12] Wakefield writes in 1812 :—" Lace
is not manufactured to a large extent in

Ireland. I saw some poor children who
were taught weaving by the daughters
of a clergyman, and Mr. Tighe mentions
a school, in Kilkenny, where twelve girls
were instructed in the art. At Abbey-
leix there is a lace manufactory, but the
quantity made is not of any importance."
—*Account of Ireland, Statistical and Political, Edw. Wakefield,* 1812.

[13] Walker was a man of literary and artistic tastes, and educated for the Church ;
but, marrying the daughter of a lace-
manufacturer, he set up in that business

who brought over twenty-four girls as teachers, and commenced manufacturing at a place in Limerick called Mount Kennet. His goods were made entirely for one house in St. Paul's Churchyard, until that house became bankrupt in 1843; after which a traveller was sent through England, Scotland, and Ireland, to take orders. Her excellency Lady Normandy, wife of the lord-lieutenant, gave great encouragement to the fabric, causing dresses to be made, not only for herself, but also for her majesty the Queen of the Belgians and the Grand Duchess of Baden. In 1855, the number of workers employed amounted to 1500; at the present time there are not above 500. The existing depression of the trade has been partly caused by the emigration of girls to America and the colonies, while glove-making and army clothing employ the rest; and indeed the manufacture, aiming only at cheapness, had produced a lace of inferior quality, without either novelty or beauty of design; from which cause Limerick lace has fallen into disrepute.

In the year of the great famine, 1846, when thousands of children were left orphans in the hands of the landed proprietors, the Irish ladies at once bethought themselves by what occupation they could be made to gain their livelihood.

Lady de Vere was the first to teach the mistress of a school on her own demesne at Curragh, Co. Limerick, the art of making application flowers, giving her own Brussels lace as patterns. The work was so good as soon to command a high price, and the late Queen of the Belgians actually purchased a dress of it at Harding's, and took it back with her to Brussels. The manufacture is known by the name of "Irish" or "Curragh point."

Various schools have since been established throughout Ireland.

That set up at Belfast by the late Jane Clarke exhibited, in 1851, beautiful imitations of the old Spanish and Italian points; among others, a specimen of the fine raised Venetian point, like Coloured Plate III. (p. 44), which can scarcely be distinguished from the original. It is now in the South Kensington Museum.

---

in Essex, working for the London wholesale trade. He removed next to Limerick, where he continued till 1841, when he sold the business; but his successor becoming bankrupt, he never received the purchase money, and died 1842, his ingenuity and industry ill rewarded. In some work (we have lost the reference), it is stated that "Coggeshall, in Essex, made a tambour lace, a sort of medium between lace and embroidery." Could this be Walker's manufacture?

Irish Brussels is made at Clones, Co. Monaghan ; Irish guipure at Carrickmacross,[14] in the same county ; and the finest Valenciennes in the schools of the Countess of Erne, at Lishnakea, Co. Fermanagh. The Irish Valenciennes closely resembles the Ypres manufacture.

There is a school at Mallow, Co. Cork, under the superintendence of the nuns of the convent.

Those of the St. George family, at Headford, Co. Galway ; of Miss Latouche, at Killmaule, Mrs. Kavanagh, at Borris, Co. Carlow, and others, are so many centres whence the lace manufacture is extending throughout the kingdom.

The Irish "lacet" is also of great beauty. It is made of flax thread, the ground-work crochet, into which are introduced flowers and patterns filled in with lace stitches of admirable finish.

Still a considerable depression exists in the Irish lace trade, caused by the impossibility of competing with inferior and machine-made lace.

It is to be regretted that the ladies presiding over the schools do not strike out into a new path, and cause such lace only to be produced as may prove remunerative to the manufacturer.

The Irish guipure might be successfully applied to the trimming of curtains, toilets, and other objects of furniture, for which ladies now purchase " Greek " and other " torchon " laces at far more extravagant prices.

---

[14] At one of the drawing-rooms of this year, a lady's dress is described as having the train, corsage, and petticoat " trimmed with Carrickmacross point lace."— *Morning Post*, 16th May 1864.

CHAPTER XXXVI.

BOBBIN-NET AND MACHINE-MADE LACE.

Fig. 147.

Arms of the Framework Knitters' Company.

BOBBIN-NET.

A SKETCH of the history of lace would be incomplete without a few words on bobbin-net and machine lace, manufactures which have risen to so much importance both in England and France, and have placed lace within the reach of all classes of society. The subject has been so ably treated by Mr. Felkin that we refer our readers to his excellent work for its full history.[1]

This manufacture has its epochs :—

1768. Net first made by machinery.

1809. Invention of bobbin-net.

1837. The Jacquard system applied to the bobbin-net machine.

It has been already told how Barbara Uttmann made a plain thread net in Germany three centuries before any attempt was made to produce it by machinery.

This invention is usually assigned to Hammond, a stocking framework knitter of Nottingham, who, examining one day the

---

[1] "History of Machine-wrought Hosiery and Lace Manufacture," W. Felkin, London, 1867.

broad lace on his wife's cap, thought he could apply his machine
to the production of a similar article.[2] His attempt so far succeeded that, by means of the stocking-frame invented the previous
century,[3] he produced, in 1768, not lace, but a kind of knitting,
of running loops or stitches, like that afterwards known as "Brus-
less ground." In 1777, Else and Harvey introduced at Nottingham
the "pin" or point-net machine, so named because made on sharp
pins or points. "Point-net" was afterwards improved, and the
"barley-corn" introduced : "square" and "spider net" appear in
succession.

But, with all these improvements, machinery had not yet
arrived at producing a solid net ; it was still only knitting, a single
thread passing from one end of the frame to the other ; and if a
thread broke, the work was unravelled ; the threads, therefore
requiring to be gummed together, to give stiffness and solidity to
the net. To remedy this evil, the warp or chain machine was
invented, uniting the knitter's and the weaver's mechanism.
Vandyke,[4] a Flemish workman, and three Englishmen dispute the
invention. This new machine was again improved and made
"Mechlin net," from which the machine took its name.

For forty years from Hammond's first attempt on the stocking-
frame, endless efforts were made to arrive at imitating the ground
of pillow lace, and there are few manufactures in which so much
capital has been expended and so much invention called forth.
Each projector fancied he had discovered the true stitch, and

---

[2] An open stitch on stockings, called
the "Derby rib," had been invented by
Jedediah Strutt, in 1758.

[3] By Rev. William Lee, of Calverton
(Nottinghamshire). The romantic story
is well known ; but whether actuated,
as usually stated, by pique at the ab-
sorbing attention paid to her knitting
by a lady, when he was urging his suit—
or, as others more amiably affirm, by a
desire to lighten the labour of his wife,
who was obliged to contribute to their
joint support by knitting stockings—
certain it is that it was he who first
conceived the idea of the stocking-frame,
and completed it about 1589. His invention met with no support from Queen
Elizabeth, so Lee went to France, where
he was well received by Henry IV.;
but the same year Henry was assassi-

nated, and the regent withdrawing her
protection, Lee died of grief and disappointment. The arms of the Framework
Knitters' Company (Fig. 147, see p. 395)
are a stocking-frame, having for supporters William Lee in full canonicals
and a female holding in her hand thread
and a knitting needle. After Lee's death
his brother returned to England, where
Lee's invention was then appreciated.
Stocking-making became the fashion,
every one tried it, and people had their
portraits taken with gold and silver
needles suspended round their necks.

[4] Vandyke had also appended the
chain to his stocking-frame, and the
zigzags formed by the ribs of his stockings were called "Vandyke ;" hence the
term now generally applied to all in-
dente l edges.

patents after patents were taken out, resulting mostly in disappointment.

The machine for making " bobbin " net was invented by John Heathcoat, son of a farmer at Longwhatton (Leicestershire). After serving his apprenticeship, he settled at Nottingham, and, while occupied in putting together stocking and net machines, gave his attention to improving the Mechlin net frame.[5] In 1809, in conjunction with Mr. Lacy, he took out a patent for fourteen years for his new and highly ingenious bobbin-net machine, which he called Old Loughborough, after the town to which he then removed.

" Bobbin-net " was so named because the threads are wound upon bobbins.[6] It was " twisted " instead of " looped " net. Heathcoat began by making net little more than an inch in width,[7] and afterwards succeeded in producing it a yard wide. There are now machines which make it $3\frac{1}{2}$ yards in width.[8]

In 1811 that vandal association called the Luddites [9] entered his manufactory and destroyed twenty-seven of his machines, of the value of 8000*l.* Indignant at their conduct, he removed to Tiverton,[10] in Devonshire.

---

[5] Mechlin net was disused in 1819, from its too great elasticity.

[6] The " bobbins " on which the thread is wound for the weft consist of two circular copper plates riveted together, and fixed upon a small carriage or frame which moves backwards and forwards like a weaver's shuttle.

[7] The Old Loughboro' employed sixty movements to form one mesh ; now obtained by twelve. It produced 1000 meshes a minute—then thought a wonderful achievement, as by the pillow only five or six can be obtained : a good circular machine now produces 30,000 in the same time.

The quality of bobbin-net depends upon the smallness of the meshes, their equality in size, and the regularity of the hexagons.

[8] Bobbin-net is measured by the " rack," which consists of 240 meshes. This mode of counting was adopted to avoid the frequent disagreements about measure which arose between the master and the workmen in consequence of the elasticity of the net. The exchange of

linen to cotton thread was the source of great regret to the Roman Catholic clergy, who by ecclesiastical law can only wear albs of flax.

[9] This association was formed by Ludlam, or General Ludd, as he was called, a stocking-frame worker at Nottingham, in 1811, when prices had fallen. The Luddites, their faces covered with a black veil, armed with swords and pistols, paraded the streets at night, entered the workshops, and broke the machines with hammers. A thousand machines were thus destroyed. Soon the net-workers joined them and made a similar destruction of the bobbin-net machines. Although many were punished, it was only with the return of work that the society disappeared in 1817.

[10] Heathcoat represented Tiverton from 1831 to 1859, colleague of Lord Palmerston.

Steam power was first introduced by Mr. J. Lindley, in 1815–16, but did not come into active operation till 1820 ; it became general 1822–23.

The year 1823 is memorable for the "bobbin-net fever." Mr. Heathcoat's patent having expired, all Nottingham went mad. Every one wished to make bobbin-net. Numerous individuals, clergymen, lawyers, doctors, and others, readily embarked capital in so tempting a speculation. Prices fell in proportion as production increased ; but the demand was immense, and the Nottingham lace frame became the organ of general supply, rivalling and supplanting in plain nets the most finished productions of France and the Netherlands.[11] Dr. Ure says: " It was no uncommon thing for an artisan to leave his usual calling and betake himself to a lace frame, of which he was part proprietor, and realise, by working upon it, twenty, thirty, nay, even forty shillings a day. In consequence of such wonderful gains, Nottingham, with Loughborough and the adjoining villages, became the scene of an epidemic mania. Many, though nearly void of mechanical genius or the constructive talent, tormented themselves night and day with projects of bobbins, pushers, lockers, point bars, and needles of every various form, till their minds got permanently bewildered. Several lost their senses altogether, and some, after cherishing visions of wealth as in the olden time of alchemy, finding their schemes abortive, sank into despair and committed suicide.

Such is the history of the bobbin-net [12] invention in England.[13] We now pass on to France.

---

[11] McCulloch.

[12] *Progressive Value of a square yard of plain cotton bobbin-net.*

1809	5*l*.	1830	2*s*.
1813	2*l*.	1833	1*s*. 4*d*.
1815	1*l*. 10*s*.	1836	10*d*.
1818	1*l*.	1842	6*d*.
1821	12*s*.	1850	4*d*.
1824	8*s*.	1856	3*d*.
1827	4*s*.	1862	3*d*.

" Histoire du Tulle et des Dentelles mécaniques en Angleterre et en France, par S. Ferguson fils." Paris, 1862.

" Bobbin-net and lace are cleaned from the loose fibres of the cotton by the ingenious process of gassing, as it is called, invented by the late Mr. Samuel Hall, of Nottingham. A flame of gas is drawn through the lace by means of a vacuum above. The sheet of lace passes to the flame opaque, and obscured by loose fibre, and issues from it bright and clear, not to be distinguished from lace made of the purest linen thread, and perfectly uninjured by the flame."—*Journal of the Society of Arts,* Jan. 1864.

[13] In 1825, Mr. Huskisson's reduction of the duty on French tulle caused so much distress in Leicester and Nottingham that ladies were desired to wear only English tulle at court ; and in 1831, Queen Adelaide appeared at one of her balls in a dress of English silk net.

FRANCE.

" To the great trading nation, to the great manufacturing nation, no progress which any portion of the human race can make in knowledge, in taste for the conveniences of life, or in the wealth by which these conveniences are produced, can be matter of indifference."—Macaulay.

Since the failure[14] of Lee, in 1610, to introduce the stocking-frame into France, that country remained ignorant of a manufacture which was daily progressing in England, on whom she was dependant for stockings and for net.

In 1778, Caillen attempted a kind of net, " tricot dentelle," for which he obtained a gratuity from the Academy of 40*l.*, but his method did not succeed; it was, like the first efforts of our countryman, only knitting.

In 1784, Louis XVI. sent the Duke de Liancourt to England to study the improvements in the stocking and net machinery, and to bring back a frame. He was accompanied by Rhumbolt, who worked in a manufactory at Nottingham, and having acquired the art, returned to France. Monarchy had fallen, but the French Republic, 1793–4, granted Rhumbolt the sum of 110,000 francs (4400*l.*). The machine he brought with him was the point net.[15]

The cessation of all commercial intercourse prevented France from keeping pace with the improvements making in England ; yet, singular enough, at the beginning of the present century, more net was manufactured in France than in England. At the time of the Peace of Amiens, 1802, there were 2000 frames in Lyons and Nîmes, while there were scarcely 1200 in England; but the superiority of the English net was incontestable; so, to protect the national manufactures, Napoleon prohibited the importation. This of course increased its demand; the net was in request in proportion as it was prohibited. The best mart for Nottingham was the French market, so the Nottingham net trade took every means to pass their produce into France.

Hayne, one of the proprietors of the " barley-corn " net, had gone to Paris to make arragements for smuggling it over, when

---

[14] See p. 396, note 3. John Hindres, in 1656, first established a stocking-frame in France.

[15] The net produced was called " tulle simple et double de Lyon et de Vienne." The net was single loops, hence the name of " single press," given to these primitive frames.

the war broke out, and he was detained. Napoleon proposed that he should set up a machine in France ; but he preferred continuing his illicit trade, which he carried on with great success until 1809, when his own agent informed against him, his goods were seized and burned, and having in one seizure lost 60,000*l.* (1,500,000 fr.), he was completely ruined and fled to England.[16]

The French manufacturers took out various patents for the improvement of their "Mechlin" machines, and one was taken, in 1809, for making a crossed net called "fond de glace ;" but the same year Heathcoat producing the bobbin-net machine, the inventors could not sustain the competition.

Every attempt was made to get over bobbin-net machines ; but the export of English machinery was punished by transportation, and the Nottingham manufacturers established at their own expense a line of surveillance to prevent the bobbin-net machines from going out. In spite of all these precautions, Cutts, an old workman of Heathcoat's, contrived to elude their vigilance, and, in 1815, to import a machine to Valenciennes, whence he removed it to Douay, where he entered into partnership with M. Thomassin. In 1816 they produced the first bobbin-net dress made in France. It was embroidered by hand by a workwoman of Douay, and presented by the makers to the Duchesse d'Angoulême. About the end of the year 1816, James Clark introduced a machine into Calais, which he passed in pieces by means of some French sailors. These two were the first bobbin-net machines set up in France.

It is not within our limits to follow the Calais lace manufacturers through their progress ; suffice it to say that it was in 1817 that the first bobbin-net machine worked, concealed from all eyes, at Saint-Pierre-lez-Calais, now, if not the rival of Nottingham, at least the great centre of the bobbin-net and machinery lace manufactures in France.[17]

---

[16] In 1801, George Armitage took a "point net" machine to Antwerp, and made several after the same model, thus introducing the manufacture into Belgium. He next went to Paris, but the wholesale contraband trade of Hayne left him no hope of success. He afterwards went to Prussia to set up net and stocking machines. At the age of 82 he started for Australia, where he died, in 1857, aged 89.

[17] The great difficulty encountered by the French manufacturers consisted in the cotton. France did not furnish cotton higher than No. 70 ; the English ranges from 160 to 200. The prohibition of English cotton obliged them to obtain it by smuggling, until 1834, when it was admitted on paying a duty. Now they make their own, and are able to rival Nottingham in the prices of their productions : a great number of Nottingham lace-makers have emigrated to Calais.

Saint-Quentin, Douay, Cambrai, Rouen, Caen, have all in turn been the seats of the tulle manufacture. Some of these fabrics are extinct; the others have a very limited trade compared with Saint-Pierre and Lyons.

At Lyons, silk net is mostly made.[18] Dating from 1791, various patents have been taken out for its manufacture : these silk nets were embroidered at Condrieu (Rhône), and were (the black especially for veils and mantles) much esteemed, particularly in Spain. In 1825, the "tulle bobine grenadine," black and white, was brought out by M. Doguin, who afterwards used the fine silks, and invented that popular material first called "zephyr," since "illusion." His son, in 1838, brought out the "tulle Bruxelles."

BELGIUM.

In 1834,[19] eight bobbin-net machines were set up in Brussels by Mr. Washer, for the purpose of making the double and triple twisted net, upon which the pillow flowers are sewn to produce the Brussels application lace. Mr. Washer devoted himself exclusively to the making of the extra fine mesh, training up workmen specially to this minute work. In a few years he succeeded in excelling the English manufacture ; and this net, universally known as " Brussels net," has for nearly thirty years superseded the expensive pillow ground, and has thereby materially decreased the price of Brussels lace. It is made of English cotton, stated, in the specimens exhibited in 1867, as costing 44l. per pound.

MACHINERY LACE.

" Qui sait si le métier à tulle ne sera pas un jour, en quelque sorte, un vrai coussin de dentellière, et les bobines de véritables fuseaux manœuvrés par des mains mécaniques."—*Aubry*, in 1851.

If England boasts the invention of bobbin-net, to France must be assigned the application of the Jacquard system to the netframe, and consequently the invention of machinery lace. Shawls and large pieces in " run lace," as it is termed, had previously

---

[18] The Caen blonde first suggested the idea.

[19] The first net-frame was set up at Brussels in 1801. Others followed at Termonde, 1817; Ghent, 1828 ; Sainte-Fosse, &c.

2 D

been made after this manner at Nottingham and Derby. The
pattern proposed to be "run in" is printed by means of engraved
wood blocks on the ground, which, if white, is of cotton; if black,
of silk. The ground is stretched on a frame; the "lace-runner"
places her left hand under the net, and with the right works the
pattern. The filling up of the interior is termed either "fining"
or "open-working," as the original meshes of the net are brought
to a smaller or larger size by the needle.[20]

In 1820, Symes, of Nottingham, invented a pattern, which he
called "Grecian" net. This was followed by the "spot," or "point
d'esprit," and various other fancy nets—bullet-hole, tattings, and
others.

The Jacquard system had been used at Lyons with the Mechlin
frame in 1823-4, for making patterned net and embroidered
blondes. This suggested the possibility of applying the Jacquard
cards to making lace, and in 1836 to 1838 Mr. Ferguson,[21] by
applying it to the circular bobbin-net frame, brought out the black
silk net called "dentelle de Cambrai," an imitation of Chantilly.
The pattern was woven by the machine, the brodé or relief
"run in."

Various patents[22] were immediately taken out in England and
France. Nottingham and Saint-Pierre-lez-Calais rival each other
in the variety of their productions. At the International Exhibition of 1874, Nottingham exhibited Spanish laces, most faithful
copies of the costly pillow-made Barcelona; imitations of Mechlin,
the brodé and picot executed by hand; Brussels needle point;
Caen blondes, and Valenciennes rivalling those of Calais; also
Cluny and the black laces of Chantilly and Mirecourt.

The French, by adopting what is technically termed eight

---

[20] D. Wyatt.

[21] Mr. Ferguson, the inventor of the
bullet hole, square net (tulle carré), and
wire-ground (point de champ or de Paris),
had transferred his manufacture, in 1838,
from Nottingham o Cambrai, where, in
partnership with M. Jourdan, he made
the "dentelle de Cambrai," and in 1852
the "lama" lace, which differs from the
Cambrai inasmuch as the weft (trame)
is made of mohair instead of silk. Mr.
Ferguson next established himself at
Amiens, where he brought out the yak,
another mixed lace.

[22] The first patents were :—

1836, Hind and Draper took out one
in France, and 1837 in England.

1838, Ferguson takes a patent at Cambrai, under the name of his partner Jourdan.

1839, Crofton.

1841, Houston and Deverill, for the
application of the Jacquard to the Leaver
machine. The great manufactures of
Nottingham and Calais are made on the
Leaver Jacquard frame.

The first patterned net was produced
1780, by R. Frost, the embroidery made
by hand.

" motives," produce their lace of a finer make and more complex pattern. The Calais lace is an admirable copy of the square-grounded Valenciennes, and is the staple trade of the manufacture. Calais also produces blondes, black and white, silver and gold, the white nearly approaching in brilliancy and whiteness the famed productions of Caen, which, by their cheapness, they have expelled from competition. She also imitates the woollen laces of Le Puy, together with black and white laces innumerable.

Almost every description of lace is now fabricated by machinery ;[23] and it is often no easy task, even for a practised eye, to detect the difference. Still we must ever be of opinion that the most finished productions of the frame never possess the touch, the finish, or the beauty of the laces made by hand. The invention

Fig. 148.

The Lagetta, or lace-bark tree.

of machine-made lace has this peculiarity—it has not diminished the demand for the finer products of the pillow and the needle. On the contrary, the rich have sought more eagerly than ever the exquisite works of Brussels or Alençon, since machinery has brought the wearing of lace within the reach of all classes of society.

The inner bark of the Lagetta, or lace-bark tree,[24] of Jamaica, may be separated into thin layers, and then into distinct meshes, bearing some resemblance to lace (Fig. 148). Of this material,

---

[23] " The machines now in use are the Cireular, Leaver, Transverse Warp, and Pusher. Out of 3552 machines computed to be in England in 1862, 2148 were at Nottingham."—*International Exhibition, Jurors' Report.*

[24] *Daphne lagetta.*

a cravat and ruffles were presented to King Charles II. by the governor of Jamaica; and at the exhibition of 1851 a dress of the same fibre was presented to the Queen, which her Majesty was graciously pleased to accept.

Caterpillars have been made to spin lace veils by the ingenious contrivance of a gentleman of Munich.[25] These veils are not strong, but surprisingly light: one, a yard square, would scarcely weigh five grains, whilst a patent net veil of the same size would weigh 262.

Asbestos has also been woven into lace; and a specimen of this mineral lace is, we have been told, in the Cabinet of Natural History at the Garden of Plants, Paris.

---

[25] " He makes a paste of the plant which is the usual food of the caterpillar, and spreads it thinly over a stone or other flat substance; then with a camel's hair pencil, dipped in olive oil, he draws upon the coating of paste the pattern he wishes the insects to leave open. The stone being placed in an inclined position, the caterpillars * are laid at the bottom, and the animals eat and spin their way up to the top, carefully avoiding every part touched by the oil, but devouring the rest of the paste."—*Encyclopædia Britannica.*

---

* *Phalæna pandilla.*

APPENDIX.

—◆—

PATTERN BOOKS FOR LACE AND EMBROIDERY.

The Notes marked with an * *show that the works referred to have been examined by the Author.*[1]

I.

Eyn new kunstlich boich, dair yn. C. vnd. xxxviij. figuren, monster ad' stalen befonden, wie man na der rechter art, Lauffer werck, Spansche stich, mit der nålen, vort vp der Ramen, vnd vp der laden, borden wirckenn sall, wilche stalen all etzo samen verbessert synt, vnd vyl kunstlicher gemacht, dā dye eirsten, &c. Sere nutzlich allen wapen sticker, frauwen, ionfferen, vnd met ger, dair uns solch kunst lichtlich tzu leren.

D Gedruckt tzu Collen vp dem Doemhoff dwrch Peter Quentell. Anno M. D. XXXVJJ.[2]

1527 (?). Cologne. P. Quentell.

Small 8vo. 22 ff. 42 plates.

Title in Gothic letters; beneath, woodcuts representing women at work. On the back of the leaf, a large escutcheon, the three crowns of Cologne in chief; supporters, a lion and a griffin. Below, " O Fœlix Colonia. 1527." The patterns consist of mediæval and arabesque borders, alphabets, &c., some on white, others on black grounds. Some with counted stitches.

Quentell refers to a previous edition. Brunet and the Marquis d' Adda mention a copy, 1529, with the portrait of Charles V., and a second edition, 1532.

2.

Liure noveau et subtil touchant lart et sciēce tant de brouderie fronssures, tapisseries cōme aultres mestiers quō fait alesguille, soit au petit mestier, aultelisse ou sur toille clere, tresvtile et necessaire a toutes gens usans des mestiers et ars dessuld, ou semblables ou il y ha C. et. xxxviij patrons de diuers ouvraiges faich per art et proportion.

1527. Cologne. P. Quinty.

---

[1] Two interesting papers were published in the "Gazette des Beaux-Arts" for 1863 and 1864, entitled, " Essai bibliographique sur les anciens dessins de dentelles, modèles de tapis-series, patrons de broderies et publiés le xvie et le xviie siècle," &c., by the Marquis Girolamo d' Adda, of Milan.

[2] Cambridge University College.

En primere a culoge (Cologne) par matrepiere quinty demorāt denpre leglie de iii roies.[3]

The same cut as the preceding, with the arms of Cologne, which seems to have been engraved for a great Bible printed by Quentell, in 1527, and is no guide for the date. Figs. 149 and 150.

Fig. 149.

Metre P. Quinty.   Cologne, 1527.

Fig. 150.

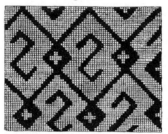

Metre P. Quinty.   Cologne, 1527.

3.

1530.
Venice.
A. Ta-
glienti.

Opera nuova che insegna a le Dōne a cuscire : a raccāmare : e a disegnar a ciascuno : Et la ditta opera sara di grande utilita ad ogni artista : per esser il disegno ad ogniuno necessario : la qual e ititolata esempio di racāmi.[4]

4to. 23 ff. 36 plates.

Title in red Gothic letters; beneath four woodcuts representing women at work. Two pages of dedication to the ladies, by Giovanni Antonio Taglienti, in which he says his book is for the instruction of each "valorosa donna & tutte altre donzelle, con gli huomini insieme & fonciulli, liquali si dilettarono de imparar a disegnar, cuscir, & raccammar."

Then follows a most miscellaneous collection of what he terms, in his dedi-cation, "fregi, frisi, tondi maravigliosi, groppi moreschi et arabeschi, uccelli volanti, fiori, lettere antique, maiuscoli, & le francesche," &c., three pages very much like the pictures in a child's spelling book, rounds (tondi) for cushions, and two pages representing hearts and scrolls ; hearts transfixed, one with an

---

[3] Paris, Bibliothèque Nat. Gravures, L. h. 13. d.*
[4] Bib. Nat. V. 1897.*—Genoa, Cav. Merli, 1528 (?).

arrow, another with a sword, a third torn open by two hands, motto on the scroll :—

" La virtù al huomo sempre li resta
Nè morte nol pò privar di questa."

On the other page hearts transfixed by two arrows, with two eyes above : " Occhi piangete accompagnete il core. Inclita virtus." Then follow six pages of instructions, from which we learn the various stitches in which these wonderful patterns may be executed, " damaschino, rilevato, a filo, sopra punto, ingaseato, Ciprioto, croceato, pugliese, scritto, incroceato, in aere, fatto su la rate, a magliata, desfilato, & di racammo," to be sewn in various coloured silks, gold and silver thread, or black silk, for " collari di huomo & di donna, camisciole con pettorali, frisi di contorni di letti, entemelle di cuscini, frisi di alcun boccassino, & scufie," &c. On the last page, " Stampa in Vineggia per Giovan Antonio Tagliente & i Fratelli de Sabbio. 1530." Brunet gives an edition dated 1528.

4.

La fleur de la science de pourtraicture et patrons de broderie. Facon arabicque, et ytalique. Cum priviligio regis.

1530.
Paris.
F. Pelegrin.

Frontispiece. Title in Gothic letters. A large figure of Sol (?), with a yoke, his feet chained, a ball, maybe the Earth, at the end of the chain. In one hand he holds a scroll with the legend. " Exitus acta probat." Privilege of " Francoys par la grace de Dieu roy de France," to " Francisque pelegrin de Florence," to publish " ung livre de fueillages, entrelatz et ouvraiges moresques, et Damasquins," for six years. " Dōne a bordeaulx le xvii. jour de Juing. L'an de grace mil cinq cens trète Et de nostre regne le seiziesme."

Ce present livre a este imprime a paris par jaques nyverd. Le iv. jour daoust. Lan de grace mil cinq cēs xxx. Pour noble hōme messire Francisque Pelegrin de florence.

On les vend a paris En la grant rue sainct Anthoyne devant les tournelles. Au logis de monseigneur le comte de Carpes. Par messire Frācisque pelegrin de florence.[5]

Small fol. 62 ff. 59 plates, consisting of graceful moresque patterns, no animals or natural objects represented. At plate 33, surrounded by arabesques, is an N, the initial of the printer.

5.

Esemplario di lavori : dove le tenere fanciulle & altre donne nobile potranno facilment imparare il modo & ordine di lavorare, cusire, racamare, & finalmente far tutte quelle gentillezze & lodevoli opere, le quali pò fare una donna virtuosa con laco in mano, con li suoi compasse & misure. Vinezia, per Nicolo D'Aristotile detto Zoppino. MDXXIX.[6]

1529.
Venice
N. Zoppino.

8vo. 46 plates.

The Cav[re] Merli quotes another edition, date 1530, in the possession of the Avvocato Francesco Pianesani, and another he believes of 1529. Mr. E. Arnold has editions of 1528 and 1530.

6.

Convivio delle belle Donne, dove con li. Nuovi raccami, &c. In fine : Finisce il convivio delle, &c. Nuovamente stampato in Vinegia, per Nicolo d'Aristotile, detto Zoppino del mese d'Agosto. MDXXXII.[7]

1532.
Venice.
N. Zoppino.

In 4to. ff. 24.

---

[5] Paris, Bib. de l'Arsenal. 11,952.*   [6] Oxford, Bib. Bodleian.
[7] Milan, Cavaliere Bertini.

7.

1537.
Venice.
N. Zop-
pino.

Gli universali de i belli Recami antichi, et moderni, ne i quali un pellegrino ingegno, si di huomo come di donna potra in questa nostra eta con l' ago vertuosamente esercitar si. Non ancora da alcuni dati altri inluce.

Frontispiece, two ladies at work ; dedication to "gli virtuosi Giovani et gentilissime Fanciulle." At the end styles himself " Nicolo d'Aristotile detto Zoppino." March 1537.

In 4to. ff. 25, printed on both sides.[8]

8.

1534.
Augsburg.
Schartzem-
berger.

Ain New Formbüchlin bin ich gnandt,
Allen Künstlern noch vnbekandt.
Sih mich (lieber kauffer) recht an,
Findst drefftlich in diser kunff stan
Schön gschnierlet, geböglet, auf gladt,
Und gold, auch schön, von premen stadt,
Es gibt dir ain prem unb ain kledyt.
Wenn mans recht aussainander schneydt,
Das kanst schneyden auss der Ellen,
Von Samat, Seyden, wie manss wolle,
Ich mag brauc̈t wern in allem landt,
Wen man mich ersücht mit verstandt.

(At the end.)

Gedruckt in der Kaiserlichen Reichstatt, Augspurg, durch Johan Schartzemberger. Formschneyder. 1534.[9]

Small obl. 20 ff. 38 plates.

Frontispiece. Title in black Gothic letters, at the foot three subjects of women at work, printed in red.

The patterns, consisting of graceful arabesque borders for embroidery, are also in red (Fig. 151 and Figs. 152 and 153.)

Fig. 151.

Augsburg, 1534.

Venice, Library of St. Mark. [9] Bib. Nat. Grav. L. h. 13. e.*

Fig. 152

Pattern book.   Augsburg, 1534.

Fig. 153.

Pattern book.   Augsburg, 1534.

9.

N. D.
Antwe-p.
W. Vorster-
man.

A neawe treatys : as cōcernynge the excellency of the nedle worcke spânisshe stitche and weavynge in the frame, very necessary to al theym wiche desyre the perfect knowledge of seamstry, quiltinge and brodry worke, côteinynge an cxxxviij figures or tables, so playnli made & set tout in portrature, the whiche is difficyll ; and natōly for crafts mē but also for gentlewemē & and iôge damosels that therein may obtayne greater conynge delyte and pleasure.

These books be to sell at Andwarp in the golden Unycorne at Willm̃ Vorstermans.

Gheprent tot Antwerpen in die camerstrate in den gulden eenhoren bey Willem Vorsterman.[10]

8vo. 24 ff. 46 plates.

Title in Gothic letters, with figures.

P. 1, dorso : Woodcut of a woman at work and a man sitting by her side.

Patterns mediæval, small black squares, arabesques, &c.

Vorsterman worked from 1514 to 1542.[11]

10.

1542.
Venice.

Giardinetto novo di punti tagliati et gropposi, per exercitio et ornamento delle donne. Ven. 1542.[12]

In 4to.

11.

1543.
Venice.

Esemplare che insegna alle donne el modo di cucire. Venetia 1543.[13]

12.

1544.
Venice.

Il Specchio di pensiere (*sic*), delle belle donne dove si vede varie sorti di punti, cioè, punti tagliati, gropposi, &c. Venetia, 1544.

In 4to.[14]

13.

1544.
Venice.

Ornamento delle belle donne et virtuose : Opere in cui troverai varie sorti di frisi con li quali si potra ornar ciascun donna. Ven. 1544.[15]

14.

1546.
Paris.
Gormont.

Le livre de moresques, tres utile et necessaire à tous orfevres, tailleurs, graveurs, painctres, tapissiers, brodeurs, lingieres et femmes qui besongnent de l'aiguille. Paris. Gormont, 1546. Fig. en bois.[16]

15.

1549.
Lyons.
P. de Ste.
Lucie.

La fleur des patrons de lingerie, a deux endroitz, a point croise, a point couche, et a point picque, en fil dor, fil dargēt, & fil de soye, ou aultre en quelque ouvraige que ce soit, en comprenant lart de broderie et tissuterie. Imprimees a Lyon, en la maison de Pierre de saincte Lucie (dict le Prince, Pres nostre Dame de Confort).[17]

---

[10] Bib. de l'Arsenal. 11,951.*

[11] Silvestre. "Marques typographiques des Imprimeurs en France, depuis 1470." Paris, 1853-61.

[12] Quoted in Cat. Cappi, of Bologna, 1829.

[13] Ibid.

[14] Ibid.

[15] Ibid.

[16] Cat. Bib. Heber. part vi. p. 258. No. 3514.

[17] Paris, Bib. Sainte-Geneviève. V.

(At the end.)

Imprimé à Lyon par Piarre de saincte Lucie, dict le Prince. 1549.

8vo. 12 ff. 21 plates.

Frontispiece. Title in Gothic letters, with woodcuts representing people at work. Below two women sitting at frames, above two others, and between a man with a frame in his hand. On each side a shield, one with crowned heart, on the other a lion, three fleurs-de-lys in chief. Patterns mediæval. At the end the device of the printer, a mountain on the top of which is a city against which a youth is placing his hand : motto, "Spero." At the foot of the mountain a cavern in which is seated a Fury. This device is engraved No. 616 in Silvestre, who gives 1530 to 1555 as the date of Pierre de Saincte Lucie.

16.

Livre nouveau, dict patrons de lingerie, cest assavoir a deux endroitz, a point croise, point couche & point picque, en fil dor, dargent, de soye & autres, en quelque ouvrage que ce soit : comprenant lart de Broderie & Tissoterie. Imprimees a Lyon, chez Pierre de Saincte Lucie, pres nostre Dame de Confort.[18]

N. D.
Lyons.
P. de Ste.
Lucie.

8vo. 24 ff. 44 plates.

Frontispiece. Title in Gothic letters ; the same shields as the preceding ; two women at work. Patterns mediæval. At the end the same device.

The copy of the Arsenal is a different impression. Instead of "Imprimees," &c., we have, "On les vend," &c.

17.

Patrons de diverses manieres
Inventez tressubtilement
Duysans a Brodeurs et Lingieres
Et a ceusy lesquelz vrayement
Veullent par bon entendement
User Dantique, et Roboesque,
Frize et Moderne proprement,
En comprenant aussi Moresque.
A tous massons, menuisiers, & verriers
Feront prouffit ces pourtraictz largement
Aux orpheures, et gentilz tapissiers
A ieunes gens aussi semblablement
Oublier point ne veuly auscunement
Côtrepointiers & les trailleurs dymages
Et tissotiers lesquelz pareillement
Par ces patrons acquerront heritages.

N. D.
Lyons.
P. de Ste.
Lucie.

Imprimees a Lyon, par Pierre de Saincte Lucie, dict le Prince, pres nostre Dame de Confort.[19]

634.* Bound in one volume with the three following (Nos. 16, 17, and 18). —Catalogue de Livres provenant de la Bibliothèque de M. L. D. D. L. V. (Duke de La Vallière). Paris, 1763. T. xi. No. 2204.

[18] Bib. Ste.-Geneviève, V. 634.*—

Bib. de l'Arsenal. No. 11,953.*—Cat. d'Estrées. Paris, 1740-46. No. 8843. 3.

[19] Bib. Ste.-Geneviève. V. 634.*— Bib. de l'Arsenal. No. 11,953.*—Cat. d'Estrées. No. 8843. 1.

8vo. 16 ff. 31 plates. Title in Gothic letters. Patterns mediæval. The copy at the Arsenal is a later impression. " On les vend a Lyon, par Pierre de saincte Lucie, en la maison du deffunct Prince, pres," &c. It has only 12 ff. and 23 plates.

18.

N. D.
Lyons.
Le Prince.

Sensuyuent lis patrons de messire Antoine Belin, Reclus de sainct Martial de Lyon. Item plusieurs autres beaulx Patrons nouveaulx, qui ont este inventez par Jehan Mayol Carme de Lyon.

On les vend à Lyon, chez le Prince.[20]

Small 8vo. 6 ff. 15 plates. Copy at the Arsenal has 12 ff.

The same device of the printer in the frontispiece and at the end of the book. " Finis."

One of the patterns represents St. Margaret holding the cross to a dragon, but in these four books the designs are copied from each other, and are many of them repetitions of Quinty.

19.

N. D.
Lyons.
D. Celle.

Ce livre est plaisant et utile
    A gens qui besongnent de leguille
Pour comprendre legèrement
    Damoyselle bourgoyse ou fille
Femmes qui ont l'esperit agille
    Ne scauroint faillir nullement
Corrige est nouvellement
    Dung honeste home par bon zelle
Son nom est Dominicque Celle
    Qui a tous lecteurs shumylie
Domicile a en Italie.
    En Thoulouse a prins sa naissauce.
Mise il a son intelligence
    A lamender subtillement
Taillé il est totallement
    Par Jehan coste de rue merciere
A Lyon et consequemment
    Quatre vingtz fassons a vrayement
Tous de differente maniere.[21]

28 ff. 27 plates. Title in Gothic letters. Dedication to the Reader, in which it states the book is for the profit of " tant hommes que femmes." Patterns mediæval. At the end of the Preface, " Finis coronat opus."

20.

N. D.
Venice.
G. A. Va-
vassore.

Esemplario di lavori: che insegna alle dōne il modo e ordine di lavorare : cusire : e racāmare : e finalmēte far tutte q̄lle opere degne di memoria : lequale po fare una donna virtuosa con laco in mano. Et uno documento che insegna al cōpratore accio sia ben servito.[22]

In 8vo. 25 ff., printed on both sides, 48 plates. Title in red Gothic characters, framed round by six woodcuts similar to that of Vorsterman ; at the foot, " fiorio Vavasore fecit."

---

[20] Bib. Ste.-Geneviève, V. 634.*—
Bib. de l'Arsenal. No. 11,953.*
[21] Paris, Bib. Baron Jérôme Pichon.*
[22] Bib. Nat. Grav. L. h. 4.*

Then follows the " Documento per el compratore," and an Address to Ladies and Readers, by " Giovandrea Vavassore detto Guadagnino," saying that he had already " fatti alcuni libri di esempli di diverse sorte."
There is no date to this copy; but in the library of Prince Massimo, at Rome, is a copy dated Venice, 18 Feb. 1546, containing 50 plates; and Brunet quotes an edition, " Stampato in Vinezia, 1556 ; " Cav. Merli also possesses an edition of the same date. Mr. E. Arnold has also copy with the same date.

The patterns are mediæval, on black grounds, with counted stitches, a large flower pot, mermaid, Paschal lamb, and a double plate representing Orpheus playing to the beasts.

21.

Essemplario novo di piu di cento variate mostre di qualunque sorte bellissime per cusire intitolato Fontana de gli essempli.   **N. D.** *Venice.* *G. A. Vavassore.*

Oblong 8vo. No date. 16 ff. 28 plates.
In the frontispiece is a fountain with the motto, " Solicitudo est mater divitiarum," and on each side of the fountain—

" Donne donzelle ch   Per farvi eterne alla
El cusir seguite   Fonte venite."

On the back of the frontispiece is the Dedication, headed, " Il Pelliciolo alla molta magnifica Madona Chiara Lipomana ; " the page finished by a sonnet ; in the last leaf, " Avviso alle virtuose donne et a qualunque lettore Giovanni Andrea Vavassore detto Guadagnino." Says he has " negli tempi passati fatto imprimere molto e varie sorte d' essemplari di mostre," &c. At the foot, " Nuovamente stampato." [23]   This work is also described by Count Cicognara with the same title, only with the date 1550. In the Bibliotheca Communitativa, Bologna, is a copy of the same date. In this last edition the author writes his name Valvassore.

22.

Vavassore Gio. Andrea. Opera nova Universal intitulata corona di ricammi ; Dove le venerande donne e fanciulle : troverano di varie opere p fare colari di camisiola & torniaenti di letti eternelle di cuscini boccasini schufioni : cordlli di piu sorte ; et molte opere per recāmatori p dipitore poreuesi : (sic) de lequale opere o vero esempli ciascuno le potra pore in opera secōdo el suo bisogno : con gratia novamente stampata ne la inclita citta di vineggia per Giovanni Andrea Vavassore detto Guadagniō.   **N. D.** *Venice.* *G. A. Vavassore.*

36 pp. sm. 4to. 13 ff. 52 designs, none of which are repetitions of the preceding. [24]

23.

Vavassore Gio. Andrea detto Guadagnino. Opera nova, etc. . . . dove le venerande donne et fanciulle trovaranno di varie opere et molte opere per recamatori et per dipintori, etc. Nuovamente stampata, etc. [25]   **N. D.** *Venice.* *G. A. Vavassore.*

Quite a different collection from the preceding. A little of everything in this volume.

[23] Bib. Nat. Grav. L. h. 4. a.*— Catalogo ragionato dei libri posseduti dal Conte di Cicognara. Pisa, 1821. No. 1818.

[24] Library, S. Kensington Museum. —Venice, Lib. St. Mark.—Milan, Bib. Marquis d' Adda.
[25] Milan, Bib. Marquis G. d' Adda.

Zoan Andrea Vavassore was the pupil in drawing and engraving of Andrea Mantegna. Towards the beginning of the sixteenth century, he worked on his own account, and his engravings are much sought after. So greedy was he of gain as to obtain for him the name of Guadigno, in Venetian patois, "covetous." He lived to a great age.

24.

N. D.
A. Paga-
nino.

Libro questo di rechami per el quale se impara in diversi modi l'ordine e il modo de recamare, cosa non mai più fatta n' è stata mostrata.

By Alessandro Paganino.[26]

20 plates, with a long explanation how these works are done.[27]

25.

N. D.
Paris.
Vve.
Ruelle.

Patrons pour Brodeurs, Lingieres, Massons, Verriers, et autres gens d'esprit. A Paris. Pour la Veuve Jean Ruelle, rue S. Jacques, à l'enseigne Sainct Nicolas.[28]

4to. 23 ff. 32 plates of mediæval designs. Ornamented title-page.

26.

1548.
Venice.
M. Pagan.

Il specchio di pensieri delle belle et virtudiose donne, dove si vede varie sorti di Punti, cioè punti tagliati, punti gropposi, punti in rede, et punti in Stuora. MDXLVIII. Stamp. in Venetia, per Mathio Pagan in frezzaria, in le case nove Tien per insegna la fede.[29]

16 ff.

27.

1551.
Venice.
M. Pagan.

1. L' honesto Essempio del vertuoso desiderio che hanno le donne di nobile ingegno circa lo imparare i punti tagliati e fogliami. In Venetia per Mathio Pagan in Frezaria al segno della Fede, M.D.L.[30]

In the South Kensington Museum is a copy dated 1550.

28.

1551.
Venice.
M. Pagan.

Giardineto novo di Punti tagliati et gropposi, per esercitio et ornamento delle donne. At the end, Venetia, Mathio Pagan in Frezzaria, in le case nove (tien per insegna della Fede) MDLI. Dedication, Alla signora Lucretia, Romana Mathio Pagan, salute.[31]

29.

1554.
Dubois.

Variarum protractionum quas vulgo Maurusias vocant omnium antehac excusarum libellus longe copiasissimus pictoribus, aurifabris, polymilariis, barbaricariis variisque id genus artificibus etiam acu operantibus utilissimus nuncque primen in lucem editus anno 1554. Balthazar Sylvius (Dubois) fecit. Jo. Theodoret, Jo. Israel de Bry excud.[32]

In 4to. ff. 23, copper-plate.

---

[26] Rome, Bib. Prince Massimo.

[27] Communicated by Prince Massimo.

[28] Bib. de l'Arsenal. 11,954 (with D. de Sera).*

[29] Genoa, Cav. Merli.

[30] Quoted by Cav. Merli.

[31] Florence. M. Bigazzi. (See also No. 39.)

[32] Paris, Bib. Nat.—Milan, Bib. Belgiosa, and Marquis d' Adda.

30.

Triompho di Lavori a Fogliami de i quali si puo far ponti in aere; opera d' Fra Hieronimo da Cividal di Frioli, de l'Ordine de i Servi di Osservantia. Cum gratia et privileggio per anni xi.[33]

1555.
Padua.
Fra Hiero-
nimo.

Obl. 4to. 14 ff. 22 pl.

Ornamental title-page. On the top, a female seated in a triumphal car drawn by unicorns, with attendants. On each side of the title are women teaching children to work.

P. 1, dorso. Dedication of the author, " Alla Magnifica & Illustre Signora Isabella Contessa Canossa," whose " Immortal Triompho " is represented in the above woodcut. Fra Hieronimo speaks of preparing "più alte e divine imprese."

Then follow three pages of verses in terzette, and p. 3, dorso, the impresa of the printer, a lion rampant, holding a sword in his fore paws. Below, " In Padou per Jacobo Fabriano, ad instantia de Fra Hieronimo da Cividal di Frioli: de l' Ordine de i Servi di Osservantia 1555."

31.

Lucidario di ricami di Guiseppe Torello. Venezia, 1556. In 4to.

1556.
Venice.
Torello.

32.

New Modelbüch, allen Nägerin, unnd Sydenstickern sehr nutzlich zü branchē, vor nye in Druck aussgangen durch Hans Hoffman, Burger und formschneider zu Strassburg. At the end, Zu Strassburg Gedruckt am Kommarckt durch Jacob Frölich. 1556.[34]

1556.
Strasburg.
H. Hoff-
man.

4to. A to G in fours. (28 leaves.)

Title printed in red and black. On it a woodcut of two women, one engaged in embroidery, the other fringing her some stuff. The last leaf (G, iii.) has on the recto a woodcut of a woman at a frame, the verso blank.

33.

Nüw Modelbüch, allerley gattungen Däntelschnür, so diser zyt in hoch Tütschlanden geng vnd brüchig sind, zü vnderricht jren Leertöchteren vnnd allen anderen schnürwürckeren zü Zürych vnd wo die sind, yetz nüwlich zübereit, vnd erstmals in truck verfergket durch R. M.[35]

N. D.
Zurich.
C Frosch-
owern.

No place or date, but it appears, both from the title and preface, to have been printed at Zurich, by Christopher Froschowern. Date probably 1560.

4to. Signatures A to F in fours. 24 leaves. On the title a woodcut of two women working at lace pillows.

Translation.

New Pattern book on all Kinds of Lace-work made and in use in Germany. For the instruction of apprentices and all other female lace-workers in Zurich and elsewhere, newly arranged and for the first time published by R. M.

A long preface, of which we give a part, as curious and important, and as giving the date of the introduction of the art into Switzerland :—

" Among the many arts which have been brought into notice for the use and advancement of the world, we must not forget that of lace-making,

---

[33] Bib. de l'Arsenal. 11,953.*—Bologna, Bib. Comm.—Cat. d'Estrées. 8843. No. 2.   [34] Mr. E. Arnold.   [35] Royal Library, Munich (?).

which was first adopted in our country twenty-five years since. It was first introduced, in the year 1536, by the merchant traders from Italy and Venice. Thereupon several intelligent women found that they could turn it to a useful account, and learnt to imitate and soon rendered it generally known. They no longer then worked from the old patterns, but invented new and more beautiful ones. By degrees this art became still more known, and other patterns and designs, together with more workers, appeared and were circulated throughout the country, so that the art was soon fixedly established, and owing to the increasing industry of the workwomen, it soon rose to its highest perfection. This new work did much to employ many hands, and besides the gain and payment, men began to see that it was more profitable than any other hand work. At first this lace was only worn on shirts, but in course of time it was used for collars, caps, to trim sleeves, aprons, jackets, tablecloths, bed-cloths, pillows, bed-covers, and after a short time for many other purposes. I need hardly say that owing to the increased demand and progress, before long, this work became very costly and an object of luxury. They began to introduce gold thread into the above mentioned articles, which, being more costly, demanded higher prices, and were very troublesome to clean, which that made with the flaxen thread was not, being easily washed."

34·

N. D.
Frankfort.
Modelbüch Welscher, Ober und Niderlandischer Arbait. Getruckt zü Franckfort.

No date, but probably at least as early as 1530. 4to. Signatures A to D in fours. 20 leaves.

Title enclosed in an elegant woodcut border.

35·

1537.
Frankfort.
C. Ege-
nolffs.
Modelbüch, von erhabener unnd flacher Arbait, Auff der Ramen, Laden, und nach der Zale.

Getruckt zu Franckfort, Bei Christian Egenolffs, Erben.

The date, 1537, occurs on one of the patterns. 4to. AA to HH in fours. 32 leaves. Title in a woodcut border. 178 patterns.[36]

36.

1571.
Frankfort
on the
Main.
N. Baseus.
New Modelbüch.

Von allerhandt Art, Nehens und Stickens, jetzt mit viellerley Welscher Arbeyt, Mödel und Stahlen, allen Steinmetzen, Seidenstickern und Neterin, sehr nützlich und kunstlich, von newem zugericht. Getruckt zu Frankfurt am Mayn, 1571.

Device and motto of Nicolas Baseus on title-page. Sm. 4to.[37]

37·

1568.
Frankfort
on the
Main.
N. Baseus.
Das new Modelbüch, &c.

Franckfurt am Mayn, 1568. Printer, Nicholas Baseus.

4to. ff. 40.

38.

1569.
Frankfort
on the
Main.
Modelbüch; Zweiter Theil: Franckfurt am Mayn, 1569.

4to. ff. 44.

Nos. 37 and 38 are cited by the Marquis d'Adda.

---

[36] Nos. 32, 33, 34, and 35, have been communicated by Mr. F. S. Ellis, London.   [37] Library, S. Kensington Museum.

39.

La Gloria et l' honore de ponti tagliati et ponti in aere Venezia per   1558.
Mathio Pagan in Frezzeria al segno della Fede. 1558.[38]   *Venice.*
                                                        M. Pagan.

16 plates. Dedicated to Vittoria Farnese, Duchess of Urbino.

40.

Il Monte. Opere nova di recami intitolata il monte, nella quale si   N. D.
ritrova varie, & diverse sorti di mostre, di punti in aiere, à fogliami.   *Venice.*
Dove le belle & virtuose Donne protranno fare ogni sorte di lavoro,
accommodate alle vera forma misura & grandezza, che debbono essere
ne mai piu per l' adietro da alcuno vedute. Opera non men bella che
utile, & necessaria.[39]

Below, the impresa of the printer, an eagle with its young; motto, " Virtute
parta sibi non tantum." In Venetia.
4to. 16 ff. 29 plates of bold scroll borders.

41.

Il Monte (libro secondo). Opera dove ogni bella donna potrà fare   1559.
ogni sorte di lavori cioè colari, fazzoletti, maneghetti, avertadure   *Venice.*
(berthes), &c., in Venetia, 1560.[40]   *G. A. Bin-*
                                                           doni.

Printer's mark and motto as No. 40 ; afterwards the dedication dated 1559,
" à Vittoria da Cordova Gio. Ant. Bindoni," in which he states, " Ho preso
arditamente di presentarvi questo secondo Monte." 4to. ff. 16.

42.

Bellezze de recami et dessegni opera novo non men bella che utile, e   1558.
necessaria et non più veduta in luce. Venezia, 1558.[41]   *Venice.*

Ob. 4to. 20 plates of patterns.

43.

Lo Splendore delle virtuose giovani con varie mostre di fogliami e   1558.
punti in aere. Venezia. Per Iseppo Foresto in calle dell' acqua a S.   *Venice.*
Zulian all' insegno del Pellegrino, 1558.[42]   *I. Foresto.*

16 plates.

44.

Trionfo di Virtù Libro novo da cucir, con fogliami, ponti a fili,   1559.
ponti cruciati, &c. Venezia, 1559.[43]   *Venice.*

16 plates.

45.

Burato.   N. D.

Consisting of four leaves, with patterns of canvas (tela chiara), in squares,
for works in " punta" of various widths, with instructions how to increase or
diminish the patterns. See p. 39.

---

[38] Cat. Cicognara. 1583. No. 4.   [41] Cat. Cicognara. 1583. No. 1.
[39] Bib. de l'Arsenal. No. 11,953.*   Bound in one volume, with six others.
—Mr. E. Arnold.   [42] Cat. Cicognara. 1583. No. 5.
[40] Florence, M. Bigazzi.   [43] Ibid. 1583. No. 6.

On the back of the last page is printed in large characters, " P. Alex Pag. (Paganinus). Benacensis F. Bena. V. V." [44]

46.

N. D.   Burato . . . . con nova maestria, gratiose donne, novo artificio vi apporto.

A second edition, without date. 4to. ff. 50; frontispiece, ladies at work, verso, Triumph of Fame. Four books of designs of great elegance and taste. The Marquis d' Adda assigns them to Vavassore.

47.

N. D.
A. Pas-
serotti.   Passerotti Aurelio Pittore Bolognese dissegnatore e miniatore figlio di Bartolommeo Passerotti circa al 1560. Libro Primo di lavorieri alle molto illustre et virtuosissime gentildonne Bolognesi. Libro secondo alle mòlto magnifici et virtuosissimi signori.[45]

In fol. obl.
67 ff. including two dedications and a frontispiece. Designs for embroidery, &c., drawn with a pen. In the title-page of the first book is the device of a sunflower, " No san questi occhi volgere altrove."

48.

1557.   Le Pompe. Opera nova di recami dove trovansi varie mostre di
Venice.   punto in aere. Venezia, 1557.[46]

Probably an earlier impression of the following. 4to. ff. 16.

49.

1559.   Le Pompe, opera nova nella quale si ritrovano varie, & diverse sorti di monstre, per poter far Cordelle over Bindelle, d' Oro, di Seta, di Filo, overo di altra cosa di Dove le belle et virtuose donne potranno fare ogni sorte di lavoro, cioè merli di diverse sorte, Cavezzi, Colari, Maneghetti, & tutte quelle cose che le piaceranno. Opera non men bella, che utile, & necessaria. E non più veduta in luce. 1559.[47]

Below, the same impresa of the eagle, as in " Il Monte," No. 40 and 41.
8vo. 16 ff. 30 plates.
A great variety of borders and indented patterns (merli). (Fig. 154.)
" Si vendeno alla Libraria della Gatta."
In the Cat. d'Estrées is noted, " Le Pompe, Opera nella quale si retrovano diverse sorti di mostre per poter far cordelle, Bindelle, d' oro di seta, di filo. 1559, fig." Probably the same work.

50.

1560.   Le Pompe, Libro secondo. Opera nuova nella quale si ritrovano varie e diverse sorti di Mostre, per poter fare Cordelle, ovver Bindelle, d' Oro, di Seta di Filo, ovvero di altra cosa. Dove le belle & virtuose Donne potranno far ogni sorte di lavoro, cioè Merli di diverse sorte Cavezzi, Colari, Maneghetti & tutte quelle cose che li piaceno. Opera non men bello che utile & necessaria e non più veduta in luce.

Impresa of the printer, " Pegasus," and below, " In Venetia 1560."

---

[44] Cat. Cicognara. 1583. No. 7.   [45] Ibid. No. 1748.
[46] Ibid. 1583. No. 3.   [47] Bib. de l'Arsenal. 11,953.*

Obl. 8vo. 16 ff. 29 plates.[48]

Mrs Stisted's copy is dated 1562, and there is one at Vienna, in the Imperial Library, of the same date.

Fig. 154.

Le Pompe. 1559.

51.

Splendore delle virtuose giovani dove si contengono molte, & varie mostre a fogliami cio è punti in aere, et punti tagliati, bellissimi, & con tale arteficio, che li punti tagliati serveno alli punti in aere. Et da quella ch' è sopragasi far si possono, medesimamente molte altre. In Venetia Appresso Jeronimo Calepino, 1563.[49]

1563.
Venice.
J. Calepino.

8vo. 20 ff. 35 plates of scroll patterns in the style of "Il Monte."

Dedication, "Alla molto honorata M. Anzola ingegniera suocera mia digniss." Francesco Calepino, wishing, he says, to "ristampare la presente opera," he dedicates it to her. In Bib. Melzi, Milan, a copy dated 1567.

52.

Lucidario di recami, nel qual si contengono molte, & varie sorti di disegni. A punti in aere et punti tagliati & a fogliami, & con figure &

1563.
Venice.
J. Calepino.

[48] Bib. de l'Arsenal. 11,953.*—Mrs. Stisted, Bagni di Lucca.
[49] Bib. Nat. V. 1901.*—Bib. de l'Arsenal. 11,973.*—Cat. d'Estrées.

2 E 2

di più altre maniere, come al presente si usano non più venute in luce. Per lequali ogni elevato ingegno potrà in diversi modi commodissimamente servirsi. In Venetia, Appresso Ieronimo Calepino, 1563.[50]

8vo. 16 ff. 29 plates of flowing borders like the preceding.

53.

1564.
Venice.

I Frutti opera nuova intitulata i frutti de i punti in stuora, a fogliami, nella quale si ritrova varie, et diverse sorti di mostre di ponti in Stuora, a fogliami, & punti in gasii & in punti in Trezola.[51] Dove ogni bella et virtuosa donna potrà fare ogni sorte di lavoro, cioè fazoletti, colari, maneghetti, Merli, Frisi, Cavezzi, Intimelle, overo forelle, avertadure da camise, & altre sorti di lavori, come piu a pieno potrai vedere, ne mai per l' adietro d' alcun altro fatte & poste in luce.

Opera non men bella, che utile et necessaria a ciascuna virtuosa gentildonna.   In Vinegia, 1564.[52]

Obl. 8vo. 16 ff. 30 plates of patterns either in dots or small squares.

54.

1564.
Paris.

Patrons pour brodeurs, lingières, massons, verriers, et autres gens d'esperit; nouvellement imprimé, à Paris, rue Saint-Jacques, à la Queue-de Regnard M.DLXIIII.[53]

55.

1564.
Venice.
D. de
Frances-
chi.

Fede (Opere nova) intitulata : Dei Recami nella quale si contiene varie diverse sorte di mostre di punti scritto, tagliato, in Stuora, in Rede, &c. In Venetia, appresso Domenico de Franceschi in Frezzaria, all' insegna della Regina. M.DLVIII.

In 4to. ff. 16. In his "Avis au Lecteur," Franceschi alludes to three other works he had published, styled "La Regina," "La Serena," and "La Speranza."

56.

1564.
Venice.
D. de
Frances-
chi.

Serena opera nova di recami, nella quale si ritrova varie et diverse sorte di punti in stuora et punti a filo. In Venetia, Domenico di Franceschi, 1564.

Obl. 4to. ff. 16. (Nos. 55 and 56 cited by Marquis d' Adda.)

57.

1581.
Lyon.
J. Ostans

Le trésor des patrons, contenant diverses sortes de broderies et lingeries, pour coudre avec grande facilité et pour ouvrer en diverses sortes de piquer avec l'ésguille, pulveriser par dessus et faire ouvrages de toutes sortes de points &ct par Jean Ostans. Lyon, Ben. Rigaud. 1581.[54]

In 4to.

---

[50] Bib. Nat. V. 1901.*—Bib. de l'Arsenal. 11,973.*—Cat. d'Estrées.

[51] Trezola, in the Riviera dialect, signifies a plait-tresse. "Porta i capei in trezola." ("She wears her hair plaited.")

[52] Bib. de l'Arsenal. 11,955 bis,*

with "Vera Perfettione," and "Fiori," of F. Franceschi, and "Corona," of Vecellio.

[53] Quoted by Willemin.

[54] Quoted in Art. "Tricot et Travaux des Dames."

58.

Ostans Giovanni. La vera perfettione del disegno di varie sorti di 1567.
Recami, et di cucire, &c. . . . punti a fogliami punti tagliati punti a *Venice.*
fili et rimessi punti in cruciati, punti a stuora, et ogni altra arte che dia *J. Ostans.*
opera a disegni. Fatta nuovamente per Gio. Ostans. Vittoria, con
gratia et privilegio dell' Illus. Senato Venetiano per anni.[55] In Venetia
appresso Gio. Ostans, 1567.

4to. obl. 4 cahiers of 8 ff. 74 plates. Letter of Ostans to Lucretia Contarini; verso, an engraving of Lucretia Romana, surrounded by her women,
signed Jose. Sal. (Joseph Salviati), who furnished thedesign, two sonnets, and
Aves. A striking example of the borrowing between France and Italy in the
sixteenth century, probably of the school of Fontainebleau. Grotesques like
A. du Cerceau, scrolls after E. de Laulne, fresco of figures from G. Tory.
Brunet describes a copy dated 1591.

59.

Ostans. La vera perfettione del desegno &ct. Venetia, M.DLXXXIIII. 1584.
presso gli heredi Valvassori e Gio. Dom. Micheli al segno dell' Ippo- *Venice.*
grifo. *Valvas-
sore's*

In 4to. obl. (Cited by Marquis d' Adda.) *heirs.*

60.

Neues Künstlicher Modelbuch von allerhand artlichen und ge- ꞌ 1582.
rechten Mödeln, &c., bei B. Tabin.[56] *B. Tabin.*

61.

Le livre de Lingerie, composé par Maistre Dominique de Sera, 1584.
Italien, enseignant le noble & gentil art de l'esguille, pour besongner en *Paris.*
tous points : utile & profitable à toutes Dames & Damoyselles, pour *D. de Sera.*
passer le temps, & euiter oysiveté.

Nouvellement angmenté, & enrichi, de plusieurs excelents & divers
patrons, tant du point coupé, raiseau, que passement, de l'invention de
M. Jean Cousin, Peintre à Paris.

A Paris. Chez Hierosme de Marnef, & la veufve de Guillaume
Cauellat, au mont S. Hilaire à l'enseigne du Pelican. 1584. Avec
privilege du Roy.[57]

In the Cat. d'Estrées, No. 8848, is ' Livre de Pourtraicture de Jean Cousin.'
Paris, 1637, in 4 fig."
4to. 28 ff. 51 plates of mediæval design.
Frontispiece, three women and a child at work, on each side of the title a
man and a woman at work under a trifoliated canopy.
Privilege for three years to H. de Marnef, "juré libraire en l'Université de
Paris."
"L'auteur aux lecteurs." He takes his pen to portray what he has seen
"en Italie, Espagne, Romanie, Allemagne, & autre païs, dont je ne fais aucune
mention à cause de trop longue plexite," that he gives at least eighty designs
for the use and singular profit of many, "hommes tant que femmes." Below,
"Finis coronat opus."

---

[55] Bib. M. d' Adda.   Mr. Gruner.
[56] Dresden, New Museum for Art   [57] Bib. de l'Arsenal. 11,954.*
and Industry.   Communicated by

Then follows a "Balade" of 28 lines. On the last page, the impresa of Cavellat, a pelican in its piety, "Mors in me vita in me."

62.

1596.
G. Frano.

Frano Gio. Libro delle mostre da ceuser per le donne.
16 engravings on wood and 8 on copper. (Cited by Marquis d' Adda.)

63.

Bologna.
A. Parisini.

Danieli Bartholomeo Recamatore libro di diversi disegni per Collari, punti per Fazzoletti et Reticelle divarie sorte. Agostino Parisini forma in Bologna.

15 leaves obl. 8vo., entirely engraved au burin, towards the end of the sixteenth century.[58]

64.

N. D.

Ornamento delle belle et virtuose donne opera nova nella quale troverrai varie sorti di frisi, con li quali si potra ornar ciascuna donna, & ogni letti con ponti tagliato, ponti gropposi, & ogni altra sorte di Ponti per fare quelle belle opere che si appartengono alle virtuose & lodevoli fanciulle.

On a scutcheon, with 3 figures below, "Libro Primo." Lib. S. K. Museum.

65.

1587.
Paris.
1st Edit.
1st Part.
F. Vinciolo.

Les singuliers et nouveaux pourtraicts et ouvrages de Lingerie. Servans de patrons à faire toutes sortes de poincts, couppé, Lacis & autres. Dedie a la Royne. Nouvellement inventez, au proffit & côtentement, des nobles Dames & Damoiselles & autres gentils esprits, amateurs d'un tel art. Par le Seigneur Federic (sic) de Vinciolo Venitien. A Paris. Par Iean le Clerc le ieune, ruë Chartiere, au Chef Sainct Denis. 1587. Avec privilege du Roy.[59]

2nd Part.

Les singuliers et nouveaux pourtraicts et ouvrages de Lingerie ou est representé les sept planettes, & plusieurs autres figures & pourtraitz servans de patrons à faire de plusieurs sortes de Lacis. Nouvellement inventez, au proffit & côntentement des nobles Dames & Damoiselles & autres gentils esprits, amateurs d'un tel art. Par le Seigneur Federic de Vinciolo Venitien. A Paris. Par Iean le Clerc le ieune, ruë Chartiere, au Chef Sainct Denis. 1587. Avec privilege du Roi.

(At the end.)

Privilege for nine years to "Iean le Clerc le ieune, 'tailleur d'histoires,' à Paris," signed 27 June, 1587. "De l'Imprimerie de David le Clerc Rue Frementel à l'Estoille d'Or."

4to.

The first part consists of 40 ff., 36 of patterns and 4 preliminary pages.
P. 1. The title-page with decorated border, in which are two ladies at work. (See title-page of this work.)
P. 2. Dedication of "Le Seigneur Federic de Vinciolo aux Benevolles Lecteurs," in which he sets forth that several authors before him having published certain patterns for work that "les Seigneurs, Dames, & Damoyselles ont eu pour agréable," he, to show "la bonne volonté que je porte à la France, laquelle m'ayant été douce et favorable, depuis certain temps que j'ay quitté

---

58 Milan, Bib. Marquis Girolamo d' Adda.
59 Bib. Rouen. No. 1313. Both parts in one vol.*

Venize, païs de ma nativité," wishes to portray the present "pourtraicts d'ouvrages magnifiques tous differēs, &non encor usitez en cette cōtree ni aultres, & que j'ay tenus cachés & incōgnus jusques à maintenant," "feeling assured that if the first you have seen 'on engendré quelque fruit & utillité, ceux cy en aporteront d'avantage,' and if I see this my invention pleases you, I will ' vous faire participer d'un aultre seconde bande d'ouvıages.' "

P. 3. Dedication "A la Royne," Louise de Vaudemont, by Le Clerc, saying that having received from Italy some rare and singular patterns, and " ouvrages de l'ingerie & en ayāt invēte quelques uns, selon mon petit sçavoir, j'ay pensé puis que ces choses là appartieñent principallement aux Dames," that he cannot do better than present them to the Queen, as if these patterns are useful (as he hears some less perfect and more rudely sketched have served and profited before), they ought to be offered to her Majesty. Signed last day of May 1587.

P. 4. A sonnet

AUX DAMES ET DAMOISELLES.

" L'un sefforce à gaigner le cœur des grāds seigneurs
Pour posséder enfin une exquise richesse,
L'autre aspire aux Estats pour monter en altesse,
Et l'autre par la guerre alléche les honneurs.

Quand à moy, seulement pour chasser mes langueurs,
Je me sen satisfait de vivre en petitesse,
Et de faire si bien, qu'aux dames je délaisse
Un gran contentement en mes graves labeurs.

Prenez doncques en gré (mes Dames), je vous prie,
Ces pourtrais ouvrages lesquelz je vous dédie,
Pour tromper vos ennuis, et l'esprit employer.

En ceste nouveauté, pourrés beaucoup apprendre,
Et maistresses en fin en cest œuvre vous rendre.
Le travail est plaisant. Si grand est le loyer."

" Morir assidouamente per virtu,
Non morirè."

Then follow the 36 patterns set off in white on a black ground, viz. 20 " Ouvrages de point Couppé," the first plate with the double λλ, according to the fashion introduced by Francis I. of using Greek monograms, standing for Queen Louise. On the second page are two escutcheons, one of France, the other with the letter H for Henry III. Then follow eight " Passemens de point Couppé," which are succeeded by eight more " Ouvrages de point Couppé."

Part 2, 24 ff. Same decorated frontispiece and 22 plates of subjects in squares for stitches like the German patterns of the present day. These consist of the Seven Planets, Sol, Luna, Mars, Mercury, Jupiter, Venus, and Saturn. Four in squares of various designs ; two of Amorini shooting stags and birds ; Neptune and the winds ; an arabesque with impresa of a column with circle and double triangle ; five borders and squares, and two " bordures à carreaux," diamond-shaped meshes. The last page contains the Extract from the Privilege.

This is the original edition of Vinciolo, of which we know but one copy existing, that in the Library at Rouen.

It was followed, the same year, by two other editions, with alterations.[60]

---

[60] We have lately received notice of there being a copy of the original edition at Turin, in the Library of the University.

66.

1587.
2nd Ed.
1st Part.
F. Vin-
ciolo.

Les singuliers et nouveaux pourtraicts pour les ouvrages de Lingerie. Nouvellement augmentez de plusieurs differens pourtraits servans de patrons à faire toutes sortes de poincts couppé, Lacis, et autres reseau de poinct conté. Dedié à la Royne. Le tout inventé, au proffit & contentement des nobles Dames & Damoiselles & autres gentil esprits, amateurs d'un tel art. Par le Seigneur Federic de Vinciolo Venetien. A Paris. Par Iean le Clerc le ieune, ruë Chartiere, au Chef Sainct Denis, pres le college de Coqueret. Avec privilege du Roy. 1587.

2nd Part. Les singuliers et nouveaux pourtraicts pour les ouvrages de Lingerie ou avons augmêté plusieurs nouveaux & differens portraitz de reseau, tout point conté, plusieurs nouvelles bordures et autres sortes differentes.

Nouvellement inventez au proffit & cõtentement des nobles Dames & Damoiselles & autres gentils esprits amateurs d'un tel art. Par le Seigneur Federick de Vinciolo Venitien. A Paris. Par Iean le Clerc le ieune, Ruë Chartiere, au Chef Sainct Denis, pres le college de Coqueret. Avec privilege du Roy. 1587.[61]

1st Part, 40 ff. The same frontispiece, dedications, date, and sonnet, as the first, the same number of patterns, only the eight styled in the first "Passemens" are here all called, like the others, "Ouvrages" de Point couppé. (See Fig. 4, p. 14.)

2nd Part, 32 ff. This part has 30 patterns, comprising the 24 of the first edition, and six additional ones, consisting of squares and two hunting subjects.

67.

1587.
3rd Edit.
No. 1.
Parts 1
and 2.

Les singuliers et nouveaux Pourtraicts, du Seigneurs Federic de Vinciolo Venitien, pour toutes sortes d'ouvrages de Lingerie. Dedie a la Royne. Derechef et pour la troisieme fois augmentez Outre le reseau premier et le point couppé et lacis, de plusieurs beaux et differens portrais de reseau de point côté avec le nombre des mailles, choze non encor veue ni inventée. A Paris. Par Iean le Clerc le ieune, ruë Chartiere, au Chef Sainct Denis, pres le College de Coqueret. Avec privilege du Roy. 1587.[62]

This must be the first impression of the third edition.

1588.
3rd Edit.
No. 2.
1st Part.

Les singuliers et nouveaux pourtraicts, du Seigneur Federic de Vinciolo Venitien, pour toutes sortes d'ouvrages de Lingerie. Dedié a la Royne. Derechef et pour la troisiesme fois augmentez, outre le reseau premier & le point couppé & lacis, de plusieurs beaux et differens portrais de reseau de point côté, avec le nombre des mailles, chose non encor veuë, ny inventée. A Paris. Par Iean le Clerc le ieune, au mont Saint Hilaire, du Chef Sainct Denis, pres le Clos Bruneau. Avec privilege du Roy. 1588.[63]

---

[61] Bib. Nat. Grav. L. h. 2.* (with Part I.): "Ex Bibliotheca illustris-imi Johannis d'Estrées Cameracensis Archiepiscopi designati quam Monasterio St. Germani à Pratis legavit. Anno 1718."

[62] Brussels, Bib. Roy. M. Alvin, Conservateur en Chef.

[63] Bib. Ste.-Geneviève. V. 634.*
—Bib. Nat. Grav. L. h. 2. b.*

68.

Les singuliers et nouveaux pourtraicts, du Seigneur Federic de Vin- *2nd Part.*
ciolo Venitien, pour toutes sortes d'ouvrages de Lingerie. Dedié a la
Royne. Derechef et pour la troisiesme fois augmentez, outre le reseau
premier & le point couppé & lacis, de plusieurs beaux et differens portrais de reseau de point côté, avec le nombre des mailles, chose non
encor veuë, ny inventée. A Paris. Par Iean le Clerc le ieune, au mont
Saint Hilaire, au Chef Sainct Denis, pres le Clos Bruneau. Avec
privilege du Roy. 1588.[64]

This must be subsequent to the Brussels impression, as Jean le Clerc has
changed his address.

In the third edition, dorso of pp. 1 and 2, we have the addition of portraits
of Louise de Vaudemont and Henry III., with a complimentary stanza of four
lines under each.

In his "Advertissement au lecteur," Vinciolo says that having promised, since
the first impression of his book, to give a "nouvelle bande d'ouvrages," and not
to disappoint certain ladies who have complained that he has not made "du
reseau assez beau à leur fantaisie," "I have wished for the third time to place
before their eyes many new and different patterns of ' reseau de point conté
que j'ay cousus et attachez à la fin de mes premières figures,' beneath which I
have put the number and quantity of the stitches." Same dedication and sonnet
as before. Privilege for nine years dated Paris, 25 May 1587. " De l'Imprimerie de David le Clerc, rue S. Jaeques, au petit Bec, devant le College de
Marmouttier."

1st Part, 40 ff. 36 places, 27 of Point couppé, two stomachers, and seven
" Passemens de Point couppé"; the same lettered "Ouvrages" as in the
preceding impression.

2nd Part, 36 ff. 50 plates. The thirty already published in the second
edition, after which follow the twenty additional of "reseau de point conté,"
announced in the Preface, consisting of " 6 Quarrés, 2 Coins of Mouchoir, 2
Bordures, 6 animals : Lion, Pelican, Unicorn, Stag, Peacock, and Griffon "; and
the Four Seasons, " Déesse des fleurs, representant le Printemps," &c.

These last twenty have the number of stitches given. (See Fig. 5, p. 15.)
On the last page is an escutcheon with the arms of France and Poland.

69.

A later impression still.

Same title, date, portraits, dedication, and sonnet ; only the Privilege is   1588.
dated " ce douzième jour de Novembre 1587. De l'Imprimerie de David le   *3rd Edit.*
Clerc, Rue S. Jaques, aux trois Mores."[65]   *No. 3.*
34 ff. 30 plates, 1st part ; 50 plates in 2nd.   *Parts* 1
                                                                                                                        and 2.

70.

Les singuliers et nouveaux pourtraicts, du Seigneur Frederic de Vin-   1595.
ciolo, Venitien, pour toutes sortes d'ouvrages de Lingerie. Dedie à la   *3rd Edit.*
Royne Douairière de France.   *No. 4.*
De Rechef et pour la troisiesme fois augmentez, outre le reseau pre-   *Parts* 1
mier & le point couppé & lacis, de plusieurs beaux & differens porrais   *and* 2.
de reseau de point côté, avec le nombre des mailles, chose non encore
veuë ny inventée.

---

[64] Bib. Ste.-Geneviève (with 1st Part).*—Bib. Nat. Grav. L. h. 2. b.
(with 1st Part).*   [65] Bib. de l'Arsenal. 11,954 *bis.**

A Paris. Par Iean le Clerc, rüe Saint Jean de Latran, à la Salemandre. Avec privilege du Roy. 1595.[66]

This impression is dedicated to Louise de Vaudemont, now " Reine Douairière," Henry III. having died in 1589.

71.

1606.   The same title as that of 1595—differing only in date.[67]
3rd Edit.   Privilege for six years, " donné à Mantes, le 3 Juillet 1593." At the foot,
No. 5.   " De l'Imprimerie de David le Clerc au Petit Corbeil 1606.'
Parts 1   The first part has 32 ff. and 36 plates ; 32 " Ouvrages de poinct couppé," and
and 2.   4 stomachers.
             The 2nd part 46 plates, same as those of 1588, only four less.
             On the last page, the escutcheons of France and Navarre.

72.

1589.   Les singuliers et nouveaux pourtraicts, du Seigneur Federic de Vin-
4th Edit. ciolo Venetien, pour toutes sortes d'ouvrages de Lingerie. Dedie a la
Turin.   Royne. Derechef et pour la quatrieme fois augmentez, outre le reseau
Parts 1
and 2.   premier et le point couppé et lacis, de plusieurs beaux et differens portrais de reseau de point conté, avec le nombre de mailles, chose non
encore veue ni inventee. A Thurin. Par Eleazaro Thomysi. 1589.[68]

Described in Cat. Cicognara with the date 1658. The first part 44 ff. and
39 plates ; the 2nd with 36 plates.
   The editions of 1613 and 1623 are described in their chronological order.
That of 1603 we have not seen ; but M. Leber states it to be equally rich
with that of 1623.
   The copies of Vinciolo in the Bodleian bear the dates of 1588, 1603, and
1612.
   Baron Pichon has a copy of an impression of 1612.
   One at Bordeaux, in the Bib. de la Ville, is dated 1588.

In a book sale at Antwerp, March 1864, there was sold the following :—

   Lot. 528. " Livre de Patrons de Lingerie dedié a la Royne, nouvellement
invente par le seign' Frederic de Vinciolo, Venitien. Paris, Jean le Clerc,
1598.—Les singuliers et nouveaux pourtraicts pour toutes sortes d'ouvrages de
Lingerie. Paris, ibid. 1598.—Les secondes œuvres et subtiles inventions de
Lingerie. Paris, ibid. 1598.—Nouveaux pourtraicts de Point coupé et Dantelles en petite moyenne et grande forme. A Montbeliard, Jacques Foillet,
1598. 4 tom. 1 vol. in-4. v. anc. fig. sur bois." It sold for 440 francs. We do
not know the editions of 1598.
   As M. Leber observes, the various editions of Vinciolo, published by Le
Clerc and his widow, from 1587 to 1623, and perhaps later, are only impressions
more or less varied of the two distinct books, the one of point coupé, the other
of lacis.
   The work of Vinciolo has been reprinted in several countries. In England
it has been translated and published by Wolfe (see No. 73) ; at Liege, by
Jean de Glen (see No. 81). Mr. Douce says that it was reprinted " at Strasburg, 1596, and at Basle, 1599, with a second part, which is rare, and sometimes contains a portrait by Gaultier of Catherine de Bourbon."

---

[66] British Museum. Grenville Lib.   [68] Brussels, Bib. Roy.—Cat. Ci-
2584.*   cognara. No. 1822.
[67] Bib. Nat. Grav. L. h. 1. a.*

In the Bib. Nat. (Grav. B. c. 22), a volume headed " Vinciolo (Federigo) Peintre Venitien et ses imitateurs," contains, with " La pratique," &c., of Mignerak, a German copy of the " nouveaux pourtraits," the work printed by Ludwig Künigs, at Basle, 1599; and a German work headed " Broderies sur filet,' 50 plates engraved upon copper.

73.

New and singular patterness and works of linen seruing for Paternes to make all sorts of Lace, Edginges and Cutworks, newlie invented for the profite & contentment of Ladies, Gentilwomen and others who are desirous of this Art. London. 1591. Printed by J. Wolfe, or Wolfe.[69]

1591. *London. Wolf.*

4to.

74.

Fiori di ricami nuovamente posti in luce ne i quali sono varii, et diversi dissegni di lavori ; Come Merli, Bauari, Manichetti, & altre sorti di opere, che al presente sono in uso, utilissimi ad ogni stato di Donne. Seconda Impressione.

1591. *Bologna. T. Pasini.*

Impresa of Mercury. Below—

In Bologna, per Giovanni Rossi. MDXCI. Ad instanza di Tomaso Pasini.[70]

Obl. 8vo. 20 ff. 18 plates like Vecellio, one " bavaro.'
Dedicated by the author to " La Signora Silveria Rossi Ghisolieri."
Mostly indented patterns on black grounds.

75.

Prima Parte de' fiori, e disegni di varie sorti di Ricami moderni come merli, bavari, manichetti, & altri nobili lavori che al presente sono in uso.

1591. *Venice. F. di Frances- chi.*

A figure of Peace. Below—

In Venetia, Appresso Francesco di Franceschi Senese all' insegna della Pace 1591.[71]

Obl. 8vo. 20 ff. 17 plates im the style of Vecellio.
Dedication to " La Signora Gabriella Zeno Michele," signed " Di Venetia alli 19 di Marzo 1591, Giovanbattista Ciotti." The last plate a figure of For-tune, with " Finis in Venetia 1591. Appresso Nicolo Moretti, ad instantia di Francesco di Franceschi."

76.

La vera perfettione del disegno di varie sorti di ricami & di cucire ogni sorti de punti à fogliami, punti tagliati, punti a fili & rimessi, punti incrociati, punti à stuora & ogn' altre arte, che dia opera à disegni. E di nuovo aggiuntovi varie sorti di merli, e mostre, che al presente sono in uso & in pratica.

1591. *Venice. F. di Frances- chi.*

Impresa of Peace differing from the preceding.

---

[69] Quoted in Watt's " Bibliographia Britannica."
[70] Bib. de l'Arsenal. No. 11,954 *ter*.*
[71] Bib. de l'Arsenal. 11,955 *bis*.*— Bib. Bodleian.

In Venetia, Appresso Francesco di Franceschi Senese all' insegna della Pace. 1581.[72]

Oblong 8vo. 36 ff. 72 plates.

Dedicated to "Signora Lucretia Contarini, per matrimonio Priula Nobile Gentildonna Venetiana," by Giovanni Ostans.

A woodcut of Lucretia working with her maidens, signed Jose Sol, 1557.

Patterns, Small Squares, Gorgets, Youth, Paris, Pyramus and Thisbe, Arabesques, Grotesqu‹s, and an Alphabet.

On the last leaf, dorso, A. B. C. D. "tutte sono quaderni." A figure again of Peace, and "In Ven. 1590."

77.

1592.   Corona delle nobili et virtuose donne. Libro primo. Nel quale si
Venice.   dimostra in varij Dissegni, tutti le sorti di Mostre di punti tagliati,
1st Book.   punti in aria, punti à Reticello, e d' ogni altra sorte cosi per Freggi
C. Vecellio. come per Merli, & Rosette, che con l' Aco si usano hoggidì per tutta l' Europa. Et molte delle quali Mostre possono servire anchora per Opere à Mazzette. Aggiuntivi in questa Quarta impressione molti bellissimi dissegni non mai più veduti.

Then follows the printer's impresa of the stork and serpent. "Voluptatum et malorum effetuu dissipatio," with a lady at work on each side, and below—

Con privilegio. In Venetia, Appresso Cesare Vecellio in Frezzaria nelle Case de' Preti. 1592.[73]

Which is repeated in the 2nd and 3rd Books.

Obl. 4to. 32 ff. 28 plates.

Dedication of Vecellio, "Alla Clarissima et Illustrissima Signora, Viena Vendramina Nani, dignatissima Consorte dell' Illust^smo Sig. Polo Nani, il Procurator di S. Marco," in which he refers to his work on costume, and says that he dedicates this book to her for the delight she takes in these works and "in farne essercitar le donne di casa sua, ricetto delle piu virtuose giovani che hoggidì vivano in questa città." Signed: Venice, 20 Jan. 1591.

Beautiful designs, among which are three corners for handkerchiefs, the last lettered: "Diverse inventioni p. cantoni dee fazoletti."

On Plate 3, within a point coupé border, is a statue of Venus standing upon a tortoise, with other figures, and above, "Conviensi, che della Donna la bontà, & non la bellezza sia divulgata," and underneath :—

"Veneer io son, de le mirabil mani
Del dotto Fidia d' un bel marmo finta.
In me vedete atti gentili, e humani,
Ch' esser dè Donna à gentilezza accinta.
Io sopra una Testugine dimora,
Perchè stia in Casa, e sia tacita ogn' hora."

2nd Book.   Corona delle nobili et virtuose donne. Libro secondo.
Nel quale si dimostra in varij Dissegni, tutte le sorti di Mostre di punti tagliati, punti in aria, punti à Reticello, e d' ogni altra sorte, cosi per Freggi, come per Merli, & Rosette, che con l' Aco si usano hoggidì per tutta l' Europa. Et molte delle quali Mostre possono servire anchora per Opere à Mazzette. Aggiuntivi in questa Quarta Impres-

---

[72] Bib. Bodleian.
[73] Bib. de l'Arsenal. 11,955* (with Books 2 and 3). "Mazzette" means wooden bobbins.

sione molti bellissimi dissegni non mai più veduti. Con Privilegio. In Venetia, Appresso Cesare Vecellio, in Frezzaria nelle Case de' Preti. 1592.

28 ff. 26 plates.

The dedication of this and the next book, though differently worded, are addressed to the same lady as the first. This is dated 24 Jan. 1591.

Among the patterns are two designs for handkerchiefs, and on the last plate a statue of Vesta, within a point coupé border.

Corona delle nobili et virtuose donne. Libro terzo. Nel quale si *3rd Book.* dimostra in varii dissegni molte sorti di Mostri di Punti in Aria, Punti tagliati, Punti a reticello, and ancora di picciole; cosi per Freggi, come per Merli, & Rosette, che con l' Aco si usano hoggidi per tutta l' Europa. Con alcune altre inventione di Bavari all' usanza Venetiana. Opera nuova e non più data in luce. Con privilegio. In Venetia Appresso Cesare Vecellio, stà in Frezzaria nella Case de' Petri. 1592.

Dedication dated 15 June 1591. Vecellio says he has added " alcune inventioni di bavari all' usanza nostra." In the copy (Bib. de l'Arsenal, 11,955 *bis*) are added instructions to transfer the patterns upon parchment without injuring the book. The last plate shows how to reduce the patterns and how to prick them (Fig. 155). This is sometimes given at the end of the first book instead of the third.

28 ff. 25 plates, two of bavari.

On Pl. 27, woman with a torch and Cupid. At Pl. 28, in a point coupé border, is a fox holding the bust of a lady, the conceit of which is explained by the verses to be, that sense is better than beauty :—

> " Trovò la Volpe d' un Scultore eletto
> Una testa sì ben formata, tale,
> Che sol le manca Spirito havresti detto,
> Tanto l' industria, e l' artefīcio vale,
> La prende in man, poi dice; O che perfetto
> Capo, e gentil ; ma voto è d' intelletto."

Fig. 155.

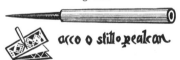

Manner of pricking the patterns. Vecellio.

78.

Gioiello della corona per le nobili e virtuose donne. Libro quarto. 1594. Nel quale si dimostra altri nuovi bellissimi Dissegni di tutte le sorte di *Venice.* Mostre di Punti in Aria, Punti tagliati & Punti à Reticello; così per *C. Vecellio* Freggi, come per Merli, & Rosette, che con l' Aco si usano hoggidì per tutta l' Europa. Et molte delle quali mostre possono servire anchora per opere à Mazzette Nuovament posto in luce con molte bellissime inventioni non mai più usate, nè vedute. Con privilegio. In Venetia, Appresso Cesare Vecellio, in Frezzaria nella Casa de i Preti. 1594.

Same Impresa of the stork and serpent.

Dedicated to the Signora Isabella Palavicina Lupi Marchese di Soragana, dated "Venetia alli 10 Novembrio 1592." Cesare Vecellio. 30 plates.[74]

Vecellio, author of the "Corona" and Gioiello," also published a work on costume, styled "Degli Habiti Antichi et Moderni. In Venezia, 1590. Presso Damian Zenero." In the frontispiece is a salamander; on the last leaf, a figure of Vesta. It has been reproduced by F. Didot, Paris.

He was not, as is often incorrectly stated, a relation or even of the same family as Titian.

These are the earliest impressions we have had an opportunity of examining of Vecellio's works, which appear to have been widely circulated. The Bib. de l'Arsenal possesses two copies of the "Corona" (No. 11,955), from a bust we have described. In the other (No. 11,155 bis), Book 1 "ultima," Book 2 "quarta," are both dated 1593 ; and Book 3 "nuovamente ristampata la quarta volta," 1592. The plates all the same.

The library of Rouen (No. 1315) has a volume containing the "Corona" and "Gioiello." Book 1 "quarta Imp.," Book 2 "ultima," both dated 1594 ; and Book 3 "quinta," 1593. The "Gioiello," 1593.

In the Bodleian is a copy of the three books, date 1592 ; and another, date 1561, was in the possession of the late Mrs. Dennistoun, of Dennistoun.

At Venice, in the Doge's Library, is a volume containing the three books of the "Corona" and the "Gioiello," dated 1593.

Mrs. Stisted, Bagni di Lucca, also possesses the three books of the "Corona," dated 1597, and the "Gioiello," 1592.

At Bologna, the library has one volume, containing the first and second books only, evidently the original impressions. The titles are the same as the above, only to each is affixed, "Opera nuova e non più data in luce," and "Stampata per gli Hered' della Regina. 1591. Ad instantia di Cesare Vecellio, Stà in Frezzaria."

The same library also possesses a volume, with the three books of the "Corona," the first and third "ottava," the second "quarta," and the "Gioiello," "nuovamente posto in luce." All "In Venetia appresso gli heredi di Cesare Vecellio, in Frezzaria. 1608."

At Vienna, in the new Museum for Art and Industry, is a copy of the five books, dated 1601.[75]

Cav. Merli cites from a copy of the four books, dated 1600. The various impressions, therefore, date from 1591 to 1608.[76] We see these different parts, like those of Vinciolo and all these old collections, have been printed and reprinted independently of each other, since the third part was at its fifth impression in 1593, while the first, which ought to have preceded it, was only at its fourth in 1594.[77]

79.

1593.
St. Gall.
G. Strau-
ben.

New Model-Buch darinnen allerley Gattung schöner Modeln der newen aussgeschitnen Arbeit auff Krägen, Hempter, Jakelet und dergleichen zu newen, so zuvor in Teutschlandt nicht gesehen. Allen thugentsamen Frawen und Jungkfrawen, Nätterinnen, auch

---

[74] Rouen Bib. Bound in one vol. with the three parts of the "Corona."*

[75] Communicated by Mr. Gruner.

[76] Mr. Lake Price has the three books of the "Corona," first edit. 1591.

[77] Note of M. Leber, who gives the dates of the dedication of the Rouen copy as follows :—B. 1, 20 Jan. ; B. 2, 24 Jan. ; B. 3, 15 June, all in 1591. The "Gioiello," 10 Nov. 1592 The volume containing the two works has 101 leaves, in addition to 10 leaves of titles, dedications, &c.

allen andern so lust zu solcher kunstlichen Arbeit haben, sehr dienstlich.

Getruckt in uerlegung George Strauben, von S. Gallem, Anno 1593.[78]

Translation.

New Pattern book, in which are all sorts of beautiful patterns of the new cutwork for collars, shirts, jackets, and such like, such as never before were seen in Germany. Most useful to all virtuous dames and damsels (needlewomen), as well as to all others who take a pleasure in such artistic works, very respectfully dedicated.

Printed for the publisher, G. Strauben.

A reprint of the third book of Vecellio's " Corona."

80.

Neu Model-Buch, darinnen allerley Gattung schöner Modeln der neuen, &c.

N. D.
Lindau am Bodensee.

Probably a reprint of No. 79.

27 plates.

81.

Les singuliers et nouveaux pourtraits, pour toutes sortes de lingeries de Jean de Glen, dediés à Madame Loyse de Perez; à Liége, chez Jean de Glen, l'an 1597.[79]

1597.
Liége.
J. de Glen.

Obl. 4to. 39 plates, mostly borrowed from Vinciolo, as well as the title. This work is described p. 112.

82.

Fior di Ricami nuovamente posti in luce. Fiorenze, 1596, ad instanza di Mattheo Florini.

1596.
Florence.
M. Florini.

4to. obl. 24 plates and 2 leaves of text.[80]

83.

Fiori di Ricami nuovamente posti in luce nei quai sono varie et diversi disegni di lavori, come merli, bavari, manichetti e altre sorte di opera. Siena, appresso Matteo Florini, 1603.

1603.
Siena.
M. Florini.

4to. obl. 27 pages.[81]

84.

Giojello &c. Nel quale si di mostra altri novi bellissimi disegni di tutte le sorte, di mostre &c. . . . . . di punti &c., cosi per fregi come per merli et rosette che con l'aco si usanno hoggi di per tutta l'Europa. Opere a Mazzette nuovamente posta in luce con molte bellissimi inventioni non mai più usate ne vedute. In Siena. Matteo Florini. MDCIII.

1603.
Siena.
M. Florini.

4to. obl.[82]

[78] South Kensington Museum.
[79] Brussels, Bib. Royale. Jean de Glen is also author of a work entitled " Des Habits, Mœurs, Ceremonies, Façons de faire, anciennes & modernes, du Monde, par J. de Glen, Linger." Liége. J. de Glen. 1601. In-8.
[80] Lyon, M. Yemenis.
[81] Turin, Count Manzoni.
[82] Cited by Marquis d' Adda.

85.

1597.
*Nurem-
berg.
B. Lai-
moxen.*
Schön neues Modelbuch von allerly lüstigen Mödeln naczunehen zu
würken un zu sticke; gemacht im Jar Ch. 1597, zu Nürmberg, bey
Balthaser Laimoxen zu erfragen.[83]

Translation.

Fine new Pattern book of all sorts of pleasant patterns for sewing, working,
and embroidering ; made in the year of Xt. 1597, at Nuremberg : to be had of
Balthasar Laimoxen.

Obl. fol. 27 ff.

5 sheets, title-page, and poem, signed J. S. (Johann Sibmacher).

Mr. Gruner has communicated to us a work with the same title, dated
1591.[84]

86.

1598.
*Mont-
béliard.
J. Foillet.*
Nouveaux pourctraicts de point coupé et dantelles en petite moyenne
et grande forme nouvellement inventez & mis en lumiere.   Imprimé a
Montbéliard par Jacques Foillet cloloxciix (1598).[85]

Small 4to. 82 ff. 78 plates.

Frontispiece with borders composed of squares of point coupé.

"Avertissement aux dames," of three pages, stating these works are all
composed of "point devant l'esguille, de point en toille, en bouclages & de
cordonnages." The writer gives patterns of roses of all sizes, "very little,
middling, large, and very large," with from one to nine "pertuis," or openings.
holes. Also Carreaux in different forms, and lastly "dantelles." "Je n'ay
voulu omettre de vous dire que pour faire des dantelles, il vous fault jetter un
fil de la grandeur que desiré faire vos dantelles, & les cordonner, puis jetter les
fils au dedans, qui fera tendre le cordon & lui donnera la forme carrée, ronde,
ou telle forme que desires, ce qu'estant faict vous paracheverès facilement.
Enoultre vous verrez qu'estant bien petites deviennent peu a peu bien grandes
jusques a la fin. Elles vous enricheront & embelliront vos ouvrages en les
applicant aux bords d'iceux." Directions, we confess, perfectly enigmatical to
us. The author finishes by exhorting the ladies to imitate Minerva and
Arachne, " qui ont acquis un grand renom, pour avoir (come à l'envie l'une de
l'autre) travaillé de l'esguille."

The avertissement is followed by an "Exhortation aux jeunes filles" in
verse, beginning—

"Si nuisible est aux humains la paresse," &c.

40 patterns of "roses" of point coupé, and 18 of "carreaux," variously
disposed.   Then follow 20 patterns of lace "bien petites, petites, moyennes &
grosses," all "à point devant l'esguille " (see Figs. 7 to 11, pp. 22–24).

At the end : "La fin courone l'œuvre." (This is the earliest pattern book
in which the word "dantelle" occurs.)

87.

1598.
*Mont-
béliard.
J. Foillet.*
New Modelbuch darinnen allerley auszgeschnittene Arbeit, in kleiner,
mittelmässiger und grosser form, erst newlich erfunden. Allen tugenden
Frawen vnnd Jungfrawen sehr nutzlich. Gedruckt zu Mumpelgarten
durch Jacob Foillet, 1598.[86]

4to. (Edition in German of the preceding.)

---

[83] Berlin, Royal Library.   L. h. 3.*—Bib. de l'Arsenal. 11,956.*
[84] Dresden, New Museum of Arts   —Bib. Ste.-Geneviève.*
and Industry.   [86] S. K. M.
[85] Bib. Nat. V. 1902,* and Grav.

88.

Fewrnew Modelbuch von allerhand künstlicher Arbeidt, nämlich Gestrickt, Aussgezogen, Aussgeschnitten, Gewirfflet, Gestickt, Gewirckt, und Geneyt: von Wollen, Garn, Faden, oder Seyden: auff der Laden, und Sonderlich auff den Ramen, Jetzt Erstmals in Teutschlandt an Tag gebracht: Zu Ehren und Glücklicher Zeitvetreibung allen dugentsamen Frawen, und Jungfrawen Nächerinen, auch allen andern, so lust zu solcher Kunstlicher Arbeit haben sehr dienstlich. Getruckt zu Basel.
In verlegung Ludwig Künigs MDXCIX.[87]

1599.
Basle.

Small obl. 33 ff. 32 plates.
Frontispiece border of point coupé. Title in Gothic, red and black.
Patterns, mostly borders, number of stitches given, " Mit xxxxvii. Bengen," &c. " Ende dieses modelbuchs."

89.

Béle Prérie contenant divers caracteres, et differentes sortes de lettres alphabetiques, à sçavoir lettres Romaines, de formes, lettres pour appliquer sur le reseuil ou lassis, et autres pour marquer sur toile et linges, par Pier. le Bé. Paris, 1601.[88]

1601.
Paris.

In 4to. obl.

90.

Modelbuch in Kupfer gemacht, Nürmberg, bei Michel Kuisner, 1601. By J. Sibmacher.[89]

1601.
Nuremberg.

91.

Newes Modelbûch fûr Kûpfer gemacht, darinnen allerhand art newen Model von dem Mittel und Dick ausgeschniden duer Arbeit auch andern kunstlichen Nahework zu gebrauchen mit Fluss fur druck verfertigt. Mit Röm. Kaiz. Maj trentich Nürmberg 1604.[90]

1604.
Nuremberg.
Sibmacher.

Translation.

New book of patterns in which are engraved on copper all kinds of new patterns for thick and thin materials, to be used also in the making of other artistic needlework. . .

Obl. 4to. 58 plates carefully engraved upon copper.
Title-page surrounded by a richly ornamented border, with two figures, one sewing, the other at embroidery ; also a second ornamented frontispiece, dedication to Maria Elizabeth, Electress Palatine, dated 1601. Nuremberg, J. Sibmacher, citizen and engraver.
Then follow five pages of dialogue, given page 6, note [25], and p. 234.
A printed title to the next plate. " The following pattern be may worked in several different ways, with a woven seam, a flat, round, or crossed Jew stitch."[91] It is probably meant for cutwork made on thin materials.

---

[87] Bib. Nat. Grav. B. c. 22. Vinciolo.*
[88] Catalogue des Livres de feu M. Picard. 1780. No. 455.
[89] Brussels, Bib. Royale.
[90] Nuremberg, German Museum.— Mr. E. Arnold.
[91] Jew's stitch is given both by

Sibmacher and Latomus (No. 95). We do not know what it is. The only parallel expression we have met with is in the rhyme of Sir Topaz, when Chaucer describes the hauberk of a knight as

" All ywrought of Jewes work."

2 F

Then follow 58 leaves of patterns, the greater number of which have the number of rows written over each pattern. Pl. 38, with two patterns, is inscribed, "The following patterns are for thick cutwork." In the upper pattern, on the first leaf, are the arms of the Palatinate; on the second, those of Juliers and Mark.

92.

N. D.   Allerhand Model zum Stricken und Nähen.

64 plates. Oblong 4to. No date.

93.

1604.   A book of models for point coupé and embroidery, published at
Padua.   Padua, 1st October, 1604, by Pietro Paolo Tozzi Romano.[92]

94.

1605.   Schön newes Modelbuch von sehr schönen ausso wählten, Kunst-
Frankfort   lichen, so wol Italiehnischen, Frantzosischen, Niederlandischen, Engel-
on the
Main.   landischen, als Teutschen Modeln, Allen Näher . . . . emstickern zu
S. Latomus. zunug. (Some of the words are illegible.)

Livre des Modelles fort utile à tous ceux qui besoignent à l'esguille.

At the foot of the last page recto, is " Francfurt am Mayn, bey Sigismund Latomus, 1608." [93]

Small obl. 100 plates (Fig. 156) and coloured title-page with figures.

Fig. 156.

Frankfort on the Main, 1605.

In the first plate is an escutcheon with this monogram (Fig. 157) surrounded with embroidery :—

Fig. 157.

Monogram.

In the Nuremberg copy it is at p. 83.

---

[92] Cited by Cav. Merli, in his " Origine delle Trine."
[93] Bib. Nat. Grav. L. h. 4. b.—Nuremberg, German Museum.

APPENDIX. 435

95.

Schön neues Modelbuch, von hundert vnd achtzig schönen kunst- 1607.
reichen vnd gerechten Modeln, Teutsche vnd Welsche, welche auff *Frankfort*
mancherley Art können geneet werden, als mit Zopffnath, Creutz- vnnd *on the*
Judenstich, auch auff Laden zu wircken : Dessgleichen von ausser- *S. Latomus.* *Main.*
lesenen Zinnigen oder Spitzen.   Allen Seydenstickern, Modelwerckern,
Näderin, vnd solcher Arbeit geflissenen Weibsbildern sehr dienstlich,
vnd zu andern Mustern anleytlich vnd verstendig.   Franckfurt am
Mayn, In Verlegung Sigismundi Latomi.   MDCVII.[94]

Small 4to. obl.   180 patterns.
Sheets A-O (the last has only 3 leaves).   On the title-page are two ladies,
one working at a pillow, the other at a frame ; in the background, other
women employed at various works.
Another copy, dated 1629.[95]

96.

La pratique de l'aiguille industrieuse du très excellent Milour Mat- 1605.
thias Mignerak Anglois, ouvrier fort expert en toute sorte de lingerie ou *Paris.*
sont tracez Divers compartimens de carrez tous differans en grandeur *M. Migne-* *rak.*
et invention avec les plus exquises bordures, desseins d'ordonnances qui
se soient veux jusques à ce jourd'hui tant poetiques historiques, qu'au
tres ouvrages de point de rebord.   Ensemble Les nouvelles invencions
Françoises pour ce qui est de devotion et contemplation.   A la Tres-
Chrestiene Roine de France et de Navarre.   Avec privilege 1605 du
Roy.[96]
A Paris, par Jean Leclere, rue St.-Jean de Latran, à la Salamandre
roialle.

EXTRACT FROM "DISCOURS DU LACIS."

" Ce chef d'œuvre divin n'est pas à l'adventure
Mais par art composé, par nombre, et par mesure :
Il commence par un, et va multipliant
Le nombre de ses trouz qu'un nœud va reliant,
Sans perdre aucunement des nombres d'entresuitte,
Croissant, et decroissant d'une mesme conduitte :
Et ainsi qu'il commence il acheve par un,
Du monde le principe et le terme commun.
Si l'on veut sans faillir cet ouvrage parfaire,
Il faut multiplier, adjouster, et soustraire :
Il faut bien promptement assembler, et partir,
Qui veut un beau Lacis inegal compartir.
Mais se peut il trouver, souz la voute azurée,
Chose plus justement en tous sens mesurée ?
Ouvrage ou il y ait tant de proportions,
De figures, de traicts et de dimensions ?

---

[94] Stockholm, Royal Library.
(Communicated by the librarian,
Mr. H. Wieselgren.) In the same
library is a work, without title-page
or date, for "broderies et de tous
autres besongnant à l'aiguille," by
Hieronymus Cock, containing, with
designs of every description, a few

patterns for Spanish point of great
beauty.
[95] Mr. Arnold and Mr. F. S. Ellis,
London.
[96] Bib. Baron J. Pichon. 2 copies.*
Cat. d'Estrées.—Bib. Nat. Grav. B.
c. 22.* (Title-page wanting.)

2 F 2

D'un point premièrement une ligne l'on tire,
Puis le filet courbé un cercle va descrire,
Et du cercle noué se trouve le quarré
Pour lequel retrouver tant d'esprits ont erré.
De six mailles se faict une figure egale,
De trois costez esgaux, pour forme pyramidale :
Et l'ouvrage croissant, s'en forme promptement
Une autre dont les deux sont egaux seulement.
Si l'on tire un des coings, se forme une figure.
D'un triangle en tout sens, d'inegale mesure.
Le moule plus tiré faict les angles pointuz,
Et l'ouvrage estendu faict les angles obtuz.
De mailles à la fin un beau quarré se faict,
Composé de quarrez, tout egal, et parfaict,
Quarré qui toutesfois se forme variable,
Or en lozange, et or en figure de table.
La bande de Lacis recouvert, à nos yeux,
Est comme un beau pourtraict de l'escharpe des cieux,
Dont chaque endroit ouvré nous represente un signe,
Le milieu, les degrez de l'Eclyptique ligne ;
 Le quarré, des vertus le symbole, et signal
De science du livre et bonnet doctoral,
Nous va representant l'Eglise et la Justice.
La façon de lacer figure l'exercice
D'enfiler une bague ou bien l'art d'escrimer.

. . . .

Le lacis recouvert sert de filet aux dames
Pour les hommes surprendre et enlacer leurs ames,
Elles en font collets, coiffures, et mouchoirs,
Des tentures de lits, tauayoles, pignoirs,
Et maint autre ornement dont elles les enlacent,
C'est pourquoi en laçant les femmes ne se lassent."

In 4to. 76 ff. 72 plates.
Frontispiece: Two ladies, with frames in their hands, labelled " Diana "
and "Pallas." On the top, an escutcheon per pale France and Medicis, supported by Cupids. Beneath, Cupids with distaff and winding reels. Between
the sides of a pair of scissors is a cushion on which is extended a piece of lacis,
a "marguerite" in progress (see page 18, and Fig. 6). Above, "Petrus
Firens fecit, I. le Clerc excud." Below, "A Paris par Jean le Clerc Rue St.
Jean de Latran à la Salamandre royalle."
Dedication of Jean le Clerc " A la royne," then Marie de Médicis, stating :
" J'avois recouvré d'un personnage Anglois tres-expert en toute sorte de Lin-
gerie ;" but who this Milour Mignerak may be, history tells not.
Then follows the " Discours du Lacis," a poem, of which we give an extract·
The privilege is signed 2 Aug. 1605.
The patterns consist of the Queen's arms and cypher, 4 Scripture subjects :
Adam and Eve, the Annunciation, Ecce Homo, and Magdalen ; 4 Elements, 4
Seasons ; Roman Charity, Lucretia, Venus, and "Pluye d'or ;" 6 "Arbres à
fruit," 6 "Pots à fleurs," 30 "Carrés grands, moyens et petits " ; 6 " Bordures,"
and, what is quite a novelty, 6 "Passements faits au fuseau " (see Fig. 12, p.
24): the first mention of pillow lace in any of the French pattern books.

97.

1613.
Paris.
*F. Vin-
ciolo.*

Les secondes œuvres, et subtiles inventions de Lingerie du Seigneur
Federic de Vinçiolo Venitien ; nouvellement augmenté de plusieurs

carrez de point de rebort. Dediée à Madame, sœur unique du roy. Ou sont representees plusieurs figures de Reseau, nombres de Carrez et Bordures tous differents, le tout de poinct conté, avec autres sortes de Carrez de nouvelles inventions non encore vues.

A Paris. Par Jean le Clerc, rue sainct Jean de Latran, à la Salemandre, 1613. Avec privilege du Roy.[97]

A scarce and valuable volume, the fullest edition of the second part of Vinciolo's work.

4to. 68 ff. 61 plates.

It contains a

"SONNET AUX DAMES & DAMOYSELLES.

Esprits rarement beaux qui fuyez la paresse,
Je vous fais un present qui la pourra chasser,
Quand vous desirez de gayement passer
Vostre temps, et monstrer de vostre main l'adresse.

Le present est utile et plein de gentillesse,
Il monstre les moyens de bien entrelasser,
Et faire au point couppé tout ce qu'on peut penser.
Cet exercise plaist à Pallas la Deesse.

Par ses enseignemens, avec l'esguille on fait
Des fleurons, des oyseaux, en ouvrage parfait,
Des chiffres et des nœuds, tels que l'amour desire.

Aymez cet exercise, et vous y occupez,
Et puis vous cognoistrez que sur les points couppez
En diverses façons quelque portrait se tire."

The author's address to the reader, and a Dedication to "Madame, sœur unique du roy" (Catherine de Bourbon, sister of Henry IV., married, 1599, to the Duc de Bar), signed by Le Clerc.

On the second plate are her arms, a lozenge, France and Navarre with crown and cordelière, and the same lozenge also surmounts the decorated frontispiece, supported on either side by a genius (?) working at a frame and point coupé drapery.

7 Scripture subjects : The Salutation, St. Sacrement, Passion, Crucifixion, Adoration of the Kings, &c.; the number of the stitches given to each.

2 Stomachers, and various patterns of " carrez " and borders. 2 of " Point de rebort."

At the end is the "Discours du Lacis," already printed by Mignerak.

98.

Specchio delle virtuose Donne, dove si vedono bellissimi lavori di ponti in aria, reticella, di maglia e piombini. Roma, 1598.[98]

Obl. 4to. 40 leaves, 38 lace patterns, title, and blank.

1598.
Rome.
I. C. Parasole.

99.

Teatro delle nobili et virtuose donne, dove si rappresentano varij disegni di lavori novamente inventati et disegnati da Elisabetta Catanea Parasole Romana.

Dedicata alla Serenissima Principessa Donna Elisabetta Borbona

1616.
Rome.
E. C. Parasole.

---

[97] Bib. Rouen. No. 1314.*—Bib. Baron J. Pichon.*
[98] Cat. Ellis, King Street, Covent Garden.

d' Austria, Principessa di Spagna, da E. C. Parasole.   Data di Roma a di 5 Marzo 1616.[99]

Other editions, 1620, 1625, and 1636.

The last is dedicated to the Grand Duchess of Tuscany, and has the Medici and Della Rovere arms in the title-page.

Obl. 4to. 47 ff. 46 plates (44 in Prince Massimo's copy) beautifully executed, the titles printed to each plate, as "Lavori di punti in aria, Merletti di ponti reticella, Merletti a piombini," &c. (See Fig. 15, p. 25.)

100.

1600.
Venice.
I. C. Pa-
rasole.

Pretiosa gemme delle virtuose donne dove si vedono bellissimi lavori di ponto in aria, reticella, di maglia e piombini disegnati da Isabella Catanea Parasole. E di nuovo dati in luce da Luchino Gargano con alcuni altri bellissimi lavori nuovamente inventate. Stampata in Venetia ad instantia de Luchino Gargano. MDC.[100]

101.

1625.
Rome.
I. C. Pa-
rasole.

Gemma pretiosa delle virtuose donne, dove si vedono bellissimi lavori di Ponti in Aria, Reticella, di Maglia e Piombini disegnati da Isabella Catanea Parasole. In Rome, appresso Guglielmo Facciotti, 1625.

102.

1618.
Frankfort
on the
Main.
D. Meyer.

Zierat Buch, von allerhandt Kutschnur, Schleyer deckel, Krägen, Leibgürtel, Passmenten, Händschug, Wehrgeheng und Schubenehen, Messerscheyden, Seckeln, Früchten, Blumen und ands. mehr.

Allen Perlenbefftern, Nederin, Lehrinngen und andern, welche lust zu dieser Kunst tragen, sehr nützlich.

Inn diese Format zusammen ordiniert und gsetzt durch Daniel Meyer Mahlern. 1ster Theil.

Franckfuhrt am Mayn, bey Eberhardt Kusern zu finden.

11 ff. 9 plates.

Translation.

Decoration book of all sorts of Cords, Veil covers, Collars, Belts, Laces, Gloves, Sword-belts, shoe-seams (?), Knife sheaths, Bags, Fruit, Flowers, and other things besides. Very useful to all Beadworkers, Seamstresses, Apprentices, and others, who take a pleasure or are fond of this art. Arranged and put into this form by D. M. M. 1st part.

103.

1619.
Leipzig.
A. Bret-
schneider.

New Modelbŭch Darinnen allerley kunstliche Virsirung und Müster artiger Zŭege und schöner Blŭmmen zu zierlichen Ueberschlagen, Häupt Schurtz Schnŭptüchern Hauben Handschuhen, Uhren (?) gehengen, Kampfüttern ŭnd dergleichen auf Muhler naht und Seidenstücker arbeit gantz Kunstlich gemahlt und vorgerissen, dergleichen sie bevorn noch nie in Druck ausgegangen. 16 Leipzicht 19.

Inn Verlegŭng Henning Grosseren, des Jŭngeren Andreas Bretschneider Mahller.[101]

Translation.

New pattern book, in which all sorts of artistic ornamentations and patterns of pretty scrolls and beautiful flowers for pretty covers for H∙ ad, Aprons, and Pocket-handkerchiefs, Caps, Gloves, Watch-pockets, Comb cases, and such like, artistically sketched from painter and silk embroiderer's work, and which nave been never before in print.

Small folio, 53 plates, and half a sheet of text, containing the dedication of the work to Madame Catherine von Dorstats, née Löser. There appear to be 3 plates wanting.

104.

A. Schole House for the Needle. 1624.[102]

Obl. 4to. Was sold at the White Knight's sale for 3*l*. 15*s*.

1624.
London.

105.

Corona delle nobili et virtuose donne. Libro terzo. Nel quale si dimostra in varii dissegni tutte le sorti di Mostre di punti tagliati e punti in aria, punti Fiamenghi, punti a Reticello, e d' ogn' altra sorte, cosi per Fregi, per Merli e Rosette, che con Aco si viano hoggidi per tutta l' Europa. E molte delle quali Mostre possono servire ancora per opere à Mazzete. Con le dichiarationi a le Mostre a' Lavori fatti da Lugretia Romana. In Venetia, appresso Alessandro de Vecchi, 1620.[103]

1620.
Venice.
Lugretia
Romana.

27 ff. obl. 8vo.

106.

Corona delle Nobili et Virtuose Donne, Libro primo, nel quale si dimostra in varij Dissegni tutte le sorti di Mostre di punti tagliati, punti in Aria, punti Fiamenghi, punti a Reticello, e d' ogni altre sorte, cosi per Freggi, per Merli, e Rosette, che con l' Aco si usano per tutta l' Europa. Con le dichiarazioni a le Mostre, a Lavori fatti da Lugretia Romana.

In Venetia appresso Alessandro de Vecchi MDCXXV. Si vendono in Venetia al Ponte de' Baretteri alla libreria delle tre Rose.[104]

1625.
Venice.
Lucretia
Romana.

Lady Wilton, in her "Art of Needlework," quotes a copy dated 1620.

Obl. 4to. ff. 27. Portrait of Maria d'Aragon.

107.

Ornamento nobile, per ogni gentil matrona, dove si contiene bavari, frisi d' infinita bellezza, lavori, per Linzuoli, Traverse, e Facuoli, Piena di Figure, Ninfe, Satiri, Grotesche, Fontane, Musiche, Caccie di Cervi, Uccelli, ed altri Animali. Con ponti in aria, fiamenghi, et tagliati, con Adornamenti bellissimi, da imperare, per ogni Virtuosa Donna, che si diletta di perfettamente cucire. Opera, per Pittori, Scultori, e disegnatori giovevole alle lor professioni, Fatta da Lucretia Romana, il quinto volume di Suoi lavori. Dedicato alle Virtuose donne, in Venetia.[105]

N. D.
Venice.
Lucretia
Romana.

Fol. 20 plates.

Frontispiece, in point coupé frame. A woman in classic attire is represented under a Doric porch, standing on a tortoise, symbol of a home-loving woman

---

[102] Lowndes' "Bibliographer's Manual," new edit. by Henry Bohn.
[103] S. K. M.
[104] Vienna, Imperial Library.
[105] Brussels, Bib. Roy.

Fig. 159.

Bavaro di ponto d' aiere, di gran bellezzi. Con figure di molti strumenti che sonano a musica, con rosete d' intorno di bella e vaga vista per ogni principessa.

Bavaro di ponto d' aere con belissime figure & altri fiori.

" Bavari," from "Ornamento nobile" of Lucretia Romana.

(see No. 77). She holds a ball of thread in her hand. Behind, on the left, are two women at work; on the right, a sculptor chiselling a statue of Minerva.

The plates, which are rich and beautiful, are each accompanied by a short explanation, as "Degna da esser portata de ogni imperatrice; " "Hopera bellissima che per il piu il Signora Duchesa et altre Signore si servano per li suoi Lavori;" "Questa bellissima Rosette usano anco le gentildonne Venetiane da far traverse," &c. (Fig. 158.)

The bavari are executed in three different stitches : punto d'aieri, punto fiamingo, and punto tagliato. This is the only author who gives Flemish patterns (punti Fiamenghi). They consist mostly of rosettes and stars (gotico).

108.

Les excellents eschantillons, patrons et modelles du Seigneur Federic de Vinciolo Venitien, pour apprendre à faire toutes sortes d'ouvrages de Lingerie, de Poinct couppé, grands et petits passements à jour, et dentelles exquises. Dediez à la Royne. A Paris. Chez la Veufve Jean le Clerc, ruë Sainct Jean de Latran, à la Salamandre Royalle. Avec Privilege du Roy, 1623.[106]

1623.
Paris.

In 4to. 56 ff.

The old frontispiece and same "Avertissement."

Dedication to the Queen, Anne of Austria.

The Goddess Pallas invented "les ouvrages de lingerie, le poinct couppé, les grands & petits passements à jour, toutes sortes de dentelles, tant pour se desennuyer que se parer, par l'artifice de ses ingenieuses mains. A raciné s'y adonna, & bien qu'inferieure se voulant comparer à elle & en venir à l'experience, mais sa presomption fut chastiée." Many illustrious ladies have delighted in this "honneste exercise." Fastrade and Constance, wives of the Emperor Charlemagne and of King Robert, "s'employèrent de cette manufacture, & de leurs ouvrages ornèrent les églises & les autels." This royal "mestier" has reached perfection through the works of Vinciolo. I reprint and again increase his work, which I dedicate to your Majesty, to whom I presume they will be agreeable; the subject of which it treats is "une invention de déesse & une occupation de Royne—vous estant autant Royne des vertus que vous l'estes de deux royaumes." Signed, "la Veufve de feu Iean le Clerc."

Same sonnet.

Privilege for six years, dated Paris, last day of March 1623.

55 ff. 58 plates, 24 ouvrages de point couppé and 8 of "Passements au fuzeau" (see Figs. 13 and 14, pp. 24 and 25), and alphabet.

109.

Here followeth certaine patternes of Cut-workes; and but once Printed before. Also sundry sorts of Spots, as Flowers, Birds, and Fishes, &c., and will fitly serve to be wrought, some with Gould, some with Silke, and some with Gewell (*sic*) or otherwise at your pleasure.

1632.
London.

London ; Printed (*sic*) in Shoe-lane, at the signe of the Faulcon, by Richard Shorleyker. 1632.[170]

Obl. 4to.

The copy in the Bodleian is probably prior to the above. It has no date,

---

[106] Bib. Nat. Grav. L. h. 2. a.*—
Brussels, Bib. Roy.—Cat. d'Estrées.
8847.

[107] In the possession of Mrs. Marryat. "Maes y dderwen."—Bib. Bodleian.

and varies in title : " Newly invented and never published before," with " crewell in coullers," &c.; and " Never but once published before." Printed by Rich. Shorleyker.

33 patterns and title.

110.

1640.   The needles excellency, a new booke wherein are divers admirable workes wrought with the needle.   Newly invented and cut in copper for the pleasure and profit for the industrious.   Printed for James Boler, &c., 1640.[108]

Beneath this title is a neat engraving of three ladies in a flower garden, under the names of Wisdom, Industrie, and Follie.   Prefixed to the patterns are sundry poems in commendation of the needle, and describing the character of the ladies who have been eminent for their skill in needlework, among whom are Queen Elizabeth and the Countess of Pembroke.   These poems were composed by John Taylor, the Water Poet.   It appears the work had gone through twelve impressions.   From the costume of a lady and gentleman in one of the patterns, it appears to have been originally published in the reign of James I.   (Douce).   From the description of the frontispiece it seems to be copied from Sibmacher.

The Needles Excellency, a new book.   10th edition.   1636.[109]
The Needles Excellency, or a New Book of Patterns, with a poem by John Taylor in Praise of the Needle.   London, 1640.
Obl. 4to. engraved title and 28 plates of patterns (Lowndes' " Bibliographical Manual," Bohn's new edition).   Another copy of the same date, marked 12th edition, is in the Library, King's College, Cambridge.   It consists of title, four leaves with the poem, subscribed " John Taylor," and 31 leaves of copper cuts of patterns.

111.

1642.   Le Pompe di Minerva, per le nobili e virtuose donne che con
Pistoja.   industriosa mano di trattenersi dilettano di far Rezze, maglia
P. A. For-   quadra, punti in aria, punti tagliati, punti a reticello, cosi per fregio
tunato.   come per merletti e rosette di varie sorti, si come oggidi con l' aco di lavorar usati per tutto l' Europa, arrichite di bellissimi et vaghi intagli cavati da più celebri autori di tal professione.   In Pistoja, per Piero A. Fortunato.

In 8vo. obl. dedicated to Caterina Giraldini, in Cellesi.   20 August 1642.[110]

112.

1666.   Dass Neue Modelbuch von schönen Nädereyen, Ladengewirk und
Nurem-   Soterleins arbeit.   Ander Theil.   Nürnberg, bey Paulus Fürsten, Kunst-
berg.   händler.

Obl. 4to. 3 sheets of text, 50 plates.
Dedicated to the Princess Rosine Helena.   Nürnberg, 20 March 1666.[111]

113.

In the Bib. Imp. (Gravures, L. h. 4. c.) is a vol. lettered " Guipure, gravures burin," containing a collection of patterns engraved on copper, 43 plates, four of which are double, pasted in the book, without title

---

[108] Quoted by Mr. Douce, " Illustrations of Shakespeare."
[109] Mr. E. Arnold.
[110] S. Marino, M. P. Bonella.
[111] Berlin, Royal Library.

or date. Pomegranates, narcissus, lilies, carnations, most of them labelled "Kreutzstich, Frantzösischer Stich, und Fadengewürck" (thread work), the number of stitches given, with Clocks (Zwickel) of stockings and other patterns.

114.

Model-Buch, dritter Theil, von unterschiedlichen Vögeln, Blumen und Früchten etc. Von und in Verlegung Rosina Helena Fürtin. Nürnberg, Christoff Gerharts, 1676.

1676.
Nuremberg.
C. Gerharts.

4 obl. engraved title and printed list; 42 wood plates, 4 large.

115.

Methode pour faire une infinité des desseins differens, avec des carreaux mi-partis de deux couleurs par une ligne diagonale, ou Observations du père Dominique Donat, religieux carme de la province de Toulouse, sur une mémoire inserée dans l'histoire de l'Académie royale des Sciences à Paris, l'année 1704, presenté par le Rev. Père Sebastien Truchet. Paris, 1722.[112]

1772.
Paris.
Père Donat.

72 geometric squares with directions how to make them useful to architects, painters, embroiderers, " tous ceux qui se servent de l'aiguille," and others.

116.

Neues Neta- und Strickbuch für das schöne Geschlecht, worinnen allerhand Zierrathen, wie auch viele neue Zwickel, nebst Buchstaben und Zahlen, sowohl zum Nähen als Stricken in zierlichen Nissen und Mustern befindlich sind. Mit vielen Kupfertafeln. Nürnberg und Leipzig, der Christoph Weigel und Schneider, 1784.[113]

1784.
Nuremberg and Leipzig.
Christoph Weigel.

26 plates. Obl. 8vo.

117.

Continuation der kunst- und fleisz-übenden Nadel-Ergötzung oder des neu ersonnenen besondern Nehe-Buchs dritter Theil, worinnen fleiszige Liebhaberinnen dieser nöthig und nützlichen Wissenschaft, ihr künstliches Nadel-*Exercitium*, beij unterschiedlich vorfallenden Belegenheiten zu haben allerhand noch nie vorgekommene Muster zu Dero Gebrauch, vorgelegt und an die Hand gegeben werden von Fr. Margaretha Helmin, zu finden in Nürnberg bei Joh. Christoph Weigel. Nürnberg, no date.[114]

N. D.
Nuremberg.
F. Mar. Helmin.

Oblong fol.

118.

Zierlich webende Minerva, oder neu erfundenes Kunst- und Bild-Buch der Weber- und Zeichner-Arbeit, worinnen treue Anweisung geschicht, wie man Künstlich wirken und schöne Arbeit verfertigen soll, von der vierschäfftigen an, bis auf zwey und dreissig-schäfftige. Nürnberg (Johann Christoph Weigel). No date.[115]

N. D.
Nuremberg.
J. Chr. Weigel.

49 plates in she ts.

---

112 Bib. de l'Arsenal. 11,956 *bis.*   114 S. K. M.
113 S. K. M.   115 S. K. M.

INDEX.

2 G

Stuart, 278; lace-worker at Chantilly, 279.

Poking sticks for setting the ruffs, Henry III. used them himself, 115; in Queen Elizabeth's wardrobe accounts, 276; frequent allusions to, in plays, *ib.*

Portugal, its lace highly esteemed, 83; offering of lace to Our Lady, *ib.*; manufacture of the Marquis de Pombal, *ib.*; lace exported to South America, *ib.*; Peniche, *ib.*

Princesses Sophia and Mary, daughters of James I., their effigies in Westminster Abbey, 285.

Protestant refugees made parchment lace 263; Alençon refugees in Holland, 225; French in Northern Germany, 231; Switzerland, 234; Protestants in England, 105, 222, 271, 288, 311, 355; at Long Island, 333.

Prussia, *see* Germany.

Punto a groppo (knotted work), 37.

Punto tirato (drawn work), 39.

Purl, lace so called, 259; A. Basset writes for edge of perle for coif and apron, 256; bequeathed by will, 275.

QUINTAIN, cloth so called, 16.

RETICELLA described, 16.

Révolte des Passemens, jeu d'esprit so called, 30.

Rézeuil, 17; of gold, 19.

Ruff of the Infanta Isabella, 89; of the French court, 115; Reine Margot, *ib.*; Henry III. *ib.*; of Queen Elizabeth, 275; wrath of Stubbs and other writers, 277; of James I., 281.

Ruffles of soldiers, 136; weeping, 142; wedding present of bride, 143; ruffles of Archbishop of Cambray and Duc de Penthièvre, 143; of Buffon, *ib.*; of Monsieur de Paris, 144; footmen, *ib.*; Queen Anne, 145; of Lord Bolingbroke, 314; of George II. 318; of the Highlanders, 377.

Russia, Oriental character of the lace, 249; point de Moscou, *ib.*; Peter the Great founded a silk lace fabric at Novogorod, *ib.*

SAINT TROND (Limburg), its lace manufacture, 113.

Samplers or samcloths, 19.

Saxony, pillow lace introduced by Barbara Uttmann, 228; her biography, *ib.*; "trellis d'Allemagne" mentioned in inventories, 230; Dresden lace, *see*; torchon lace of the Saxon Erzgebirge, 231; modern Saxon lace, *ib.*

Scandinavian barrow, lace found in, 3.

Scotland, 370; gold and silver "pasment" of King James V. *ib.*; the passement bond, 371; Mary Stuart's lace, *ib.*; her inventory and will, *ib.*; sumptuary acts of James VI. 374; pearling, Scotch term for lace, *ib.*; laced cap of Scotch lawyers, 375; packets of lace from Saint-Germain, 378; smuggling originated the Porteous riots, 379.

Scotland, 381; its lace manufacture at Hamilton, *ib.*; Edinburgh Society for Promoting Arts give prizes for lace, 382; lace-making occupation of the Jacobite ladies, 384; efforts to improve thread manufacture, 385; lace of Renfrew and Glasgow, 386.

Shirt or smock, lace-trimmed, in which Henry VI. was assassinated, 117; William the Silent, 228; caterpillar and oak pattern of Queen Elizabeth, 272; saffron tinted of Irish, 388.

Shoes, lace rosettes on, 120; anecdote of James I. 293.

Sienna, its lace, *see* Florence.

Smuggling of lace, 320; by dogs, 92; in loaf of bread, 321; seizure of lace, 322; lace concealed in coffin of Bishop Atterbury, *ib.*; escape from seizure of a Brussels veil, 323.

Spain, its laces made for church use, 71; splendid lace of the Madonna, and office of her mistress of the robes, *ib.*; point d'Espagne of gold and silver, 72, 79; lace alb given by Ferdinand and Isabella, 73; letter of Sancho Panza's wife, *ib.*; unfinished work of Spanish nuns, 74; Prince Charles' visit to Spain, 77; lace-trimmed dresses of Spanish lady, 77; point d'Espagne worn in profusion at the French court, 78; point d'Espagne banner of the Inquisition, 79; on the uniform of the Maestranza, *ib.*; Châtelain introduces manufacture into France, 80; blonde made in Catalonia, *ib.*; at Barcelona specially, *ib.*; the national mantilla, 81; coloured Spanish lace, *ib.*

Starch, clear starcher of Queen Elizabeth,